Are We Downhearted?

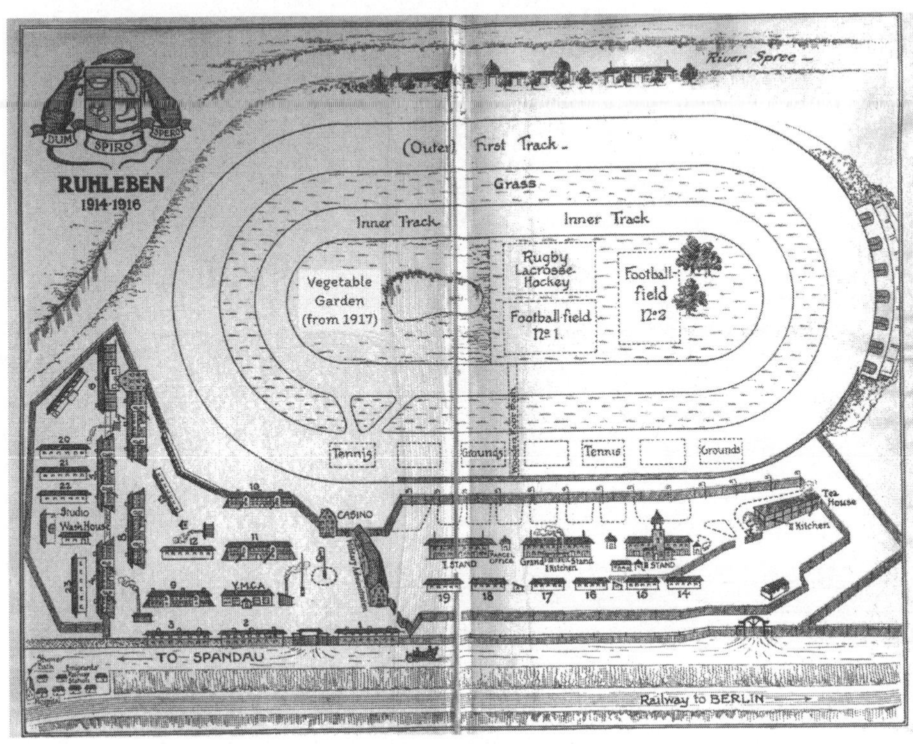

Map of Ruhleben Camp in 1916

Are We Downhearted?

The Diaries and Letters of Michael Stewart Pease from Ruhleben Internment Camp, Germany, 1914–1918

Transcribed with notes by
Sarah Kimbell and Rowan Pease

Copyright © Sarah Kimbell and Rowan Pease 2020
The moral rights of the authors have been asserted

Published by The Poplars Press
thepoplarspress@gmail.com

ISBN 978-1-8381599-0-0

Printed by Print2Demand
Westoning, Bedfordshire

To our grandparents,
Michael and Helen

The old catchphrase 'Are we downhearted?' was a rallying call for those interned in Ruhleben Camp – and the response was always a resounding 'No!' It was shouted or sung out defiantly when groups were gathered, despite (and because of) the objections of the camp authorities. It was used to greet new arrivals or as a farewell to those who were being released, and was a reinforcement of camp solidarity.

He [Michael] *has faced the discomforts and monotony of the Ruhleben life better than anyone I know and his energy and strength of character to make the best of a deplorable sort of existence was a lesson to a great many of us.*

Arthur Dodd
Letter to Michael's mother, written in 1918

CONTENTS

ILLUSTRATIONS

ABBREVIATIONS

ASU	Arts and Science Union
Bar.	Barrack (stable)
B of S	Board of Studies
CUFS	Cambridge University Fabian Society
DT	Daily Telegraph newspaper
ILP	Independent Labour Party
PC	Postcard
PG	Pro-German
RCS	Ruhleben Camp School
RHS	Ruhleben Horticultural Society
SP Circle	Social Problems Circle
TP	Thurloe Place (Central Prisoners of War Committee)
M	Usually Tom Marshall
J	Usually Douglas Jones
S	Usually Felix Schlesinger

Preamble

Michael Stewart Pease was born in Aberfeldy, Perthshire on 2nd October 1890, the eldest child of Edward Reynolds Pease and Mary Gammell Pease (known as Marjory). Edward was a notable socialist, one of the founders of the Fabian Society and its secretary for many years. He was raised as a Quaker, but resigned from the Society of Friends when he was in his mid-twenties. Marjory had a Scottish Presbyterian background, and was the only daughter of the Reverend George Smyttan Davidson, minister of Kinfauns, Perthshire. Also a socialist, Marjory joined the Fabian Society in 1886 where she met Edward. The couple married in 1889 and in 1895 the family moved to Limpsfield, Surrey, where they lived for the rest of their lives.

Michael and his younger brother Nicolas were educated at Bedales School, a progressive, co-educational boarding school. Michael then took his Natural Sciences Tripos and Diploma in Agriculture at Trinity College Cambridge in 1909–1913. In 1914 he was working at the Plant Breeding Institute, part of Cambridge University's School of Agriculture. He had a three year scholarship from the Board of Agriculture, working under Professor Rowland Biffen.

In the summer of 1914 Michael (aged 23) was on a trip to Germany when war broke out, and found himself unable to return home. He stayed in his guesthouse in Jena for a while, before being arrested and sent to Ruhleben Civilian Internment Camp on the 25th November 1914.

The camp was located on a racecourse in Ruhleben, a district west of Berlin, and housed 4000–5000 men from Britain and the colonies. The men were mostly accommodated in 11 adapted stables (known as barracks), each consisting of two rows of horseboxes (each box sleeping six people in tiers) and a hayloft, which held about 100 internees. Michael spent the majority of his time in Ruhleben in Barrack XI, Box 17. Because of overcrowding, the stables were later supplemented by a further 12 wooden barracks. There were public areas in the grandstands and on the track itself, where a great range of intellectual, cultural and sporting activities took place.

The camp is well documented: having held several thousand internees, there are diaries, letters and accounts galore. Left much to their own devices, they seemed to have formed a microcosm of British male society – with many of its class, race and social boundaries, and a flourishing bureaucracy. Michael seems to have kept his spirits up by not worrying about the things he couldn't control – like his imprisonment and the war – and instead threw himself into camp life. He was heavily involved in establishing the Camp School and running its biology department. He gave talks on a variety of topics when asked (for example a well-received talk on syphilis in 1918), served on various committees, and played for his barrack's hockey team. He was well enough known to have been given a mention on a page of spoof adverts in the 1916 summer edition of the Ruhleben Camp Magazine: 'PEASE - The Old English Morris Prancer' as a result of the Morris dancing lessons and shows he gave, and his talk on Elizabethan dancing.

In addition to a busy round of organised activities, the diaries and letters reveal voracious and wide-ranging interests in literature and ideas. The insights they provide into his personality are all the more revealing because he was not writing for posterity and does not seem to indulge in self-deception. He abhorred alcohol, perhaps unsurprisingly given his Quaker and Presbyterian roots, and his po-faced account of the 1915 Christmas celebrations is just one example of this. The occasional casual use of racist language is painful to read, though of its time. He has little respect for the British Camp Captains ('knaves') and gets exasperated with the posturing that goes on in many of the camp committees. The overall impression, however, is of a man with a hugely enquiring mind, a sense of humour and remarkable resilience. He formed a wide range of friendships which lasted well beyond his internment. These included academics, musicians and people from other walks of life (one of his best friends – Arthur Dodd – was a professional golfer). As an aside, he obviously cared little for his appearance: he is consistently the worst-dressed man in the photos we have of him in the camp (see pages 111 and 222 for evidence).

For his children and grandchildren the account (on 28th Dec. 1915) of his receiving his first letter from Helen Bowen Wedgwood is fantastic: 'a wench of some guts' no less! Thoughts of her keep him awake that night. In a letter written to Helen after the war he confesses 'it afforded me hours of hard thinking trying to visualise the authoress, but it was all in vain!' Helen (the eldest daughter of Josiah Clement Wedgwood MP) came from a similar social background; her siblings were educated at Bedales, and she herself was at Cambridge University (1913–1916), overlapping for a short time with Michael, where she had obviously spotted him at political and social events. Their letters express a shared political and pacifist commitment, and many common interests.

Sometimes, reading about the intrigues of committees, the goods he receives from home, or his anxiously awaiting the delivery of dresses for a play he was producing, it is hard to imagine that the world was at war, and his brother Nicolas serving in France. The Camp School, the Horticultural Society, listening to the camp musicians and improving his language skills gave him a sense of purpose and small pleasures.

Over the course of the war, as camp life became more routine, Michael seems to have adjusted to internment surprisingly well, becoming immersed in his botanical research and teaching. Perhaps the experience of boarding school helped him cope with dormitory living and the lack of privacy. He seems to have been determined to remain cheerful and positive, but does occasionally give signs of being 'downhearted', for example on his 27th birthday (2nd October 1917) when he writes 'the last birthday I was alive I cycled from Cambridge to home' (Limpsfield – a journey of over 80 miles). In the latter half of the war Michael had opportunities to stay outside the camp, but returning was hard. In 1918, as the war dragged on, there is a real sense of decline in the camp. Many friends and camp stalwarts had left under exchange schemes, and amongst remainers morale was low. At the beginning of July 1918 the Spanish flu struck Ruhleben and over half the camp were taken ill, though fortunately there were only two reported deaths. Michael stops writing his diary without explanation on July 8th; maybe he contracted the disease and didn't get back into the habit after his recovery.

Re-telling Michael's Ruhleben story

Michael brought back a wooden chest that he'd made at Ruhleben, in which he kept his diaries, letters, postcards and memorabilia relating to the camp. After Helen died in 1981 this passed to his eldest son Sebastian Pease, and it sat, unopened, for the next three decades. Although we knew that our grandfather had been interned in Germany during the First World War, when we finally opened the chest after Sebastian's death and started reading Michael's recollections, written about 30 years after his release, we became fascinated by his story.

Our book starts with these recollections, which help to fill the gap between his arrest and the start of the first diary in November 1915. Following this, we have some letters from his first year of incarceration. During these months the camp was still being set up, and conditions were very primitive. The first surviving diary starts abruptly, as if in mid-flow, and reveals that the camp infrastructure is almost complete, mostly organised by the internees themselves.

The diaries are interleaved with agendas, programmes, invitations and sundry documents that are noted in the transcripts. We have also included some personal letters, inserted between the diary entries on or around the dates on which Michael sent and received them. This includes all the surviving correspondence between him and Helen Wedgwood during these years.

We can't always read Michael's handwriting, but have transcribed his text as closely as possible. Letters on pages 29, 243 and 390–392 were originally in German and were kindly translated for us by Günter Kowa. We have checked many names against the *Ruhleben Story* website (http://ruhleben.tripod.com/) and used Matthew Stibbe's excellent 2008 book *British Civilian Internees in Germany: The Ruhleben Camp 1914–18* to inform the footnotes.

Finally, there are several appendices: letters Michael received from his family and friends; correspondence between Michael and scientific colleagues; official correspondence; petitions for his release; and some family trees.

The Ruhleben Chest

Recollections

The following recollections were contained in a typewritten document found in the chest, annotated by Helen Pease, who thought they were probably written in 1952 and were unfinished.

In the middle of July 1914 I left home for Germany. It had been my intention to spend three weeks in Jena, learning German, and then to proceed to Vienna, where I was to meet my father[1] at the International Socialist Congress. I crossed from Folkestone to Flushing, where I got into the wrong train, but eventually got safely to Jena with my luggage, (what a lot of luggage one travelled with in those days – I took a tennis racket and white flannels, evening dress and half a dozen boiled shirts). I stopped with a certain Fraulein Zeiss, who had been recommended to me by John Layard.[2] She was a motherly old soul, who lived in a detached house with a very large garden, indeed the street was called Gartenstrasse, just outside the western gate of the old city walls. She took in English students who had come to learn German, casually (like me) or by attending regular vacation courses for foreigners. Margaret and Billy Darwin [Cambridge friends] had been there. She was at the last remaining descendant of the famous Zeiss family; Carl Zeiss had left all his fortune to the Factory, constituting it a "Cooperative Institut." Thus it came about that this good lady had been left to earn her own living. She had an adopted daughter, then about fifteen, with whom I have remained on friendly terms ever since.

In the July days I just caught a glimpse of the Old German University student life. The streets of Jena were then dominated by the students. They wore highly coloured distinctive caps for their different corps. They walked about the streets in groups, ceremoniously raising their caps to each other, and to senior members of the University. They sat conspicuously in the market place and elsewhere drinking beer. Their faces were scarred with wound marks; and particular objects of attention were those with freshly bound up wounds – where students congregated there was usually an odour of iodoform.

---

[1] Edward Reynolds Pease, founding member (and secretary) of the Fabian Society, and member of the Independent Labour Party.

[2] At Bedales School with Michael.

With singularly ill-timed obstinacy I did not read any newspapers – so that it came as shock to learn that Austria had declared war on Serbia, and that on the following day German mobilisation had been ordered. I consulted Fr. Zeiss' brother, who was a lawyer; he advised me that it was impossible to travel without a military pass (because of mobilisation) and that when that was over I could then leave and go home. He took the prevailing view that England wouldn't fight: I felt sure we would be drawn into the war – but not, I thought, at once.

In the meantime Jena was in a state of turmoil. Being a garrison town there was considerable military activity, and many wild rumours about spies, especially Russian spies. On that day, there happened to me my first personal lucky encounter during the war. Walking across the crowded and excited market place, I met Miss Schlesinger[3] who had been in charge of the San. at Bedales; and as she played in the orchestra and sometimes sang solo parts she was well known to us boys. She told me that she was staying with her brother,[4] who lived in Jena, where he had a job with Zeiss, and that they were all just off for a fortnight's holiday in the Wald. She was in a hurry, and with these few words we parted. I never saw her again, but the consequence of that chance meeting meant much to me.

The next day England declared war. I made the acquaintance of another Britisher, a Scotsman called Arnold Whyte,[5] a Cambridge man and a hockey blue, who had just graduated. He, like me, had just come to Jena to learn German – he was stopping in rather mean lodgings in the town. He was a very pleasant fellow, and we got on well together. We decided to try to get out and we were told soothingly that we had 48 hours to cross the frontier, the police gave us passes allowing us to travel "to England". We were recommended to go to Berlin where no doubt the English would be collected and sent home. A train for Berlin left about noon.

We boarded this train, not without difficulty. It was packed to the doors with returning holiday makers from south Germany, Austria and Italy. The train crawled slowly, stopping at every station. After about an hour's

---

[3] Lettice Ruth Schlesinger, under-matron in Bedales school sanatorium in the 1901 census.

[4] Felix Schlesinger (fn 11) who lived in Jena with his (English) wife and their two children.

[5] William John Arnold Whyte, 1892–1967 (*Ruhleben Story* at http://ruhleben.tripod.com).

journey we reached the main line from Berlin to Frankfurt and the west front, where we changed trains. Here we saw mobilisation in full swing, working with clockwork precision. While we waited in the station, every few minutes there passed us, going west, huge long troop trains, carrying men and horses; there was no motorised transport: it was horses, beautiful horses, gleaming new harness, everything, uniform and equipment shining bright in the afternoon sun, as yet untarnished by battle. It was a splendid spectacle, but hardly a cheering one.

We boarded the Berlin train and jogged on; clearly at this rate we would not reach Berlin till 2 or 3 in the morning. An inspection of papers brought an anxious moment; the official paused at ours, but happily handed them back without comment. We passed the big and important junction of Halle. As darkness fell we stopped at a wayside station, it seemed interminable. I suppose somewhere near Wittenberg the cause of the stoppage soon became clear to us – it was an examination of passes. This time we were taken off the train and marched up to the guardroom – there were others, I think, mostly Russians. And here chanced my second lucky encounter. The O.C. of the station was a Cambridge graduate whom I had known well; we were both interested in politics and we had met at the Union debates, where he was a frequent and I an infrequent speaker. He told us emphatically that it was madness to go to Berlin; that no English were being allowed out, and that the diplomatic train had long since gone. His advice was to go back to Jena, where we were "known to the police", (a frightening phrase to English ears) and bide our time quietly there. He wrote out railway passes for us back to Jena and told us to present them to the police there. This we did and next morning found us back in Jena. Fr. Zeiss was surprised but welcomed me warmly, saying she would keep me without payment during the war; for money was a problem. It is difficult to realise that in the enlightened times of 1914 there was no bother about foreign money, an Englishman's cheque was accepted in every civilised continental town. So it came that when the war started I had four or five gold sovereigns in my pocket and a cheque book, now worthless.

To begin with Whyte and I were left entirely alone. We applied our minds to mastering German and to keeping our bodies fit: swimming every day in the Saal and taking long walks through the very attractive wooded hills which surround Jena. About ten days after our return to Jena we were hauled before the police for examination, the Prof. of English being present. We were examined closely on our particular family background, education and our activities at the University, reasons for coming to Germany and so forth. The Professor brightened up when he heard that my father was secretary of the Fabian Society. In the event I passed and was told not leave Jena. Unfortunately Whyte had been in the O.T.C. [University Officers' Training Corps] at Cambridge, and because of this he was regarded as a military prisoner and was swept off to an officers camp at Celle [Schloss Celle, Lower Saxony]. Some years later they decided that he was not an officer, and brought him into Ruhleben, where we renewed our friendship.

Thereafter I was very much on my own. All through the August sunshine the bells and the flags proclaimed victory after victory for the German army. It was difficult to see how our side could possibly win the war. In September however the bells no longer rang, though the flags remained in the streets. The little pin flags, on the big public buildings, of the western front remained neglected for days on end, and the newspapers for what seemed a long time were completely silent about the war in the west: the daily bulletins were from the Eastern Front. When the reports on the western front started to reappear they told of German victories, but these victories were a long way east of the August line. No explanation was given and very few Germans at the time realised what had happened.

It was at that time a very solitary life that I led. The Zeisses, (mother and daughter) were kindness itself to me, but they were deeply involved in war work, and I felt it kindest not to obtrude an enemy alien upon them. But I enjoyed the fresh air and the exercise, my increasing command of German enabled me to read more quickly, and to understand more fully the conversation in the streets and on the market place.

I made the acquaintance of a Russian student, who like me was an enemy alien: or rather it was he who insisted on knowing me. My knowledge of Russian refugees of the Free Russia movement led me to regard Russians as incompetent and unreliable and apt to get into scrapes; I didn't wish to be involved in any foolishness of his. Nonetheless, he was a bright and cheerful fellow who lived with a pretty and sympathetic concubine in pleasant rooms. He was a law student and we found we had interest in history, politics, music and pictures. Characteristically he was cocksure the Russians would be in Berlin by Christmas and that he would be in the Market Place in Jena to receive the Cossacks when they entered the town! It was his utter inability to make an objective judgement that made me distrust him. I took care to avoid being seen going about with him in daytime: but I enjoyed my evenings with him and his girl, and the conversation improved my German, for though he wanted to talk in French I insisted on talking German.

My next move was to try to make touch with the Schlesingers. The post office directory disclosed some dozen Schlesingers resident in Jena. I copied out the addresses and armed with them set out to prospect. After eliminating a builder, a shoemaker, a lodging-house keeper and several others, I reduced the list to three possibles. At the next likely looking house I summoned up my courage: my ring was answered by a friendly little woman who listened to my story. She told me to cheer up, that the war would soon be over, and directed me to the Frau Schlesinger I was looking for.

One important event sometime in September disturbed my quiet and eventless existence. One day two men, (one a policeman) turned up at Frl. Zeiss' and were ushered into my room. The policeman introduced his friend who related his story thus. He had just had news that his soldier son was prisoner of war in British hands at Frimley in Surrey [Frith Hill P.O.W. Camp]. Was I in touch with my parents in England? Could I get a message through to the boy in the camp? This I was of course very glad to do, and since Frimley was near to Limpsfield, I told him that my Mother would doubtless organise a visit. My visitor was a certain Otto Neumeister, a master tiler, with whose family we have kept it up ever since. By the time Mother got my message Walter [the son] had been moved from Frimley to Ireland [Templemore]. Mother with her usual determination mobilised Aunt Louise,[6] who visited the camp and reported Walter well and sound. Uncle Jonathan Hogg[7] was also mobilised to send food parcels.

---

[6] Wife of Marjory Pease's brother John, who lived in Kinsale, Ireland.

[7] Jonathan Hogg, widower of Edward Reynolds Pease's half-sister Margaret, who lived in Dublin.

Letters November 1914 – October 1915

....

Letter from Frau Zeiss to Marjory Pease (received 13th November), sent via Leonard Ornstein in Holland:

Jena, Gartenstrasse 3

Afternoon of 6th Nov, 1914

Dear Mrs. Pease,

I am sorry to have to tell you, that 10 minutes ago an official of the police came to take away your son into the building of our town court. This is a consequence of England's not having answered to the German proposal to set the German civil people free, who are being kept as prisoners though they have nothing whatever to do with the war. We knew that a response was claimed for November 5th at latest under the menace that all English civil people living till now in Germany without being bothered, would be interned if the proposal was not accepted. Today a telegram was affirmed that no answer had come from England, and so we were quite prepared to see your son being taken away. We are very sorry to lose him, for we think very highly of him and like him much, but these things cannot be helped, and they say that exceptions are not possible. The one thing I can assure you is that your son will be treated well, that his health is safe and that he will have every comfort that is to be expected in this situation. Surely he will miss his nice walks, but the German Government is very exact and fair. Probably he is allowed to take care of his own boarding, – I mean that he pays a daily small sum; – at all events do not be very much in anxiety. He has not done anything wrong and nothing really bad will happen to him. It is simply a matter of lack of comfort for some time. This I write in a hurry after finding a letter [below] *in his room, which I think better to send off.*

Yours very sincerely, Lilla Zeiss

Enclosed letter from Michael Stewart Pease (MSP) to Edward Reynolds Pease, written just before his arrest:

bei Fraulein Zeiss, Gartenstrasse 3, Jena

Nov. 6th

My dear Father,

Many thanks for your letters which I am sorry I've not answered directly before – if however I had thought you would consider yourself to have been neglected, you would have had an answer long ago. All your news, domestic, local and imperial is very welcome. Here nothing much happens and the days slip by very quickly, though I confess I don't find life as a hostage very reposeful.

Yesterday I got mother's letter from Cambridge, and rejoiced greatly at the news therein, though in many ways it's the more irritating to hear that one's experiments are turning out interesting! I felt sure I'd got hold of interesting material, but I think the analysis of the present generation [of plants] *will be hard, especially for a new man just turned on to the job. I have also piles of reserve seeds, kept in case of accidents, but I confess I didn't think of the "accident" taking the present form!*

I hope to send you shortly an order on my Cambridge Bank, which you can avail yourself of. Keep what I already owe you, and, subject to your approval, I suggest you send £5 to the Hanbury-Aggs fund for assisting Germans in England. I thoroughly appreciate the awkwardness of their situation! The rest you can send over to me here as I require it. At present I have plenty, since, as I have already explained, I've very little to spend it on. It's very decent of the Board [of Agriculture] *to go on paying me – as for the future, we must just wait and see.*

About the nitrate – I should think it will soon mash up the tin tub to pieces! I suppose the soil was too dry, and, if you put on solid nitrate, it withdrew the water from the seedlings in order to dissolve. Hope they're all right again. I long to be in our garden again: I take no interest in this garden here, primarily because the only things I'm allowed to do are so childish. I've done a certain amount of leaf sweeping up, a job you can bear witness, I've thoroughly abominated and always 'cut' at home!

Yes I've read little bits of Prothero,[8] *but was not much impressed. However I want to read the whole book sometime, more especially as I'm beginning to think quite seriously of taking up farming as a profession. I shall be interested to see your draft report on Co-op: I haven't been at all satisfied with most of the written stuff that has appeared to date, though I can't really say what is wrong. One can only say, I think, that the problem, as far as England is concerned, is far more complicated than most people suppose, and that short of some definitely collectivist scheme on a large scale, I don't really see what can be done. Affectionately, Michael Pease*

---

[8] Probably Rowland Edmund Prothero, a British agricultural expert, journalist, author and politician.

Note stuck on this letter, covering a small section that had been physically cut out:

Dear Mr. Pease. I have had to take away some part of this letter. I hope that my restoration of the other side [of the letter] *is in order. Truly yours, Ornstein*[9]

The neutral attitude of Holland did not allow to forward the lines written on this side.

....

MSP to Marjory Pease:[10]

12th Nov. 1914

Stadt. Gefangnis, Berlin [Stadtvogtei Prison]

My dear Mother,

I hope the papers have not been giving very alarming accounts of our imprisonment here. I can say that up to now I have been treated with as much consideration as was in the circumstances to be expected, and that the officials that I have so far come in contact with have done everything to make the proceedings as bearable as possible. My one concern has been you and D. I only hope you have not been worrying: remember I am strong and can stand much in the way of physical discomforts.

Well here is the account of my adventures. On Friday (Nov. 6th) midday the notice was posted up that the English were to be arrested. So I went up and warned the Schlesingers, went for a walk on the hills, came back through the town, getting my money and buying necessary clothing, and returned to my rooms to find a plain clothes policeman in possession. I packed my bag and followed down to the police station where I found Schlesinger.[11] *After a longish wait there we were taken up to*

---

[9] Dr Leonard Salomon Ornstein, a Dutch physicist. In 1914 he was Chair of Theoretical Physics at the University of Utrecht. He appears to have had a connection to the Peases and became a conduit for some of their correspondence. A photo of him, his wife and first child was also in the Ruhleben chest (page 361).

[10] Parts of this letter were published in the *Surrey Mirror* 4 Dec 1914, in an article titled 'An Englishman in Germany'.

[11] Hermann Felix Emil Schlesinger (1873–1964), brother of Miss Schlesinger, whose chance meeting with Michael is described in the Recollections (page 6). He was living and working (at Goertz optical instruments) in Jena in 1914 and was interned in Ruhleben with Michael, where they became close friends. A talented amateur cellist he often played in camp concerts. Ironically, as his father was German, Britain would have regarded him as a German national, despite being born and raised in England, and it is likely that he would have been interned as a German civilian during the war if he had been in Britain in August 1914.

the prison in Jena everything taken from us and we were locked up, mercifully together. It was a biggish cell, about 8yds by 2 and well lighted (but no artificial light) and moderately clean, though the sanitary arrangements were primitive. Apart from the beds (which weren't really so awfully bad) the only furniture was a table and two stools, all melancholy and depressing to view. The "Tages ordnung" [daily regime] *consisted of rising at 7am and cleaning the cell. An enormous loaf of bread (each) and "coffee" comprised breakfast. Soup at 11 am, walk in the yard 12–1pm and "coffee" (5pf* [pfennig] *without milk, 10pf with) at 6pm. On our walk on Saturday we reviewed our fellow prisoners – mostly jailbirds of the lowest type. We were given the books we had brought and told that we could order what food we liked. The jailmaster's wife interviewed us on the point, as she herself was cook. So on Sunday we had the finest dinner I've had since I came to Germany and only 1 mark at that!*

On Monday we were told we were going to Erfurt [capital city of Thuringia], *and a barber was sent in to shave us and off we went that afternoon with two plain clothes officers. After being before two different authorities we were taken to the town jail, and locked up. This however was a much more social proceeding. We had a whole wing, as it were, to ourselves and were not shut up separately. Here we met about 20 other English, amongst whom, two Trinity fellows whom I knew. Also one Jones,*[12] *a great friend of Uncle Gerald's.*[13] *We were practically all tourists in Thuringia. This was a most lively and exhausting proceeding as we told our adventures unceasingly. Supper was ordered in from a neighbouring restaurant and we had a gay time. Just as well too, since the prison was hardly clean, and swarmed with fleas and beetles. We were told to be ready at 2.30 a.m. to leave for Berlin, but we didn't start till about 5 a.m. We marched in procession to the station and there we met more English and received a military escort. The journey to Berlin was pleasant, and instructive from an agricultural point of view, and we saw some quite interesting spots in Berlin as we came through. When we were got out we were told that the concentration camp was already full up and we had to wait in the station for further orders. After about 1/2 an hour we were marched in formation through the streets of Berlin to this place, which I gather from the linen is the town jail. It is a colossal building and altogether defies description: everything is spotlessly clean and attendants very nice and civil and we can have all our luggage, books and everything with us. We are also provided with lamps (which unfortunately have to be given up at 6.30). Most of us are in single cells but*

---

[12] Possibly Douglas Doyle Jones, a Barrister at Law in London (see fn 88).

[13] Joseph Gerald Pease – Michael's uncle, a barrister in London.

some of us are in large quarters and of course have a much better time. Cooking is excellent: rations consist of soup and bread. Yesterday we had a 2½ hours walk in the yard and saw our fellow English. About half of us are sailors taken off ships in Hamburg and there are a certain number of artisans. A few can't speak a word of English! Ludicrous situation! The other half of us are students and tourists, and I suppose we are about 200 in all (300 more expected last night). I don't know how long we are to stay here, but the authorities seem to think only a day or two.

It isn't really half as bad for me: the worst blow fell when I couldn't get back to Cambridge for my work. It has been, of course, awful for Schlesinger. He has lost his job, taken away from his wife and family and broken up his home. Mrs. S and children hope to get back to England but are no means sure: if they do you will hear of me from them.[14]

Nov. 15th. Today [Michael always wrote this word as 'to day'] *we are allowed to send off letters, but as they will have to be read by the authorities and most of us will be writing, I don't know how long this may be till it gets off. They seem to think now we may be here for some weeks, but as one has no say in one's future, one doesn't worry about it. I've got into a resigned, a sort of stupid and torpid state and don't really feel this present change so much as I felt being separated from home and work in the first place. One sleeps away a lot of the time and while it is light I can read. The food is sufficient but monotonous (it is reported that we are allowed to order food from tomorrow onwards, but I don't anticipate that material delicacies can really do very much to enliven affairs).*

Don't fret about me, it can't do any good. That it can't last forever and that we shall meet again sometime is the one hope that keeps the fire alight within me. Don't expect to hear from me for at least a week as I gather we may only write on Sundays, at least for the present. With love,

Affectionately,

Michael Pease

....

Michael was sent to Ruhleben 10 days later, on November 25th.

---

[14] Non-German women and children were allowed to leave Germany under the terms of an agreement signed in October 1914.

Edward Reynolds Pease to MSP:

The Pendicle, Limpsfield, Surrey

Tues. 17th Nov. 1914

My dear Michael,

We were very sorry to hear of your fate, tho' it was quite what we expected. Fraulein Zeiss sent me your letter written just before you were sent away. I hope you will not suffer much hardship, and you will no doubt exchange books and walks for plenty of company and I expect, more occupation. Your mother has gone to Scotland for the week-end, but Nicolas [Michael's brother] *was home as usual, so I have not been solitary. Write as often as you can. I fear we may not be able to hear so often from you.*

I have been lately planting out your wallflowers and primulas. The nitrate is too strong for wallflowers: they are too big, especially those you pricked out earliest. Today we have our first sharp frost, and the nasturtiums have gone at last. They were very gay round the house. I only go up [to London] *2 or 3 days a week, as I don't find much to do at the office. The Shaw lectures after all have gone quite well: the hall is full, tho' largely of paper, but we shall take £350 and clear £100 profit. In these times this is not bad. –*

I am writing on the future of agricultural labour with much interest. It always surprises me what a lot one discovers as soon as one begins to think about a subject. For example I don't think it has hitherto been observed that whereas a factory turns over its capital twice or thrice in a year (i.e. capital £50,000, annual production £100,000 or more) a farm in England produces only 1/8th of its capital (e.g. land £25 per acre: farmers capital £7 = £32; average output £4 per acre!). Of course the exact figures vary enormously, but the general effect is as stated. –

The manured cabbages all died, but I had plenty to replace them. The ground was apparently damp enough, but I expect your explanation is correct.

A letter came from the German prisoner (Neumeister or some such name) in Ireland which I sent on to your mother. So we can now send him money and news. The delay in reply from Frimley was no doubt due to his having left. He sent your translation of his letter. –

I hope you have got warm clothes. I fear in your new status you will get very little news. That must be a serious loss. I am afraid it is no good for us to write of public affairs: the letters would be stopped.

Well, goodbye and good luck to you.

Affectionately Edw. R. Pease

P.S. Are you sure the nitrate will damage the zinc tub? I can see no trace at present. The warrant from Sir S.O. [Sydney Olivier[15]] *on your account has just come.*

....

Marjory Pease to MSP:

The Pendicle, Limpsfield, Surrey

18th Nov. 1914

Dearest Michael,

How I long for news of you. Since I got Fr. Zeiss' kind note written 10 minutes after you were arrested I have not a single word about you. Fr. Zeiss' letter arrived on the 13th and she kindly enclosed a letter you had left in your room written that morning to your father. I do so wonder where you are and if you get my letters and if you have companions. I also wonder where Mr. Schlesinger is. I got home this evening travelling from Scotland all night – cold journey, train 3½ hours late owing to fog. I worked in my office all day and came down here at 6. Your father is up in town hearing G. B. Shaw lecture. The Kylie Hills, Drummond Hays, McDonalds and many others enquired after you. I am finding out if Cook[16] *will take parcels to Germany, if not I will try and send you some warm things by the Geneva Red Cross. I am now in correspondence with* [Walter] *Neumeister who is in a camp near Tipperary. The commandant says he will see that he gets whatever I like to send him. I have already sent him 10/- and asked him if I can send him warm clothes. If Mrs. Neumeister cares to send him a parcel of things addressed to me care of The Baroness de vos van Steenwijk, Palace Hotel, Mont Pelerin, Vevey, Switzerland, I will gladly send it on to Ireland. Shall I send you some of your warm tweed suits and vests and drawers? By the way an account has just come for you Lilley & Co. Cambridge for a suitcase got on July 13th. £1-14-6. Shall I pay it or did you already pay it? There is a note from Mrs. Crosthwaite wanting to meet me in London. She is back now from Zurich and I hope better. Mrs. Stepniak*[17] *writes for news of you. Your grandmother has written to a very old friend of hers Mrs. Schwartzman in Stuttgart about you. Possibly she will write to you. I hope Prof.*

---

[15] Sir Sydney Olivier was the Permanent Secretary to the Board of Agriculture and Fisheries in 1913–1917. A member of the Fabian Society and the Labour Party, he was a friend and neighbour of the Peases in Limpsfield.

[16] Thomas Cook's?

[17] Fanny Stepniak, widow of the Russian revolutionary Sergey Stepniak, who had lived in Limpsfield.

Wendt[18] *has been to see you. I think Prof. Biffen*[19] *is making an elaborate report for you. He told me that all your notes were so exact and so carefully kept that your work would not suffer. I do so hope you are allowed to work at your mathematics – I have read with great interest "The Way of all Flesh".*[20] *It came too late for me to take it to Switzerland and here I get less and less time for reading. Nicolas is bringing Cohen here next weekend.*

Nov 19th. Still nothing from you, but I remember Mrs. Whyte was kept a long time without news of her son though she often hears of him now at Celle [Schloss Celle officers prison camp]. *I have a letter from the Templemore*[21] *Commandant this morning saying I can come and see Neumeister and he will give him whatever I like to send. I am trying to find out if other Jena men are there and will let you know their names. The Cecil Smiths of Titsey have just heard their son is a prisoner in Germany. He was reported wounded and missing early in September and then heard nothing more of him till they got this message yesterday from Switzerland. You are never out of my thoughts,*

Your loving Mother

P.S. Mrs. Charles Leveson Gower called to ask for you while I was in Scotland. Hope you have got a letter from Peggy Scott.[22] *She tells me she has written to you via Holland. I am writing to Herr Bernstein.*[23]

....

Marjory Pease to MSP:

The Pendicle, Limpsfield, Surrey

4th Dec. 1914

Dearest Michael,

I can't help feeling that camp life in spite of its trying conditions is really much better than being shut up in a cell alone. You will get fresh air and exercise and companionship and I do hope you are allowed to get extra food. I have sent you a

---

[18] Possibly Hans Hinrich Wendt, Professor of Theology and Rector of Jena University.

[19] Sir Rowland Biffen, Professor of Agricultural Botany at Cambridge and Director of the Plant Breeding Institute (Michael's supervisor).

[20] Semi-autobiographical novel by Samuel Butler that attacks Victorian-era hypocrisy.

[21] German POW camp at Richmond Barracks, Templemore, Tipperary, Ireland.

[22] Peggy Scott – an old Bedalian and sister of George Klaassen Scott (fn 324).

[23] Eduard Bernstein, a German social-democratic Marxist theorist and politician who had links with the Fabian Society and the Labour Party.

book and shortbread and am sending you Blenheim oranges tomorrow. Your p.c. written on Nov 26th from the camp reached me on the evening of Dec 2nd and your letter of Nov 22nd reached me on the morning of Dec 3rd. I am so thankful you got all the letters I wrote to you in Jena. Do ask Frl. Zeiss to buy you warm clothes and blankets and tell me what I can send you. If you are only allowed to write 2 p.c. a week I will only expect to hear from you once a week. I have been writing to Neumeister and sending him chocolate, cigarettes, money and books. The commandant wrote me a very nice letter about him which I sent on to Fr. Zeiss. Nicolas is kept hard at work and I doubt he will be home this weekend. Mrs. Scott[24] *asked most kindly after you and got your address for Peggy who has now left Bedales. I have a very kind letter from Mrs. Green today asking for news of you. Your Uncle Jonathan* [fn 7] *also writes about you and your cousin Enid.*[25] *Mrs. Howard's brother who was butler to some old lady who recently died has been left £300 by her! Our Land Club meets on Tuesday. Poor old Cornford*[26] *very broken down now – Furzedown*[27] *(Percy Sharman's old home) is used for wounded soldiers. Some fine Highlanders are there and come often to see us. We have not yet been asked to Cote Bank*[28] *for Xmas, but don't mean to budge. I am going to stay on here and work. Prize giving at Merle Common School on the 18th when Mr. and Mrs. Charles Leveson Gower*[29] *attend! The school goes on excellently – such a good infant teacher now.*

5th Dec. Just going off to meeting about soldiers' wives at Rectory, I will post this on the way. Prof. Biffen writes such a nice letter about you. He is going to make a special study himself of your cabbages. He writes he has 8 students in his senior class! We had sanitary com. yesterday and issued closing orders for 7 houses in Tatsfield and 1 in Tanridge. The M.O. reported that 12 houses should be erected in Upper Warlingham and we adopted his report so we are getting on! I'm so glad you went to a dentist in Jena. I must visit McDonald soon, but can't find the time. Nicolas can't get home this weekend. Am sending off a few apples and a little chocolate and will send more when I hear this reaches. Looking forward eagerly to your next p.c.

---

[24] Mother of Bedalians George, Peggy, Tommy and Violet Scott. She was married to Prof Dunkinfield Henry Scott FRS, who wrote the classic guide *Introduction to Structural Botany*.

[25] Enid Lucy Pease Robinson – Michael's 1st cousin.

[26] In 1911 census of Limpsfield there is a George Cornford, aged 72, who is a 'jobbing gardener'.

[27] Furzedown Auxiliary Hospital, Limpsfield. A military convalescent home 1914–1918.

[28] Pease family home in Westbury-on-Trym, Bristol.

[29] The local bigwigs who lived at Titsey Place, Limpsfield.

Your loving mother, M. Pease

....

Engländerlager
Ruhleben=Spandau
Xmas 1914.

Mr. M Pease
XI Barrack.

WITH HEARTIEST XMAS AND NEW YEAR'S WISHES
from
Captains

TRINKS, No. 1.
SWIFT, No. 2.
DEXHEIMER, No. 3.
NICHOLSON, No. 4.
COCKER, No. 5.
KATZ, No. 6.
HALLAM, No. 7.
RUSSELL, No. 8.
ROBSON, No. 9.
POWELL, No. 10.
THORPE, No. 11.
AMAN, No. 12.
BEAUMONT, Tea House.
JONES, Secy.

Christmas card from the Barrack Captains

....

Edward Reynolds Pease to MSP:

The Pendicle, Limpsfield, Surrey

Monday after Xmas [28th Dec. 1914]

My dear Michael,

Your letter of Nov 27th interested us much. I confess I am surprised that you go the whole hog of pacifism. I admit killing is a horrid business, but there are worse. I can't put the Egyptians, the Bengalis, and the Armenians at the head of the nations of the world. I can't condemn as bloody men Cromwell and Washington, Garibaldi and even old Kruger. Non-resistance is a possible creed for those who believe in a providence that shapes our ends accordingly, and who do not care for evidence. In fact the meek inherit nothing, and like the Incas, go under when the proud come along. You may put your trust in God if you like, but it avails you nothing unless you keep your powder dry. Fighting is silly and disgusting and out of date. But as the world is (tho' I trust it will not long remain so) it has got to be done, and those who leave it to others, like J.R.M [James Ramsey Macdonald] *who says we must not make peace till – all sorts of things are achieved – and yet won't lift a finger to achieve them, well, have not my respect. –*

We've had the Greens for Xmas; Mrs. G. fills every pause with anecdotes of David, which pall. I've cut the creepers and so on. I don't suppose I shall cut the sycamore. I shall have to go to town some 5 days a week, and the other 2 days will be needed to keep the garden going, without extras. The removal of the thorn and laburnum makes a great clearance in that region. The Fabian defalcation is a great business. It has been going on for a year. Sanders was careless in not keeping a sharper eye on the accounts. He might have discovered it two or three months ago. The youth, a very pleasant fellow, has certainly taken £70, and probably £90 or £100. I've got the books straight, and other things will be got through!

Don't stint yourself for money. We have plenty: you have your own: the B of A [Board of Agriculture] *will pay if necessary. Your health and comfort are more precious to us than anything else. So just let us know what you can make use of. Webb and Shaw have gone through my book and added lots of things. Shaw calls it "jolly good"! The publishers are off: probably I shall publish at my own expense. I am sure to get the money back, and may make a handsome sum. The publishers agreed to 20% royalty on a 6/- book, – then backed out on a side issue.*

Yours affectionately Edw. R. Pease

P.S. I admire your taste in books, and read some of those bought for you. I've just got Benj. Franklin's autobiography which is very good. Would you like it? Gibbon I have just read, and find it excellent.

....

1915

Marjory Pease to MSP (letter number 15[30]):

27th April 1915

Kinfauns, Perth [Kinfauns Manse, Marjory's family home]

Dearest Michael,

I posted you a card at Victoria on Sunday night when Nicolas and I were there. He returned to Epsom and I went on to Euston and took the midnight train here. All

---

[30] Marjory started numbering her letters to Michael – presumably so they could see when any went missing.

here are in their usual way. George[31] *(Edinburgh) is here. He is now 6 ft 1. A fine handsome youth. He will be 15 months more at Fettes and hopes to get a scholarship at Oriole College Oxford. He is doing classics and hopes to go in for Indian Civil Service. Alastair and Jock are well* [Marjory's nephews]. *Your grandmother is well and will be going to Aberdeen soon* [where her son James lives]. *I leave here on Thursday night and visit Neumeister at Leigh.*[32] *The commandant says I can come whenever or as often as I like and stay as long as I like and see Neumeister alone or with a friend of his own choice to translate. I shall thus be able to write a satisfactory account to his father.*

Did I tell you Professor Ornstein writes enquiring for news of you and sending on a letter from Herr Schmeisser's niece? By the way, does not Schmeisser remind you of Scheu and also of Funnell? I have got the "official" correspondence about Ruhleben camp and I see you can buy certain foods, but probably this varies from week to week. I gather bread from home is appreciated? I wrote to Mrs. Jones telling her her son now gets parcels. I hope he is alright now? I left a cake, walnuts, and a cheap pocket knife which your father would post yesterday and I will send you a box of biscuits from Perth tomorrow.

Your Cote Bank grandmother writes for news of you. Aunt Dora describes Cote Bank as a backwater! I don't feel as if I could stand the life there at present. I have written to Collier[33] *and given him extracts of your letters. I am also writing to Miss Taylor and Mrs. Sambrook* [Bedales School staff].

The garden here is gay, but very untidy. I find things here are quite as far on as at Limpsfield, which is surprising, but then we have had very cold nights at Limpsfield. Did I tell you the casual ward of our workhouse was burnt down on Saturday – no one hurt. It was the best thing that could have happened as now we will get a new building and this was badly wanted. Forgive a scrappy letter written under difficulties. Everyone here is full of enquiries about you and send the usual messages. I am so thankful that you are among congenial friends and that you can read.

Your loving mother.

....

---

[31] George William Smyttan Davidson, Marjory's nephew. Enlisted in the Queen's Own Cameron Highlanders in August 1915 and was killed at The Somme in 1916.

[32] Lilford Mill POW camp at Leigh, Lancashire, located in a disused mill. Opened in Feb. 1915, German POWs were transferred there from Templemore a month later.

[33] Laurence Collier (1890–1976), who had been at Bedales school with Michael.

Marjory Pease to MSP (letter 70):

17th August 1915

Limpsfield.

Dearest Michael,

Very glad indeed to have your pc of July 31st this morning and to know that you are getting all my parcels and letters. I wonder which bread is best – Selfridge or Birmingham? I hope you like my war biscuits. I sent biscuits, cake, jam etc to Leigh, and Walter used a German adjective which Miss Gruner said meant he licked his lips twice. What an extraordinary flow of adjectives both he and his father employ! My letters must seem very colourless to them. I will write to all the people you name and thank them for you.

George Scott and John Russell [school friends of Michael] *are still in England. The owner of the Carlile's Limpsfield House*[34] *is now in the Adonis' native city while his wife and children are at Eastbourne. The R.D.C.* [Rural District Council] *is moving into the house on the Station Road near the laundry. This is more convenient for me by about 7 minutes.*

I have sent your message to Guildford. I'm hoping to meet G's companion in London on Friday. Probably at Murray Stewart's rooms. I should rather like Collier to meet him and give me his impression of him.

Your father is busy in the garden but we have thunderstorms every day now and far too much rain. He rather takes to the idea of cutting down the sycamore but I think it will end by us doing nothing till you return!

I have a letter tonight from Mrs. Thompson who has sent off the books you wish. I hope they reach you alright. I have sent Mrs. Thompson a copy of Neumeister's letter with which she is greatly delighted. She is a very kind-hearted nice woman. I hear the Osmastons have let their house and will be away for 6 months. Miss Gruner is now on a visit to the Adams. The entire Adams family entirely share our views at this time and so does Mr. Badley.[35]

It was very nice having Nicolas for 24 hours. We propose going to Cote Bank on August 27th till September 6th and Nicolas will join us there for 24 hours. Did I

---

[34] Colonel Maurice Pascal Alers Hankey, Secretary of David Lloyd George's War Cabinet and of the Imperial War Cabinet, who lived at Hailie, Limpsfield, previously owned by the economist William Warrand Carlile.

[35] John Haden Badley, founder and Head of Bedales School, the first public co-educational boarding school in England.

tell you N is now over 5 ft 10 inch and holds himself well? He does not put on flesh much but then he works very hard. It is rumoured he is going to India but I think France is more likely.

Can I send you an acetylene lamp for your "study" now that the nights are drawing in? Also can I send you any warm clothes? I have all your clothes here and you have quite a lot of tweed jackets etc. I showed Mr. Pye your card today about your Napier and he was interested to know you had met. He was going to write to Lady Napier. David Pye has had an operation but is getting better and will be at Priesthill next week. I sent two copies of Nature and one copy of Board of Agriculture Journal in your parcel yesterday.

Many loving thoughts from your loving mother

....

Marjory Pease to MSP (letter 82):

12th September 1915

Limpsfield

Dearest Michael,

Your letter of August 21st is my last news of you. I do hope you are well and having the same beautiful weather that we have here. All this week has been lovely and Fanny [Stepniak] *has so enjoyed the country. She goes tomorrow to Frog Hall to "Ferg-ab" to stay a few days and then back to stay with the Turpins. Nicolas came yesterday and will be here a week. I'm so glad he will have a real good rest and get long nights. His future movements are unknown.*

Murray Stewart came today and we talked of Miss Sellers and you and Collier! Your father went off at 5.35 p.m. train for his work at Woolwich and after he had gone we all went up to see the Oliviers. We found Sir Sydney and Lady Olivier down for 24 hours, their tenants having departed. The four girls [Olivier's daughters] *are all down in Dorset – Daphne is better physically but quite broken-hearted and devoid of interest and no wonder. They all feel poor Bekassy's*[36] *death terribly. It is terrible to think of all these young lives so full of promise being cut down before they have ever reproduced themselves.*

Monday. Going up to town today to meet the Blackpool boys [nephews – sons of her deceased brother Andrew] *at 1.40 and buy them clothes and bring them*

---

[36] Ferenc Bekassy (1893–1915). A Hungarian national, who was at Bedales (1905–1911) and Cambridge (1911–1914) with Michael. He returned to Hungary at the start of the war and died fighting the Russians in the Ukraine on 22 June 1915.

down here for the night. They go off to Reigate per omnibus tomorrow while I go to school managers' meeting. After that I devote myself to Nicolas. When he leaves on Saturday your father goes to the Curries and I go to Miss Sellers for "a few days rest" at Bournemouth.

My most exciting domestic news is that Mrs. Howard has virtually resigned and I am so thankful. She has been so sulky and bad tempered, and "slack" and because I ventured to say that she ought to inform me when she can't come in to cook supper instead of letting me return at 7 and find nothing prepared, she writes me a long rigmarole.

As the Ashtons are leaving Robbs cottage for a new council cottage next month I'm arranging for the Howards to apply for it and I hope to install Mrs. Gibbs (widow of the Cohen's late gardener) and to retain the two new rooms for the use of our visitors. I have a great plan for establishing Fanny there. One clings to one's old friends in these days. Meanwhile I am so thankful to get possession of the cottage. Howard will continue to have buildings and land for the present, but I have schemes for dealing with this later.

I expect this letter will reach you about 2nd October [Michael's birthday] – *a day on which you will be very much in my thoughts, but indeed you are always in my thoughts wherever I am. Your grandmother (Kinfauns) is sending you shortbread and I am trying to get you a reading candle as I fear an acetylene light may be forbidden. I have not sent you carbolic as I thought it dangerous to send poison by post but I have sent boracic lint etc and sundry other things which I hope reach you. Isabella Ford*[37] *wishes to send you something too! Every week I now send you 1lb of Irish butter and 4lbs of Birmingham bread. I have sent you the land enquiry report and the mentally deficient report follows on Wednesday.*

Every good wish and loving thought,

Your mother.

....

[37] Isabella Ormston Ford. Daughter of Hannah Ford (nee Pease). Michael's first cousin once removed. A socialist, trade unionist and member of the Women's Labour League.

1915 Diaries and Letters

The Y.M.C.A. Hall and Barrack XI (on the right). The hall was built in the autumn of 1915 and the photo taken in 1918.

FIRST DIARY

Barrack XI Box 17

Nov. 7th *Fuoco*[38] coming to an end fairly rapidly, but poor stuff! 10 a.m. hockey match against Bar. [barrack] 8 – poor game and badly beaten 8–1. 1.30 Henry's[39] lecture, but at 1.50 no sign of H; left, and to cubby hole[40] where studied Mental D. Report. 4–6 p.m. meeting of constitution-

[38] Possibly *Il Fuoco* (The Flame) by Gabriele D'Annunzio, published in 1900.

[39] Leigh Vaughan Henry (1889–1958), composer, conductor, critic and author. Taught music in Florence pre-war and was on a visit to Germany in 1914. He escaped from Ruhleben in Feb. 1918 but was caught and sent to Havelberg Camp. In the 1930s he became a renowned die-hard fascist and was placed under surveillance by MI5.

[40] Cubby holes were originally the racecourse betting booths, located under the first grandstand. Camp students were allowed to book one for two hours a day (*In Ruhleben Camp*, No 8, Sep 1915).

mongering committee to approve final draft of proposed constitution for Ruhleben camp. Butterscotch[41] speaking a lot, showing no signs of contrition for the severe snubbing he got last time – very lachrymose about his democracy and democratic principles. I shall be surprised if the time spent in drawing up and discussing the scheme is rewarded by any change. Evening read Racine – *Andromaque* and in bed Wells' *Boon*. Gurgled over the sketch for a novel by Henry James.

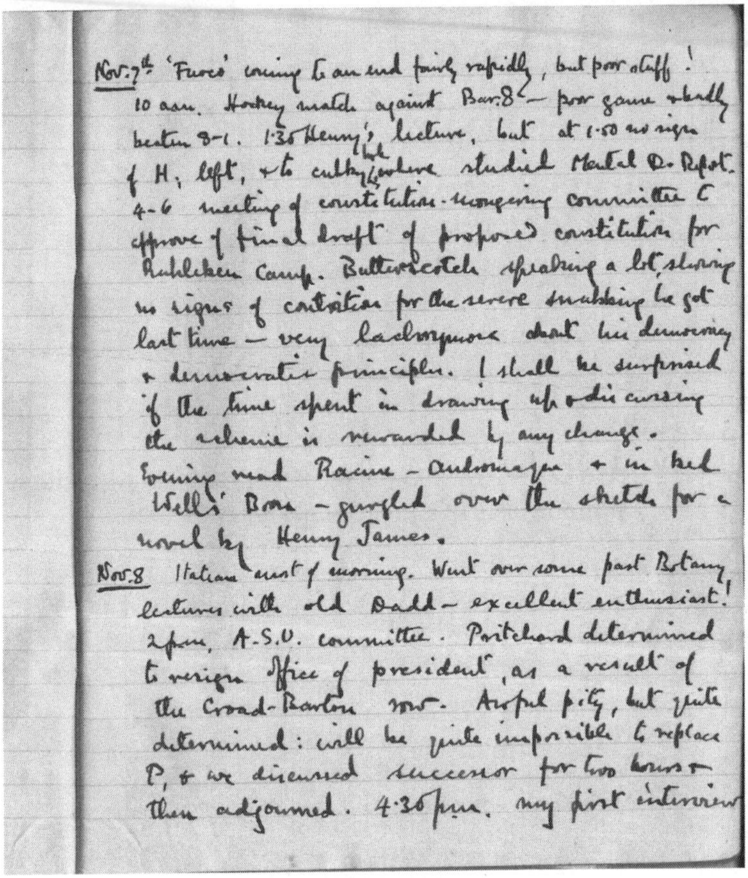

First page of the diary

[41] Walter Butterworth (1862–1935), founder of the Ruhleben Literary and Debating Society, a member of the Recreation Committee (and various others), as well as teaching Dutch and Dutch literature in the school. Director of a Manchester glass-manufacturing company, he was in Germany for the Bayreuth Music Festival when war broke out. The Ruhleben Camp Magazine for May 1916 has a whole page on him. Michael often refers to him as 'Butterscotch'.

Nov. 8th Italian most of morning. Went over some past Botany lectures with old Dodd[42] – excellent enthusiast. 2 p.m. A.S.U. [Arts and Science Union] Committee. Pritchard[43] determined to resign office of president, as a result of the Croad[44] – Barton[45] row. Awful pity, but quite determined: will be quite impossible to replace P, and we discussed successor for two hours and then adjourned. 4.30 p.m. my first interview with the new camp dentist – an *internierte*[46] [internee]. A young fellow, but seems competent and, in any case, has a most up to date fit out. Just put in temporary stopping – return again in three weeks. 6.30 p.m. took Chair for A.S.U. lecture on Parasites and Putrefaction by Lechmere[47] and Lochhead.[48] Appreciative audience and good lectures: we had a home-made lantern, made out of cigar boxes, and it worked excellently. "Pea nuts"[49] produced "some incident" at going to bedtime. He wanted to spend the night in our Bar., and when forcibly ejected, tried to stab Thorpe[50] with a dinner knife.

---

[42] There were several Dodds mentioned in the diaries; two golfing brothers, Arthur (a good friend of Michael's) and Walter, and a Mr (or 'old') Dodd whom Michael teaches.

[43] Matthew Stewart Prichard (1865–1936), an art historian, critic and philosopher, who was a leading figure in the Arts and Science Union. He also taught Italian in the camp school. Michael misspells this name throughout as Pritchard.

[44] Robin Bruce Croad (1891–1968), a chemist studying at Leipzig University in 1914. He taught chemistry in the camp school and was involved with the A.S.U.

[45] Probably Thomas Arthur Barton (1889–1950), a journalist involved in the Education Committee.

[46] Stibbe (2008, p. 84) writes how part of the camp community feeling was created by special lingo, which often dropped in bits of German. It's scattered throughout the diary.

[47] Dr Arthur Eckley Lechmere (1885–1919) had just finished a research scholarship on plant diseases studying under Prof. von Tubeuf in Munich and found himself trapped in Germany. After his arrest he was sent to the salt mines in Bavaria before being transferred to Ruhleben on the 6th November 1914. Whilst there he helped set up the Science Union and was head of the camp school Biology Department. He was also a talented costume-maker for the Ruhleben Dramatic Society. A close colleague of Michael's, he is often referred to as 'L.' in the diaries. Lechmere suffered from bouts of ill-health during his time in the camp, and died in the influenza pandemic on 14th February 1919, shortly after his return to England, aged 34 years.

[48] Allan Grant Lochhead (1890–1980), a Canadian citizen who had just finished his doctorate in plant bacteriology/pathology at the University of Leipzig when war broke out (*Ottawa Naturalist*, Vol. 32, November 1918). He taught bacteriology and Italian in the camp school.

[49] William Jacko (Joeanis Apashay, born 1892 Cameroon). A ship's steward whose ship got impounded in Hamburg. Sold peanuts in the camp, hence his nickname. A death is registered in Berlin on 3rd Jun 1916 for a 'Jakob Williams Jacko Apashaÿ' so he may have died in the camp.

[50] John Hobbs Thorpe (1885–1967), captain of Barrack 11 and Chair of the Entertainments Committee. An engineer who, at the outbreak of war, was director of the Otis Lift Company in Berlin. He also taught in the camp school Engineering Department.

Eventually carried howling to the *Wache* [guardhouse], and then put in the cells,[51] the Baron Powell,[52] sundry police and sentries in attendance. He then proceeded to howl and moan for about half an hour, but finally subsided. Finished *Boon*: good, but rather hastily written, it seemed to me.

Nov. 9th The excitement today was an unexpected visit from Bernstein [fn 23] this morning. We had a bare half hour's talk in the guard room and spoke most in English, in German only when the soldiers came near. Very friendly and kind; said he had put in a *'gesuch'* [petition] for me – but on the whole I'm not so sure I wouldn't just as soon stay here as be free outside. However the *gesuch* is sure to be *abgelehnt!* [rejected] We talked about the camp and I told him fairly straight what I thought of it all: we also talked of the war and the prospects of peace: he thinks peace may come quite unexpectedly, but that at present France is the stumbling block. We talked about poor Hardie[53] and in next to no time the half hour was up [letter from Bernstein to Michael's father on facing page]. Went round to the French Circle at 3 p.m. but found it postponed. The n*****s have at last been removed from the far end of Bar. 6 and so this will presumably now be free for the school. However some of the Jews had immediately seized on it and were having a "*wohnung*" [lodging] built in one corner.[54] Ford[55] was there and jostled them out, timber and all, assuring that nothing could be done without the permission of the Education Committee.[56] It's always the way: we have to wait weeks before we can get a shelf put up for the school, but any Jew can get a house put up at a moment's notice! 7 p.m. Hatfield[57] on Butler's *Way of all Flesh* at the Literary Circle. Very "Hatfieldian" – thinks

---

[51] There were cells at the end of Barrack 11, Michael's barrack.

[52] Joseph Powell (1875–1925). The British overall captain of the camp. Each barrack had its own captain, appointed by Baron von Taube, the German deputy to the camp commandant. It's not clear from the diary if both a German officer and Powell were in attendance, or Michael was using the term 'Baron' sarcastically.

[53] Probably Keir Hardie, Scottish socialist and leading pacifist who died on 26th September 1915.

[54] The orthodox Jews were already housed in Bar. 6, ostensibly segregated for dietary reasons. The loft had been deemed unfit for habitation, and the occupants rehoused, but space was at a premium.

[55] Probably Arthur Clow Ford (1883–1952), a schoolmaster before the war, he became chairman of the Camp School. A regular in the diary, he talks late into the night, cadging cigarettes.

[56] Education in the camp was divided between the Camp School (teaching) and the A.S.U. (lectures and circles) – the Education Committee was hierarchically above the School and A.S.U. Committees.

[57] Dr Henry Stafford Hatfield (1880–1966). Inventor, academic (electricity and electro-chemistry), and broadcaster. Heavily involved in the ASU and the Ruhleben Dramatic Society.

S.B. is the last word in everything. Miserable discussion so came away not much the wiser, but I couldn't have looked H. in the face again if I hadn't gone! Started *Pride and Prejudice* this evening.

....

Eduard Bernstein to Edward Reynolds Pease, sent via E. B. Schattner, a British engineer born in Berlin and living in London:

Berlin Schöneberg

At last I had a chance today to visit Michael Pease in Ruhleben. To my joy I can say that I found him in good health, looking fine and in a good mood. For half an hour we were able to talk unsupervised so that he could have told me, had he wanted to, about any complaints. But he said nothing which may have to do with the fact that he is a very reasoned man who will easily accept what he cannot change. To me his whole appearance and the clear gaze in his eyes were proof to me that he did not suppress any thoughts, at least not to me. We spoke about all kinds of things, also about the war and its possible outcome. In the camps they get the German newspapers, and in the past Pease used to read the "B.Z. Am Mittag" which was terribly jingoistic, and now the "Berliner Tageblatt" which, although it leaves much to be desired, does run the occasional article of worth. It appears that he has no lack of things to read, but what he's missing is the ample opportunity to write to his loved ones! I had oranges, chocolate and such things with me and could hand them over to him unchecked, so it looks as if one is able to send him locally all kinds of agreeable things. I am happy to attend to any wishes his parents may have in this respect. My wife and I send their heartfelt greetings.

Ed Bernstein, Berlin Schöneberg

....

Nov. 10th 8.30 my German conversation hour with Hohenrein.[58] Then Italian till '*Appell*' [roll call] at 11.15 a.m., and then Schimper.[59] On duty at school office 2.30 and then hockey. 5 p.m. Dante Circle. Saw Hatfield and

---

[58] There were a father and son Hohenrein at Ruhleben. The Hohenreins had emigrated from Germany to Hull in 1850. George and his family returned to Germany in 1909, but were interned as British citizens.

[59] A German botanist, best known for *Pflanzengeographie auf Physiologischer Grundlage* (Plant Geography on a Physiological Basis), published in 1898.

discussed the President of A.S.U. question; also *The Knight.*[60] I hear the cubby holes are to be heated after all, but I can hardly believe it.

Nov. 11th Lined up for tickets for *L'enfant Prodigue* and got bad seats for two nights. Finished *Fuoco* and spent the morning on Schimper. 1.30 p.m. informal committee to discuss fitting up the far end of Bar. 6 as a lab. Much talk and eventually a subcommittee of Blagden,[61] Higgins[62] and self appointed to draw up plans. Very important to get ourselves fixed up in there before the authorities can put new people in there. We bought timber on the spot to put up the first partition. 3.30 Merritt[63] came to tea to discuss *The Knight.* Glad he concurs in turning down Harry[64] as Merrythought: he would be a dreadful handful. Decided on Bainton's[65] protégé Bell.[66] Read Scotch [Scottish] report of feeble-minded commission and quiet evening with Victorian verse.

Nov. 12th Got Bainton to introduce me to his protégé Bell; think he'll do excellently for Merrythought – gave him the part to read. Quiet morning with Italian and Schimper. 3 p.m. Italian with Pritchard. Saw Higgins in the evening about the proposed new lab. He's drawn up very elaborate plans – an excellent person to have mobilised for the job.

---

[60] *The Knight of the Burning Pestle,* a Tudor parody by Francis Beaumont, was eventually performed in June 1916. Michael was a co-producer with George Merritt, and the play features prominently in the diaries until then.

[61] Dr John William Blagden (1873–1940), a Cambridge Natural Sciences graduate who had been living in Germany since completing a PhD at Würzburg University in 1896. He was working as a research chemist for Boehringer and Soehne in Mannheim when the war broke out. He taught chemistry in the camp school and was head of the Mathematics and Physical Sciences department.

[62] Dr Eric Berkley Higgins (1885–1959), a chemical engineer and inventor, working in Hamburg when war broke out (obituary in *Nature* by fellow Ruhlebenite H. Stafford Hatfield). In 1916 he was the head of the Arts and Science Union (ASU) and director of the research labs in Bar 6.

[63] George Merritt (1890–1997). Involved in over 50 plays in Ruhleben. He was in Magdeburg studying German theatre and teaching at the Berlitz School at the outbreak of war. Became an actor after the war – often in authoritarian roles – and worked to a ripe old age.

[64] Possibly Harry Stafford (1883–?), interned with his brother Frederick, who acted in various productions whilst in camp. The Stafford brothers were in Germany with Fred Karnos' 'Mumming Birds' Continental Company when war was declared.

[65] Edgar Leslie Bainton (1880–1956), Professor of Music at Newcastle Conservatoire, was in Germany to attend the Bayreuth Music Festival when war broke out.

[66] Colin Bell, listed as singing folk songs on a programme for the Y.M.C.A. concert on 8th Jan. 1916.

Nov. 13th Got two parcels of books today. Cobbett from Bellot,[67] and Prothero and Doncaster's *Determination of Sex* by request. Italian and Schimper in the morning. Afternoon German with Hohenrein. Then saw Higgins and Blagden about Bar. 6. H. hard at work putting up partition. Evening to *L'enfant Prodigue* with Ponsonby.[68] Of its sort it was wonderfully good, the music executed wonderfully. Not very subtle though, in composition. Henry would have awful things to say about it. Finished *Pride and Prejudice*.

[Inserted into diary: programme for *The Prodigal Son,* produced by H. G. Hopkirk]

Nov. 14th Hockey match against Bar. 10 this morning. We had a complete walk over (7–0), and it was a poor game. 1.30 Henry's lecture on the Italian futurist musicians in which he expounded to some extent the anti-traditional philosophy of these people. He played some nice pieces and also repeated some of the Finnish pieces I missed last time. Went round to Bar. 6 to look at our lab only to find that the new people from Sennelager[69] had been put in there! If we had only had a few days more we could have fitted it out so as to make it uninhabitable. Really it is maddening the way they go on humbugging us about that loft. However since they are not n*****s they may get shifted but it probably means waiting again till after Dec. 6th. Went to *L'enfant Prodigue* again with Jones.[70] Started re-reading Cobbett's [*Rural*] *Rides,* sent to me by Bellot – he's a charmingly garrulous old chap.

---

[67] Probably Hugh Hale Bellot, a friend from Bedales School.

[68] Arthur Gordon Ponsonby (1892–1978). A Trinity College graduate who was visiting relatives in Germany in the summer of 1914. He worked in the camp library, taught French and history, and devoted himself to learning languages, which equipped him for a subsequent career in the Consular Service. He played 'a boy' in *The Knight*. His aunt had been a close friend of the Cote Bank Peases.

[69] The P.O.W. camp at Sennelager was initially used to house merchant seaman, mostly British trawlermen taken prisoner after German raiders sank their ships in the North Sea. Many were transferred to Ruhleben.

[70] There were a number of people surnamed Jones in Ruhleben, but the ones most connected with Michael are Douglas Doyle Jones (fn 88), Cecil Duncan Jones (fn 94) and John Phillips Jones (fn 102).

Nov. 15th Saw Higgins this morning who says the engineers personified in Lockyer Roberts[71] are furious because space has not been allotted to them in Bar. 6. I don't know if they think they can set up an oil engine in that rickety old loft: however in the meantime nobody can do anything, though Higgins says the people are to be twisted out today. Spent most of the morning seeing people about the A.S.U. Bainton and Bell[72] very down on the Hawkins[73] proposal. Managed to mobilise Lechmere, Pritchard and Treharne[74] in support of our scheme to have no president. At the meeting, by bad management Bainton put in the chair, Treharne back slid and my proposal beaten by 5–4. Finally Lechmere literally forced to take it. Very rough on him as naturally he doesn't want the responsibility of keeping Hatfield in order! Don't think the business is at an end by any means yet: general meeting on Sunday and all sorts of things may happen between now and then! 3 p.m. Italian with Pritchard, and 6.30 p.m. to first rate lecture on Canada by Bell.[75] Really very able and illuminating paper though far too long: he went on for 2 hours and 10 minutes and then didn't finish, but it wasn't a bit dull the whole time. He dealt with the economic, educational, racial and imperial problems. By a long chalk the most interesting person I've met here, Bell is. Large parcel of bulbs from Mrs. Scott – these people seem to think I've a palace to decorate with flowers!

Nov. 16th Devoted most of the morning to digging up one of the flower beds in front of the Barracks and planting Mrs. Scott's gifts of bulbs – a few I also buried in tins. Planting bulbs collected a huge crowd of people, most of whom laughed at the notion that we should be here at Easter. One most persistent gossiper burbled on about a dear old lady of 90 who used to

---

[71] Cuthbert Lockyer Roberts (1889–?). An engineer working for W. P. Digby Consultant Engineers in Germany at the outbreak of war. *Ruhleben Story* mentions his lectures on wireless telegraphy and engineering. He played Mistress Merrythought in *The Knight*.

[72] H. Alfred Bell, who was active in the camp school. He taught French and commercial subjects, and served on the school Finance Committee. He was also on the Entertainments Committee, and was heavily involved in the French and German dramatic societies.

[73] Horatio John Nelson Hawkins (1874–1928), Chair of the Education Committee, released in 1916.

[74] Professor Bryceson Treharne (1879–1948), a Welsh musician and composer. He was a professor at the University of Adelaide, and was released from Ruhleben in December 1915.

[75] Winthrop Pickard Bell (1884–1965), a Canadian philosophy student who had just completed a doctorate at Göttingen University, sitting his final examination whilst in custody. Michael was good friends with Winthrop during their internment and after the war. In the diaries it is sometimes hard to distinguish which 'Bell' Michael is referring to – Winthrop or Alfred (fn 72).

send him flowers for his indigestion, and of the casino pass the Baron had given him! Had a long talk with [H. Alfred] Bell about the A.S.U. business. Lechmere very sick at the result, as he really doesn't want the responsibility of coping with Hatfield. Saw Pritchard and arranged for a meeting of our faction tomorrow. Read Prothero most of afternoon. Pender's[76] and Jones' lectures in evening. Ingleby[77] summoned for 11 a.m. to be photographed so he looks like getting out!

Nov. 17th Today being "*Putztag*" [cleaning day] we had the *Appell* at 8 a.m., much to the discomfort of the late risers. At caucus meeting of A.S.U. Pritchard frankly gave his reasons for resigning from Presidency – namely the worry and strain of keeping Hatfield in order. Lechmere resolved to send in his resignation and we all agreed to follow suit. Continued Prothero most of morning. 2 p.m. meeting of the constitution mongering committee. Powell received the deputation with every show of friendliness, but subsequently said there were difficulties. Committee appointed to treat with Captains. 3 p.m. hockey in miserable hail and snow. 5 p.m. Dante. Saw Lechmere who said Hatfield abused him furiously for resigning. Henry came round summoning general meeting of A.S.U. for 2 p.m. tomorrow. When I expostulated about the short notice, he first said they knew nothing of L. resignation and then that "we" had decided to throw the presidency open to the free nomination of the meeting. Saw Blagden and explained the crisis to him. Quiet evening reading Prothero and then Cobbett in bed – that wonderful passage of his ride all through the Bedalian Country.

Nov. 18th 1.30 Committee of A.S.U. called to consider the report; Hatfield's draft here attached. I moved to omit words in square brackets in penultimate paragraph. Seconded by Bainton, violently opposed by Henry and lost on vote by 5–3, Lechmere not voting and Pritchard in Chair. Agreed that in reading our report, our dissent would be indicated. No time for further criticism of report as general meeting at 2 p.m. Croad in Chair. Fired off with report and attack on Bainton for wanting to wind up the

---

[76] Robert Herdman Pender (1890–1970), a teacher of modern languages at George Heriot's School who left Scotland for a fortnight's holiday in Germany in July 1914 – only to find himself trapped after war broke out (*Edinburgh Evening News*, 1 July 2015).

[77] J. Ingleby, released from Ruhleben on 7th December 1915 along with another 150 or so unfit internees.

Union. I gave our reasons for not supporting the words in controversy. Wimpfheimer[78] moved that report be not adopted, amendment by Rawson[79] to delete the offending words lost, and W.'s motion passed by 25–21. There followed discussion on Presidency. Pritchard made delightful speech explaining his resignation, and talked about divergence on views of art! Rawson moved to dissolve the Society and after much discussion only mustered 7 supporters. Hatfield proposed for Presidency and carried. Pender for Secretary and Croad for Treasurer. Great difficulty in getting a committee together as no one would serve. Eventually mustered 7 inter alias Kapp[80] and the unfortunate Higgins; I'm sorry for the latter! Meeting terminated at 4.45. It was very amusing, more especially as there was no open ill feeling or abuse. Patchett[81] came nearest to abuse when he held forth on futurism. Well, it will indeed be a comfort to have Monday afternoons freed from these terrible committees. Heard earlier in the day that the military had once more turned down our application for heating the cubby holes. Just as I feared. Quiet evening with Prothero and later Cobbett.

[Insert: secretary's report to the A.S.U. General Meeting, November 18th]

Nov. 19th Everyone very pleased with A.S.U. meeting and seemed thoroughly to have enjoyed it: had a good laugh with Farmer[82] and with Blagden about it. Not feeling quite up to scratch with cold coming on. Played hockey in selection game and felt too tired and sore for much the rest of the day. Saw Lechmere about the dresses for *The Knight* and Bainton

---

[78] Maximilian Wimpfheimer (1878–1952), often called 'Wimpfy' in the diaries, was a barrister who set up the camp's Department for Commercial Subjects, where he taught classes in subjects such as business problems and commercial law. After the war he changed his name by deed poll to Maxwell Wimpole.

[79] Wyatt Trevelyan Rawson Rawson (1894–1980), a graduate of Trinity College Cambridge, was studying music and philosophy in Weimar at the outbreak of war. After the war he became a school master, teaching languages.

[80] Norman Gisbert Kapp (1887–1927), involved in the ASU and the Ruhleben Dramatic Society.

[81] Professor Ernest William Patchett (1878–1936), who taught German literature and philosophy at Ruhleben. A Cambridge graduate (Modern Languages) he had just returned to England from Canada to work at Southampton College. He had married a German girl in Heidelberg in 1910 and was presumably visiting family in Germany when war was declared.

[82] Eric Farmer (1888–1976), a Trinity College Cambridge graduate. He wrote an article after the war for the *Quarterly Review* (Volume 231, April 1919) entitled 'The Psychology of a Prison Camp'.

tells me that Keel[83] will arrange the music for it, so we seem like getting on a bit.

Nov. 20th Felt rather rotten with cold, so quiet morning with Prothero. 1.30 German with Hohenrein, 3 Italian, 5.30 History Circle (paper by Wimpfheimer on a Franconian Manor, the property of his family) and 7.30 School Committee. Not much doing at the latter – vaguely discussed the lab, but the whole thing is held up by the Sennelager people. At bedtime S.[84] tells me the Schloss-Celle people[85] have come in here, including Whyte [fn 5] and Colonel Mitchell of Brotchen [German bread roll] fame! Too late to look up the former till the morning.

Nov. 21st Hustled round first thing after breakfast and found Whyte and another fellow in loft Bar. 5. They seem very pleased at the prospect of being here, as Schloss Celle was very confined. It appears they have been brought here by mistake: it was intended to bring the remaining sailors from Sennelager, and instead the order went to Celle, so they sent a bunch of officers, including General Bradley, and sundry other big nuts. Long conference with Lechmere and Merritt about *The Knight*. Then prepared lecture for Tuesday. Henry's lecture 1.30. Dodd in to tea – we talked about his big farm in B.C. 7.30 p.m. Edge[86] on Boy Scouts at the S.P. [Social Problems] Circle. Finished Cobbett in bed: well worth re-reading.

Nov. 22nd Quiet morning with only parcel *hohling* [fetching?] nuisance. Photos of Godstone R.D.C. [Rural District Council] cottages came through: they look very fine. Made formal application to Entertainments Committee for production of *The Knight*. 3 p.m. scratch game of hockey. Whyte playing, though somehow not so brilliantly in spite of his blue. To Pender's lecture on Maeterlinck with dramatic illustrations by Henry – the A.S.U. Monday

---

[83] Professor Frederick Keel (1871–1954), a composer of art songs, a baritone singer and an academic. Professor of Singing at the Royal Academy of Music in London, he was on a family holiday in Germany when war broke out. He wrote his own memoir *Life in Ruhleben, 1914–1918* in 1920.

[84] Probably Felix Schlesinger [fn 11]. Often referred to as 'S.' or 'Schl'.

[85] An internment camp for officers at Schloss Celle (Celle Castle) in Lower Saxony.

[86] Stephen Rathbone Holden Edge (1893–1955), one of the camp school Biology Department teachers, who gave a series of lectures on animal physiology (including the human body). The *Staffordshire Sentinel* of 20th December 1918 has a short article stating that Mr Stephen R Edge was an Oxbridge graduate studying in Germany in 1914 and had been interned at Ruhleben.

evening affair. A very indifferent ill prepared exhibition – very glad that I am no longer an auspice. It seemed so strange having a Monday without the tiresome A.S.U. Committee. Read *Zukunft* in bed: it's a very sound commentary.

[Insert: programme for illustrated lecture "Maeterlinck as Dramatist" by R. Herdman Pender]

Nov. 23rd Got card at breakfast saying plants arrived. 8 a.m. lecture – rather an ordeal by ice, but a plucky ten or so turned up. 9.30 a.m. hockey match against Bar. 5, beat them 2–1, good game though I got damaged in first minute. Appalling and most disconcerting discovery that the Special Orders Department have got me 106 Marks worth of bulbs; made a botch of the order somehow. Dootson[87] says he'll try to get them returned, but hardly held out much hope. I spent much time and energy in going round to other Barracks to get promises of purchase. Bar. 8 guaranteed 25 Marks and the others would see what could be done. Much perturbed about it, as I shall be ruined if I have to pay. The music for the sword dances came today, so we shall be ready with them when the artists' shed is ready and we get permission. 3 p.m. Italian and 7 p.m. Jones'[88] law lecture. Saw Bainton who tells me *The Knight* has been accepted for Jan. 27th (Kaiser's birthday!) so must set to in real earnest. Read Creighton's *Queen Elizabeth* in bed.

Nov. 24th Still rather in a stew about these beastly bulbs. The devil is, that it's no good refusing to pay because they hold all my money and will simply dock it off, and to make matters worse 108 Marks has this morning arrived for me! Except Bar. 8 none of the others held out any hopes, and Dootson has not yet seen about getting them returned! Finally put the cuts for *The Knight* right and handed the copy over to the typist. 2–3 p.m. on duty at school office. 3 p.m. scratch game Hockey. 6 p.m. we treated Dodd[89] to supper in his loft – we carrying over all the food and he providing the

---

[87] Percy Dootson (1888-1966), a chemist from Lancashire, who also worked in the camp library.

[88] Douglas Doyle Jones (1886–1980), a Cambridge graduate and London barrister who was visiting clients near Gotha at the outbreak of war. He was a close friend and box-mate of Michael's (photo on page 111). Often referred to as 'J' or 'D²J' in the diaries, he was active in the Camp School's Commercial Department.

[89] Arthur Edgar Dodd (1879–?), a professional golfer who was living in Wentorf (near Hamburg) with a German wife and daughter at the outbreak of war. He was an amateur musician, and one of Michael's close friends who appears regularly throughout the diary (photo on page 111).

room. After supper music – a Gade trio consisting of him, Lindsay[90] and Riley.[91] A poorish sort of thing, but quite nice to listen to.

Nov. 25th A year today since we first saw Ruhleben! Spent morning writing out small parts for *The Knight*. Italian 3 p.m. and evening 7 p.m. reading Italian plays. Saw Keel about the music for *The Knight* and got him mobilised. He's sending for his books and I shall write to Paul[92] to see if he can get any of the music that was used for the Cambridge performance. Heard nothing more yet about those infernal bulbs!

Nov. 26th Morning doing small parts for *The Knight*. Too bad for hockey in afternoon – snow and mighty cold. Went to Hatfield's famous production of *The Master Builder* [Ibsen play], which wasn't really so badly done – but why on earth choose the *MB* to introduce Ibsen to the camp?

Nov. 27th Wrote letters in morning and got Mützenbecher[93] to post letter direct through to Ginny[?] for Merrythought's songs. 3 p.m. Italian. Went up to Dodd's loft where read an appalling account of camp at Witenberger [probably Wittenberg] – simply awful. 7.30 School Committee. Hear the Y.M.C.A. hall is ready to be begun next week.

Nov. 28th Mighty cold: buzzed up and down the promenade with Bell discussing *The Master Builder*. Then froze in cubby hole. Curled up in rugs all afternoon in cubby hole. Reading *Leila*. 4.30 S.P. Circle, good paper on unemployment insurance. Quiet but cold evening in cubby hole.

Nov. 29th What Schl. calls a "brass monkey morning". Curled up in rugs in cubby hole and read Italian with my breath frozen on my beard. Saw Merritt about *The Knight* – sundry difficulties with small parts. Copied out rest of small parts in afternoon and further conference with M. 4 p.m.

---

[90] William Lindsay (1882–?), a professional pianist who won the Mendelssohn Prize at the Leipzig Conservatory before the war. He appears on many concert programmes in Ruhleben. After the war he became Professor of Music at Minnesota University.

[91] Walter Riley, a professional violin player.

[92] Paul Denys Montague (1890–1918). A good friend of Michael's at Bedales and Cambridge. Montague was a member of the Cambridge Marlowe Society, a student drama club founded in 1907 to produce relatively unknown historical plays. We think Michael saw their 1911 performance of *The Knight* (maybe even helped out) and therefore chose to produce it at Ruhleben.

[93] The camp officer in charge of censorship of all post. According to Stibbe (2008), he made the internees' lives considerably easier with his sympathetic attitude.

Pender on Racine [French dramatist] at 7 p.m. Read Goldoni's plays in school office – miserably cold! Pritchard is wonderful the way he reads – he was an irate uncle this time.

Nov. 30th Still cold and sleeting to boot. Read Italian in morning and had further conference with Merritt. Ought to have lectured at 8 a.m. this morning but I scratched last night – too much of an ordeal by ice. 3 p.m. Italian. 6.30 p.m. to a squash in Dodd's loft where Treharne gave some of the music he has composed in camp. Part songs to words of Henry and Duncan-Jones[94] and solos, two of which Fergusson[95] sang. All very weird futurist stuff, though one of the solos – a dirge – very attractive and interesting. On the whole, the effect was distinctly depressing. Button holed by Hatfield after meeting who wants me to come on A.S.U. Committee instead of Treharne who is leaving. Went up into his "*wohnung*" [lodging] and explained why I couldn't. Hatfield is so nice that you can tell him things to his face without his taking offence! Also discussed *Master Builders*.

[Insert: membership card for Ruhleben Lawn Tennis Association, Season 1915]

Dec. 1st As a result of partial thaw and frost, the whole place a sheet of ice and walking most dangerous. 8.30 German jaw with Hohenrein: then parcel *hohlen*; went up and looked at stage with Merritt. At midday our friend "Peanuts" went "loo" again and was carried howling to the *Wache*. However, his *lieben Onkel* [Dear Uncle] (The Baron) took his side saying he was a "*ganz harmloser Mensch*" [very harmless person] and he would like him to *schlag* [beat] one of us *tod* [to death]!! So a scapegoat was found and another n****r put in the cells for 72 hours. This afternoon the prisoners from Wittenberg arrived, about 40 sailor fellows. Hung Grannie's pictures in the cubby hole. The place <u>looks</u> very nice and cosy – would it were as warm as it looks! The Education Committee far too busy squabbling over

[94] Cecil Duncan Jones (1883–1918), a novelist, poet and actor. He produced a number of plays and helped organise a Shakespeare Festival whilst interned. He had been in Alsace Lorraine recovering from an operation when the war broke out. Due to ill-health he was released and sent to Holland in Oct 1918, but died on 10th Nov 1918, shortly after his return to England.

[95] George William Fergusson (1864–1947), a professional baritone singer who was teaching at a German repertory in Berlin at the outbreak of war *(Bournemouth Graphic*, 28th February 1919).

Hatfield to turn its attention to the heating question. 5 p.m. went to the Dante Circle but Cutayar[96] had such a bad cold and throat that his voice gave out after ½ hour; adjourned. 7 p.m. to Science Circle where Lechmere held forth on Spectromicroscopy. I sampled the new ref. library this afternoon; presented the vol. of Fabian tracts and Wells' *New Worlds for Old.* Paid 4 weeks deposit and took out a Marrett's *Anthropology*:– rather fatuous reading. Today it was my turn to have a row with Wagner [a box-mate]. At tea time, I left the door open, thinking Bickerstaffe[97] was just going out, when W. turned on me with the most filthy and abusive language I've ever had addressed to me. I just stood there, smirking, with my hands in my pockets and let him swear away purple in the face and his eyes bloodshot and bulging. It's intolerable to have to be mixed up intimately with such low down crass curs.

Dec. 2nd Fairly quiet morning mostly reading Italian. 3 p.m. Italian class with Pritchard. Whyte and Hill[98] into supper: a pleasant "*schmaus*" [feast]; heard all W.'s history. Merritt came along to say that he wants to put off *The Knight* and do a play of his own in that date. The *geschichte* [saga] is fairly complicated; I showed fairly clearly that I didn't like the change but he failed to take the hint. However, see what the morrow brings forth. Just saw Bainton for a moment or two about it, who says doesn't think Entertainments Committee will consent to any such change. Read Marett in bed – interesting on primitive languages.

Dec. 3rd Still in a tiresome state of uncertainty about *The Knight*, as Merritt can't find out for certain about dates. Anyhow got the typed copies, put them together and marked them – only to find some sheets had been left out. Read *Leila* in the afternoon, Dante 5 p.m. and quiet evening with Victorian verse.

---

[96] Mario Cutayar (c1885–1982), a professional tenor singer. According to an article in the *Bournemouth Graphic* on 28th February 1919, he was arrested as a spy and tortured before being sent to Ruhleben. At the time of the article he was performing in an opera in Bournemouth with fellow internees Fergusson and Webber.

[97] Harold Douglas Bickerstaffe (1895–1965). Was a ship's clerk in his father's Steamship Company. In the 1930s he became chairman of the Blackpool Tower Company, the tower having been built by his uncle (*Liverpool Echo*, 24th August 1965).

[98] Alfred Hill (1887–?). A graduate of Aberdeen University, he was an agricultural chemist working for the German Potash Syndicate in Berlin at the outbreak of war (*Aberdeen Journal*, 28th April 1916). He ran practical classes in the testing of agricultural seeds in the camp school biology laboratories.

Dec. 4th Long talk with Merritt: he's still very unsettled about his *Passers By.*[99] Must get that settled up very quickly. Also terribly up the spout for "Jasper" [character in *The Knight*]. 1.30 German with Hohenrein – Italian off, because of Pritchard's lecture. 5.30 History Circle – Leigh Henry on the Elizabethan Era – an awful rag. Delivered of course in the usual L.H. style – unprepared halting and appallingly meaningless involved sentence – "to actually come to actualities" etc. Absolutely nothing in the paper and very much taken to task by Patchett, Wimpfheimer and others – of course L.H. is a complete ignoramus on matters of historical fact. The finishing touch was when Winzer[100] moved that no communication about the activities of the society should be made to the press without the approval of the president. This was aimed, of course, at Henry's article in the *Musical Times* in which he ascribed all the musical, dramatical, and lecturing activities in the camp to himself! The motion caused tremendous merriment and poor Henry looked dreadfully taken down. Hope it did him some good: I only wish Pender and Kapp and other of his admirers had been there. 7.30 School Committee – everyone still chortling over the Henry baiting rag. Re-reading Graham Wallas' *Human Nature and Politics* in bed. I got today Coulter's *Sex in Plants* from an unknown donor in Cambridge. Read about half of it – doesn't strike me as illuminating or profound. Mr. Ingleby is on the list to get out on Monday, so that reduces our box to 5.

Dec. 5th Played hockey against Bar. 2: not a bad game at all, but beaten. Quiet afternoon reading Italian. Merritt still in a state of irritating uncertainty! 4.30 S.P. Circle – Bell on Emigration – not so illuminating as I had anticipated. At supper Schlesinger brought best bit of news I've had for a long time – to whit Wagner has arranged an exchange between himself and Milner.[101] This will be great – we can have the window open and above all, that awful state of strain, of keeping up an appearance of pleasantness with that rough cur to avoid a hopeless rupture. After tomorrow may I never have to speak to him again – much less rub shoulders with him all day! What an unspeakable relief it will be though

---

[99] A play by Charles Haddon Chambers.

[100] Charles Freegrove Winzer (1886–1940), a painter and lithographer, who was working for the French Red Cross when he was arrested by the German authorities in 1914.

[101] Frank Clifford Milner (1889–1943), a teacher who was working in Thüringen when war broke out. He taught bookbinding in the camp, and was a box-mate of Michael's.

I'm awfully nervous lest some hitch should arise. Millington and his crew in the box opposite had a great binge on and kept all our half of the Barrack awake till long after midnight – just the sort of selfish dogs that one of these fine days will get the soldiers [German guards] brought back. Went to concert this evening – not bad, but not very great. Dodd got a tremendous reception.

Dec. 6th Ingleby went off at 6 a.m. this morning and we spent the whole day *umgruppieren* [rearranging] in the box. Wagner, thank the Lord, moved out without any unpleasantness, and Milner came in in the afternoon. In the meantime we made one bed *verschwinden* [disappear] and put the other 5 up, with 2 below and 3 above. A most exhausting proceeding: not finished till suppertime. Quiet evening with poetry and then to bed mighty pleased with the change – first night with open window for many weeks! The whole atmosphere, physical and spiritual so different within the box.

Dec. 7th Gave my last lecture of the course at 8 a.m. this morning: only 6 turned up including Mr. Dodd [fn 42]. Rather an early morning ordeal in these demoralised days of the *Zivilverwaltung* [civil administration]. Wasted a lot of time looking for Merritt, and for Jones[102] to settle up about those famous bulbs! Kremnitz[103] got some plants sent to him today which we put in our bed. Afternoon spent in erecting shelves but much handicapped by the lack of timber in camp. 6 p.m. went to Jones' law lecture. Saw Bainton this evening who tells me Merritt wrote a very strong letter to the E.C. [Entertainments Committee] saying he'd no interest in *The Knight*(!) and wanted to have his play instead on Jan. 27!! I think that's treating me very inconsiderately: the *Master Builder* is all very well on the stage, but his attitude of ruthless push is very trying in real life.[104] Infernal binge again in the box opposite.

Dec. 8th Spent practically all day timbering up shelves and boot racks and so forth in the Box. Life is altogether different now! Also spent endless time

---

[102] Possibly John Phillips Jones, Chair of the Finance Department.

[103] Brothers Harry and Frank Kremnitz were in Barrack 11 loft. Their father was German and mother English. Harry (1874–?) was an engineer and became a UK citizen in 1896 (Inst. Mech. Engineer records). After the war Frank (1878–?) became a farmer in South Africa. and it seems that both took their mother's maiden name (Buckton).

[104] Reference to Ibsen's play – comparing Merritt's behaviour with the Master Builder's.

trying to find Merritt and Jones – still rather grumpy about the former. The drunk swine were put in the cells at *Appell* time, but the situation is not improved by their friends coming and shouting to them. Quiet evening reading poetry. In bed finished Wallas and started a novel of Hauptmann's. Another drunk put in the cells: this specimen very talkative and held forth for a long while on P.G.ismus.[105] The captains adopt the usual attitude towards the drunks question. They know how it comes in, but haven't got the courage to stop it at its source. They're as bad as politicians on prostitution. Talking of captains, after much electioneering Masterman[106] has been elected for Bar. 10. That will be some new type [*sic*], and may make things buzz in the Captain's office.

Dec. 9th I joined the *baden*[107] [bath] party this morning, as I'd nothing better to do. It's a tiresome waste of time, but nice to get a hot spray now and again. Went and saw Merritt and I'm afraid we had rather a brusque interview but I was rather ruffled, I confess. However I don't think we quarrelled, as he was certainly somewhat ashamed of himself over the proceeding. Saw Dootson about those famous bulbs, who says that Jones has induced the Military to inquire into the matter. 3 p.m. went to Pritchard's for Italian but read English papers instead till 4 p.m. as P. was having interview with Mützenbecher. Quiet evening re-reading Emily Bronte's poems. Drafted a letter to Entertainments Committee about *The Knight*, but failed to find M. for his approval. Read the *Vorssische Zeitung* [a German newspaper] in bed. Fine speeches by Scheidemann and other socialists on Peace, and a very good leader, criticising the Chancellor's speech – this is much more significant than the socialist speeches. However, if only some of our poor weak kneed chalk and water leader writers had the guts to speak up..... Lord, when I was reading the *Chronicle* this afternoon I was reduced to such a state of contempt and despair by the sentiments expressed therein. Why can't they have a concentration camp

---

105 Pro-German prejudice. Some internees (known as PGs) were German born and/or raised, but were classed as British due to their parent's nationality and were sent to Ruhleben.

106 John Cecil Masterman (1891–1977), a regular in the diary, was captain of Bar 10 and a leading athlete and academic in the camp. He was an exchange lecturer at the University of Freiburg in 1914 and after the war he became a tutor in modern history at Oxford and an international sportsman. In 1957 he was appointed Vice-Chancellor of Oxford University.

107 Hot showers were located outside the camp at the Emigrant Control Station by the railway (where pre-war emigrants from the east started their journey to the USA).

for journalists? I'd like to shove some of those glossy recruiting agents in here!

Dec. 10th Saw Merritt this morning, who was friendly. He had heard from the Entertainments Committee, so further communication was useless. Parcel with *Nature, Bedales Chronicle* received. Wrote letter home in the afternoon. 5.30 went to French play – *La Petite Chocolatiere*. Learnt much French, but it passes my comprehension how people can go night after night to that sort of stuff for the sake of the play itself. Read Hauptmann's *Atlantis* in bed.

[Insert: programme for *La Petite Chocolatiere*, produced by H. Alfred Bell]

Dec. 11th Played a most murderous Hockey Match against Bar. 10A. Lost, but good game notwithstanding. 3 p.m. Italian, during which Hahlo[108] was carried in with his knee crooked and stiff, the result of the hockey match. He seemed in considerable pain, so we sent for a *sanitäts* man who felt it round, said it was only a bad bruise and gave us a wet bandage for him. He was a particularly nice friendly man, chatted away smoking cigarettes while we held candles round for him to see! We made him a present of a box of biscuits when he went off. 7.30 School Committee. Hear that the Y.M.C.A. Barrack will be ready by end of January, but that there is little hope of the end of Bar. 6 being cleared for Lab purposes.

Dec. 12th 10 a.m. went to Pritchard's first lecture on Art entitled "Greek and Byzantine ideals". He started by criticising the Greeks, pointing out that their appeal was always to the intellect, and that white marble was soulless stuff to work in. But when he came on to the Byzantine work he waxed eloquent, maintaining that the Byzantine art appealed to the sentiments and the soul, ending up with a great peroration on the High Mass. One of the most interesting lectures I've heard here, or elsewhere for that matter. Quiet afternoon with Schimper. 4.30 S.P. Circle. Warkentin[109] on Canadian education. 6.30 Bainton's first symphony concert – not up to very much – the wind instruments were appalling. The captains are

---

[108] Sidney James Hahlo (1897–1971), a schoolmaster from Manchester. After the war he changed his name by deed poll to Sidney James Harlowe (*London Gazette*, 12th September 1919) and became a psychologist.

[109] Isaak Johann Warkentin (1885–1971), a Canadian school teacher, who was studying pedagogy in Leipzig University when war broke out.

showing up in their very worst colours over the constitution-mongering business. What contemptible, unaspiring, unimaginative fools – or rather knaves – they are.

[Insert: programme of Symphony Concert, Sunday Dec. 12th. Conductor Mr. E. L. Bainton]

Dec. 13th Quiet morning reading *Leila* and started Marriott's *English Land System* with a view to a paper for the Historical Circle on what I don't quite know. This afternoon we got our supply of timber at last so Schl. and I set to work on shelves again, and worked till bedtime.

Dec. 14th Read some Italian in morning and timbered up a shelf and a plate rack. Box really looks very nice now. 3 p.m. Italian with Pritchard. 7 p.m. Jones' law lectures. From letters today I hear that N.[110] is now in the trenches.

....

Marjory Pease to MSP (letter 114, received 14th Dec):

The Pendicle, Limpsfield, Surrey

16th Nov. 1915

Dearest Michael

We were very pleased to get your letter written on October 31st and to know you are well in spite of the horrid cold winter which seems to have begun so early this year. Your letter has come quickly as things go nowadays and it is a great relief to know you are well. Do always let me know how you are. I am thankful that sleeping bag has reached you as I know it will be a real "comfort". Do use it for keeping yourself warm when you sit reading. Snow fell here last night – 2 inches – but mercifully it has nearly all melted and there is no wind.

London 17th Nov. To continue– I have sent your letter to Bellot and will write to Lesley tonight. A PC from Nicolas date 15th saying he is well and evidently in France, though this is not stated. And it is only an official printed card, to which he has signed his name. In some ways, I shall hear less of his doings than I do of you, but I am getting my passport and have a plan of perhaps going to work in France. In any case I get my passport so as to be able to get at Nicolas if he is

---

[110] Nicolas Arthington Pease, Michael's brother.

wounded. Peter Eckersley [an Old Bedalian] *is at Salonika. I have sent you a parcel today containing quince jam and bramble jam, carefully done up in tins. I also sent a copy of the Bedales chronicle which I hope reaches you. It contains an interesting letter from Jarintzoff*[111] *in Gallipoli. We called on the Dudley Wards on Saturday but only the lady was in. She is a Prussian – very anxious to know about you and to help you to get books via her mother who lives in Munich. I have written to Mrs. Spencer Mumby*[112] *about your books and I will also write to the Baroness. I asked her to send you bulbs not books! Glad you got the bulbs from Barrs. Who is Lechmere? I remember you mentioned his name and told me he knew the Southeast Coast. What glorious days those were. My last bicycling in France alone with Nicolas was a very pleasant time that I think was four years ago last Summer.*

Mrs. Gibbs is perfect. At last I've hit upon the right sort trained by the gentry! She remarked "if you do not give me more work to do I will not feel I'm earning my money!!" Forgive this scrappy note. I go north on Monday visiting Neumeister en route taking him apples, jam cake etc.

Ever your loving mother

....

Dec. 15th Read Italian in the morning. 2–3 p.m. at school office making out report of department. 5 p.m. Dante. Quiet evening reading Marriott. 4 p.m. meeting at Hatfield's about research room which has been given to us by the Educ. Dept, one of the rooms in the roof of the new Y.M.C.A. building. Thing in charge of Higgins. One hardly believes it, but the authorities are charging the Y.M.C.A. rent for the site of the hall!! The unspeakable meanness of these people passes one's comprehension!

Dec. 16th Quiet morning with Italian. Parcel from home with Joffnette cooker in which was enclosed some eggs which caused the usual stinking *schweinerei* [mess]. 3 p.m. Italian with Pritchard. Quiet evening: began famous Land Enquiry Report. We are invited to a champagne Xmas dinner with Dodd. Feel more like celebrating Xmas on bread and water at present. How I loathe Xmas and all its disgusting brawling and insincere sentiments.

---

[111] Dmitri Jarintzoff, a Bedalian school friend of Michael's who was a 2nd Lieutenant in the 10th Battalion of the East Lancashire Regiment.

[112] A Pease family friend living in Switzerland.

Dec. 17th Quiet morning. Went to picture exhibition in afternoon. Poor, I thought, not so good as last one. The work pertaining to the camp was mostly "funny" and much of it gross. The rest consisted mostly of back numbers of the professional artists who put them up in hope of getting them sold. Of the camp studies only two attracted me, one of which I bought, a little fragment by Hotopf.[113] Helped S. construct a ladder for his top bed. 3 p.m. scratch game hockey. Quiet evening reading poetry.

Dec. 18th Hockey match this morning against Bar. 3. Good game but lost 3–4. 3 p.m. Italian with P. 5.30 p.m. Historical Circle lecture on the mad King Ludwig II of Bayern. 7.30 p.m. School Committee. Patchett on the war path again about our science research scheme. He's really animated by a desire to spike Hatfield's scheme, and it was bad luck that Wimpfheimer just happened to mention it. I tried to adjourn the discussion at one stage on the score that the report should be first considered, but by further bad luck the draft wasn't ready and so that dodge fell flat.

[Insert: list of members and papers from the Ruhleben Historical Club, December 1915, President: J. C. Masterman, Hon. Sec: H. M. Andrews]

Dec. 19th 10 a.m. Winzer's lecture on Poussin. Interesting to the uninitiated, but of course I was not able to judge critically. 2.15 School Committee to approve of draft report. 3 p.m. teachers meeting: very uneventful. Jones elected on committee for commercial dept. in place of Wimpfheimer who resigned. 6.30 p.m. repeat of Bainton's last concert: much better this time in spite of the appalling woodwind. [On this day he posted the 1915 Ruhleben Xmas postcard to his mother, which arrived on January 4th 1916].

Dec. 20th Quiet morning reading *Leila*. Afternoon ditto: spent some trying to pitch on suitable subject for Historical Circle. 7 p.m. Social Problems Circle, poor turn out and worse paper by Lockyer Roberts. Cold snow. Postcard from old Bowman[114] and from Ingleby.

Dec. 21st Uneventful day, cold.

---

[113] Ernst Herman Friedrich Hotopf (1878–1946). An electrical engineer, born in England to German parents. Taught French in the camp school and also designed programmes. After the war changed his name to Ernest Frederick Holden (*London Gazette,* 21st January 1919).

[114] Edward Allinson Bowman (1860-1931), released with his son Noel on 6th September 1915.

Dec. 22nd Very cold -16°C. Walked up and down all morning, talking with Bell mostly. Bright and wonderfully dry like Switzerland. Got the parcel of books I ordered from Geneva three months ago. 1.30 p.m. meeting of Committee for the School Conversazione, drew up program (including a Morris jig!) and a play produced by Winzer. Saw W. shortly afterwards who says he's given up all intention of producing the said play! 5 p.m. Dante Circle. Quiet evening. S. very rotten with a huge boil on his leg.

Dec. 23rd Not nearly so cold today. S. very bad with his great boil. Went to the doctor and was put in the *Schonungsbaracke* [sanatorium, located in Bar 19], where I saw him in the afternoon. Expects to return tomorrow. Looks as if the Y.M.C.A. hall really will be finished by tomorrow, a remarkable triumph, but I hear Butterscotch is being tiresome about the '*verwaltung*' [administration] of the building and wants the Ed. Dept. kept out of it altogether. In any case we can't have the research room there. Saw Lechmere in the evening and discussed the biology and the new lab. There is one beautiful roman hyacinth out. The bulb business with the Special Orders Dept. still hangs fire! Finished *Atlantis*; the rottenest novel it's ever been my fate to read. Started Trevelyan's *England in the Age of Wycliffe*.

Dec. 24th Great thaw today, rain and unspeakable slush! Quiet morning. S. returned from *Schonungsbaracke* able to get about now. Saw Lechmere and made out list of stuff we want Seward[115] to send us. 2 p.m. constitution mongery committee, rather a poor turn out. Report of deputation to captains, who turned the scheme completely down in the most idiotic way. Agreed to draw up a résumé of the scheme and submit this to the committee and then get all the signatures in camp worth having. This afternoon the Y.M.C.A. mission hall was opened amid much hymn singing and pretty speech singing. While they were singing "Onward Christian Soldiers", within a stone's throw the real article was going past in trainloads to spread a little Christianity in Kurland! S. and J. went and had a *schmaus* [feast] with Dodd (J. considerably the worse for it!) and I dined off bread and butter to show my contempt of Xmas. I retired to cubby hole with rugs and read quietly. Allowed to stay up till 10 p.m. Considerable row

115 Albert Charles Seward, Professor of Botany at Cambridge University 1906–1936. Their correspondence is in Appendix 2.

and drinking in the Barracks, though ours was relatively very quiet – at least down stairs.

Dec. 25th As warm as spring, and unspeakable slush. Quiet morning writing Xmas letter home and composing a "funny story" for the Italian Circle on Sunday. Beer handed out at lunch, to the great excitement and mighty content of people in general! Quiet afternoon and a pleasant Xmas supper with Dodd – Ford, Williams[116] (the cellist) and Manning also there. Pleasant but neither eventful nor interesting. A great spread of all the usual fare, including champagne. The soldiers [guards] must have coined fortunes over the amount of drink brought into camp during the last few days. Hot punch – about millinormal – handed out in the Barracks, but produced no bad effects. Ours was <u>very</u> quiet, but in other Barracks I hear pandemonium reigned. The Baron came through about 10 p.m., found all well with us, but I wonder what he saw and heard elsewhere!

Dec. 26th Everyone looking sort of rather after-Xmas-dinnery today. Composed letter to Seward. Quiet afternoon reading. Very nice concert in evening. Carols etc arranged by Bainton.

Dec. 27th Uneventful day. Started Machiavelli's *Principe*.

Dec. 28th Fairly quiet day. Saw Jones about these famous bulbs, which the firm has refused to take back. I volunteered to take 40 Mks worth and his dept. will try to sell the rest. Warner[117] of Bar. 8 declines now to take any and prophesies complete failure. Tremendous post, including a letter from one Helen Wedgwood of Newnham Coll [see facing page] whom I don't remember ever having seen. Most affectionate and really writes something worth reading – not the usual flippant tosh. Also nice letter from Biffen and from Tony Clarke. Supped with Dodd and read English papers. Assailed by Pritchard and carried off to Italian play reading. Not very thrilling! Went into loft Bar. 6 and conferred with Ford, Blagden and Higgins re proposed lab. for research and teaching purposes. Really looks like getting underway at last! To bed and read *England in the Age of Wycliffe*. Woke up in night and started thinking about the Wedgwood letter: can't

---

[116] Arthur Williams, a Welsh musician who was released in the autumn of 1917.

[117] Lionel Percy Warner (1879–1948), working for the Dunlop Tyre Company in Germany in 1914.

remember ever having seen or talked to her – anyhow she ~~wants~~ deserves some reply – she looks like a wench of some guts. Finally I turned on light and went on reading – wonderful account of Peasants' revolt.

……………………

Helen Bowen Wedgwood [HBW] to MSP (received 28th Dec):

Newnham College, Cambridge.

10th Dec. 1915

Dear Mr. Pease,

You will not be likely to remember me, but I used to see you at the Morris dancing and elsewhere in Cambridge just before the war; and as my brothers are at Bedales and I have many Bedalian friends I have heard a good deal about you. I thought I would write as Miss Lapthorn and Miss Schuster have gone down, and as I am secretary of the Fabian Society [Cambridge University branch] *it might amuse you to hear from someone how things are going.*[118] *Of course it has been very difficult to manage with so many people away, and of course it will get worse; but on the whole we have not done so badly. To begin with the Newnhamites have been doing their share nobly – poor Miss Clough*[119] *has had a dreadful time as she has been growing steadily more Tory since the war began; and it must be trying at her age to see the young persistently treading the broad road to destruction.*

The study circles have been properly started and we are all industriously engaged in teaching other people what we don't know ourselves; but after all that is a very good way of learning. The discussions are occasionally good and frequently acrimonious, especially when Cole's[120] *disciples, or the solitary Land Taxer begin to air their views. Members of the I.L.P.* [Independent Labour Party] *join in a good deal, and we see quite a lot of them, but they are rather a scattered band, and not active at present; still if we can help them just to exist till the end of the war, it will be something. It is the most hopeful thing about the war, the way in which everyone is trying to do a little hard thinking for themselves. Cambridge is a battle ground of conflicting views. We had Clifford Allen*[121] *down last term. He made a violent anti-war speech, (though he had promised to confine himself to*

---

[118] Michael was President of the Cambridge University Fabian Society in 1912-13.

[119] Blanche Athena Clough, A Newnham graduate who was Vice-Principal of the College at this time.

[120] George D. H. Cole, a Fabian economist.

[121] Former Chair of the Cambridge University Fabian Society, in 1914 he was manager of the *Daily Citizen*, and Chair of the No-Conscription Fellowship (NCF).

social questions!) The meeting was <u>*not*</u> *broken up, whereat he was much disappointed, and, I am afraid, thought us very degenerate. What will, we fear, annoy many of our absent members, is that we have changed our name. We did it partly because the central society wanted money and we hadn't got any, and partly because the followers of Cole are getting the upperhand. It was rather a shame to do it when so many members were away.*[122] *We felt very brave and independent at the time, but took care to safeguard ourselves by retaining a Fabian Group. So far it does not seem to have made much difference, and you can always re-convert us when you come back!*

It is a pity you are not in Cambridge now, as agriculture is becoming an extremely fashionable pursuit, – especially if presided over by a real live Belgian professor of intensive cultivation. Those who cannot get a Belgian have to put up with the English article. The results seem to be about the same in both cases. The really patriotic ruthlessly dig up their lawns; at Newnham we unfortunately found the remains of an asphalt tennis court underneath, but "nothing could stop that astonishing infantry" and we attacked it with pickaxes. As you may imagine, the tangible results, in the form of cabbages, is small, as a rule, but the moral and muscular force developed is well worth the effort.

When you come back you will find splendid chances of getting people to understand better methods of agriculture. Putting aside the fads of the Cambridge ladies, people at large do really seem to be beginning to grasp the fact that growing food is not an "unskilled" occupation to be left to anyone too stupid to do anything else, but should be studied by everyone and bought into touch with the best scientific theories.

It must be fearfully boring being shut up at Ruhleben, but you can console yourselves by thinking that there is a grand clearance of rubbishy old ideas going on here, and imagining what a fine time we shall have building up something better on the ground so cleared. The war doesn't seem <u>*quite*</u> *so bad when one thinks about that hard.*

Yours sincerely,

Helen Bowen Wedgwood

……………………

[122] The Cambridge University Fabian Society became the Cambridge University Socialist Society in June 1915 dedicated to 'complete political and industrial democracy [and] supersession of the capitalist system'. It was pacifist, affiliated to the NCF.

Dec. 29th Spent most of morning trying to find Jones to settle up that bulb business finally. Went over the actual stuff but as no invoice was forthcoming I made another appointment for 2 p.m. This time I went with Dr Lloyd[123] and we carted off 40 Marks worth of bulbs, narcissus, crocus, and tulips – fine bulbs: it was wicked to have them wasted so. We planted them there and then – or some of them, rather – surrounded by the usual crowd of loafers whose minds were so material that they all thought they were onions! I ought to have been at a constitution-mongery committee: it approved of the résumé and so we are to collect influential signatures. Kapp came in after supper and yarned away a bit, mainly to say that he's great friends of Margery Fry's.[124] Lab. scheme step forwarder this morning. Meeting of Blagden, Ford, Smith,[125] Venables,[126] Pennington,[127] approve of our plans. Quiet evening reading de Vigny poems and so to bed almighty relieved to have settled the bulb business, even so unsatisfactorily as dropping 35 Mks and planting after Xmas.

Dec. 30th Bath 8.30 a.m. till nearly 10. Went up and measured out the space and made estimate for timber for fitting up lab. Finished planting the famous bulbs and darned socks till lunch. Went round and secured the required timber and made a beginning with Lechmere. Crowd in to tea as usual: Dodd and Marshall[128] there, discussed Pritchard on music. Went round to Dodd's and read Xmas eve leaders in the *D.T.*[129] which reduced me

---

[123] John Alexander Lloyd (1878–1960). Working in Germany at the outbreak of war. Whilst at Ruhleben he taught Physics, studied leatherwork and bookbinding, and took part in amateur dramatics. He lived in Barrack 11.

[124] Michael's 1st cousin once removed, Sara Margery Fry, daughter of his great uncle Sir Edward Fry.

[125] Possibly F. H. Smith, requisites manager of the Camp School and one of the physics teachers.

[126] R. E. Venables, an engineer from Oxford, who taught in (and was the representative of) the Engineering Department of the Camp School.

[127] Allan Mather Pennington (1889–1955), a teacher in (and representative of) the Handicrafts Department of the Camp School.

[128] Thomas Humphrey Marshall (1893–1981), a graduate of Trinity College Cambridge, he was studying German in Weimar at the outbreak of war. A close friend of Michael's at Ruhleben, he also was a talented amateur musician. After the war he worked in the London School of Economics Social Science Department, and later for UNESCO's Social Science Department.

[129] Presumably *The Daily Telegraph.* Newspapers were smuggled into the camp, thanks to Mützenbecher turning a blind eye.

to an indescribable state of pulp. Composed letter to Neumeister.[130] Yarned all evening with Rawson and so to bed and finished *Wycliffe* with mighty content.

Dec. 31st Busy morning. Fearful *antretenei* [line up] for parcels, then School Committee 9.45 till lunch. Afternoon in Bar. 6 putting up lab. bench. After tea composed reply to Miss Wedgwood and quiet evening – till bedtime! Went to bed feeling rotten with headache, but no peace, for pandemonium prevailed. No officers in camp and Mohr who was in charge, drunk, went round to the Barracks arm in arm with prisoners, followed by drum and fife band and made speeches. He said *"Vor allen Dingen wollen wir Frieden"* [above all, we want peace], that it laid with the German government to offer terms, that when we went back to England we should always think of our good friend Mohr, and that if England wanted help, he, Mohr, would *unterstutzen* [support] England. If only the Hauptmann [captain] could have pictured the scene! Practically everyone was blind drunk, but about 4 a.m. peace reigned again. Not a very elevating proceeding when all said and done, though it had its comic moments.

[130] The Neumeister family adopted Michael Pease as a prisoner, reciprocated by Michael's family caring for their son interned in Britain (see page 9). Michael was later allowed to visit them in Jena.

1916 Diaries and Letters

Jan. 1st Tired after sleepless night. Wrote letter home in morning. Quiet afternoon. Dodd into supper. He had just been out in Berlin for 24 hours to see wife and family and consequently rather exhausted. Says life in Berlin is same as ever – dare say it is for the millionaire.

....

Marjory Pease to HBW:

The Pendicle, Limpsfield, Surrey

26th Jan. 1916

Dear Miss Wedgwood,

I am sending you a message from my son in Ruhleben which is in a letter he wrote to me on New Year's Day. I am so glad you wrote to him and I hope if you have time you will write again as I know how much he has appreciated your letter.

I do hope your brother is in some less dangerous place than the Dardanelles now. My younger boy is in France and I anxiously await news from this German offensive.

Yours truly

Mrs. Pease

The following was transcribed by Marjory under the heading "Extract from letter written by M. S. Pease on New Year's Day from Ruhleben".

My greatest and pleasantest surprise was the letter from Miss Wedgwood: it struck an entirely different note from most of the others. Please send her the following message:

I was deeply touched by your kind letter and extremely interested in all the Cambridge gossip. No I don't remember having met or spoken to you ever but just so much the more does that make me appreciate your kindness in writing. And in addition let me thank you for having really grasped my state of mind and therefore having refrained from relating "funny" stories or telling me to "cheer up". It is such a comfort to find someone who realises that one's object in life here is <u>not</u> to kill time and that one's brain is, if anything the more active and eager for serious work. Your account of the C.U.F.S. [Cambridge University Fabian Society] *does indeed revive happy memories. I'm glad you are showing such good signs of vitality. We have started a Social Problems Circle here which will, we* *think, be of some real value. After life at Bedales and at Cambridge I find the tone here revolting – especially so at Xmas. The vast majority smoke, spit, gamble, grumble and whine for parcels of victuals to save the trouble of walking 200 yards for the food provided. The shopkeeping class from whom the so called "Captains of the Camp" are drawn, as a body makes a fine display of selfishness. And over and above this the whole place is pervaded by this desolating kill time spirit. Of course, among the University and professional classes there are tip top people and around the so called camp schools an entirely different spirit prevails – a spirit which has called forth practically the only serious unselfish effort in the camp. And to the school I devote nearly all my public energy. At present I'm hard at work with timber and tools fixing up a "lab" for the biological department.*

Yes I know you are experiencing a great change of atmosphere at home. Is it I wonder really a change of heart? And in any case ought one to "think about that hard" and forget that it is very likely as it were an outgrowth – perhaps only a temporary outgrowth from something which is wrong and wicked at core, which is inconsistent with all that is noble in life? May it not all be like the beautiful foliage of a dying tree, all rotten through at heart? I've just been recovering from the state of pulp to which I was reduced by reading some Xmas Eve leaders in the Daily Telegraph. I looked in vain for any change for the better in the sentiments therein expressed. I wonder if the fight with the real powers of evil will be any less slow and tedious afterwards! I rather picture J.B.[131] *slamming his fist down and saying "good old J.B. muddled through all right in the end! Don't talk to me about science, education and all that rubbish!" However in the meantime you must make the best of the prevailing spirit at home; we here can only stand and wait and equip ourselves for clearing up the mess and for building up a goodwill, understanding and friendship which shall prevent such another disaster.*

....

Jan. 2nd Worked in Bar. 6 all morning and got a good firm bench put up: looks very nice and I long to get to work there. Lechmere very bucked with it. Quiet evening reading de Vigny's poetry and in bed Vernon Lee [a pacifist] on the war. The latter v. much to the point.

Jan. 3rd Spent all day fixing up screens and shelves in Bar. 6. Lechmere not much of a hand at it, so I'm glad to be really of some use to him. Got the place finished now except for putting American cloth on the bench. Made

---

[131] Possibly John Bradbury, Permanent Secretary to H.M. Treasury and chief financial advisor.

out our order of apparatus and handed it over to Blagden. Quiet evening reading poetry and in bed started Green's book – not much catch so far.

Jan. 4th Quiet morning only interrupted by parcel *hohling*. Started bookbinding in afternoon with Lechmere's tackle and sewed up *Mauprat*. Worked at our new lab. bench. Wrote letters to Biffen and "business" letter home. This business letter scheme is a wonderful device![132]

SECOND DIARY

Jan. 5th German walk with Hohenrein, then rather an interrupted morning trying to find people and fetch parcels. Glued the back of *Mauprat*. Played hockey in selection game: good, but got my right hand bashed up a bit – very annoying. 5 p.m. Dante Circle. Dodd into supper and we talked *"kultur"* at length. Quiet evening reading poetry. Finished Green's book – alright for newspaper articles but not nearly good enough for book form – too rambly and aimless. Jones tells me of the fate of our reform scheme at the hand of these despicable captains. They got at the military and said it means riot and revolution, so von Brocken[133] comes along in a towering rage. Has an interview with Blagden, Cotterill[134] plus Powell and Co and says they've got to stop and won't listen to anything. Fine specimens of the freedom-loving Englishman – too funky to fight the scheme openly so they get out the officers and shield themselves behind Prussian militarism.

Jan. 6th Spent morning bookbinding – in fact on and off bookbinding all day. Quiet evening reading poetry. Miss Rose's present of Thoreau's *Walden* in bed.

Jan. 7th Fearful rain continues. School Committee in morning – very prolonged – Pennington on the warpath again. Ponsonby got a game knee and cried off Morris dancing for the school show so mobilised Roberts

---

[132] According to Stibbe (2008), prisoners were limited in the numbers of letters they were allowed to send (2 postcards a week and 2 letters a month), but a 'reasonable number' of business letters were allowed by Mützenbecher.

[133] Rittmeister von Brocken, assistant Camp Commandant.

[134] Probably Harry Dougan Cotterell (1866–1920), founder and owner of HD Cotterell of Hamburg (http://www.cotterell.de/en/historie).

instead. Had a practice in Bar. 6 loft. Spent afternoon binding. Quiet evening.

Jan. 8th Pouring rain all night and day. German prowl with Hohenrein again then on duty with school. Great enrollment day. I sat in lab and received several new names, but other sections, e.g. French had over 200 new names in – very encouraging. After lunch again at school – I did mostly bookbinding, as I had already unearthed practically all the biologists in camp. In evening the School Conversazione took place – very successfully. Very select audience – place being full, – and much appreciated in spite of somewhat dismal recitations! Our item [Morris dance] came off without untoward incident and was well received.

Jan. 9th Interviewed electrician about lighting in new lab. And then at 11 a.m. very prolonged School Committee. Mighty cross examination of Venables by Pritchard about the great studio in the Y.M.C.A. hall which we want for drawing classes on two days a week. This seems to conflict with the Y.M.C.A. "principle" of letting anyone come in any time. What happens to this principle, I wonder, if so many come that there is no standing room! Eventually passed strong resolution on subject to Education Committee. Pennington, also with a grievance, making a scene. Quiet afternoon darning and mending and then bookbinding – long yarn with Hatfield about the eternal woman question which is very much on his brain now.

Jan. 10th Morning bookbinding and parcel *hohling* – a great bally leather waistcoat from granny C.B. [Cote Bank, i.e. Susanna Pease]. Still raining furiously. Afternoon bookbinding in Bar. 6 and missed *Appell*, but nobody seemed to mind. Shows what a farce the silly proceeding is. Evening repeat of School Conversazione:– good, but not such a select audience this time. Dancing caused much merriment. Letter from Y.M.C.A. allowing use of hall for Morris dancing for 3 <u>nights</u> a week – they must have written p.m. for a.m.

Jan. 11th Saw Sheldon of [Y.M.C.A.] Control Committee re Morris dancing and found p.m. was written for a.m., and 7.30 a.m. at this season is "*so eine sache*" [such a business]. Spent most of the day bookbinding on and off: evening reading poetry. Started *Pamela*[135] in bed. It appears this evening

[135] Novel by Samuel Richardson.

Rüdiger[136] came into the Barracks, lined everyone out and just casually went through and picked out ancient looking people to be photographed – I'm sure this casual business *"gegen die Fortschrifften"* [is anti-progressive?] and is very unbecoming to *Preussische ordnung*! [Prussian order]

Jan. 12th German prowl 8.30 and Lechmere first zoo lecture 9 a.m. Then some bookbinding. Dentist 1 p.m. Dante 5 p.m. Quiet evening reading Schimper and poetry. Have been put on a committee to celebrate Shakespeare's tercentenary!

Jan. 13th Miserable day of melting snow and mud. Quiet morning reading and did a little binding in Venables' famous handicraft room: felt like the first that ever burst into that silent room! Pritchard into tea who jawed away talking of his fights with Powell. Social Problems Circle – Bodin[137] very abstract. Mobilised Morris set 7.45 a.m. but find they've changed our time to 8.15 to 9 a.m., really rather better – much more chance of getting a turn out.

Jan. 14th Marshall to breakfast 7.30 and then Morris dancing in the Y.M.C.A. hall. Started the sword dance with the wooden lathes – goes quite well. Miserable snow and slush. 1.30 first practical botany class, but only arranged time and explained programme. Blagden is in Berlin today buying our requisites. 2 p.m. meeting of Shakespeare's Tercentenary Committee. That dreadful man Leon[138] very much in evidence but very effectively snubbed in the end – so much so that he resigned. But was only with difficulty restrained from making a furious personal explanation. Decided to accept Hopkirk's[139] *Othello* and Duncan Jones' *12th Night* for festival week, and a musical or a "jaw" evening. Dodd into tea and then went to his loft to hear music and read papers. Bell into supper and long talk: he's a great but very interesting talker.

---

[136] A vengeful and malicious lieutenant who, according to Stibbe (2008), would cruelly raise internees' hopes of release. He was eventually dismissed.

[137] Alexander Hastie Bodin (1887-1948), Assistant Professor of Logic at Glasgow University, who was visiting Germany in August 1914. Taught in the Camp School and was a box-mate of Michael's.

[138] P. Sylvester Leon (1883–1975), a Jamaican actor (http://thefamousjamaicachoir.weebly.com/--sylvester-leon.html). He performed in many plays staged by the Ruhleben Dramatic Society and was secretary of the Literary and Debating Society.

[139] Hubert Gordon Hopkirk (1894–1966). Born in Jena to English parents. An actor/comedian of the silent era and active in the Ruhleben theatre. He played 'Jasper' in *The Knight*.

Jan. 15th Nice bright morning. German prowl 8.30. Got concert tickets for party and rest of morning reading. Ditto afternoon. 6 p.m. Historical Circle: Pritchard repeated lecture on Greek and Byzantine ideals. Very good indeed especially on second reading. Everyone rather demoralised by last night of famous pantomime [Cinderella]. Several of leading parts so blind drunk that they had to be understudied. Great binge after it was all over. S. went to the feed and came in none the worse about 10 p.m. Saw Blagden who says he had a very successful day in Berlin and that [lab] apparatus will be here on Monday or Tuesday.

Jan. 16th 10 a.m. Pritchard's second lecture on art – "The Place of the Picture in Art". Interesting and very suggestive, though not so clear to the uninitiated at first. Great abuse of the classicists, or rather, of those who merely copy them. 11 a.m. meeting of School Committee but immediately adjourned on account of *Appell.* Speech by Baron on candles and policemen: remarkably restrained. Nothing about "*blutiger Hunde*" [bloody dogs] this time. School Committee 1.45, not much on – slight contretemps. Blagden and self versus Pennington. 3 p.m. Mackenzie's[140] constitution mongering committee: report by Blagden and Cotterill on interview with von Brocken. Decided not to dissolve committee but to hammer away and devise new methods. 5 p.m. went to tea with Ponsonby and Co – 6.30 p.m. concert. Good – though it's a terrible hall to hear music in.

[Insert: programme and song sheets for the Chamber Concert, Jan. 16th]

Jan. 17th Early start with Marshall to breakfast and then Morris dancing. 9 a.m. Lechmere on fungi, then parcel fetching. Spent afternoon sorting out apparatus that has come from Leitz and making arrangements for the practical course: really think we'll have to divide up again and make three instead of two sets. Started de Vigny *Grandeur et Servitude Militaire* and *Elizabeth and her German Garden* in bed.

Jan. 18th S. taken to *Schonungsbaracke* again today on account of boils. Rough luck on him. Nice tulips out now and first narcissus just showing through. Afternoon in lab getting ready for course and 7 p.m. to Jones on law. Finished *Elizabeth and her GG* – very good indeed – I love her

---

[140] W. F. Mackenzie, who became captain of Barrack 5 in March 1916, but was 'sacked' by Powell a month later.

philosophy of flowers and solitude and her love of flowers in clumps, not straight lines!

Jan. 19th Lechmere 9 a.m. then parcel *hohling* and letter writing. *Appell* till lunch. At lab, then hockey 3.15 and Dante Circle at 5 p.m. Conference with Blagden about accommodation report for science room – ultimately drafted a report which we both agreed to. Resumed *Pamela* in bed.

Jan. 20th S. was taken off to the *Lazarett*[141] today poor fellow, to be under more careful supervision. I suppose in one way for him the worse he is the better. Great do at *Appell* today about law and order in the barracks. The candle rule to be stringently enforced – a nuisance. Fitted up S's accumulator for box use. Goes very nicely. 1.30 first practical botany class. 4 people turned up and it went off quite well. Dentist at 3 p.m., doing more of Mr. D's work over again. Quiet evening with de Vigny.

Jan. 21st Early start with Hill and Swale[142] to breakfast and then Morris dancing. Hill's playing is rather distressing! Then Lechmere 9 a.m. and darned till lunchtime. Invigilated at library 12–1 and practical botany 1.30 to 4. Glanced through the English papers at Dodd's and quiet evening reading. Must always have my natural minimum of solitude.

Jan. 22nd German prowl 8.30, hockey match 9.30, change, *Appell*, lunch. Botany 1.30, dentist 2.30. Returned to botany class, wrote p.c. home. Ponsonby to tea 5 p.m. History Circle 6 p.m. School Committee 7.30 and so to bed reading *Pamela* – a book that takes some getting *fertig* [done] with!

Jan. 23rd Adjourned School Committee 11 a.m. 1.30 extra botany class which I left mostly to L. Prowled round course with J, Dodd and Philips,[143] who came into tea. Up at Dodd's reading papers and to concert 6.30 p.m.

---

[141] Camp hospital, situated in the old Emigrants' Railway Station, just outside the camp.

[142] William Eric Swale (1890–1980), an electrical engineer working at Mannheim at the outbreak of war. His unpublished memoirs of Ruhleben are held in the Liddle collection at Leeds University, and Michael's Ruhleben chest contains his list of some of the internees.

[143] Probably St George Haigh Phillips (1890–1983). The son of a singing teacher, born in Germany and raised in England. He was working as a bank assistant in Hamburg in 1914. An amateur musician, he worked in the BBC music department after the war. Michael misspells his name throughout the diaries as 'Philips'. Photo on page 111.

[Insert: programme for Third Symphony Concert, Sunday Jan. 23rd. Conductor Mr. Charles Weber]

Jan. 24th Morris dancing 8 a.m. Swale and Ponsonby to breakfast. Got parcel from Seward today with botanical specimens. Much alarmed the parcel soldier! Jones got a permit for us to visit S in *Lazarett*, and at 10 p.m. we sallied forth. Philips joined us and after long waiting there we saw him. Looks alright and cheerful though it must be terribly boring there. No fresh complications, but doesn't know how long he must stay there. Place wonderfully improved since last Summer! 1.30 p.m. botany, 5 p.m. Cutayar on Petrarch and 6.30 A.S.U. show on Strindberg. Really quite good. *The Creditors* was very well done – very glad I went.

....

MSP to Prof. A. C. Seward, The Botany School, Downing Street, Cambridge

Jan. 25th 1916

Dear Prof. Seward

We were overjoyed to get the great bottle of Botanical material, which turned up yesterday, perfectly safely. I haven't had time to open it up and sort it out yet, but Dr Lechmere and I have turned it over and over, and eyed it eagerly from the outside. We are extremely grateful to you and your department coming to the rescue and helping us with the Ruhleben Camp School. The help which we get from folk at home and the response with which we meet among our fellow prisoners here are enormous encouragement to us to persevere in our educational experiments. In the biology department there are some very promising students. I've fitted up a very nice bench and with our six microscopes, we take 20 people in 3 relays. Your material will be invaluable, and both of us send our most grateful thanks to you.

I think we're fairly near solving the embedding problem by using a Dewar flask and an electrical thermostat. If we can manage this we shall try our luck with some Cytology.

I won't trespass on your valuable time any more, except to thank you again very much indeed. With kind regard to Mrs. Seward, and best wishes to all of you.

Yours sincerely

Michael Pease

Jan. 25th Moderately uninterrupted morning. Botany as usual 1.30. 6.30 p.m. went to Burns concert; concert itself not bad, but the heat, squash and discomfort was so intolerable that I left before the end. Moreover, it was like the irony of Ruhleben that I celebrated Burns amongst a bunch of Bar. 6-ers jabbering their guttural ungrammatical German!

[Insert: programme for Burns Night concert]

Jan. 26th 9 a.m. Lechmere. Saw Blagden about sundry R.C.S. [Ruhleben Camp School] matters. 1.30 botany. 3.30 dentist. 5 p.m. Dante Circle and thank goodness a quiet evening!

Jan. 27th Today being Kaiser's birthday, no bathing allowed, or permission to visit S in *Lazarett*. Extra big do at *Appell* with a military *Kontrolle* [check] and of course nothing "*stimmened*" [correct] and we had to have a second *Appell* in the afternoon. All the officers pranced about in their full get up and there was a great service in the Y.M.C.A. Saw Blagden on school business at 7 p.m. Social probs with Pearce[144] on overcrowding – not bad.

Jan. 28th Early start with Morris dancing 7.30. Hill rather better today! Lechmere 9 a.m. and morning rather uninterrupted. Got parcel of E.R.O. papers. 1.30 botany 3.30 dentist. And then thank goodness a quiet evening. Finished de Vigny's *Grandeur et Servitude Militaires*. I hear Benthin[145] has turned down all the lighting arrangements in Bar. 6. What do they expect us to do? I hear they call him the stormy petrel, excellent name.

Jan. 29th Surprise today is visit from Neumeister. Very friendly, kind and affectionate. Brought a large box of foodstuffs. It's really awfully kind of the dear old chap to come and see me, and the pathetic thing is that there is so little to be done when he does come. We talked for a long time on health and the camp and touched gently and in the most general terms, on affairs of state. My lavish praises of his homemade sausage result in a sausage end being produced and bit cut off which I had to eat in full view of the guard! Typically German, *nicht*? 1.30 Botany. Cut the Historical Circle and

---

[144] Reverend Christopher John Pearce (1883–1964), a British clergyman interned at Ruhleben. Active in the Ruhleben theatre, and one of Ruhleben's 'popular actors'.

[145] Sub-lieutenant Benthin, according to Powell and Gribble (1919) he was also nicknamed Benzene because of his explosive temper.

7.30 School Committee. Rather a do on about finance and so meeting adjourned to Sunday.

Jan. 30th The famous Christmas number of the camp magazine came out this morning – usual facetious stuff! 10 p.m. adjourned Committee of School. Seems that Education Committee refused to accept grant from Finance Committee on score that the money has been illegally raised, i.e. that Powell and Co have no right to tax the camp without its consent. So we have to raise our own money and hence long jaw on proposal for fees, subs, shows and appeal to British government. 12–1 Invigilated at library. Quiet afternoon and evening – didn't go to concert.

Jan. 31st Started morning with Morris dancing and then 9 a.m. Lechmere. 10 a.m. went down to *Lazarett* to see S. but kept waiting a tremendous time. Conversed with Darbishire[146] for some time who also came down to see S. Eventually we got in. We found he was coming up today. So we brought up some of his property and came away. 1.30 Botany. Had long interviews with Roker[147] about *The Knight*. Difficult to persuade him that one can't make a detailed estimate of cost until one knows what the Education Committee already has or rather will have in 6 months' time! 3.30 dentist. 5 p.m. Petrarch. 6.30 School Committee until bedtime. S really did turn up again in the afternoon.

Feb. 1st Quiet morning reading Boccaccio. 1.30 Botany in spite of a famous count up of bowls, towels etc – just let that rip. Jones' law lecture and so to bed as cold coming on, worse luck. Got copy of Molière from Kul via Lechmere and read *Les Precieuses Ridicules* in bed.

Feb. 2nd Felt not quite A1 when I got up and by lunch I was sorely afraid that I was in for flu. However, scratched lab duties, wrote home and turned in early and worked up a record fever in the evening.

---

[146] Francis Vernon Darbishire (1868–1932). An Oxford graduate working at the Berlin Sugar Institute in 1914. He gave lectures on botany and chemistry at Ruhleben. A committee member of the Ruhleben Horticultural Society, he worked at RHS Wisley after the war.

[147] John Kelland Roker (1885–1946) was the ballet-master at the Metropol Variety Theatre in Berlin when the war broke out. Roker was on the Entertainments Committee and became the theatre's Stage Director, as well as producing and acting in several shows. He was released in May 1918 and continued working in theatre (a well known pantomime producer according to his obituary in *The Stage*, 25 April 1946).

Feb. 3rd Dozed quietly in bed most of the day. No headache, but feverish.

Feb. 4th Still in bed. Read *Children of the Dead Ends,* Aunt Margaret's[148] gift.

Feb. 5th Still in bed, but really no fever, only irritatingly weak. Read Mrs. Ritchie's *Two Sinners*. I've no patience with moral cowards who can't make up their minds and have to be steered through life by omniscient and benevolent R.C. clergy!

Feb. 6th Much better in the morning but stayed in bed till the forenoon. Read Gibbons autobiography – good. Just fancy that while I was a Bedales I went so often to Buriton without knowing the famous man lived there! Invigilated at the library 12–1. Sat out in the sun for an hour in the afternoon. Went out to supper with Swale and Pearce and turned in early. Hear the Adler[149] concert was not so bad and that the Baron made a great speech about our dear friend Adler – not the usual attitude of a Prussian officer to a Jew!

Feb. 7th Got up after breakfast. Bad news today is that Mützenbecher is to leave the camp – really the worst news I have heard for long. The other news is Dodd has flu, probably got it from me. Went down to Botany in afternoon. 5 p.m. Petrarch. 6.30–8.30 terrible long School Committee.

Feb. 8th Started the day with Morris dancing at 7.30. Then moderately quiet morning. Botany in afternoon. In the cubby hole I picked up Wells' *Research Magnificent* and started reading. His style is attractive even if his point of view is stale. I don't think it added anything new to my view of the world or of Wells. Curious however to know who was the original of the ménage at South Harting and who he had in mind for Proteus. Awful rumour that we are to be evicted from the cubby hole for the new camp newspaper. Hatfield and Wimpfheimer came hustling round about it.

Feb. 9th The great victory this morning was getting the newspaper officers shoved off into somebody else's cubby hole: great comfort to be saved the trouble of moving! Botany as usual and quiet evening getting notes

---

[148] Cyril Arthington Pease's wife.

[149] Frederick Charles Adler (1889–1959), born in London to German parents, he was living in Germany in 1914. A conductor, who studied with Gustav Mahler, he was the camp orchestra's first conductor, and gave his opening concert on 6 Dec 1914.

together for my eugenics paper. That newspaper article[150] on gardens for the camp is a great nuisance!

Feb. 10th S. was summoned to the doctor today only to be told that he couldn't be recommended for exchange on account of his being an engineer. Rough on him: afraid he is rather down in the mouth about it. Paper by Higgins at the Social Probs. Circle. Not at all bad, and in fact the best we've had, I should think. Started Carlyle's *Frederick the Great* in bed.

Feb. 11th Morris dancing 7.30. Lechmere 9 a.m. 12–1 library. 1.30 Botany which I deserted for School Committee 2–3. Dodd into tea then reading English papers and Molière 6–7. Wrote p.c. home and so to bed and to *Frederick the Great*. We got our "fishing license" today – permit to fish the pond for algae.

....

Marjory Pease to MSP ((letter 144, date of receipt unknown, but letters seem to be taking about 3 weeks to arrive):

The Pendicle, Limpsfield, Surrey

22nd January 1916

Dearest Michael,

Last night we had the annual meeting of the Land Club here so I couldn't write any letters. Today I have been at a meeting in London to protest against the economy in education as now practised by L.C.C. but the speeches made by the various teachers were so narrow and ignorant and selfish that I came away despairing of reform. The last thing some of the teachers think about is the education of the child. The Reverend W. Temple was in the chair and struck the right note.

I do hope Aunt Kate[151] *will remove her charming girls from this wretched high church school. I took Mary and Betty* [Kate's daughters] *to East Grinstead on Thursday and left them in a dreary looking place. They are not allowed out on Sundays – all I can do is to go and see them on Saturdays. I went on to the Coopers*

---

[150] Michael had a letter published in the March issue of the Camp Magazine, calling for the creation of public gardens to beautify the camp (reproduced on page 77). The letter was preceded by an article titled 'Gardening' written under the pseudoname 'Forget-me-not'. This may be what he refers to, although articles by Forget-me-not in subsequent issues are not mentioned in the diaries.

[151] Kate Davidson, Marjory's widowed sister-in-law.

and had tea with them – Stuart is in hospital in France with influenza. I am still without latest news of Nicolas from January 12th and anxiously watch the post. By the way, Miss Rose told me she had sent some books to you for Christmas and Uncle Jonathan [fn 7] *writes "I have been sending Michael food through the Civilian Prisoners Help Committee for the past six weeks. I hope it gets to him. I know you send, but I thought it would give him pleasure to have more to distribute."*

I do hope you have got the top coat and the leather waistcoat. Here the weather is very mild – crocuses and snowdrops and lots of other little flowers showing and birds singing – lovely moon this evening. I think of you and Nicolas constantly. I saw Mrs. Culley[?] *in London today and she tells me poor old Hinder has had a paralytic stroke and has lost the power of one side and has almost lost her power of speaking. Is it not sad. She says she is very cheerful and bright.*

Betty has given her very precious cat "Stripy" to the Argyll and Sutherland Highlanders for a regimental pet and is very excited about it! By the way the cake I sent you on the 24th was almost entirely made by Betty for you.

I saw Miss Whyte for a few minutes yesterday. She says her brother much prefers his present quarters and the society he gets. I have not heard the Colonel Mitchell tale though Mrs. Bowman refers often to him! I expect Whyte can relate it!

Sunday. Your father will post this on route to Woolwich. I am thankful to say I have a "field p.c." from Nicolas on the 19th saying "I am quite well" and for this I am more than relieved. He has had 10 weeks of it now and one hopes before very long he may get a few days at home.

Your loving mother

....

Feb. 12th 8.30 German jaw as usual, then parcels, *Appell*, lunch, botany. 4 p.m. Ford's Molière lecture, and then quiet evening. No School Committee for some strange reason.

Feb. 13th 10 a.m. Teachers meeting about this finance show. Eloquent appeal by Pritchard not to touch the Captain's ill-gotten money and this was well received. Then considerable wrangle about the voluntary versus compulsory subscription of a mark a month from pupils; finally voluntary and huge moral pressure carried almost unanimously. Little Wimpfheimer in great form, grinning and giggling away. Popping up and making nice legal points at intervals. 12–1 invigilated at library, browsed through Plato's *Republic* with a view to something after *Frederick the Great*. Lovely afternoon. Walked round the field with Ponsonby. Then read Holmes' *In Defence of What Might Be*. Very good and goes right to the rock bottom of the problem. Then to Bainton's concert – individual items alright; but an awful hotchpotch of a programme. Marshall played very well.

[Insert: programme and song sheets for concert. Conductor Mr. E. L. Bainton]

Feb.14th Moderately quiet morning. Botany as usual but very poor turnout, on account of the cleaning out business. Read papers at Dodd's and then to Hunt's[152] Grieg evening. Very good indeed; Conn[153] played better than I've ever heard him. Graf,[154] Baron[155] and Baronin [his wife] there.

[Insert: programme and song sheets for illustrated lecture on Grieg, by Mr. Horace Hunt]

Feb. 15th *Appell* at 8 a.m. this morning, which bust up Morris dancing. Then moderately quiet morning. Botany as usual but without Lechmere. Found some moulds in all stages of usual reproduction – very interesting. Set to work on that famous article for the camp magazine on gardens. The spirit didn't move me a bit. Nice letter from Bellot: then Jones' law lecture and so to bed.

Feb. 16th Today the appalling thought of spring cleaning was very much in the air, and as it snowed and rained alternately all day, the prospect for the morrow is not attractive. We carted many things over to Dodd's loft packing up our odd groceries in great biscuit tins – perfectly enormous supplies! Wrote letter home and went to hear Bell at the Banking Circle on agricultural credit. I really ought to have gone to hear Duncan Jones at the English Lit. Circle and the situation was rather tragic when D-J, thinking I had been there, asked me my opinion of his paper!

---

[152] Horace George Hunt (1886-1981) was studying the piano in Berlin when the war began. After the war he went to the USA and became a choral teacher, conductor and organist.

[153] James [John] Peebles Conn (1883–1960), a conductor and violinist from Edinburgh. In 1906 he took the post of 'Konzert Meister' in the Hulter Orchestra at Dortmund and was still working there at the outbreak of war. After the war he continued as a professional violinist and conductor in Scotland (his biography is in the *Dundee Evening Telegraph,* 23 March 1937).

[154] Graf [Count] Schwerin, the elderly Camp Commandant who was generally popular with the internees.

[155] Baron von Taube, Deputy to the Camp Commandant.

Feb. 17th Today the great cleaning day. Representations having been made about the stupidity of starting so early we didn't get underway until about 6 and our box didn't start till nearly 8. However it didn't take so long to move out most of the stuff and scrub down and wash out. By lunch we were pretty well properly installed again, and endless cartloads of rubbish had to be carried away. Went down to Botany class, and spent the evening finishing up the box and writing the article for Philimore.[156]

Feb. 18th Early morning *Appell* today with great scene by the Baron. Bar. 11 was very exhausted after the great cleaning and about 8.15 only a dozen odd people out, Thorpe looking very worried and Baron stamping up and down calling us "*dumme Bengeln*" [stupid villains] with obsequious Feldwebel saying "*Ja, ja*". Eventually Baron makes a dash into the Barracks to sort people out! Finally after ½ hour we get lined up and counted by two soldiers, and after much calculating the thing "*stimmens*" [is correct]. Botany as usual. Farmer and Ponsonby in to tea. Dante 5–6 and then Milner's Molière – latter very poor as M. wasn't there and we only finished reading *L'ecole des Maries*. Our 2nd Leitz order came this afternoon and I and Blagden had no end of a do over it. Went up into the casino to interview the "*Zahl-meister*" [paymaster] and Co – a bunch of "*unter officiers*" with a minus quantity of brains. However B. jawed away excellently and did them out of their 10 per cent "*zuschlag*" [surcharge]. I dreamt last night very vividly of Jarintzoff – dreamt that he was wounded and dying and that I was taking his dying messages for Peggy Jacks [another Bedalian] (as was)!!

Feb. 19th Early *Appell* again, but without much adventure except that it took us ages to "*stimmen*." Then German jaw to 9.30. Botany as usual. 8 p.m. interview with Welland[157] and Pearce about hiring dresses for *The Knight* and also with Boyd and Roker about estimates for property. Filled in a great and alarming form and put my signature to contract! 3.30 dentist, 4–5 Ford on Molière, and 6 p.m. Jones at Historical Circle on 'History of Inns of Court'. Pritchard in the chair. Pritchard opened the discussion giving

---

[156] Possibly Louis Egerton Filmore (1872–1939), one of the camp magazine's editors.

[157] Ralph Archibald Welland (1888–1922). In the 1911 census he was helping his father in his map engraving business. After the war he became an actor with the Shakespearean Repertoire Company (*Hastings and St Leonards Observer*, 28 August 1920).

amusing account of his early days in the Temple – this was quite new to me. Wimpfheimer made a lachrymose speech, weeping over the good old pre-kriegal days. I had to fly early to write my postcard before end of postal month. After bed, Coates announced about election of committee to consider reply to Gerard's[158] comments in the White Book[159] on Ruhleben. Powell and Co got into a nasty mess over that, as they virtually admit that they praised Gerard and in any case they saw the thing in proof before the offending letter was sent.

[Insert: hand-drawn map of Holborn/Inns of court]

Feb. 20th Spent morning in Lab sorting out Seward's Cambridge jar of material and got frozen to the bone. 12–1 invigilating in library, 2–3 walk round field with Ponsonby whom I advised to take Smith's physics class to get some notion of scientific method. 3–5 R.C.S. Committee. Open tea with Farmer where we discussed future careers. May be chance for me if I kid people up I can make 2 blades grow where one did, but none for someone who wants to persuade you that the one blade is a mere figment of the imagination! 6.30 concert – mighty fine – specially the Tchaikovsky string variations. Keel sang "The Keeper" excellently.

[Insert: programme for Symphony Concert, Sunday 20th Feb. Conductor Mr. E. C. MacMillan]

Feb. 21st Bright cold morning. 9 a.m. Lechmere Botany as usual. Then Doddering.[160] Merritt to supper to discuss *The Knight*.

Feb. 22nd Fairly nippy. Started with Morris Dancing then quiet reading Oltmanns [German botanist]. Botany single handed this afternoon and mighty cold in the lab to wit +3°C – this morning it was -6°C and all the water frozen. Milner's French Plays at 6 p.m. – not at all bad: Balfour[161] acted excellently – a great discovery.

---

[158] James Watson Gerard, the American diplomat in charge of British interests in Germany.

[159] The 'White Papers' were the correspondence between the British Government and the US Ambassador at Berlin.

[160] What is 'Doddering'? It becomes a regular activity.

[161] John 'Jock' Balfour (1894–1983), son of the Conservative politician Sir Charles Balfour, was an Oxford student studying German in Freiberg when war broke out. He was involved in the A.S.U. and

Feb. 23rd Very cold, snowy and easterly gale. Notwithstanding this we had an *Appell*. Lechmere 9 a.m. Botany as usual. Dante 5 p.m. and Banking Circle 7 p.m. when I held forth on Credit Banks. Silly people denied that the Raiffeisen system [mutual societies] had ever been tried in England.

Feb. 24th Still very cold. Bath expedition 8.30. Quiet morning studying Oltmanns and long encounter with the dentist 2–3.30. Walked up and down all evening; then Social Probs Circle 7 p.m. – Good paper by Boggon[162] on Municipal Trading. Very nice letter from Seward [page 373].

Feb. 25th Lechmere 9 a.m. Sent off a 3rd Leitz order by *Eilbrief* [express mail]. Invigilated 12–1; then Botany and went to theatre to see Merritt's piece *What Happened to Jones*. Not bad of its sort (but I don't like its sort) and very well staged.

[Insert: programme for *What Happened to Jones*, producers H. G. Hopkirk and George Merritt]

Feb. 26th "*Nichts neues*!" [nothing new]

Feb. 27th Quiet morning. 12–1 invigilating. Sunday grind with Ponsonby. 3 p.m. School Committee. Quiet evening – started my essay on Eugenics.

Feb. 28th Day much as usual: finding much enjoyment in Oltmann's *Algae*: makes the subject very interesting. Went to A.S.U. lecture on Greek Drama by Howard. A very enthusiastic lecture; the best I've heard for a long time. The acting was not bad either, but The Leader [of The Chorus] looked rather astray without his chorus!

[Insert: programme for lecture by Arthur E. Howard on Greek Tragedy, followed by two scenes from *The Electra*]

Feb. 29th Morris dancing early. Then spent rest of morning reading *Ecole des Femmes*. Botany single handed. I hear that the lab. was inspected by Schwerin, von Brocken and Benzene this morning. The lighting and the window have been "*genehmigt*" [approved]. Benzene distinguished himself

---

the Camp School during his internment and published his *Ruhleben Poems* in 1919. After the war he had a successful career in the Foreign Office as a diplomat.

[162] Keith Maitland Boggon (1891-1971), a bank clerk in the 1911 census, he working in Germany at the outbreak of war.

by pointing at our neat row of worn out dry cells and saying it was *verboten* [forbidden] to charge cells from the mains (A.C.)!! That's the sort of specimen they have in charge of electrical arrangements, no wonder they go astray! A great parcel of provisions from Mrs. Scott; rather tiresome to be beholden in that quarter! Letter from Helen Wedgwood [see below]. Jones' law lecture in evening and after that went in to the lab where I found Hoffmann[163] of the Embassy looking through mics [microscopes] and talking away with Lechmere. Seems he's a soil bacteriologist in Kansas!

....

HBW to MSP (received Feb. 29th):

Newnham College, Cambridge.

Feb. 12th 1916

Dear Mr. Pease,

Thank you very much for the long message you sent in reply to my letter. I hardly hoped you would be able to answer, but wrote just to tell you we are keeping the flag flying, which is about the only consolation we can give to you unfortunate captives; so it was very jolly to hear my letter was the right sort.

Perhaps it is the result of having such rotten people round you that makes you hopeless about whatever the new spirit there is here. But there really does seem to be a new desire to think things out and feeling that every individual is responsible for putting things right, and building up a better state. People have been startled out of their indifference and forced to see that there is something radically wrong, and even if they get hold of the wrong ideas, still they do care very much now, and after all, it was the great mass of indifference that was so hard to fight, rather than open opposition. And the best way to encourage this seems to be to treat it as permanent and normal and not to remind people that it might be only temporary. It should be the normal state of things; do not think of it as the 'foliage of a rotten tree'. It is people's natural goodness getting a chance of appearing, now that they have been startled out of the 'Livelihood-getting' groove. They must get now into the new habit. Alas, we are almost as unable to make any real alterations at present as you are. The war naturally occupies everyone. It is also used as an excuse for everything by our opponents, so that, in spite of our new keenness, we are losing much for which we have fought, so sometimes one feels

---

[163] Conrad Hoffmann – a pioneer (along with colleague James Sprunger) of the War Prisoners' Aid branch of the Y.M.C.A.

rather despairing. Still things will never be the same as before; perhaps they will be worse, but there are so many of us who believe in better things, and society will be so shaken, and people are now so used to shocks as to be less afraid of change, that with a good shove we ought to be able to knock down our beautiful civilisation and build something better. That is where you people in Ruhleben will have the advantage of us, for you will be fresh whilst we may be already tired of fighting.

Just now we are rather 'on the stretch' wondering what may happen to some of our friends, who are likely to get into trouble for their views on taking life. It is hateful being obliged to disagree with people at a time like this, and knowing they must hate or despise you. (It is not so bad in a way for us women, though it is annoying to be confined to showing your convictions by offering 'to pass buns through the bars', – a truly feminine occupation which ought to recommend us to the anti-suffs – but it doesn't). Perhaps you say, "serve you right" (since father, who never used to be able to open his lips in the house without mentioning the Liberty of the Individual, has not only become actively military, but a conscriptionist, I have lost all faith in the stability of human principals).

However, you will envy us our form of war-antidote. For we have discovered that Sunday picnics on the Gogs [Gog Magog Downs] *are just the thing. So when it is fine a group of "the elect" go up to the Roman Road, and there build a fire, cook eggs in damp earth, and sit round toasting our toes (and getting the smoke in our eyes) and suck oranges and hold forth on our private ideas of the perfect state, and discuss the witty remarks to be made to the tribunals, or read Edward Carpenter and "Songs of Freedom". Then we go for a windy walk along the ridge where the geologist of the party pretends to find fossils, until we go back to Cambridge able to meet the worst (which will probably be most disappointing). Last time Bekassy,*[164] *who is living in Cambridge, came too, and he and several others, including the president of C.U.F.S., held a tree climbing competition, and got themselves into a fearful mess. Bekassy won easily – Bedales training I suppose. Is climbing trees "strengst verboten" in Ruhleben? I hope not, because it is a splendid way of escaping from one's kind, and you must want to do that or commit murder.*

---

[164] János Bekassy, younger brother of Ferenc (fn 36) was also educated at Bedales. As a Hungarian national, Janos was interned in England at the outbreak of war, but was given into the care of Josiah Clement Wedgwood (HBW's father) for the duration (Wedgwood's sons had also been at Bedales). János (known as Doge) married HBW's sister Rosamund after the end of the war.

Heretics[165] *is going strong. The other night Hardy of Trinity read a paper on "The Value of Knowledge", challenging several unfortunate professors to justify their studies. Poor Prof. Eddington got up and defended himself as best he could. A verdict was passed of "useless, but harmless", Hardy passing the same sentence on himself. It was like the session of a secret tribunal, with Ogden blinking over his spectacles as the impassive and cynical judge, – So you see even the Dons are expected now to be some practical use to humanity!*

Good luck to the Social Problems Circle, just rub in to your people that we here think with relief of there being some good 'rebels' safe, when so many will be gone, and we count on them to preserve our old ideals, and to come out fresh, and ready to help us take up the work where we left off.

Yours sincerely,

Helen Bowen Wedgwood

....

March 1st German jaw; then Lechmere 9 a.m. Spent morning investigating some of Seward's material. Then Botany as usual. Long walk up and down and quiet evening with Oltmann's *Algae*.

March 2nd Quiet morning with Oltmann's. It is a wonderful comfort to have a slave for parcels – fool that I was not to manage it before.[166] They brought two small Russian children aged about 9 and 11 into the camp today. Captured in Warsaw – no doubt a "*grosser Sieg*" [big victory]. In the evening there was the school public meeting. Simon[167] in the chair. Speeches by Ford, Henricksen,[168] Butterscotch, Cotterill and above all by Pritchard – in tremendous form! I don't think they really made the matter clear at all! But anyhow there was no opposition and everything carried nem. con. and the money M.1500 easily raised.

---

165 Cambridge Heretics Society, active 1909–1932.

166 It became common for some internees to pay others to queue to collect their parcels.

167 Philip Frederic William Simon (1868–1943). A German, born in Paris he became a naturalized British citizen in 1894. Simon was an engineer, and in 1906 became the first works manager of the Singer sewing machine factory in Wittenberg. He was still working there at the outbreak of war. He was repatriated in March 1918 as an 'over-45er'.

168 Chief Officer of the SS Wardane, who taught navigation and engineering in the camp school.

....

Postcard from MSP to HBW:

Ruhleben, March 2nd 1916

Very many thanks for yours, coming, as it did, just after the news of Snowden's efforts,[169] *it puts much spirit and determination into one. Alas how can I answer it all within the crucial limits of these 9 lines? Yes I feel it very much that in the hour of trial so many of my friends, including my parents, have bowed the knee to Baal – hopelessly stampeded and bamboozled I suppose. Do you remember Disraeli's famous remark to Bismarck at the Berlin conference? Yes I do envy you your picnics on the Gogs. I, too, have done that many times: you should try further afield. My present war anti-dote is sea-weeds! Best wishes to all.*

MSP

....

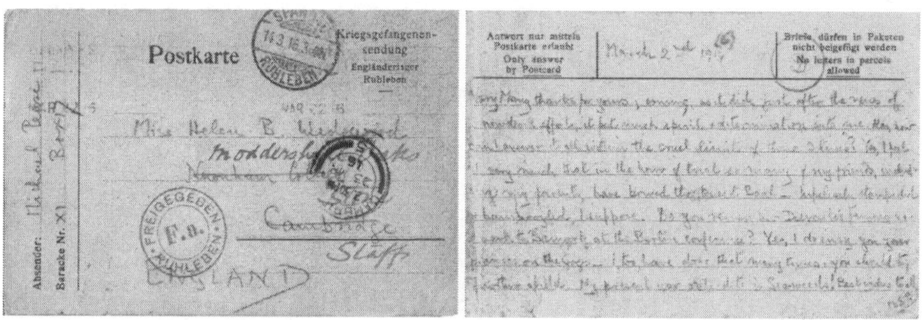
Postkarte
Kriegsgefangenensendung
Engländerlager Ruhleben
Absender:
Baracke Nr. X1
F.a.
Antwort nur mittels Postkarte erlaubt
Only answer by Postcard
Briefe dürfen in Paketen nicht beigefügt werden
No letters in parcels allowed

The first postcard sent by Michael to Helen Wedgwood

March 3rd Morris dancing; Lechmere; then odd darning and mending. Invigilating 12–1. Botany as usual. Milner's Molière reading 6–7 – otherwise quiet evening.

[Insert: Ruhleben Camp School prospectus for Easter Term 1916]

March 4th German prowl 8.30. Then spent the morning planting and bestowing the new bulbs on various people. Botany as usual. 4 p.m. Molière with Milner, then quiet evening. The most distressing news is that Mützenbecher [fn 93] has left for good: wrote a very pathetic letter to

[169] Philip Snowden, a Labour MP campaigned against conscription and voted against the criminalisation of men evading military service.

Balfour. Appears he had a row with von Brocken. I don't think his country realises how much he did for it here – bringing a real spirit of friendliness and helpfulness, of good manners and good breeding into this place.

March 5th Took some extra people in the lab this morning – including the great Mr. Dodd. Invigilated 12–1: then Camp School Committee 3–6 p.m. I didn't realise Bodin was a religious mono-maniac. Been stampeded, no doubt, by Hoffmann's "Stunt" evening! Then a walk and a great "*schmaus*" [feast] and a quiet evening with Goethe.

March 6th Lechmere 9. Then interrupted morning. Books from Elijah Johnson [Cambridge bookshop], but sent the wrong Davenport – a piffling little pamphlet: wrote again and got it through without delay. Nobody in Mützenbecher's place yet. Botany as usual: then walked about – very bleak and harsh. 6 p.m. "The Hunt is Up". Very much better evening than the last: Hunt himself played very well. And so to bed with mighty content.

[Insert: programme and song sheets for the A.S.U. Fourth Music Evening. 'Characteristics of Grieg's Work'. Illustrated lecture by Horace Hunt]

March 7th Morris dancing early. Then quiet morning browsing in Bower – very attractively written. No parcels today, owing to the sinking of the "Mecklenburg"[170] – hope the books I'm waiting for haven't gone down. Botany mighty cold. Then Doddering. Evening in Lab. by way of to help L. fix up some apparatus for the Science Circle evening – but mostly did the looking on. Beastly snow blizzard.

[Written on facing diary page: Handed in formal applications for *The Knight* to Tapp.[171] Merritt, has, after all, thrown over his *Passers By* project!]

March 8th Unspeakable *schweinerei* of melting snow. Lechmere 9 a.m. Then quiet reading. Botany as usual. Electrician came up to me about lighting: seems to be a real good sport and chattered away, mimicking Benzene. Delighted with the story of B and the Batteries. However, after all these

---

[170] Should be Mecklenburgh, the Dutch cargo liner that struck a mine on 27 February 1916. There was no loss of life, so Michael wasn't being too hard-hearted in worrying about his books.

[171] Bernard Eve Tapp (1877–1955), known as Bert Bernard, was the Entertainment Committee's administrator. Pre-war he was manager of touring theatrical companies, and at the outbreak of war owned picture palaces in Berlin (*Sheffield Independent*, 29 March 1918). He was released from Ruhleben in May 1918.

months of waiting excellent to get the job done so quickly. 5 p.m. Cutayar Italian. 7 p.m. Science Circle. I demonstrated three of L's cytology slides telling the same old story 30 times over to all and sundry.

March 9th Quiet morning, super lunch, Botany, Doddering. Social Problems Circle 7 p.m. Ponsonby on "Church and S.P." The sadness today is that Marsh[172] has been shot – notice in *Nature* by Tansely:[173] what aching voids there will be when it's all over. I hope they're proud of their bloody men!

March 10th Lechmere 9 p.m. Then reading. Starting invigilating in library but at 12.30 goods arrived from Leitz and I had to receive them. Find Jones, the camp cashier, get money and mobilise L. to check the microscopes. Sent one too many microscopes so had to be sent back with long explanation. However, eventually got the stuff *kontrolliert* [controlled] and things carted down to lab. 5 p.m. Dante Circle, – then to supper with Kell[174] and company, Lechmere and MacMillan.[175] Very nice to have a slack evening telling yarns – mostly of old Dons!

March 11th Morris dancing early. Line up for concert tickets. Sunday sewing – then quiet. Botany, 4–5 Ford's Molière – rather prosy. Cut History Circle and quiet evening reading Tredgold,[176] which arrived this morning.

March 12th Morning reading Tredgold. Doesn't really seem to have grasped the principle of Mendelism and is very casual about accepting evidence that he likes and rejecting what he doesn't. 12 p.m. invigilated. Then usual "Grantchester grind" with Ponsonby. 3 p.m. R.C.S. Committee and then to

---

[172] Alfred Stanley Marsh (1892–1916). An ecologist who graduated in Natural Sciences (Trinity College) in 1909. At the outbreak of war he was acting as lecturer and demonstrator in the botany school. A Captain in the 8th Somersetshire Light Infantry, he was shot through the heart by a sniper's bullet in the trenches of Armentieres on 5 Jan 1916.

[173] Arthur George Tansley, FRS. Botanist and pioneer ecologist who was a lecturer at Cambridge.

[174] Joel Foster Kell (1887–1983), an exporter and manufacturer from London.

[175] Ernest Alexander Campbell Macmillan (1893–1973). A Canadian musician and composer. In 1914 he was studying music in Paris and was caught at the Bayreuth Festival when war broke out. After the war he directed the Toronto Symphony Orchestra and was Dean of the Faculty of Music at the University of Toronto (obituary in the *New York Times,* 8 May 1973).

[176] Possibly Alfred Frank Tredgold's *Eugenics and the Future Progress of Man*, published 1911.

concert. Quartette very good, but an ill put together program. Dale's[177] composition very attractive. Very much dislike singing sort of sandwiched in anywhere in a concert program.

[Insert: concert programme for Sunday 12th March 1916]

March 13th Lechmere 9. Quiet making out syllabus for my Botany lectures – about which I don't really enthuse very much. Botany as usual, continued Tredgold and so to bed.

[Insert: R.C.S. membership card for March/April 1916]

March 14th Morris dancing, *Appell,* resumed dancing. Then hockey selection game – first for months. At 2 p.m. there was a great straw sack filling parade which I designed to cut, but S. and Milner seized both my sacks and filled them up so that I could scarcely squeeze into bed. It appears Roberts, Coote, Hawkins and one other getting out on special exchange; went round and saw [W.A.C.] Roberts who says they are booked for Saturday. Mighty exciting for them. Decided to get more tea roses for the garden.

March 15th Ordered tea roses. Otherwise the only event was that Leon asked me to speak on Heredity vs. Environment at the debating society on Tuesday. It's a futile subject to discuss even for an intelligent and instructed audience – but for the Butterscotch club – .... Lechmere is to second me.

March 16th Cut the bathing expedition: worked till 9.30 then hockey selection game. Very energetic game. Botany: we decided to share the afternoons, I taking Tues, Thur, Sat and L. the others. With class till 5.30, just 4 hours on end. The notice of that dreadful debate gone up, so now too late to back down, I suppose. Wrote letter to Seward for more specimens: spent the evening putting together stuff for my botany lectures. I hear

---

[177] Benjamin James Dale (1885–1943), a composer and teacher at the London Royal Academy of Music. He was on his way to the Bayreuth Music Festival when war broke out. Dale was heavily involved in the Ruhleben Musical Society, and among other compositions wrote a Country Dance for 4 violins, 2 violas and 2 cellos as the Introduction to Act 3 of *The Knight of the Burning Pestle*. After the war he became Warden of the Royal Academy of Music in London.

Beaumont[178] of Bar. 5 is among those to be exchanged, a real good riddance. He's the strongest and most ill mannered of the arm band mob!

Camp Garden Plots.

Sir,

No self-respecting Town Council in England is without its Parks and Gardens Committee; surely in Ruhleben, too, some public energy, and public funds, could be devoted to beautifyng the Camp? With such a body in existence, some organised effort could be made with the happiest results, in the direction of utilising the spaces available for floral decoration. Some bright colour, for example, introduced round the arc lamps in the compound, and by the gateways, and in that dismal waste between the "village pump" and the dentist's surgery would be a source of untold joy to all, throughout the summer and autumn, and would be one of the few beautiful things to which we could look back in Ruhleben. The thing is worth doing, and worth doing well; each Barrack should set to work to contribute its share of colour to the compound. Though not every one, like Wordsworth, is moved beyond tears by the contemplation of a primrose, nearly all feel the fresh, graceful, and innocent appeal of flowers. "A Garden", says Bacon, "is the purest of human pleasures; it is the greatest refreshment to the Spirit of man."

Yours truly,

March, 1916.

M. S. PEASE.

Letter published in the camp magazine in March 1916 – possibly the catalyst for the formation of the Ruhleben Horticultural Society

March 17th Much complaining going on about the reduction of relief money from 5 to 3 marks and the boiler house plastered with anonymous posters. It's lamentable the way people growl and grumble. Another good incident today calculated to make one proud of one's fellow countrymen is

[178] Lewis Grote Beaumont (1873–1940), a Liverpool merchant (metal broker) before and after the war. Vice-Captain of the camp.

that today Bar. 2 were beaten at football by the P.G.[179] Barracks, whereupon the true British sportsmen turn on the P.G.s with mud and filth.

March 18th Morris dancing early; then quiet morning. Saw Roberts who said they had no news of their leaving yet, but later in the day heard they have orders to leave tomorrow. Sent letter off to Seward and this afternoon got long friendly letter from Biffen [page 384] also offering to send stuff. Here there's a huge row on by Hopkirk and Co. over our decision about *Othello* at the Shakespeare Committee. Quiet evening writing letter home.

March 19th A really prize day of committees. At 11 a.m. Shakespeare Committee. Hopkirk now as sick as hell with his hasty action and wants to go on with his play and save his face. Hence a long ramble on concocting grievance of unfair treatment, disgraceful boorish outbursts by Merritt, many personal explanations by sundry people and much technical jaw about flats. Pearce raising technical points of order about rescinding resolutions passed at our last and Welland obviously anxious not to be done out of the glory of being the producer of *Othello*. After very much talk I got up and asked whether Hopkirk would give us a direct answer as to whether he would in any circumstances produce his play, if for example we met him on every point and smoothed all his difficulties for him. Confusion worse confounded, he declined to answer the question. Then he left the room, Merritt knifed on his behalf. M. by his appalling manners very nearly lost his client's case. I put my questions again to M. and M. replied in the affirmative. Motion by Hatfield to invite Hopkirk to return; carried after protest by Pearce and Welland. Hopkirk returned, rather contrite, apologised, but not gracefully, and said he would produce *Othello* unconditionally. Welland now getting very angry – made a speech in the worst possible of taste, saying he was being unfairly treated, that it was depriving him of glory to which he was due, for all the world as bad as Leon at the first meeting. Pearce took the bull by the horns, moved we stick by W. Only 3 voted for including W. There upon W. and Pearce flounced out resigning from the whole show. Finally Hopkirk appointed, and vote to call Welland and P. back to committee passed. Lasted till 1.45 and never seen such an exhibition of bad feeling and worse manners. Next encounter at R.C.S. Committee 3 p.m. All went smoothly till we came to Bodin and the

179 The pro-German barracks.

S.E. corner room. Then ensued an enormous pow wow – whole committee vs. Bodin. Because he had accommodated Jones' classes in his art room, he could not see that by handing over the S.E. room to the Y.M.C.A. we were doing anything but a compromise, as he would call it. At 5.30 I moved the previous question which was carried and we adjourned for tea. Resumed 6.30 and when all the business done, we suspended standing orders and reopened the discussion – I alone voting against. After ¾ hours further discussion Bodin moved we accept his "compromise" but found no seconder. So the matter remains where it was, negotiations still going on between Education dept. and Control Committee. The most important news today is that Roberts, Coote etc. left at 7.30 this morning.

[Insert: agenda for R.C.S. Committee meeting, Sunday 19th March]

March 20th As a result of yesterday's long committee my lecture was very scrappy at 9 a.m. Then put things together for the Butterscotch debate. Very glorious day at last.

March 21st Morris dancing. Then quiet morning marshalling material for Butterscotch club. As I am to propose I wrote out speech complete and timed it. Then learned it practically by heart – made abstract to speak from. No easy matter to talk about a technical matter to a non technical audience: to be accurate and yet clear, and withal only 20 minutes. However finally got the thing ship-shape, and when the time came it went off absolutely "*programmässig*" [as planned]. An attentive and alert audience but easily tickled by silly jokes – my reference to K-brot was most effective. Uncle Patters [Patchett] was rather pompous, very learned, quoted Plato, William James, and Sully; but evidently knew nothing of heredity, nor indeed did anyone else. He talked exclusively psychology. There also spoke sundry people – a theosophist, the inevitable teller of smutty stories, Pearce spoke for me – Leon looking very smart claimed acquaintance with Shaw and Olivier. On the whole I was pleased – think I did well, though motion lost. Two interesting bits of news. (1) Roberts, Coote and Co held up on the frontier[180] (2) Jones has been appointed legal adviser to the Captain's body and is now one of the privileged lot. This is surely Mackenzie's doing. Got

[180] The group (six in total) got back to England on the 24th March.

official intimation that *The Knight* has been sanctioned for May 31st. Cotterill had already mentioned the matter to me unofficially on the field.

[Insert: approval for the production of *The Knight of the Burning Pestle* from the Entertainments Committee, signed by John H. Thorpe (Chairman)]

March 22nd Been much complimented on my effort last night, among others by Harris.[181] They are starting this tiresome clearing out business again. I was on this morning, so no lecture from Lechmere. Played hockey this afternoon – poor game, not a full side, otherwise a good rush about. Shakespeare Committee again at 4 p.m. Long but not so bitter this time – in fact but for a few boorish remarks from Merritt, went off smoothly, though Hopkirk is awfully difficult to deal with. Then quiet evening, thank goodness.

March 23rd Quiet morning preparing lecture. Botany as usual. Quiet evening.

March 24th *Nichts neues.* Dante 5 and Molière 6–7. Jones very much in demand with his new post. Lechmere and I went fishing in the pond for the first time this year. Very cold and nippy, but fairly bright.

March 25th No Morris dancing – Catholic service. Quiet morning putting lecture together. Jost[182] is good – glad I invested in him. Botany class fairly prolonged. Got the two new people underway. Quiet evening with Tredgold.

[Insert: agenda for R.C.S. Committee meeting on Sunday 26th March]

March 26th Nice bright morning and finished lecture – planted gladioli. Handed in formal contract for *The Knight.* Kapp will take Venturewell – good. Then invigilated. Examined the pond material – full of all sorts of thrilling things. Ulothrix, Oedogonium, crowds of diatoms, and chrysophyceae [all algaes]. 3 p.m. R.C.S. Committee – not so prolonged today. Bodin quiet, but Patchett much to the front. I agree with Pritchard – the man's an utter ass. He's the cotton woolliest old chump I've ever struck. Warkentin in at 5.30 and concert at 6.30. Conn got the orchestra in great

---

[181] Probably Leslie Harris (1879-?), an Australian violinist who is mentioned in many concert programmes and played chamber music with Michael's friends Dodd and Marshall. He was completing his music studies in Germany when war broke out (*Western Argus*, 19 June 1917).

[182] Dr Ludwig Jost's *Lectures on Plant Physiology.*

form. Overture to Rosamunda, a serenade for strings (by ?), Scotch Symphony, songs by Weber, Schubert's 2 Grenadiers, and Overture to Merry Wives by one Nikolai. Very enjoyable.

March 27th Nothing much on. Crocuses in the garden looking very gay, but they are yellow, not blue, only a few white. Awful old swindler. Morning looking at pond takings.

March 28th Morris Dancing – then hockey match. Poor game and got knee slightly damaged. Botany class. Then conference with Merritt and Hopkirk about *The Knight*. M. very keen now, but wants to juggle round with the cast. Hopkirk wants to take Jasper, if only his English weren't so weak it would be excellent. Finished Tredgold: good – a very handy book of reference.

March 29th Milner crocked up with water on the knee – in the *Schonungsbaracke*. Read paper on sex to Science Circle – one I wrote about a year ago for A.S.U. meeting. Huge crowd and went down well. Today there was a sugar line reaching up to Bar. 3!

March 30th Nothing much on.

March 31st Lechmere at 9. Lab inspected by American doctors brought round by the Baron. The latter showing the place off as if he had made and provided it. They seemed moderately intelligent and fairly enterprising – actually went right into the latrines and by good luck it was at its worst, just being cleaned out! Roses came today from Haage and Schmidt – excellent plants. In hope of good results. Dante at 5 p.m. Mobilised Marshall and Gilbert for the Shakespeare Morris set. Quiet evening.

....

Marjory Pease to MSP (letter 163, date of receipt unknown):

The Pendicle, Limpsfield, Surrey

5th March 1916

Dearest Michael

No letter from you yet, perhaps one will come tomorrow. I am so relieved to think of Nicolas in a place of comparative safety after 3 and a half months of tremendous hardship. I can't think how he has lived through it. What changed times we live in! I have just been conducting a long telephone talk with Mr. Cohen about a man working for him who is threatened with eviction from the moat farm cottage. Mr. Cohen is now as advanced in his housing views as Montague Fordham[183] *in the old days of David Nicholl!*[184] *Don't think I have become reactionary, it's the others who are rushing ahead!*

Tomorrow we go to a meeting at the Duke of Westminster's to hear Lord Milner and others discourse upon women workers for agriculture. On Wednesday I lunch with Christopher Turner and draw up with him resolutions for our rural education conference.

I hope the censor will allow the circular about the Rupert Brooke[185] *memorial to pass. I am sure that you would like to subscribe to it, but as the list does not close, I will wait till I hear from you.*

Monday, London. Minute enquiries for you from Stuart Davidson with whom I've been walking along Victoria Street and from Cyril Jackson whom I saw at the station. If you have as bitter a wind at Ruhleben as here you will be glad of the despised leather waistcoat. Stuart Davidson is very optimistic and my conversation with him makes me hesitate about sending you sweet peas.

How is Whyte? I have missed seeing Miss Whyte the last time or two she called. She is still under this roof.

Forgive this hastily written letter. Just sent you off bread, marmalade and walnuts and ordered more butter from Cork.

Will write whenever I hear from you. February 5th still my last news of you.

Your loving mother

....

April 1st Morris Dancing – Gilbert will take some coaching. *Appell* 8 a.m., and then the usual monthly silly inventory business at 11 a.m. Botany, Doddering, quiet evening writing home. Bed at 9.45 this evening. Great tension about rumours of Holland[186] coming in.

[Insert: agenda for R.C.S. Committee meeting on Sunday 2nd April (with notes on school financial matters scribbled on the back)]

---

183 Montague Edward Fordham, an agriculturalist and advocate of rural reform.

184 Possibly David Nicholl, an anarchist active in Britain, who participated in the Socialist League.

185 Rupert Brooke, who died in April 1915, was known to Michael through the Cambridge University Fabian Society and the university's Marlowe Society.

186 There were hopes that some prisoners could be released to Holland for internment in a neutral country.

April 2nd Free morning. Invigilated 12–1. Then pottered around trying to secure corner house for rehearsals. 3–5 School Committee. Put on subcommittee, much against my will, to consider relation between R.C.S. and Educ. Comm. Patters in a particularly cantankerous mood and more cotton-woolly than ever. Concert at 6.30. Trio excellent, but didn't much care for the other things. Wrote to Biffen in the evening.

[Insert: concert programme for Sunday 2nd April 1916]

April 3rd Lecture 9 a.m. Then quiet morning. Cut lunch and made long job of it; got another copy of *The Knight* from Carlyle and pasted up acting copy. Thorpe tackled me on question of further gardening activities. Bulbs at present very gay indeed. Have come very well indeed in spite of my anxious misgiving.

THIRD DIARY

April 4th Morris set mobilised in the morning. Then first rehearsal of *The Knight*. Burgoyne[187] will do, but Bell is rather a terrible let down: I don't think he'll do at all – very tiresome. However, give him another chance. Botany. Quiet evening. Heard the most amazing tale from Jones. Amelunxen[188] is a wine merchant in private life. Sends an order to the captains requiring them to arrange for the sale of Moselle in the camp! To be bought with "tickets," like hot water, in a kiosk on the field and in the compound. I didn't think such a flagrant piece of commercialism possible, even here! Awful meeting with Wolf[189] and Patters today about the R.C.S. – the former jawing interminably and bursting with ill digested and fantastic schemes. I tried in vain to get them to formulate a definite preamble of grievances.

---

[187] John Edgar Galbraith Burgoyne (1893–1966). An Edinburgh University student on holiday in Germany in 1914 who played the citizen's wife in *The Knight*. After the war he became a teacher at the Royal High School, Edinburgh.

[188] Captain von Amelunxen. According to Powell he was unpopular with the soldiers and the prisoners.

[189] Spelt variously as Wolff, Wolfe and Wolf. Probably Oswald Wolff, who is listed as a Spanish language teacher and department representative in the RCS September 1916 prospectus.

April 5th Lechmere, then quiet morning. Hockey league match 3.30 against Bar. 5 which we won! So we're in for the cup-tie! Farmer and Bell into supper and pleasant evening thus, gossiping. Flowers in the garden very gay and much admired by many. The red tulips out: the last sending of pot bulbs is very poor – mostly rotted: I had my doubts. These unreasonable people persist in shutting the field at 5.30, just when one wants to get away out of the dusty old compounds. Letter from Norah S[chuster – a Bedalian].

April 6th Morris dancing: I think the set will manage something, but not brilliantly. Finished lecture for Monday. Botany as usual. Quiet evening. Had 2nd rehearsal with Bell – very doubtful if he'll do. Reynolds[190] is all right, without doubt.

April 7th Lechmere. Quiet morning. Cold and rain. Read Bower. Dante 5 p.m. Tea with Ponsonby. *Sonst nichts neues* [nothing else new].

April 8th Morris dancing 7.30. Rehearsal 9. The man Wilson[191] and Roupell[192] will do. Stopped by Wolff about the R.C.S. business: drafted a minority report for myself. This was approved of by Ford and by Pritchard and later by Blagden. I showed it to Patchett who was nice, rather lachrymose, and presumed that it meant I resigned from his committee, to which I agreed. However see what happens. Botany as usual. Doddering. Quiet evening, sorting out some music for *The Knight*. Will try to get Hughesdon.[193]

[Insert: agenda for R.S.C. Committee meeting on Sunday 9th April]

April 9th Went to hear rehearsal of Dale's concert. Then R.C.S. 10 a.m.: Patchett pretty well snubbed by committee. My report accepted without comment. I resigned from Patchett's sub committee and I don't know what

---

[190] F. C. Reynolds played 'Ralph' in *The Knight*. A member of the Dramatic Society and associate of Duncan-Jones he acquired the nickname 'Andy' after playing the title role in *Androcles and the Lion* in March 1915.

[191] Thomas W. Wilson (1894–?), played 'Humphrey' in *The Knight*. One of Ruhleben's 'popular players' he was a woollens representative for Binberrys in Breslau at the outbreak of war.

[192] Charles Frederick (de Coetlogon) Roupell (1897–1980). From a military family, he was in Germany studying for the Sandhurst entrance examination when war was declared. He joined the RAF after the war, and then became a tennis pro and coach.

[193] Frederick William Hughesdon (1883-1936), an insurance clerk before the war, he was a singer in the camp. In the end he doesn't appear on the programme for *The Knight*.

they'll produce. Poor old boy: I feel sorry for him – he means well, but has such a fuzzy old cotton woolly head. Played hockey final against Bar. 10, and got what we expected 12–0 an inglorious licking. Saw Hughesdon about *The Knight*: quiet evening reading *Frederick the Great*. Just halfway through now!

[Insert: memorandum from Michael Pease on relations of the R.C.S. with the Education Committee]

April 10th Lechmere. Then moderately uninterrupted morning. Went down to botany lab to give L. a hand. Doddering – Budget, so interesting for once in a way. Paid for the roses this morning only 6.90 under protest – they've made a mistake again, but to my advantage this time. Fiendish wind and dust. Quiet evening reading *Didone abbandonata*, an 18th century Italian opera. Glad to see no one has "*abboniert*" [subscribed] for the wine yet.

April 11th Morris set to begin with: it won't do brilliantly, I'm afraid: it will just "*gehen*"[go] – that's all. An enormous match queue this afternoon reaching right down to the Spandauer latrines.[194] Very much annoyed by Benzene: comes up and turns us out of the lab at 8.30. Like them, down to the ground, let us put up an expensive installation at our own cost, then won't let us use it. Arranged rehearsal for Hughesdon. Went to reading of *Didone Abbandonata* – not much catch.

April 12th Rehearsal at 9 a.m. Bell very much improved. May possibly do, which will be a comfort. Put in some plants that Kremnitz had sent to him. Drew up report of Bio. Dept. for R.C.S. Doddering: quiet evening preparing lecture and reading *Frederick the Great*. Enormous sugar lines this afternoon, but owing to fearful dust and rain I didn't line up. A mercy I was brought up on drinks without sugar.

April 13th Started with usual breakfast party and then Morris dancing. Then rehearsal of *The Knight*. Hughesdon will do all right, if need be. Ponsonby passed. Then quiet reading Bower. Botany, Doddering, Rawson into supper and then Social Probs Circle.

---

[194] Whilst most places in Ruhleben were named after London landmarks, the two latrines on either side of the camp were named after the Berlin suburbs Charlottenburg and Spandau.

[Insert: internal postcards for collection of two parcels ordered by Pease – 'roses' and 'goods']

April 14th More or less interrupted morning. Coached Bell 11–12. Took L.'s botany class for him, as he's very busy with *12th Night* dressmaking. Went to the meeting of the so called Sociological Circle which Rawson spoke of. The usual gang of I.L.P.ers [Independent Labour Party persons], with sundry stray anarchists and Spencerians. However they seemed very keen someone read a chapter from *New Worlds for Old* [H.G.Wells book] after which a very poor discussion followed. I switched them on to Fabian Essays as a text book of Socialism. They seem to be run by one Brown, who has spent most of his life in America. Jones tells me the most amazing tale. The captains had petitioned to have Ettlinger and Ellison [imprisoned for attempting to escape from Ruhleben] released from the Stadtvogtei[195] and sent back here. Whereupon the Graf calls a meeting of the captains and makes a harangue, saying he can't possibly allow it, because we are so ungrateful for all he does for us, and in particular because someone wrote a very unfavourable account of how the mothers and wives interviews are allowed to take place. He stated the facts, so far as I know, that you sit four at a table, with a garrison of soldiers standing by. For this the man has got 4 weeks in the bird cage and Ellison and Ettlinger are to linger in prison! Blagden tells me von Brocken has the sack, that the Baron has been hauled over the coals, and that Amelunxen has been given long *Urlaub* [leave], ostensibly for an *entfaltung kur* [development course?] but probably as a stepping stone to dismissal. Of course, if this wine deal becomes known it would probably be a wholesale scrap of the staff. It is ridiculous to put such an old dodderer in such a responsible position.

April 15th Morris dancing. Then *Knight* again at 8.30. Wish I could make up my mind about Bell. Then went fishing in the pond: very nice to have a little outing. Much upset the coots there. Botany and then Doddering. *DT*[196] of 10th with report of Wittenberg camp. I only read half of the thing but such a tale of insane cruelty and cowardice passes my comprehension. It is the most harrowing thing I've read for ever so long. No wonder the *Nord.*

---

[195] The prison in Berlin.

[196] *The Daily Telegraph.* News reports came out at this time of conditions in this camp and the typhus epidemic.

Deutscher Alf. Ztg. [North German newspaper] thought it necessary to counter report by quoting the report of the American commission which visited the camp 6 months after the atrocities! There has been another great *"gesinster"* [hostile] stunt in the P.G. barracks. Have Warkentin coming to tea tomorrow to tell us about it!

April 16th Quiet morning. Tried sitting out, but very windy and dusty. Finished Bower. Invigilated 12–1. Searched through pond water and made some preps. Then Doddering. Warkentin and Bell to supper 6 p.m., and heard the true story of the new P.G. segregation. This time the distinction is definitely political, i.e. do you want to become naturalised.[197] They seemed to manage to raise about 100 odd from the P.G. barracks. Concert good – much enjoyed the Bach *Vorspiel.* Heard them last in Jena Church.

[Insert: programme for Palm Sunday Concert, conducted by Mr. E. C. MacMillan]

April 17th Lecture 9 a.m. Saw Ford and Bell about Shakespeare program. This dancing business is an awful nuisance. Stuff from Seward. Took L's Botany for him. Then to Mozart evening. Pritchard gave a very lucid exposition of his philosophy of music, contrasting the selfish effect produced by Beethoven over the altruistic produced by Mozart. Quartette very good, and so to bed with mighty content. I did hear today from Ford that we are all to be exchanged in July!

[Insert: programme for A.S.U. Fifth Musical Evening – Mozart. Monday 17th April 1916]

April 18th Breakfast party and then Morris dancing. Unfortunately Ponsonby put his knee out in a galley, and, as our last spare man is out, that is *schlim* [bad]. I'm sorry for P. – rotten for him to be laid up. Saw Ford and Bell about altering the Shakespeare program, and undertook to write them an essay on the subject instead. Gather from Jones there was a stormy captains' meeting – came back saying *der Teufel ist wieder los* [all hell is breaking loose again], which he repeated ad lib, but nothing *weiter* [further].

---

[197] Pro-German internees could be released if they accepted naturalisation and volunteered for military service.

April19th Lechmere. Then terribly interrupted morning. Saw Wimpfheimer about using cinema for Edge's lectures and chased people round camp. Then Botany. Saw Hopkirk about dresses for *The Knight*. Went to *The Younger Generation*, with a view to getting ideas about this old stage for *The Knight*. A poor play, stale theme, and not treated with any subtlety.

April 20th I hear there are great doings in the captains' body. MacKenzie has been ordered to resign [as Captain of Barrack 5] because he refused to recognise Powell as the elected head of the camp. *Grosse Unruhe* [great unrest] in Bar. 5 and in camp generally. Baron in conversations with Masterman said the Ed. Com. were a lot of stinkers and intriguers – whereupon Ed. Com. resigns en bloc (joy for Patchett). Blagden in to supper and discussed the *allgemeine lage* [general situation]. Jones says there will be great doings tomorrow. School Committee most of the morning. Rather long drawn out. Patchett well snubbed for his constitution mongery; otherwise nothing of importance.

[Insert: agenda for R.C.S. Committee meeting on Thursday 20th April]

April 21st Captains have proved a miserable weak-kneed set of fools – knuckled under to Powell with only a feeble show of fight. D.D.J. very disappointed. Masterman resigned, after the Baron called him a stinker and so there is the old situation with Powell installed and recognised as elected Captain of the camp. However, agreed that J.P. Jones (who is hand in glove with P.) to be chairman of the meeting. When this was announced by Thorpe in the Barrack, the part about P. was received with groans and derision. General meeting of school teachers in the afternoon, to which I didn't go for more than 5 minutes. Gather it went off perfectly *programmässig* [as planned].

[Insert: invitation to the dress rehearsal of *Twelfth Nig*ht from C. Duncan-Jones]

April 22nd Up betimes and starting lining up for the Shakespeare tickets at 6.10 a.m. – I was about 65th, even at that early hour. D^2J [D.D.J.] relieved me at 8, when I turned in for some breakfast! Came out again and got my tickets about 10.15 – also about 4 hours. Sowed sweet peas in the garden and to *12th Night* dress rehearsal at 1.00. There we sat through 1½ hours scene changing. Didn't get away till 5.15. Very good acting in parts, but some very indifferent. Very much enjoyed Henry's scenery and dresses, but that scene changing is a great mistake. Hughesdon lamentably bad and Andy [F. C. Reynolds] not at all good. Wilson as Malvolio excellent. Walked up and down with Keel and talked *The Knight* and sundry things, and so to bed mighty tired. D^2J sent in resignation to captains. I hear Pritchard is to be elected for Bar. 10. It will be interesting to see the upshot.

April 23rd Spent nearly all day writing my essay on Elizabethan dance for the Shakespeare week, and got the first draft finished, thank goodness, all but the opening paragraph. I hear *12th Night* was a tremendous success – for which I own I am mighty glad as D.J. was rather down about it after the dress rehearsal, and I don't blame him too! It is true that Pritchard has been elected for Bar. 10. It will be interesting to see the upshot.

April 24th Got my essay on Elizabethan dance finished for which the gods be praised. This night I did go to the play house and did see a mighty fine play. There was no comparison with the dress rehearsal. Andy is still bad (I have serious misgivings for Ralph) but Eden[198] as Malvolio was excellent. Goodhind [199] [as Olivia] looked wonderful, but acted like a statue. Thoroughly enjoyed the evening. Today we got the extra window put in the lab., which is a great improvement.

April 25th Rehearsal of *The Knight*. Bell doing very much better. Saw Keel about his songs. Spent morning putting board edging round garden; got grass seed from Cooper[200] and gave him some of my extra stuff.

April 26th Not much excitement. Everybody very pleased with the success of *XIIth Night*. Down at the R.C.S. taking names, enrolling new pupils. Rather a slow game. At it again afternoon, talked with Egremont[201] about stage for

---

198 Sir Timothy Clavert Eden (1893–1963). Brother of Anthony Eden who became Prime Minister in 1955.

199 Harold Goodhind, a frequent and popular actor in the Ruhleben Dramatic Society. He also taught French in the camp school.

200 There were a number of 'Coopers' in Ruhleben, Michael is probably referring to Walter Roylands Cooper (1885–1963) who seems to have been a keen gardener. Walter was an engineer who lectured on oil engines and steam power plant during his internment. After the war he joined the editorial board of '*The Engineer*' magazine and in 1931 was one of the founding members of 'The Engineers German Circle'.

201 Hobart Godfrey Egremont (1879–1946), an Australian architect and artist (*Adelaide Observer,* 2 Sep 1916) who was studying architecture in Karlsruhe when war broke out. In 1934 he was a lecturer in German at the University of Melbourne.

The Knight. To Shakespeare Concert, and mighty fine it was, too. Keel is really wonderful and the Nicolai[202] miserable wash.

[Insert: Tercentenary Shakespeare Festival Programme (April 23rd–30th): *Twelfth Night, Othello*, concert and talks]

[Insert: invitation to the dress rehearsal of *Othello* from H. G. Hopkirk]

April 27th Rehearsal at 9. Bell much improved with the Songs, but Andy is v. doubtful. I don't know what we shall do. I would hate to sack him. Then to R.C.S. 2nd day enrollment. 1 p.m. to dress rehearsal of *Othello* (secured Neville[203] to enrol folk). Hopkirk did not speak, practically only did dumb show. The dresses were magnificently gaudy. It will be a good success. People enjoy the simple melodrama. Then our "*sponterei*" evening:[204] the audience were very patient to sit through 2 hours' jaw. I think my paper went down all right. At least, it drew many laughs (not hard to do with Ruhleben crowd) and as usually happens after such occasions, accosted by unknown people who say how interested they were.

[Insert: R.C.S. prospectus for summer term 1916]

April 28th Put in some seeds in garden today: then rehearsal. Complimented by Bainton and Keel on paper.

April 29th To *Othello* in the evening. Merritt indistinct but acted well, I thought. The setting was poor and Hopkirk's accent really not at all bad.

April 30th School Committee in the morning. Longish, and not much catch. Early morning *Appell* nuisance, though when all said and done it's as good a time as any. Somehow seemed to waste a lot of time in the afternoon. The two men who escaped yesterday are still unheard of – one was Gaunt. Finished Ruggles Gates[205] in the evening – a poor book, I think.

---

[202] *Merry Wives of Windsor* overture by Otto Nicolai.

[203] Possibly Guy Neville, a young gardener at Kew at the outbreak of war. Taught theoretical and practical botany, and gave lectures in plant pathology in the Camp School (*Kew Guild Journal* 1919).

[204] Talks by Pease, Marshall, Howard and Ford on Elizabethan England, with songs and Morris dancing. A favourable review (despite reporting some heckling from the audience) by Hatfield was published in the July edition of *In Ruhleben Camp*.

[205] Reginald Ruggles Gates, a botanist and geneticist.

....

HBW to MSP: (received some time during late April/early May)

Moddershall Oaks, Stone, Staffs.[206]

April 15th 1916

Dear Mr. Pease,

Many thanks for your postcard. How annoying it must be to see ones friends going wrong and not to be able to get at them and show them the error of their ways! Argument however is useless in most cases: I know Father is quite impervious to it.

Please don't think me cheeky, but it is jolly for us to know that there is one more man who has not changed his views. We are so few that we hail each supporter with cheers, even though they can only sympathise. It is a shame you are not here to be in the fight too (are you an "out & outer"?). Send them your sympathy. They need it, and will need it more. Things are going to be hard, but everyone is staunch, and the spirit perfectly splendid. It is wonderful too, what a stand a few determined people can make; and there are far more of us than anyone expected. I suppose, even in Ruhleben, you hear something of what is going on, so you will know that things have been pretty lively. (I dare not tell you anything really interesting.)

Term is just over, and has of course, been rather exciting – too much so for those of us with Triposes [exams]. *C.U.F.S has been as flourishing as could be expected. The study circles were very strenuous. Overton, Huckle and Wright (Ind. Lab. Pers) sometimes come, and enliven them considerably.*

They were glad to get your £1, and more for the thought, I imagine; they must be feeling rather low, seeing everything for which they have worked crumbling in a few months. They have done their best too to back up many of our members under the difficulties of present circumstances, and many of the boys have been glad of the encouragement of older and experienced men (a thing not too easy to get now.)

The best meeting we had was addressed by George Lansbury.[207] *He spoke on Guild Socialism, and he was a rather refreshing change from Cole or Melor. Perhaps it is unjust to them, but they seem to regard Socialism too much as the "class war", and as dealing exclusively with the means of living, instead of more broadly as a*

---

[206] The Wedgwood family home built by Helen's father in the style of a South African bungalow.

[207] Sometime Labour MP and editor of the *Daily Herald* – a pacifist, left-leaning paper.

struggle against all injustice. However it may be, Lansbury put a new spirit and inspiration into it. He ended up characteristically by saying that neither Guild Socialism not any other sort of Socialism is any good unless people rid themselves of the old ideal of "getting on" and substitute that of serving the world – a commonplace almost, but it does need rubbing in. The meeting was very enthusiastic, and ended with the Red Flag. It was the best we have had; you would have enjoyed it.

The remnant of the University Federation conference has just been held near Wroxham. No men, for various reasons, so the women did the business, and got a fine lot done. The women's groups will have to carry on next year. Half Newnham is away this Vac. "working on the land". It is wonderful how anxious the good people who used to bid us "mind the baby" are to get us out at work now! Well they won't get us back again in a hurry. Though I must say, 8 hours a day and 13s a week does <u>not</u> attract me and some of us intend to give the farmers a lively time.

I hope the lab. is getting on well. You must feel rather like the early chemists who had to heat their retorts with candles! How do you manage to get seaweeds in Ruhleben?

Now the days are long the botanically inclined socialists are going to picnic on Fleam Dyke, and look for the pasqueflower. I've missed it every year, so far.

I hope you have good news of your brother. Mine is just back safe from Egypt and thank goodness, with no military 'swagger'.

Yours sincerely

Helen Bowen Wedgwood

....

May 1st Got up to new time this morning. *Appell* at 6.50 and kept standing 25 mins. Rehearsal 9 a.m. Then sowed sundry seeds in the garden. Fishing in afternoon with plankton net: fine catch of cyclops etc. Merritt to supper and discussion of *The Knight*.

May 2nd Usual early *Appell.* Rehearsal 9 a.m. Played first game of tennis 10.15. Then Shakespeare Committee 2 p.m. Many complaints and grievances against the stage staff. Appointed committee to investigate and report.

May 3rd Hear (1) the escapees [Gaunt and Colston] are safely across, lucky dogs (2) that they are going to pinch the extra money that we get on account of the unfavourable rate of exchange on Amsterdam. Edge's first lecture 8 a.m. – huge crush. Unsatisfactory day – poor rehearsal. Saw Ford about sundry details: messed about in the lab.

May 4th Rehearsal 10 a.m. Merritt approves of Bell, so now it's merely a matter of blazing ahead. Saw Roker about the staging. Must give up the draw curtains notion, and revert to a drop with an opening. Tennis at 3 p.m. and then to Shakespeare Committee – still sitting. Dodd to supper. Came away from committee with Hopkirk who wants me to write him some butter for the press.

May 5th Rehearsed Wilson at 9.30. Then full rehearsal at 10. Went to Roker for stage measurements which I took down to Egremont and had a long talk with him. Then writing Hopkirk's butter for him. In the evening to Lubinsky's circle where they were discussing the next part of Shaw's Fabian Essay – walked up and down with Brown who is an excellent talker. Very excited about the exclusiveness of the tennis club.

May 6th Rehearsal 9 a.m. Roped in Dannhorn[208] and Nash[209]. Then finished off Hopkirk's butter and then found he wanted me to sign it and send in the whole thing as my effort. However, this I declined to do. I wrote the letter for him and made him sign it, and packed him off to the censor. Tennis at 2 p.m. and came back to find a great rat hunt raging in my garden and considerable damage being done – swore fairly vehemently at them. Dale and Evans to tea. Supper with Bell and spent the evening talking. Article on the Shakespeare festival in the *Berliner Tageblatt.*

[Insert: newspaper cutting on the Shakespeare festival from the *Berliner Tageblatt*, which mentions Michael's Elizabethan dance talk]

May 7th Tennis 9.30. Then School Committee at 11. Got times for stage rehearsals and spent afternoon sending out calls. Quiet evening reading *Frederick.*

May 8th Masterman's first German history lecture 9 a.m. on grandstand – great crowd and very good. 11 a.m. interview with new candidates for pract. botany in lab. Four in all who have to be given special coaching this

---

208 Albert John Dannhorn (1892–1972). An Englishman of German descent, he was an engineer in the 1911 census, and after the war he became a journalist.

209 L. Nash played one of the 'boys' in *The Knight.* He also taught French in the Camp School.

week. Then starting putting up strings for sweet peas in the garden. Paid 2.70 for a ball of string! Continued same all afternoon. To lecture by Dodd on birds in grandstand – not bad, but slides awful. Today the following notice was posted in the Barracks. "As a retaliatory measure against depreciation of German currency in enemy countries it has been decided to pay postal orders received through foreign countries at the flowing rates:" Then follows schedule and for £1 only 20.40 is offered instead of 24.00. A piece of the most impertinent robbery.

May 9th Rehearsal at 12–1 and then again 3–5. Fairly exhausting.

May 10th Edge's lecture in the cinema 8–9. Rehearsal 12–1. Otherwise *nichts neues.*

[Insert: programme for the Ruhleben Society for German Drama and Literature evening, 10 May 1916 – *Flachsmann als Erzieher* (a comedy by Otto Schmidt)]

May 11th Lochhead's lecture 8–9. Keel on German folksong 9–10 (mighty fine) and then my class of new candidates till 12. Then Merritt into lunch before rehearsal at 1. But news comes that we are to have 48 hours arrest. Rüdiger alleges that two buttons were stolen off his cap; hence honour has to be avenged. Laid up store of books and retired to box. Read *Lucrece* and wrote letter. The two fellows[210] that escaped were brought back and shoved into the cells. Poor fellows – sorrow for them, but they were stupid to go with no knowledge of German. The camp treats the arrest as a great joke and is in the best of spirits.

May 12th Arrest continues, though rumours of relaxation are rife and in fact at 1 o'clock release was announced "owing to the uncertainty of who committed the crime". Annoyed at missing two rehearsals but otherwise all right. Walked round with Keel and discussed *The Knight.* The two escapees were taken off to the Stadtvogtei this afternoon – poor fellows.

[The following entries appear to be written in a great hurry, possibly as Michael was busy with rehearsals]

---

[210] Chalmers and Leatham, according to *Wyndham's War.*

May 13th Edge at 8 – then Dufty[211] and Co at 9, tennis at 11 and rehearsal at 12–1. Gave up my Sunday time to Pemberton[212] for Driven. Went fishing in the pond in afternoon. Dodd to supper and quiet evening reading *Frederick* – I dislike the Carlylean style more and more.

May 14th Fixed up rehearsals for *The Knight* – nothing till Wednesday. School Committee 10.30. Quiet afternoon. Bell and Philips to supper and then to German play. Very good. Lot of work put into it. Makes me anxious for *The Knight*! Tried to screw up Merritt to seeing Eden.

May 15th Started lectures today and practical work, Lechmere made some ripping drawings for *The Knight.* Saw Merritt who seems still to be letting the Venturewell[213] matter slide! Blagden got the glass house scheme *genehmigt* [approved] by Benzene, who said, first of all, *gibts nicht. Nichts zu Machen* [do not exist. Nothing to do] etc. The excitement in camp today is that Foster Kell, a leading light of the Y.M.C.A., has been sent for a month's imprisonment for the "abominable offence not to be mentioned among Christians".

May 16th Lechmere at 8 a.m. Then practical botany all morning. Conferences with Merritt about *The Knight* and Venturewell – he seemed much more taken up with poker at that juncture. Eventually decided to ask Hatfield. Left the matter to him.

May 17th Edge 8–9. Poor rehearsal of *The Knight.* Hatfield as I feared very indifferent. Quiet afternoon. Tennis at 5 and so to bed mightily discontented.

May 18th Lochhead 8–9, he's one of these murmurers when he lectures! Botany till 12. Then rehearsal at 1 p.m. Roberts is weak. Dodd to supper and so to bed.

May 19th Rushed round to see Pearce about the dresses and find it's all right. Then rehearsal at 10–12. Conference with Merritt and Hopkirk re

---

211 Francis John North Dufty (1866–1940), a schoolmaster who taught French whilst at Ruhleben. He was repatriated in 1917.

212 Christopher Gale Pemberton (1892–1972), editor of Ruhleben Camp Magazine. Living and working in Hamburg with his German wife and their baby at the outbreak of war.

213 A character in the play.

wigs dresses and cuts – regret we'll have to cut Andy very much – Hatfield not so bad. Then further conference with Pearce about dresses. He is mighty energetic and obliging about it.

May 20th Got Neville to dep for me, and sat in the library to listen to Adler's dress rehearsal of Verdi's *Requiem*. Not nearly so bad as I had been given to suppose it would be by Schlesinger. Rehearsal 1–3, tennis 3.15 and quiet evening. The excitement in camp today is still further about F. Kell. Owing to the Baron being made a *Hauptmann* [Captain] all prisoners were released. Whereupon K. protests he is innocent and his friends Butterscotch and others mobilise Jones and go to Powell, look at the "evidence" and find it is hearsay and gossip. K. demands an enquiry. Next thing that happens is K. is caged again and made to sign a statement that he wants a trial in a German court! What prize fools P. and the B. are!

May 21st Rehearsal 10–12. Merritt and Wilson both so much the worse for a binge the previous night that they couldn't turn up. However, in spite of this we did some good work. Tennis at 2. Sat in the Library for Adler's *Requiem* – some of the choruses were really excruciating!

May 22nd Lecture 8–9. Then Wimpfy on the 30 Years War – not bad. Then practical till 1 p.m. Worked in lab, went out on pond and got inter alia some Equisetum spores. Then Doddering. Spent evening with Keel and Dale fixing up music for *The Knight*. Saw Egremont about posters and sundry props. Morrison[214] was in Berlin and brought in many things from Leitz, and reports the rest are to follow this week.

May 23rd Rehearsal at 10 – not very satisfactory. Pearce reports that Beckers'[215] [team] were very sniffy at Lechmere's drawings, want to read the play and make suggestions for themselves. Quiet afternoon. Doddering – then Dodd and Philips into supper and spent the evening gossiping. Very hard to settle down to concentrated work with this play hanging round.

---

[214] George Herbert Morrison (c1895–1935). The son of the Reverend George Herbert Morrison of Wellington Church, Glasgow. His obituary in the *Dundee Evening Telegraph* (31 August 1935) says he was studying German in Berlin when war broke out. He was repatriated to England in early 1918 on account of ill-health. After the war he studied medicine at Edinburgh University and then worked in London.

[215] Beckers is listed as an artist in *Ruhleben Story*, so maybe he and his team were designing costumes or scenery for *The Knight*.

Hoffmann and the *Rittmeister* [Captain] were round at the lab today and granted us permission to take a lead from the Y.M.C.A. building and thus get continuous current, day and night.

May 24th No attempt to celebrate Empire Day this year. Botany at 9–12. Rehearsal 1–3, much better today.

May 25th Bainton's lecture on Bach 9–10. Very fine – Keel sang a Cantata, which was also mighty fine. Then Botany. Merritt and Wilson to lunch, and then rehearsal. Act 1 put ship-shape.

May 26th Lechmere at 8. Then Botany and then rehearsal – fair. The Kell affaire is a good illustration of Master Powell's dealings. Having promised him an open enquiry, he then gets a German *Rechtsanwalt* [lawyer], goes to his prison with the so called witnesses without giving him notice or letting him call his witnesses or anything. However, in spite of this K is *freigesprochen* [acquitted], so there's one in the eye for P. and B. Ferns came today.

....

MSP to HBW:

Ruhleben, May 26th 1916

Your letter is most welcome; I too hail with cheer each kindred spirit – even an unknown one! That is why it is so refreshing to hear from someone who doesn't tell me about Johnnie, who looks so smart in his uniform and isn't it wonderful, and brave, and beautiful of him – and so on. I send "them" my sympathy – if it helps, with all my heart and soul. Remember me warmly to the Camb. I.L.Pers. I hope the Tripos is treating you well. My work here still continues as a great source of joy. I wonder how you like hoeing turnips? Good luck. Remember that if you start by lying low, you will end up by lying lower still! Best wishes – farewell MSP

....

May 27th Edge at 8–9 then set Botany going and then tennis 10–12. Rehearsal 1–3 – fair. Then tennis again and quiet evening writing letter except then Adler took me by the arm and explained how he did it when he conducted the *Meistersänger* and *Götterdämmerung*.

May 28th Heard Dale's overture rehearsal – very jolly, but hard to play. Rehearsal at 10 a.m., by arrangement with Pearce. Finished letter and prepared lecture. R.C.S. Committee 7.15 p.m. – discussed the [electricity] current question – and so to bed.

May 29th Saw Pearce before going to Berlin. Then lecture 8–9 and practical Botany all morning. Quiet afternoon – tennis 4–6 and then to Bröse's[216] production of Florentine tragedy.

May 30th Conference with Egremont and Roker about stage. Then rehearsal at 10 – not bad. Quiet afternoon – planted out the Azolla and Salvinia in the pond.

May 31st Tennis 10–12 – played rottenly. Rehearsal 1–3 – fairly good, but Roberts was bad. Farmer and Dodd to supper.

June 1st [no entry]

June 2nd Play postponed a week owing to success of *Liberty Hall* – good in some ways, rotten in others. I want to get to work again. Dale rather sick about it. Rehearsal not bad. Order in at last from Leitz. First rose out today! Lab. inspected yesterday by the doctor – very friendly and offered to help all he could.

June 3rd Rehearsal today – went fairly well.

June 4th [no entry]

June 5th No rehearsal. L. took my lecture as per arrangement. Very slack day – caught frogs in the pond. Tennis 5–6. Hear that Hoffmann has volunteered to advance the money necessary for bringing the lead [electric cable] from the Y.M.C.A.

[8 days missing from diary]

[Insert: blank postcard invitation to dress rehearsal of *The Knight*, on Tuesday 13th June, from Merritt and Pease]

---

[216] Henry Herman Leopold Adolph Bröse (1890–1965), an Australian-born physicist. He was studying mathematics at Oxford University in 1914 and visiting relatives in Hamburg when war broke out.

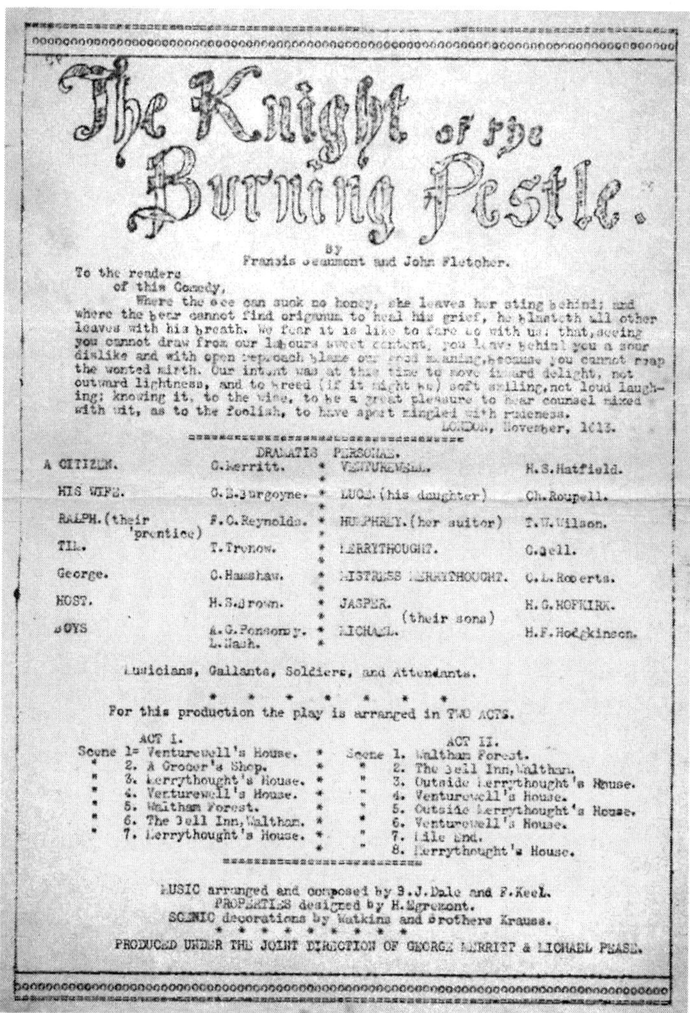

The Knight of the Burning Pestle.

By
Francis Beaumont and John Fletcher.

To the readers
of this Comedy,

Where the bee can suck no honey, she leaves her sting behind; and where the bear cannot find origanum to heal his grief, he blasteth all other leaves with his breath. We fear it is like to fare so with us: that, seeing you cannot draw from our labours sweet content, you leave behind you a sour dislike and with open reproach blame our good meaning, because you cannot reap the wonted mirth. Our intent was at this time to move inward delight, not outward lightness, and to breed (if it might be) soft smiling, not loud laughing: knowing it, to the wise, to be a great pleasure to hear counsel mixed with wit, as to the foolish, to have sport mingled with rudeness.

LONDON, November, 1613.

DRAMATIS PERSONAE.

A CITIZEN.	G.Merritt.	VENTUREWELL.	H.S.Hatfield.
HIS WIFE.	G.E.Burgoyne.	LUCE.(his daughter)	Ch.Roupell.
RALPH.(their 'prentice)	F.C.Reynolds.	HUMPHREY.(her suitor)	T.W.Wilson.
TIM.	T.Trenow.	MERRYTHOUGHT.	G.Bell.
George.	C.Hamshaw.	MISTRESS MERRYTHOUGHT.	C.L.Roberts.
HOST.	H.S.Brown.	JASPER. (their sons)	H.G.HOPKIRK.
BOYS	A.G.Ponsonby. L.Nash.	MICHAEL.	H.F.Hodgkinson.

Musicians, Gallants, Soldiers, and Attendants.

* * * * * * *

For this production the play is arranged in TWO ACTS.

ACT I.	ACT II.
Scene 1= Venturewell's House.	Scene 1. Waltham Forest.
" 2. A Grocer's Shop.	" 2. The Bell Inn, Waltham.
" 3. Merrythought's House.	" 3. Outside Merrythought's House.
" 4. Venturewell's House.	" 4. Venturewell's House.
" 5. Waltham Forest.	" 5. Outside Merrythought's House.
" 6. The Bell Inn, Waltham.	" 6. Venturewell's House.
" 7. Merrythought's House.	" 7. Mile End.
	" 8. Merrythought's House.

MUSIC arranged and composed by B.J.Dale and F.Keel.
PROPERTIES designed by H.Egremont.
SCENIC decorations by Watkins and Brothers Krauss.

* * * * * * * * *

PRODUCED UNDER THE JOINT DIRECTION OF GEORGE MERRITT & MICHAEL PEASE.

Programme for the Knight of the Burning Pestle

June 14th Much happened since last entry. Very full with the play. On Saturday rehearsal with music. Just before rushing out hailed by Neumeister from the *Wache.* Poor man rushed up specially to see me and I could only give him a hurried 10 minutes. He was full of enquiries and brought a great parcel. Then a damned bad rehearsal. Merritt is very trying – the casual way he treats the affair! Even when Dale was there with the orchestra. Sunday – no rehearsal. Monday, put up stage with Roker and Egremont. M. turned up and swore a bit, but went away again and we got the thing put up fairly well – looks nice with the green curtains. Then rehearsal at 1–4.30. Not bad – if only M. knew his lines. Tuesday – Pearce in Berlin to swear about the clothes. None turned up and we had to have an "undress" rehearsal – going rather better, again if only M. knew his lines! Pearce came back and reported that no possibility of dresses till midday on Thursday. Scratched performance for Thursday night.

June 15th Waited about all morning for dresses and by dint of frequent telephoning found that they could not get a taxi to come here, roads too bad! Turnbull[217] came in at 3.45 to say that he had telephoned and that the dresses had been put on a cart and would be here at 6. War council with Merritt and Wilson and agree to mobilise the cast at 5.30 and get them made up. At 6.10 p.m. the dresses were at the gate and in 5 minutes up at the theatre. Pearce got them out and then we hurled them at people and got under way at 7.15 – no swords, guns, or purses. I rushed down and got socks. Went well though not as I wanted it. Wilson is abominably vulgar. Roberts forgot all his part, Hatfield about half, but otherwise it went ~~excellently~~ down well. Towards the end a gang of Roupell's friends started shouting but otherwise it was received well. Dale very sick at the orchestra, which gaped at the play instead of playing.

June 16th Comments on the play very mixed – seems to have been thoroughly enjoyed in spite of its shortcomings. Others said the programmes weren't worth printing. It was badly done: Wilson's "stunts" get much on my nerves. Spoke earnestly to him on the matter and tonight it went much better. Hopkirk fainted in the first scene, that was the only tragedy. Roberts remembered nearly all his part and it was well received, except by one gang who shouted at Roupell in the "strike" scene. Merritt told them off in great style! No abuse – just told Hopkirk to stop, and asked if the gentlemen wanted to come up and act. Absolutely effective. There seems to be a big row brewing about the school and A.S.U. – very tiresome. Anyhow they are at last laying on the continuous current for the lab.

---

[217] Charles Esmond Turnbull (1879–?), aka Charles Esmond Amos, had been living in Hamburg since at least 1903 (when he married a German girl). He was Vice-Chair of the Entertainments Committee.

June 17th Every one pleased with last night's play. Hear that old Logie[218] is upset at the indecent jokes, but Bainton and Keel and others were enthusiastic over it. Haven't heard D.J. but as he's said nothing, I should think he doesn't approve. It is still a pity Wilson trades on his cheap stunts. Heard there was going to be an organised rag tonight but nothing came of it. It went extremely well and was greeted with great cheers at the end. If only we had not been rash enough to dash in on Thursday! Really happy about the play now. Even Tapp congratulated me!

June 18th Mobilised the cast for the photo [see below, Michael back row rhs] and got it done in costume, only Wilson protesting, Merritt, of course, wouldn't dress, but otherwise it went off without contretemps. The performance in the evening went off excellently – no drag or anything of that sort, and kept the fun up the whole time and it was thoroughly appreciated. Very glad we carried it through to a successful conclusion.

Cast and crew of The Knight of the Burning Pestle

June 19th Great relief to have the play over and to know we made a good job of it – congratulated by all sorts of people whose judgement I trust. D.J. been very glum, so I suppose he doesn't approve. Bell criticised severely,

---

[218] Dr Logie was interned with his son George Kirkland Logie (1891–1944) a well-known international tennis player. According to Swale's memoirs, Dr Logie was running an Officers' crammer (language?) school in Leipzig at the outbreak of war, and taught English Literature in the Camp School.

but Blagden, Masterman, and others were warmly congratulatory. Tennis 2–4 and then walking round the field with Hatfield discussing the R.C.S. and A.S.U. row.

June 20th Still miserably cold. Botany in morning. Then started odds and ends of accounts for *The Knight*. Spent afternoon composing letter to Neumeister, and making the money affair an excuse posted it as business letter. Warkentin in to supper and laughed over the silly letters he's been having from the good people Mother has turned on to him. I find that that ass Nebel[219] is a great friend of the Blands![220]

[Insert: programme for Promenade Concert No 6, Tuesday June 20th]

June 21st Edge 8 a.m. and then Botany. Neumeister's letter returned *Als geschäftsbrief nicht zulässig* [not allowed as business letter] and secondly because I enclosed young N.'s letter.[221] Very annoying to have to spend a letter over N. Decided to do so after much lucubration. Light arrangements in Lab completed. Read D's book[222] and so to bed, mighty tired.

June 22nd Lochhead in morning 8 a.m. Then botany after dullish lecture by Woods on Germany and French Revolution. Tennis 2 p.m. and then caught by Hatfield about row, joined by Pender, Hunt and finally Croad and no end of a jaw. I cited Croad's great report on the school, and then the fat was fairly in the fire, and Croad and co. fairly stormed away. However, I didn't give in or retract, but got heartily sick of the jaw. Dodd and Mackenzie to supper between whom a great stock exchange deal was concluded. Mac. to sell Dodd Mk40,000 Kriegsanleihe [war bonds] at 76¼ to be delivered two months after signing of peace!

June 23rd Cut Lechmere in order to go through accounts of *The Knight* only to find that Redmayne[223] wasn't ready. Botany at 9, tennis 11. Everyone

---

[219] Roland Hans Nebel (1883–1958), an electrical engineer prior to his internment, he was the son of a German engineer who moved to England in the 1870s.

[220] Hubert Bland and his wife (the author E Nesbit), both founding members of the Fabian Society.

[221] Walter Neumeister, the son being held as a POW in England whom Michael corresponded with. Letters sent to the Pease family by Walter were copied by the Imperial War Museum and returned to the Neumeister family in 1978.

[222] *History of the Fabian Society*, by Michael's father (see letters in Appendix 1).

[223] Harold Redmayne (1887–1981), a chartered accountant working in Berlin at the outbreak of war.

very bucked with the group of *The Knight*. Finished D's *History of the FS*. Meeting of R.C.S. E.S. [Education Sub-] Committee to which I went somewhat against my heart. Wolff to give the first lecture and I was commissioned to find someone for 2nd: saw Smith on this and then tried Heather.[224]

June 24th Edge 8 am. Then Botany. Studying Scott's fossil types. Saw Heather who recommended me to try Venables; this I did and I think he'll do. Then tennis 3–4 and 5–6 – very hot and somewhat tired. Parcel of shoes and tennis balls arrived. Saw Bell who tells me that pending enquiries the Captains have upheld the exclusive right of the A.S.U. to Monday evenings.

June 25th Everybody stays in bed on Sunday and the camp is quite peaceful for the first hour or so. Even J is always just a bit sorry about getting up. Played about with the aquaria, washing and etc, and the R.C.S. Committee. Milner resigned. Asher[225] there and long report on A.S.U. row. Quiet afternoon but noisy night owing to a very talkative drunk being brought in. Very insistent that Davies had robbed him. What with the two drunks the night before, this is really a great nuisance!

June 26th Lecture 8–9 then botany. Didn't go to Patter's lecture – couldn't bear the thought of his making so interesting a subject dull. Then by appointment to dentist who is very gloomy about the wisdom teeth. Then wrote letter home and quiet evening. Finished *Frederick the Great*. The camp was inspected by Gerard, also by Hoffmann, Hart and the famous Mott[226] "of America". Saw Lechmere so we went arm in arm and got hold of and thanked Hoffmann for the lighting – very friendly. Then he introduced us to Mott, a big, ugly, intensely moral American. He talked like the organiser of funeral. Then Dr Logie came up and I shrunk off relieved. I gather the Ambassador got it fairly hot and lots of people rubbed it in about Master Ford. Ford had an hour with him and talked sense. Most people mainly howled about the food.

---

[224] Aubrey George Foster Heather (1879–1966), an electrical engineer who taught Spanish in the Camp School.

[225] Possibly Sol Ascher who was captain of barracks 6, 20 and 22, and also on the Camp's Health Department Committee.

[226] Dr John Raleigh Mott, leader of the Y.M.C.A. and the World Student Christian Federation.

June 27th Lechmere 8–9. Then botany – spent most of the time putting the aquarium in order. Then quiet afternoon. Ambassador here again receiving complaints. Butterscotch and co. formulating a written statement of complaints – Jones as secretary. Had my first crack with Moresby White.[227] And so to bed beginning Rose's *Napoleon.*

June 28th Botany in morning – reading Bayliss[228] in afternoon, then dentist 2.30 (job finished for time being) and then tennis 4–6. The whole camp has been placarded with ads of the great Dr Mott ~~who is to address us~~ of America – the greatest world personality and so forth. Found an invitation lying on my bed, so I went and was never more bored in my life. Apart from the hymn singing and prayers the man had nothing, or at least only platitudes, to say and said it badly. Jones has been sitting all day on a commission to enquire into the conduct of the objectionable policeman Scott – they have decided to recommend that he is an unfit person for the post.

[Insert: invitation from the Y.M.C.A. for talk by Dr John Mott of New York]

June 29th Raised cash for *Knight* expenses from Jones (performance came out Mk80 under estimate). Botany in morning. Reading in afternoon: meeting of R.C.S.E.S.C. at 4 p.m. re A.S.U. row. Bainton and Bell very much on the war path and on for writing to A.S.U. and demanding that posters of Pritchard's Mozart evening should be taken down. Ford and I taking a more conciliatory line and after 1½ hours a letter drafted – I didn't altogether approve of the tone which it adopted. Coached Moresby White and couldn't prove PV=RT!

June 30th Lechmere 8–9. Then Botany and tennis 11–12. Reading in afternoon. Walk round with Farmer and Lochhead to supper. Bar. 4 got arrest for having dust up with Becker at *Appell.* Great exchange rumour again!

---

[227] Extra tuition for John Moresby-White (1896–1979), a Rhodes scholar from South Africa (and keen rugby player).

[228] Probably W M Bayliss – *Principles of General Physiology.*

July 1st Edge 8–9. Peaceful morning preparing lecture. Tennis 4–6. Reminded Rawson of our "double or quits" bet for being here on July 1st 1916: prolonged till July 1st 1917.

July 2nd R.C.S. Committee photo today 10.30. Invigilated 12–1: picked up Lowes Dickinson's *Modern Symposium* and read it right through in course of afternoon – very stimulating of thought. Dodd and Philips to supper. Promenaded with Blagden and so to bed.

Camp School Committee (back row, 3rd and 6th from left: T H Marshall and D D Jones. Front row, 1st, 4th and 5th from left: MSP, A C Ford and E L Bainton)

July 3rd Lecture 8–9. Then Weber[229] on the opera. Lavish praise of Wagner, one of the many things that must be attended to afterwards is my knowledge of opera – would that I had been born of musical parents! Then tennis with Bell, very hot and languid. Quiet reading. Camp very excited

229 Charles Henry George Weber (1875–1954), born in London to German parents. In the summer of 1914 he was an assistant conductor in Bayreuth. Arrested as a spy in November he was eventually sent to Ruhleben (*Western Mail* 17 October 1922). Weber was a founding committee member of the Ruhleben Music Society and is often mentioned as an accompanist in concert programmes. After the war conducted the Carl Rosa Opera Company.

about the *grosse* [big] offensive.[230] Then to Mozart evening: same lecture and different program – orchestra very good. Read the Cambridge list through and relieved to find that so far only [Alfred] Marsh and [Rupert] Brooke are the only two casualties that affect me personally.

[Insert: programme and songs for A.S.U. "Second Mozart Evening" Monday July 3rd]

July 4th Today is the famous day when the so-called English ultimatum is supposed to be up – however nothing happened. Dropped my brand new watch on the floor and smashed it. Botany all morning. Tennis 3–4, Dante 5–6 and Moresby White 8 p.m. and so to bed.

July 5th Lechmere still fairly ill; anyhow in bed looking rather a wreck and says it's only nerves. Talking of nerves, Milner says that Bradney[231] has gone mad – poor fellow. I wonder what about Taunton. Edge 8–9 – demonstrated slides for him. Then Botany all morning. Very wet and cold. This old lecture on the F.S. [Fabian Society] for Friday is a beastly nuisance.

July 6th Botany in the morning, working at lectures in afternoon. Dodd to supper. *Sonst nichts neues* [otherwise nothing new].

July 7th Lechmere still ill, so no lecture. Botany and then prepared notes for the F.S. lecture. The P. Ger. [pro-German] Hughes who is always so friendly to me, came and as we walked away explained to me the reason for his P.G. ism – which I daren't commit to writing! Had the man Ball[232] to supper and then gave the lecture. Went fairly well but not much discussion. A young fellow whom I know by sight however spoke with some understanding. Mobilised Morrison to put up shelves in the green house.

July 8th Jones has a great rumour, and rather serious too. Gerard having asked for a written memorial on the camp and having given an undertaking not to pass it through the military – apparently has done so – anyhow Powell made a speech about it at the captains' meeting – poor old Graf dreadfully worried. Perhaps it means Stadtvogtei. Paragraph in *B.J.*

---

[230] Start of the Battle of the Somme.

[231] C.E Bradney – he appears to be well in later diary entries. A French teacher in the Camp School.

[232] There are three men named Ball in *Ruhleben Story* and one, L. J. Ball, is mentioned as being in favour of Trade Unions.

[*Berlin Journal*] about possibilities of exchange: everyone rather excited about it. Tennis 11–12. Dante 5–6 and Ponsonby and Nash in to supper. For tea this afternoon I got down a tin of what I took to be shortbread, but on opening turned out to be a stink bomb of eggs – been reposing there since Xmas.

July 9th R.C.S. Committee 10.15 – long but peaceful. Finance[?] rather suffering from hot weather. Put flowers in new greenhouse. Tennis 4–6. Dodd to supper. Exchange rumours galore.

July 10th Lecture 8–9. Then practical and cut Andrews'[233] history lecture – far too prosy. Tennis 2–0: quiet reading. Doddering. Lecture by Higgins on Tech. Research. Hear that Moresby-White, Urry and Eden going home by special exchange. Saw White and said goodbye – saves me the trouble of coaching! Exchange reports very high!

July 11th White and Co went off this morning 6.45 am. Urry got considerably booed on account of the Relief business.[234]

July 12th Edge 8–9, then Botany. Reading in afternoon Webb's *Towards Social Democracy.* Some Italian verse. Dodd to supper. Rumours still very rife!

July 13th Lochhead 8–9. Tennis 11–12, Moderately interrupted afternoon. Dodd in to supper and talked fruit prospects in Canada. Distressed to find that my bank balance is less by about 100 marks than I thought it was: good resolution to keep accounts strictly in future!

July 14th Lechmere 8–9. Then tennis 10–11. Quiet afternoon – theatre in evening. Play had lots of good acting and some very indifferent. Milner was

---

[233] Henry Maxwell Andrews (1894–1968). A banker who was in Hamburg when war was declared. His letters home to his mother were published in a book *In Ruhleben* under the pseudonym Richard Roe. In Ruhleben he lectured in English literature and history, and taught French and Latin. In 1930 he married the author Dame Rebecca West.

[234] Sidney Hamilton Urry (1880–1950). A banker working in Hamburg at the beginning of the war. According to *Ruhleben Story*, Urry was a member of the camp's Finance Department, whose remit was to control camp funds and distribute monetary relief. The *Western Mail*, 21 June 1916, has a photo of the Ruhleben Canteen Committee which includes Urry, Beaumont, Platford, Jones and Powell.

good, but the best acting was Perrot.[235] Very hot and stuffy. Great speech by Pritchard and much worked up feeling and enthusiasm. Special end up with *Marseillaise*.

[Insert: The 14 July National French Festival leaflet for a promenade concert, songs, speeches and the play *Mlle Josette ma femme,* presented by Mr. Peebles-Conn]

July 15th Edge, then botany. Tennis 3–5 – Bell very grumpy and weather v. disagreeable. Dante 5–6 then writing letter home. *B.Z.* [*Berliner Zeitung am Mittag*] says exchange is off. I'm afraid some fellows will go clean off their heads.

July 16th Spent most of the day preparing lecture on ferns, and drawing out scheme of classification. Invigilated 12–1, read *Nan*. Beastly cold and bleak. Orless[236] into supper – he's a very quiet unenthusiastic youth, but nice.

July 17th Lecture 8–9 – then hung about for tennis at 10 but was none till 11. Dresel[237] of American Embassy here to interview the camp committees and we were summoned at noon. Got there and hung about: A.S.U. Committee also assembled. Ultimately we returned at 2 pm for interview. All went in and Ford made a speech and then each one of us was examined by Dresel. Powell – damn his impertinence – was there. Lasted about an hour. Then moderately interrupted afternoon. To A.S.U. concert 7 p.m. – the Mozart and Schumann good, one advantage of our move has certainly been to galvanise the A.S.U. into a perfervid state of activity! In bed Jones gave a great tale of the iniquities of Gerard. He was here today and summoned to see him, Ford and Logie and several others about their memorandum. In the presence of the military and the captains he threatened them that if complaints were made they would be sent to military camp.[238] However they all spoke up well and showed no funk – told

---

[235] Maurice Perrot, a student born in France. He acted and produced French plays, and also taught French in the camp school.

[236] J. Orless was the Ruhleben Camp School treasurer in 1916.

[237] Mr Ellis Loring Dresel, an American lawyer attached to the U.S. Embassy in Berlin.

[238] Conditions in the military POW camps were far worse than in Ruhleben, and so one punishment was to suffer a spell either in German prison or the POW camps.

him that it was he himself who had asked for a written statement of complaints. Logie in particular got up and made a great speech. What a contemptible lot they are – the captains, the military and the Embassy!

[Insert: programme for piano-duo evening, Monday 17th July, by Mr. Leland A. Cossart and Mr. Gordon Short]

July 18th Lechmere 8–9: then botany. Moderately quiet afternoon. Tennis 5–6. Awful night with a drunk. I had just turned in after reading *Napoleon*, and was then woken up by shouting and singing: this started about 11.30 and continued till 3 a.m. when they took the man back to his barrack. I walked round the compound in despair from 1–2 – till I was cold and tired. Going round the last time noticed there were voices coming from the German room in the Y.M.C.A. I didn't feel strong enough to deal with the situation myself so reported the matter to the police and turned into bed. Singing and shouting still going on, but went to sleep in spite of it.

July 19th Edge 8–9. Then set the Botany going and returned to Box to wait for Bernstein. I picked some sweet peas for him. He turned up punctually at 10 and we had a pleasant chat. We were not severely *kontrolliert* [controlled], so he talked German and I English. I told him freely about the conditions in camp and we discussed on the situation outside. He held out very little hopes of peace. People had committed themselves to too much. Rather sleepy all day – not strong enough for work so read and finished Rose's *Napoleon.* Took it back to Ponsonby whom I found was in the *Schonungsbaracke* with a bad leg; poor fellow. Went out to the pond and found any amount of the Azolla growing there, but no Salvinia. Jones tells me that the people in the Y.M.C.A. rooms last night included the famous policeman Scott all drunk. So he's resigned. Makes the captains look silly! He's the man that they declined to sack because he's so valuable a member of the force!

July 20th Cut Lochhead lecture – I'm afraid he's not got the necessary enthusiasm and charm for lecturing! Then to Silberman's[239] lecture on romanticism in German art in 19th century. Good. Then Botany. Quiet afternoon reading Bayliss – rather a rambling book, but very sound –

---

[239] Two Silberman brothers (Ernest & F) are listed in Swale's memoirs as 'prosperous city merchants'.

chapter on nutrition seemed to touch on everything under the sun including Mendelism, and an outburst on the stupidity of the conspiracy of secrecy with regard to sex. Tennis 5–6 and quiet evening.

July 21st Lechmere 8–9. Then Botany. Took out some Salvinia and planted it in the pond in a cigar box anchored to the side. Otherwise quiet day, reading Bayliss.

July 22nd Edge 8–9. Tennis 11–12. Caught after lunch by a gloomy policeman Fitzpatrick, who was one of the alleged drunks in the Y.M.C.A. Says it is a base accusation; did I start it, what did I see on that night and so forth. I explained my part. It seems that the alleged drunks having resigned now have been induced to rejoin and an effort is being made to whitewash the affair. Anyhow he kept on saying they were very sensitive, to which I replied that Scott didn't on a previous occasion act as a sensitive man and that by resigning they had practically admitted their guilt! However, he didn't seem to want to pursue the matter.

July 23rd S. wanted a group photograph [see facing], at which I was rather grumpy but went through with it looking rather more of a fearsome creature than ever! Then School Committee – everyone very sleepy and without settled convictions except when it got to nearly 12 o'clock when there was a general move for lunch. Adjourned till Tuesday and important matter of finance left till then. The Embassy has placed Mks20,000 at disposal of R.C.S. and A.S.U. and the main thing is to prevent a squabble. However, there will be some talk before the matter is settled. Invigilated 12–1, read Shelley's *Prometheus Unbound* on advice of Isabella Ford[240] from whom I had a kind letter. Tennis 5–6.

July 24th Lecture 8–9. Then Dale on Brahms and Schumann – very good lecture, illustrated by Lindsay, Keel and Ludlow[241] – the latter very much off form. Then botany. Very wet afternoon. Walked round field in pouring rain. Bell in to supper. Promenaded with Blagden and discussed the school finance question and agreed to lead a revolt. Then joined by Masterman and Jones and discussed A.S.U.

---

240 Isabella Ormston Ford (fn 37; see her letter on page 306).

241 Godfrey Randolph Ludlow (1893–1956), an Australian concert violinist who had been working in Dresden.

Michael and friends: Back row: Michael Pease, St George Haigh Phillips, Douglas Jones. Front row: Arthur Dodd, Felix Schlesinger.

July 25th Lechmere 8–9. Last lecture on worms. Then peaceful morning. Spent afternoon mobilising people for R.C.S. Committee to vote against paid teachers. By bad luck Blagden, our strongest gun, was playing in the proms concert and could only be there at beginning. However, he set the thing going. I proposed that the departments which simply paid teachers should pay for them separately. Violently opposed by Wolff, Bell and Patters. W. very noisy and P. letting off big shots about Nietzsche's atomic doctrine of society. Ultimately no decision arrived at, and adjourned till next day – four proposals being made, typed and circulated. Long jaw with

Ford after *Appell,* and pointed out that solutions must be found as compromise.

[Insert: report of Finance Committee and various finance proposals to be considered on Wednesday July 26th, including one proposal that R.C.S. should not accept any money from American Embassy].

July 26th Discussed compromise of R.C.S. business with Blagden, Bainton, and Ford, and decided to go back on the recommendation of the Finance Committee. Patters is very grumpy over last night's affair and won't come again to meeting to argue with school boys! That of course simplified things enormously and in fact the meeting went very simply – there was no argumentation and no quoting Nietzsche and so forth and we transacted a considerable amount of stuff. After *Appell* a great announcement: to wit arising out of the alleged stonethrowing affair,[242] the matter has been reported to Berlin and it has been ordered that all games and amusements are to be stopped for 8 days. The amusing thing is that the Graf believing us to be innocent of the "crime" as much as says so in the order, and as compensation we are to be let off early morning *Appells*! He also hoped that we would take the punishment in the quiet and dignified way we have done our other (undeserved) punishments! Irritating not to be able to get out on the field away from the worst of the stench but I suppose we'll survive. Notice that Devereux[243] has been killed, poor chap.

July 27th No *Appell* so wonderfully quiet in morning. Lochhead 8–9. Then Botany. Very hot, so remained in cubby hole practically all day.

July 28th Started taking a serious early morning run up and down the promenade before breakfast instead of my usual trot. Very hot, but nice and cool in cubby hole. Dresel came today with other two youths and looked round the lab. It was hot enough to melt.

July 29th Wrote letter home in morning. Dante 5–6. Lecture by Butterscotch to Historical Circle on local government – a poor paper – no thesis – but an interesting study in Butterscotchism. The one good thing

---

[242] Someone had thrown a stone at a sentry according to Wyndham Richard's diaries.

[243] Possibly Lieutenant Humphrey William Devereux, a Cambridge man killed June 1916.

was that he told Duncan Jones he'd never trust a committee of parsons. Order from Leitz arrived. I hear that the Mk20,000 from the Embassy is *rein aus der Luft gegriffen!* [simply plucked out of thin air.]

July 30th Moderately quiet morning putting lecture notes together. Invigilated 12–1. Read Shelley's *Queen Mab*. Rest of day reading.

July 31st Lecture 8–9. Then Botany. Quiet day. Great leader in the *Vorsische*[244] on *die Engländer* in Ruhleben. In *D.T.* Gerard's letter to Grey: contains many good points and a fierce tone.

Aug. 1nd Botany class. Hauled up before RCS Finance Committee to explain the finances of the Bio. Dept. Wolff, after very much noise and shouting, discovered that I had been pursuing the method which he advocated. Sent off the two photos home and discovered that Bernstein's book must be sent through censor. Otherwise quietish day. Dante 5–6. Wrote to Seward to ask for specimens for next term and by a strange coincidence received a letter from him by today's post. Heard two good stories about the Baron today: 1. From Higgins. A man asks for leave to go out to see dying wife – refused by Rüdiger. Applies to Baron. "Very sorry, can't do anything, these war times are very trying – my wife can't get any manure for her garden!" and 2. From Bell. Baron conducting visitors round camp takes them to Bar. 15 where Tilly[245] and Warkentin and Co. having tea outside. B pointing to the food – "*Schönes abendessen*!" [nice dinner] Tilly replies "*Ja, alles aus England*" [Yes, everything from England]. B restrains himself in presence of visitors but afterwards came back and gave Tilly a furious dressing down!

Aug. 2nd Took Botany class in morning: sent off letter to Seward. New English censor seems very nice. Talked perfect English and seemed interested in the school. Quiet afternoon. Rawson in to supper and discussed S.P. Circle. Ford came in to the box after bedtime and we stayed and discussed the R.C.S. and subsequently the war. Letter from Helen Wedgwood today [Y tails off to bottom of the page].

---

[244] A Berlin newspaper.

[245] Possibly William H. E. Tilly. An Australian who went to Germany in 1892 and ran a cramming German Language Institute in Berlin. He, his son and his British pupils (including Ford, Roupell and others) were all interned in Ruhleben on 6th Nov 1914, where according to Wyndham Richard's diaries, they were known as 'Tilly's Boys'.

....

HBW to MSP (received Aug. 2nd):

Old Jordan's Hostel, Beaconsfield, Bucks.

11th Jul. 1916

Dear Mr. Pease,

Many thanks for your postcard. You are only allowed to send a limited number aren't you? So please don't trouble to send one each time. Perhaps I could share with one of your other friends? Cambridge, alas, is now over for me. The three years do go dreadfully quickly and these last terms have been too exciting for good work or for making the most of the place.

Thank you for sending "them" your sympathy. They have been perfectly splendid. Their possible fate, has, as you may imagine, hung over us for some time, but you must not think we go about with long faces. It has drawn us all so closely together. I think most of us never realised what friendship could be. When there may be so little time too, one does not waste conversations but seem to make friends at once. I am glad we kept on C.U.F.S. now, if only as a nucleus for this. Will you sing the last verse of the Flag with us in spirit. We always used to laugh to hear English people sing that, it was so much too melodramatic! Now it is a bit too real. You can imagine that we, who cannot go through the worst, are anxious to start work. We are not going to 'lie low'. Half Newnham is now on the land, and I intended to do that too. But I am now torn between my long cherished dream of a market garden (combined with tub thumping on the village green) and a new born "call" to help in organising women into Trade Unions. They do seem to want workers badly, and they can't pay them much, and I have enough to live on and could do it, I think. So I'm afraid it will have to be that. All my socialist friends (not being agriculturalists) advise it, at any rate until women are better organised than at present. You would get a great surprise to see what a number of things women are doing; and there is certain to be a great upset, not to say row, after the war; so one feels one must do what one can. The market garden will have to be reserved for me in the "perfect state".

I do hope it is not all true about the state of affairs in Ruhleben. It must be dreadful if it is as the papers say. People swear a lot at the Germans, but if it comes to that, I suppose we are doing our best to starve them. Oh damn. Isn't it all <u>stupid</u> and cruel and unnecessary.

I have been here for a few days at a gathering of about 30 people to talk things over. I wonder if you know the place; it is a sort of Quakers' Mecca, besides a place for gatherings. The house was William Penn's; and the country round is glorious. The party dispersed all too soon, but we did get some good discussion and got to conclusions. Don't think because you hear nothing that reasonable people are being idle. It is true though, unfortunately, that many are only just waking up.

All sorts of interesting people were there, besides some University men, whom I expect you know. Mr. Henderson[246] *was one of them; also G.D.H. Cole and his satellites from Oxford. He is an autocrat, and also 'unsound' on the woman's question, which I think shows something radically wrong. All the same there is something rather attractive about him. Perhaps he will grow out of his academic Oxford manner!*

Mrs. Russell[247] *showed us some of your Ruhleben magazines which were interesting and amusing to look at. Only how dull it must be to be always having to play at things. Margaret Russell was there also. She is lovely. I have been wanting to meet her for ever so long. There were a good number of socialists. It is very funny to see how the Quakers are being forced to come to our point of view, and how apologetic they are for never having done anything before the war!*

I am sitting writing this in the old Quaker cemetery, opposite the grave of William Penn, having just finished a hot discussion with a Manchester socialist on the Land Question. He is not so unsound as most! (It is no good you trying to confute me as a Single Taxer on a postcard!)

I cannot tell you any of the really interesting things; but I daresay the German newspapers have more than I could tell!

Best wishes,

Yours sincerely

Helen Bowen Wedgwood

P.S. It is so annoying being told one has seen someone when one has no recollection of the fact, so perhaps I had better mention that I was at the last fancy dress dance at the Malting House in a sort of orange Indian dress, and in mauve at the gala, – and that my dancing was very bad. I believe I asked you if you could come to a Fabian tea at Newnham. (We have had some very successful ones by the way). If you have ever seen my Father, [Josiah Wedgwood M.P.] *I am very like him, with black hair. So if you can, pick me out of fifty similar descriptions.*

……………………

---

[246] Fred Henderson, author of *The Case for Socialism* (1911).

[247] Mother of Bedalians John and Margaret, and wife of Rollo Russell (fn 326).

August 3rd Ruhleben at its worst – fiendish wind and dust all day. Took *History of Fabian Society* to Forester who said it was too dangerous to send out but he'd try to get the censor to pass it next week. R.C.S Committee at 10.15 – lot of detailed and drudgery work. Adjourned at noon and resumed at 7: discussion on draft reports.

August 4th Wind and dust still rampant. Botany at 9. Borrowed and read Wells' *Bealby* – poor, very. Ford to tea. Jones wants to resign committee. Field open again.

August 5th Hear there's likely to be a row at the school meeting, organised by A.S.U. Long talk with Higgins over things in general – can't make him out: he's got his knife into Ford, thinks he's dishonest. Meeting came off at two. Very boring and stupid. Bröse led the attack with a veiled attack on Ford about his meeting Dresel with Logie and Butterscotch. Very prolonged and persistent and turned the whole meeting against himself. Ultimately agreed after very much talk to appoint a committee of 3 to treat with the A.S.U. Never, never have I sat through 3½ hours such drivelling talk, by Gourvitch,[248] Wechsler,[249] Ll. Roberts[250] aided and abetted by Higgins, Bröse and Hunt. Ultimately we adjourned, and worse luck too!

August 6th R.C.S. Committee 10.15. Discussed proposed new reading room building on 3rd grandstand, and adjourned meeting of teachers. Personally I don't know how to treat Bröse's move to put himself on the committee and squash out me: the thing is so very plausible – Biology is so small a department. Ford came in after supper and we discussed the whole thing. Harris seems to be acting as a mediator. It's damned regrettable to say the least of it. I must say if we had only realised what a hullabaloo they would make of it, we certainly should not have wasted our time on the venture.

---

[248] Isaac Gourvitch (1889–1963), a school teacher from London. Son of a naturalised Russian, he changed his name to 'Goodridge' in the 1920s.

[249] Abraham Wechsler (1888–1973), A graduate of London University, teaching in London in the 1911 census. In Ruhleben he lectured on physical and inorganic chemistry, and after the war he published a paper on the teaching of micro-chemical methods with Blagden. Changed his name to Wexler after the war.

[250] Cuthbert Lockyer Roberts? (fn 71).

August 7th Set to work cleaning up the lab. Tennis 2–4. Jones been at conference with A.S.U. and seems like coming to some agreement. Ford came in about 7 and discussed it further in box and then resumed conference at 8.30. J. and I drafted proposed constitution for new body.

August 8th Continued lab cleaning. Jones sitting on reconciliation committee all morning – they won't agree to being rushed into a settlement but agree to an ultimate amalgamation. In the meantime we agree to assign to them our Monday evenings in return for 80 Mks a month. Higgins came in to tea and was very friendly. Saw Blagden about the Bröse business – whether Bröse means to press his motion for squashing the bio dept on the committee and assures me this is all right – so my personal little bit in this lamentable business seems free from attack so far.

[Insert: postcard invitation from the Historical Circle, dated 8th August, to an exhibition of Mr. Winzer's drawings]

August 9th Went round to RCS Committee 9.30 and found the photographer in possession to photograph the lab.[251] So with great pulling down of screens and arranging of things we got the place shipshape. That over, returned to committee meeting where draft agreement was agreed to. Patters alone against. At 2.15 resumed teachers meeting. Altogether new tone. Jones made a statement about agreement and at once put meeting in a good *stimmung* [mood]. I had to explain the constitution committee. Pritchard and Ford had a big set to over a very trifling matter of drafting a resolution in which P. scored debating points but lost I think in everyone's estimation. Came away and talked with Andrews and then with Pritchard, who now seems very anti A.S.U. Great scare today. Two chaps tried to escape and were caught and announced that in future 4 *Appells* a day – mercifully this was cancelled: the persons in question alleged that they did not intend to escape, but only had an appointment with some whores on the other side of the netting!

August 10th Moderately quiet day. Scrubbed down the lab. benches and made out Leitz order and spent afternoon in cubby hole reading Bielschowsky's *Life of Goethe*.

---

[251] A photo of the biology laboratory was printed in the school's autumn 1916 prospectus, which is referred to here. Other photos (e.g. pages 222, 275 and 276) may also have been taken at this time.

August 11th Great inspection this morning by war office – a great bunch of pink striped officers were conducted round by The Graf & Co. Came round the lab, but didn't make any very intelligent observations. Great Switzerland rumours on foot this evening.

....

MSP to HBW:

Ruhleben, August 11th 1916.

Very many thanks for yours – most welcome and very cheering. So many benevolent people bore me with their kind but colourless letters: but I only hear from very few kindred spirits who share my views in this dismal and stupid business; I am always anxious to hear how it goes with you all. Interested to hear of your T.U. work – are you being taken in hand by Susan Lawrence?[252] *Don't lose sight of your market garden though! No, the senses are jarred by ever present ugliness, and then, we have to play at life instead of living – the lot of all prisoners. My best wishes to 'them'. Good luck*

MS Pease

....

August 12th Quiet morning writing home – then A.S.U. meeting at 2. Went off very quietly. Patchett was not there, and the only tiresome people were the invariable Ll. Roberts, and Wechsler. A good report – quite sure it wasn't drawn up by Hatfield. Agreement accepted without discussion, though I've a strong feeling that that committee doesn't intend to amalgamate. Andrews moved for a re-election of committee, but was countered by a vote of confidence – always a mean low down trick, though I hardly think it was intentional this time as it came from old Kremnitz. I didn't sit it all out. Mr. Dodd was next to me, very worried because he couldn't follow all that was going on and very irate against the school. Exchange rumours very rife again tonight, though seems to concern only the 45-ers[253] now. Ford came into the box and yarned away very late.

---

[252] Newnham College alumna, a member of Fabian Society and activist for Women's Trade Union League. She became a Labour Party councillor and eventually an MP.

[253] People over the age of 45, and therefore not considered likely to serve as soldiers.

[Insert: hand-written letter from A. Richardson,[254] of the R.C.S. Office requesting a list of department equipment]

August 13th Very quiet day – no R.C.S meeting. Tennis 11–12, invigilated 12.30–1.30 (I always try conscientiously to put in my hour, even if I start late!!) Dante 7 p.m.

August 14th Quiet morning reading *Goethe*. Tennis 3–4. Went to Winzer's picture show. Some priceless caricatures, e.g. King and Maloney, and a cruel one of Duncan Jones and Hughesdon. Dodd in to supper and walked up and down with Bainton. And so to bed, where I found Blagden and Ford in box discussing the prospect of another row with Patters. An offensive expression in the proposed prospectus about P.Gers. Read Merejkowsky's *The Forerunner* in bed. The last "drunk" we had is back in the cells again, brought in about 7 p.m. Only got out of bird cage this afternoon. Sold the 8 parcels that had arrived for him and goes on the burst[?] and brought in expostulating vehemently that he is a **** Englishman!

August 15th Quiet morning at nothing in particular, mostly reading *Goethe*. 50Mks today from Mrs. Mumby. Afternoon reading – in fact didn't do much else all day. Ford in again to discuss R.C.S. matters. Pritchard wishes now to reconstruct an Education Committee under his presidency and so discussed schemes for circumventing it.

August 16th Tennis 9–10. School office about next term's prospectus. R.C.S. Committee at 2. Approved of joint committee proposal as a counter to Pritchard's scheme. Marshall in to tea and Ford to supper. Exchange rumour very hot indeed tonight.

August 17th Morning considerably broken up by R.C.S. work in office. Afternoon quiet. Tennis 5–6 and Bell into supper. Exchange rumours still very rife. Also great rumour about ultimatum to Roumania [*sic*].

August 18th Wrote letters to Biffen and D. about money and took them off to censor. Quiet afternoon – went with Lechmere to see Squire about the electrical heater for the embedding bath. Apparently old Seal Tusks[255] has

---

[254] Alexander Richardson (1888–?), the camp school requisitions manager. He also taught German in the school and was a regular actor in the German Dramatic Society's productions.

[255] Probably Count von Schwerin, the Camp Commandant, who sported a fine moustache.

got into a funk about the *D.T.* [*Daily Telegraph*] – anyhow it doesn't turn up now. Went to meeting of S.P. Circle to discuss plan of action for winter. After some discussion agreed on a series on education.

August 19th Quiet morning. Saw Croad – friendly, offered to try to get Turnbull to get the hot plate for me. Tennis 2–4. Wrote p.c. Dodd to supper and then quiet evening reading. Got a great greeting from O.B.[256] gathering today.

....

Isabella O Ford to MSP:

30th July 1916 (date of receipt unknown)

Adel, Yorks

My dear Michael,

I have been at Cote Bank for a night and I read everything I could about you – your letters and so on. How I wish you were here with us. It is a very difficult world – Aunt Pease was well for now and cheerful and so delightful to talk about all we are working at as was May [Marian Fry Pease]. *We had such an interesting meeting on the Downs at which May was present. I, and another woman, were the speakers. Very interesting meetings are being held and deep interest grows.*

You remember the stories about the last day of the sheep and the goats – well the sifting out of goats is extraordinary now. You find the whole flocks are mixed up as one never before realised – oh how asleep we have all been. How selfishly idle – I suppose now till death there is continual educational work before one – I only wish I were your age – somehow, nothing else matters now but all this. But there are hopeful things on too.

Everyone is quite well. Heaps of people are growing rich – not us of course – we are becoming poor. But England is extremely prosperous.

It is lovely weather. Bessie and I are sitting on our verandah writing. Emily [another sister] *and all the orthodox are at church – what a useful place church is. It makes Sunday morning so peaceful and quiet for us sinners!*

We think of you very much indeed, but of course letters are not very "conducive" just now I fear. So all very dull reading for you. I get your messages from your mother. I haven't the courage to see her.

---

256 Old Bedalians – alumni of Bedales school.

Nicolas is well I hear, and Tom[257]

Best wishes and my love,

Your affectionate cousin,

I.O. Ford

Bessie sends her love

....

FOURTH DIARY

[Insert: plan of Barracks 6 and 7. Handwritten note on rear: *I shall not be in to tea D.D.J.*]

August 20th Very quiet Sabbath reading away at *Goethe*. Invigilated 12–1, read the Home University Library series on The American Civil War – good. Tennis 5–6. Then reading again and talk with Wechsler.

Aug. 21st Again very peaceful day. Played tennis with Wigg[258] 11–12 – otherwise reading *Goethe*.

Aug. 22nd Thoroughly enjoying quiet peaceful holidays. Reading all morning. Croad has not managed to negotiate the heater, but will try again. Roberts wants me to speak for the Debating Society on the Marriage question. Rawson to oppose. Thought it over and refused – not worth wasting my time with an ass like Rawson.

Aug. 23rd Played tennis at 10 but gave my back a nasty twist, which annoyed me all day. Explained my position re debate to Roberts, who seemed quite contrite about it. Dodd into supper.

[Insert: letter from Hon Sec of the A.S.U.: Your letter re the cubby holes will receive our best attention. A lock has been ordered for some time. The suggestions for the winter will be carried out, excepting as regards the heating, for

---

[257] Michael's cousin Thomas Ormston Cave Pease who was serving in the Middlesex Regiment.

[258] Possibly John Wiggin (1865–1941) an English artist who made many sketches of camp life. According to *The Sporting Times* 29 July 1916 he was living with his wife and daughter in Uccle, near Brussels in 1914, and was the starter at the Brussels race track.

which we will do our best, and a letter of permission reading: *Erlaubnisschein: Den herren Dr Lechmere und Pease ist das betreten des geländes um den teich zwecks entnahme von biologischen untersuchungsobjekten aus dem letzteren bis auf weiteres gestattet.* [The gentlemen Dr Lechmere and Pease are allowed to enter the land around the pond for the purpose of taking biological objects of investigation from the latter until further notice]]

Aug. 24th Back not all it might be, so not playing tennis today. Got R.C.[259] Report, Shaw's book etc. today. Spent day reading his preface on Christianity.

Aug. 25th Spent most of the day reading Shaw's book. Somehow not Shaw at his best. His great preface is too long and discursive, and *Pygmalion* is certainly poor as a play. Saw *The Daily News* today at Dodd's for a change – awful rag. Bell in to supper. Solemnly announced by Thorpe in the Barrack that negotiations re exchange were in progress!

Aug. 26th Another quiet day. Wrote letter home. Terrific thunderstorm this afternoon, office boy struck and considerably damaged. Rumour has it now that only the 45-ers to be exchanged.

Aug. 27th Peaceful Sabbath. Read Pope's *Essay on Man* in Library. Farmer and Hodgkinson into supper and long yarn. Ford came in after bedtime and had a huge yarn; didn't leave till nearly midnight. He appears to have been in Cambridge for the summer vac. geography course.

Aug. 28th Awful day of thunder. Otherwise nothing of importance.

Aug. 29th They gave a man 3 days in the cells and 30 in the Cage for giving some biscuits to the children down at the baths today. Hear that all leave to Berlin has been cancelled.

Aug. 30th Very tired this morning as J. would say. Interrupted morning. Tennis 2–4 – played abominably. Doddering. Finished Bielschowsky's *Goethe* this evening.

---

[259] E. R. Pease writes on 19th July that he is sending Shaw's new book, so the R.C. report could be something from home (possibly the Rural Conference Report, which Marjory was involved with).

Aug. 31st Spend most of morning manufacturing a tea-cosy out of Elsie Rose's fish basket: it turned out a wonderful affair and will be a very effective thing, I think. R.C.S. Committee 2.30–5. I got very much on the war path about finance – payments being made by the camp cashiers without the necessary signatures. Bell very much on the high and mighty about his French examination system. Put on a subcommittee to arrange a R.C.S. conversazione.

Sept. 1st Can't think that anything much happened today. Letter from Helen Wedgwood – rather alarmed at my being an "out and outer". Ford came in a talked and smoked my cigarettes for a considerable but not appalling time: thank goodness they've forgotten to send us to bed at 9 on Sept. 1st as they did last year!

....

HBW to MSP: (received Sept. 1st)

Moddershall Oaks, Stone, Staffs.

August 17th 1916

Dear Mr. Pease,

How you Ruhleben people must be praying that this exchange takes place. The prospect of perhaps another year or more would have been to awful to contemplate.

Father tells me that Mrs. Pease, among others, wrote to him asking him to press the House for an exchange of prisoners, and altogether it looks as if something will be done at last.

Are your views really as extreme as some of our friends? Because if so, won't your position when you are exchanged be rather difficult? I hope you won't think me impertinent to mention it, but one can't help speculating about the attitude of people with unusual views, and I was not sure from your postcards whether you are an 'out and outer'. Lots of people are sympathetic, but comparatively few feel that they ought to refuse to fight, and if you <u>*are*</u> *one of these, things will be hard, I am afraid. Also we have been wondering what will happen to Bekassy when he goes back to Hungary at the end of the war, as he too has become an extremist, and he has not served his years in the army yet. It looks pretty awful for him. But things may be very different by that time and probably he can make some arrangement. You see, when times are as difficult as now and people take up all sorts of unexpected points of view, one falls into a habit, which some might resent, of thinking and talking about other people's private affairs. The trouble is, being practically a Quaker myself, one doesn't quite know what to wish for other people. I do hope things will turn out all right for you. You have had about your share of ill luck I should think! I am afraid there is very little to tell you in this letter, as we have been in the depths of these Staffordshire woods, with only one or two short visits to London. The very belated daily paper alone unites us to 'civilisation', and the most exciting event to us at present is the capture of a huge water beetle for our aquarium, and the mysterious death of all the sticklebacks, – sunstroke we think (the beetle was in another jar, so he is innocent.)*

Father is home after 6 months absence in East Africa, chiefly employed, we gather, in disconcerting encounters with lions and other beasts. He is very keen on the place and is trying to get the Colonial Office to adopt a reasonable scheme of Land Settlement. Now he is making himself a nuisance in the House in quite his old style. He is, alas, more militarist than ever, but he has not, like many people, lost all notions of justice in his desire to crrrrush [sic] *the Germans. Also he is extremely nice about the way my sister and I look at things which is a great relief. You have no idea how terribly bitter differences of opinion make many people now. Of course it is natural because the war touches everyone so nearly, and it is often difficult not to be bitter with one's opponents, when one cares very much; so really one should be surprised people are not worse. But we are glad Father is all right. The trouble is that the people one really admire are divided, (most of them are on the other side) so that one often feels one must be mad to differ from so overwhelming a majority.*

I start working at the Women's Trade Union under Miss Bondfield[260] *in September. At present it does not seem an attractive prospect, – dingy streets and factories seem so horrible, especially when one is in the country, but they say it is very interesting and extremely jolly getting to know people; and it does want doing. The amusing thing is that it is now quite respectable and patriotic to be an 'agitator' for women's unions. They really ought to train one from infancy to the habit of spouting from a butter tub; I am sure it is a most important branch of knowledge. They should train for it in C.U.F.S – take it in turns to address imaginary street corner crowds and learn how to answer the heckler, and then start in real life. It is the only way to be much use as a socialist. Only a few very active members learn it now. People say one ought to take economics for work like mine; but I wish everyone were brought up on natural sciences, the scientists seem to be almost the only people who can think things out impersonally, and one*

[260] Margaret Bondfield, a British Labour politician, trades unionist and women's rights activist.

learns not to twist one's evidence and to hate bad arguments and to inquire into reasons. It is a pity though that most scientists cannot be scientific outside their own subject!

With best wishes for a speedy release from Ruhleben,

Yours sincerely

Helen Bowen Wedgwood

....

Sept. 2nd Moderately interrupted morning. Tennis 11. Caught by Eglington who wants literature for marriage debate – so I gave him the two R.C. [Rural Conference] reports and sundry Eugenics stuff. R.C.S. com. on "conversazione" 1.30. Dale and Evans to supper 7 p.m. After languishing considerably during the last few days the exchange rumour had a great boom last night, but people are still awaiting the announcement! Lechmere got hold of a pregnant rat this evening and dissected out 10 fairly advanced embryos. R.C.S. programmes actually turned up in time.

Sept. 3rd R.C.S. Committee 10.15. Pennington in one of his worst and cantankerous moods and what annoyed us particularly was that by supporting me in my scheme for getting Bröse on the committee the thing was lost. Invigilated from 1–2 and finished *Essay on Man*. Dodd in to supper and he brought an immense pie with him! Exchange rumour as regards the 45-ers again very strong, but there is also a growing "all off" rumour. Ford came in again and stayed some time and smoked my cigarettes.

[Insert: programme for Special Orchestral Concert, conducted by Mr. W Pauer on Sept. 3rd]

Sept. 4th Spent most of the day enrolling for the R.C.S. Old gang very slack at turning up and only several new people. To A.S.U. concert and then a very prolonged *Appell* combined with blanket check. Exchange rumour rather waning again. Got German books today – much taken with Eichendorf.

[Insert: programme for A.S.U. First Chamber Music Evening, Monday 4th Sep, with introductory lecture by Mr. Gordon Short]

Sept. 5th All day enrolling in the lab, very quiet most of the time. Tennis 5–6 and then quiet evening. Confess I can't make much of *Faust part II.*

Shelley which I'm now reading in bed much more entertaining. Photo of Mary today but as she sends one of herself and a school friend together I don't know which is which!

[Insert: photo of two young women]

Sept. 6th Main excitement today is that at 3 this afternoon notice given out that in future not more than 4 in a box to be allowed and that by 4 p.m. the names to be handed in of those to leave, and failing agreement, the person last to arrive has to leave. Very rotten for Milner, when so obvious that Bickerstaffe should leave. But B declined point blank, so I suppose there is nothing to be done. They are prize fools; after two years they proceed to do this at one hour's notice and the turned out are to go to Bar. 14 which is to be emptied into the T.H. [Tea House]. The Official notice is headed "*Auf verlangen der Amerikanischen Botschaft*" [At the request of the American Embassy]. Went to first meeting of Science Circle at 6.30 – paper by Lechmere. Come across an extraordinary apt quotation in Faust this evening "*Da geht es den dem fünften schlecht*" [The fifth then doesn't stand a chance].

Sept. 7th Milner in a great state of nerves about moving and after much parlaying and uncertainty nothing is ultimately done and we remain as before, plus a very considerable estrangement between ourselves and Bickerstaffe. Bar. 14 is now full again, and uncertain what is to happen to the rest. Went to the *Pirates* with Jones. Very good for Ruhleben – but I don't enthuse over Gilbert and Sullivan, especially an amateur production.

[Insert: programme for *The Pirates of Penzance* produced by John H Corless]

Sept. 8th Rather a disturbance in the morning because someone wanted our spare bed, and it was some job getting it out and the four bed boards that belonged to it. Otherwise *die Lage is unverändent* [the situation is unchanged].

Sept. 9th Morning writing letter and then took out deckchair and sat in the sun for about first time this year. Read *Also Sprach Zarathustra*: it's extremely witty – alas how it makes me think of Bekassy[261] – I can't bear to think of him dead. Eventually had to give up owing to the offensive noise

---

[261] Ferenc Bekassy (fn 36).

and chatter of the wine line. Then tennis 5–6 and quiet evening reading Shelley.

Sept. 10th Photo of camp gardeners today – really getting ludicrous all this photographing. Out at the pond getting algae for class. Invigilated 12–1 and then basked in sun. Dante 7–9. Pritchard in very critical mood – Vincent[262] not nearly up to it! Three people went out to Berlin last night and were caught on the return journey – came back too late. The regrettable thing is that young Greene gave away the soldier whom they had bribed.

Sept. 11th Quiet morning. Saw Blagden about the alcohol *erlaubnisschein* [permission].[263] New Botany class 2–4 then prowled around field. Went to A.S.U. concert, or rather we went rather discreetly when the jaw was over and listened to the illustrations. Rumour very persistent that the Baron has got the sack.

[Insert: programme for A.S.U. Ninth Musical Evening, Sept. 11th. "Hugo Wolf" by Mr. Roland Bocquet]

Sept. 12th Blagden tells me for certain that the Baron goes. And also that Benzene goes too. Reason not clear, probably the Dresel report and nothing to do with the recent escapes. This evening we saw the Baron and wife paying a last visit to the pumpkins and to their gardens and then they just walked out of the far gate without any ceremony or anything. Amelunxen also on *urlaub* [leave] so the camp is now in charge of the English censor who took *Appell* in the evening. Blagden will try to wangle the alcohol through the doctor in the interregnum period.

Sept. 13th Rumours very rife about the Baron's dismissal – everything ranging from accepting butter to Dresel's note freely talked of. Blagden couldn't see the doctor about alcohol, but on the other hand the Heizpatrone [cartridge heater] has come in, so now we're getting one stage forwarder. Dodd and Bell to supper and Ford in after bedtime who smoked and talked till late.

---

[262] Eric Reginald Pearce Vincent (1894–1978), who was studying German at Gotha at the outbreak of the war. He taught Italian in the Camp School and after the war he became Professor of Italian at Cambridge University. In WW2 worked at Bletchley Park as an Italian cryptanalyst.

[263] Alcohol was needed for botany laboratory work.

Sept. 14th Doctor says he can't manage the alcohol question so formal application for leave sent to Kommando, whoever he may be. Appears to be Rüdiger: has commenced his career well by going round the lofts in rubber boots to catch people smoking, and got a huge crowd including Bocquet[264] and Oppe – all marched off to the cage. Botany class 2–4, tea at Ford's and Dodd into supper. Having another read at *Faust* to see what can be made of it.

Sept. 15th Doing some Hertwig's *Zoology* in the morning. Tried to play tennis 2–3 with Kapp – frightfully windy, dusty and rainy. Meeting of medical students in evening. Embedding baths getting on finely.

Sept. 16th Feeling just a bit off colour this morning and in addition it was a foul day of cold, rain, and wind. 8 a.m. went to dress rehearsal of Adler's concert – very scrappy. Then Botany 2–4. After *Appell* today officially given out about Havelberg – 1000 to be moved on October 1st. Great petition to be put in [this order was rescinded on Oct 5th]. Got a strange parcel today from Marks in Manchester. The new Kommandant appeared today – doesn't look a bad specimen, Dodd says he looks as if he meant well! Letter from Seward [page 377].

Sept. 17th Chilly morning – walked around the field till 9.30. Then R.C.S. Committee till 11.15. Not very much on. Invigilation 12–1 and then in the lab preparing material for the microtome.[265] Ponsonby to tea and tennis 4–6 and quiet evening reading Nietzsche. Drunk brought in at 11 who proved quiet but the fun began later. Let out at 3.30 for expedition to Spandau [latrines] and on returning he walked in at our box door – asked plaintively for cigarettes. The soldier – a very effete specimen – simply whined "*das gibt nichts*" [there is nothing] and funking to collar the man went over to the *wache* to get help, and in the interval the drunk just hooked it. When he came back he insisted that we were hiding the drunk in the box and searched under the beds and so forth in vain. Then ensued a great pow-wow and stamping about and conference and eventually I went to sleep.

---

[264] Roland Bocquet (1878–1956) a British composer, pianist and teacher who for most of his career was based in Dresden. In the camp he was Chair of the Ruhleben Music Society and a performer.

[265] Instrument for cutting extremely thin slices (sections) of material.

Sept. 18th Chilly this morning. Tennis 10–11. Botany in afternoon. To chamber concert – the music was very good, especially the Cesar Franck, but Short's[266] jaw was very dull. Bröse who was to have played in the Tchaikovsky trio was bird-caged for writing on someone else's p.c. and was not released – rough on him. Ponsonby and Marshall in to supper.

Sept. 19th Started collecting material for my Botany lectures. Got Montessori's *Il Metodo della Pedogogia Scientifico* today from Mrs. Mumby. Dante 5–6. Dodd into supper, brought with him a loaf of bread baked in camp – top hole – I feel tempted to mobilise myself in bread making!

Sept. 20th Reading and in the lab in the morning. Tennis 2–3.30. To the Italian evening 5.30–7.30. Singing only so so and play quite good – trifling of course. The new Kommandant turned up for the play. Shed was full of smoke and naked lights but he didn't seem to mind in the least. After the official programme great patriotic haranguing by Cutayar and then a very Butterworthian speech by Butterworth.

[Insert: programme and invitation to the Italian Circle's "Trattenimento Musicale", 20 Sept. 1916. Introduction by M. S. Prichard.]

....

HBW to MSP (received late Sept?):

Moddershall Oaks, Stone, Staffs.

10th Sept. 1916

Dear Mr. Pease,

Thank you very much for the postcard. I am so glad my letters are the right sort. It is just as well our views do agree, isn't it? Because it would be rather hard on you to have to reply to a four page argument in nine lines. If my sense of fair play were not so strong I should certainly take the opportunity of holding forth on Single Tax, or Individuality versus State Socialism, or even perhaps on the proper method of growing potatoes (we have a small patch which we have dug, in an excess of patriotic fervour, from a very stony field, so we all hold very strong views on the really correct method – only unfortunately they were divergent). Your remarks however would not be so complimentary if I so abused my power, and the

---

[266] Gordon Short, a pianist from Adelaide who was studying music in Berlin at the outbreak of war (*The Adelaide Chronicle*, 4th Dec 1920).

censor would be horribly bored. It is a relief to hear that the starvation is not material, but to many people ugliness is nearly as bad and one can guess what a camp like that must be. It makes one feel horribly selfish to be living in this beautiful place when the rest of the world is in prison or trenches or slums. You may imagine us living an Arcadian existence in the thick of scrub oak and silver birches, with a view forty miles across Staffordshire and Shropshire to the Wrekin and the Welsh hills. The new president of C.U.F.S (Miss Dunn) is lying on the ground in a most unpresident-like attitude studying one of Father's Single Tax articles and annotating it vigorously. Father is, I think, composing an article on 'The Brotherhood of War'. The others are not so intellectually employed and are making a fearful row on the whole, I fear the "simple living" is considerably more apparent than the "high thinking". All too soon however we remove to London and I start T.U. work under Miss Bondfield. Then I hope to have more to write about than I have now; "Impressions of a Lady Trade Unionist" or "what I saw in the East End" will be the correct thing then, – in the best Fabian style, of course. You need not tell me though, not to lose sight of the Market garden. The vision of it becomes more enticing every day. But I must be in London with Father.

Our friends affairs are much the same, they try of course to split us and crush the few extremists, but the sport is excellent, and come what may we must face it out. It is the one thing worth doing now. If the idea for which we stand is crushed there is little hope indeed. Only it is awful the way the brunt falls often on the weakest, and then the strain is so long. One does get tired of fighting and sometimes it all seems so futile here, where everything is so peaceful why on earth can't people let each other alone?

My brother is just playing a Beethoven sonata. Isn't Beethoven splendid, he lifts one out of oneself and makes one see big things and not be afraid. I hope they allow you music in Ruhleben.

We hear that you have Morris dancing. A lady came to Newnham to lecture on folk dancing (as a means of regenerating the world) and mentioned that "a Bedales man was teaching it in Ruhleben", and that must have been you; so you see even now your exploits are not hidden from the world. The dances are jolly things. Josiah (my brother) has been teaching us some, only as he has to be musician and teacher as well it is rather hard work. As an ardent Bedalian (we remarked with admiration how you and other O.B.s used to champion the cause of co-education at Heretics) you will be glad to hear that my small sister [Camilla] *is going there. The poor child is rather dreading it as the boys and others have been rubbing in to her what a very high standard is expected.*

Keep your hearts up in Ruhleben. We are doing our best here to keep the flag flying. Don't be misled by reports of what idiots like Lord Selborne say about how "the workers will have to realise that the interests of Capital and Labour are one" and "all classes will have to realise after the war, that hard work is necessary if we are to 'beat German Trade" etc. Much hard work he's ever done. You should hear the complimentary remarks the soldiers make about that sort of thing. Most of the best people are in the army (or elsewhere) so it is only the drivellers who are heard; but when it is over we will show them their proper place. The only work we can do at present is to get the women's organisation on a solid basis. It is much better than it was.

With best wishes

Yours sincerely, Helen Bowen Wedgwood

....

Sept. 21st Tennis 10–12. Great pot of material came from Seward today. Saw Blagden again about getting forward with the alcohol question. Botany 2–4 and then tried my first effort at party in Ruhleben with a great pie. Very successful and hugely appreciated by Dodd and the others.

Sept. 22nd Lechmere's first lecture today on Echinoderms 9–10. Then tennis 10–12. Wrote letter to Seward in afternoon. It appears that the sailors off the "Brussells" and the other ships captured on the high seas are to be sent out of the camp, about 60 in all.

....

MSP to HBW:

Ruhleben, Sept. 22nd 1916

Very many thanks indeed for yours and all your good wishes. No, of course I don't resent your enquiries, but you mustn't expect me to answer accurately and completely on a card. It will have to suffice to say that I suppose I'm what you call an "out and outer", though I hesitate to identify myself with any particular brand. Here, strange as it may sound, the matter is, like nearly everything else, as academic as Faust or Fossil Ferns (the other topics with which I find myself occupied). How goes your T.U. work? How I envy you your life of activity, even in dingy slums! I'm just getting under way with some botanical research, but the delays are awful! Again many thanks: best wishes! MS Pease

....

Sept. 23rd Tennis 10–11. Then to meeting of gardeners to consider what should be done with the seeds sent to the camp by the Queen [Princess] of Sweden via Hoffmann of Y.M.C.A. When I arrived they were making arrangement to have a barrack flower show competition. However, I suggest a general mutual camp gardening effort, and this suggestion was adopted. Then to English censor with Seward's letter but found Rüdiger in possession, so came away in vain. Botany 2–4, then to "*Alt Heidelberg*" at 5. A most miserable production – could see no artistic, literary or psychological value about it at all, though Bainton's songs were good. Then to R.C.S. Conversazione Committee at 9.30 – great discussion as to whether to repeat it or not – Bainton very much against and Ford strongly for; undertook to organise the police for the hall. Then to Barrack somewhat late and got cursed at by the Barbarossa for having a bath under the tap. Dodd's *boxengenossen* [box comrades] seem to be in a querulous mood again

[Insert: programme for *Alt Heidelberg*, produced by Mr. Joseph Stein]

Sept. 24th Got up and went straight to the lab at 6.30 am, only to find the place locked up and key not in Ascher's room [captain of Bar. 6]. Climbed in through the window and set the embedding bath going. It didn't go all absolutely *glatt* [smooth] as there wasn't enough low m.p. [melting point] wax, but I ultimately got in all right and crawled out through the window again. Rather cold, but all right again after bath and breakfast. Lovely morning walking round the field. Invigilated 12–1, finished letter in afternoon. Didn't go to Linsday–Ludlow concert, though I should have liked to have heard Keel sing. In any case it would have meant standing. Transferred the embedding stuff, set and cut into chunks for the microtome. Farmer into supper. Then Conversazione sub-com at 9 p.m. to which Blagden and Jones turned up. Ford very on for repeat and eventually got his way, to the considerable discontent of Bainton.

Sept. 25th Mobilised the various people for door-keepers and so forth, otherwise quiet morning. 2–4 botany, Ford into tea: went up to hall and took charge. Hall very comfortably full and very appreciative audience. The musical part was very good and so also was the play, but I had to go out and stop people walking on the top of the grandstand. Marshall into supper and then to meeting of gardeners at 8.30 to form a Horticultural Society. Pritchard there and more or less conducting affairs. Warner elected president and Howat[267] secretary I couldn't on the spur of the moment see any way of effectively opposing Howat but I much object to his Y.M.C.A. connections. A very un-businesslike meeting, but eventually a committee of ten elected on which I headed the poll.

[Insert: programme for R.C.S. Conversazione evening, 25 Sept 1916]

Sept. 26th Quietish morning preparing lecture, except for Lechmere on embryology 9–10. Horticultural Committee at 2 in the famous house of Lazarus,[268] very opulent cigars handed around. Not very businesslike but moderately practical. A long argument ensued when I objected to the committee confirming the minutes of the first general meeting, but eventually got my way. Very beautiful evening walking round course till 5.30 then came in to take charge of hall for R.C.S. Conversazione. Hall again comfortably full – Kommandant there. Keel didn't sing again but for the rest it went off very well. Play good, but Goodhind rather weak. Given out at *Appell* that Dresel reports that 45-ers negotiation going on well and hopes to make announcement in a few weeks and at bedtime that Fisher[269] had been elected vice captain of camp.

Sept. 27th Very nice warm morning, so deliberately cut work and sat in the sun reading *Dichtung and Wahrheit*. Tennis 2–4 with Vincent. Went around and saw Henry about cubby holes: proposed to have Marshall and Morrison in, but stipulated for table and chairs. Made party and then to lab; walked round the field with Philips and discussed pacifism and then to supper, Dodd and Philips as guests. The following priceless notice has been posted in the Barracks "Will you kindly ask your men to line up at the *Appell* a little sooner. As most of you will have noticed, soldiers were put into Bar. 18 today on account of their not lining up on time, which was only countermanded on my petition. The new camp officer wishes for the *Appell* to be got over a bit smarter. I feel certain that a little good will on all sides and a little consideration for one's fellow prisoners who are punctual

---

[267] Thomas Howat (1888–1957) was a manager before his internment. He was living in Germany prior to the war, and had married a German girl in 1912. He stayed in Germany after his release.

[268] Possibly Frederick Herbert Lazarus (1872–1942), listed as a Vice-Chair of the R.H.S. in 1916/7. The famous house could be the 'Summer House', a shed behind the 3rd Grandstand where a club was established by well-to-do businessmen in 1915. There was also an Isaac Lazarus in camp.

[269] George Frederick Fisher, Captain of Barracks 3 and 22, Chair of various committees.

everything could be carried on satisfactory. Everyone has to line up as soon as the bell goes and are not allowed to dismiss untill (sic) the second bell goes (signed) Powell." !!!

Sept. 28th Ford out in Berlin today – gave him instructions with regard to Leitz: the order incidentally came in in the interval but of course without alcohol. Tennis 10–12, Botany 2–4. Seemed to waste a lot of the evening doing odd jobs, but got started on lecture notes for Monday. Dodd into supper who told the most astounding tales of people who wangle things in this camp. Then at work on lecture and so to bed. Mightily tired for some unknown reason.

Sept. 29th Ford very full of himself as a result of his Berlin visit – ordered the Minot.[270] Lechmere 9–10. Work at lecture in the morning. Afternoon pond expedition and successfully used the new leave[?]. Lecture work; Dodd into supper. I put about 1 cc of oil of cloves in the apples this morning with disastrous results – nearly blew Dodd's head off! Ford came in after bedtime and yarned. Talking always tires me last thing at night! Jones very scornful at the Captains of the Relief Fund muddle: he attended special meeting of the Finance Committee. A great medical examination of the whole garrison (officers included) but haven't heard any gossip yet.

[Insert: finance statements for R.C.S. expenditure]

Sept. 30th Continued lecture work. Tennis 11–12. Botany 2–4. Wrote p.c. Dante 5–6. Warkentin into supper, Historical Circle 7–8, Masterman on English Parties, Jones in the chair. *Appell* and then walked up and down until bedtime.

Oct. 1st Did what J. calls *"bis spät einschlafen"* [sleep in] this morning. Lecture work – tennis 11–12, concert 6–8 and bed at the ridiculous hour of 9 p.m. I don't like Ludlow's florid efforts at all but Keel was splendid.

[Insert: programme for Sunday Evening Concert, 1st Oct. 1916]

Oct. 2nd Birthday was very full of routine business, so much so that I forgot about it until I was prowling down to my opening lecture on gymnosperms.

---

[270] The Minot is a type of microtome invented by Charles Sedgewick Minot around 1886 for the preparation of biological specimens (in 1912–1913 Minot was Harvard Exchange Professor at Berlin and Jena).

Saw Richardson about Leitz order. Tennis 11–12, then Botany as per usual 1:30–4. Made a great birthday pie, but not accepted at the cookhouse as they were too crowded. Had a row with Chadwick[271] about the title of my paper for the Science Circle. Then to work on the paper and so to bed. Ford came and talked, smoked and thoroughly upset a quiet evening's reading.

[Insert: bill from a Berlin laundry company (for shirts, towels, bedsheet etc) – Mk1.66]

Oct. 3rd Lechmere 9–10. Then assisted with the absurd monthly *"Kontrolle"* of chairs, tables etc. Tennis 11–12. Botany 1:30–4. Set about lecture for Science Circle. Dodd and Bell to supper, walked up and down after *Appell* till bed, read *Dichtung und Wahrheit.*[272]

Oct. 4th Prepared lecture in morning – tennis 11–12, Botany as usual, then finishing touches on lecture. Dodd to supper and lecture at 6.30. Went fairly well, it was more extempore than I should have liked, but an amusing discussion arose on the proper way to hold rabbits and hens. Walk with Ponsonby, and borrowed Morley's *Gladstone* off him. Very strong exchange rumour today, emanating it appears from Rüdiger.

Oct. 5th Hustled off to lab at 6 am and set some material on the embedding bath. Spent morning with C&C' [a book?] preparing Botany lecture, and got that done except for diagrams. Botany class 1.30 as usual. Long walk with Marshall 4–6, Dodd to supper, spent evening embedding the material and much annoyed by fire bell which came right at the critical moment with one lot and spoiled it. Rather a slump in exchange rumour this evening – only ½ dozen or so going home tomorrow.

Oct. 6th Cleared up last night's mess in the lab. Lechmere 9–10. Walked round field with Chadwick, and to cubby hole. Botany as usual, wrote letter, Doddering, D to supper and then went up and listened to quintettes – Dvorak and Brahms: never came across Speed[273] before – he is an excellent

---

[271] James Chadwick (1891–1974), a physicist who was working with Hans Geiger in Berlin as a research fellow when war broke out. He received the 1935 Nobel Prize for Physics, after discovering the neutron.

[272] Goethe's autobiography.

[273] Arthur Speed (1870–1940), a professional musician. Living in Germany for many years before the war. After the war he was a music teacher at Harrow School.

player. Ford in and yarned – I read Morley and said nothing but he talked on. S. snored and J grunted now and again.

Oct. 7th Rather tired this morning, result of Ford's late visit. Wrote letter home and prepared diagrams for lecture. Botany as usual with an interval in which I made a pie crust. I hear censor has struck out glycerol and paraffin from the Leitz order. Dodd to supper, and I went to Historical Society. The 'discussion' consisted of a speech by Butterscotch – that's all and was rather boring. I didn't go but walked up and down, and read Morley in bed.

Oct. 8th R.C.S. Committee 10.15–12. Good work done and arranged only to meet monthly. Cut the library and walked round with Ponsonby. Investigated some of Seward's material. Walked up and down and to concert: not good except for the Schumann. Letter from D[ad] today, looks as if Board were not paying me anything for being interned. However, he's got some cash out of them which he's sending me.

[Insert: Symphony Concert programme for Midsummer Night's Dream overture, with rather sweet fairy on back]

Oct. 9th Lecture 9–10. Then cleared out the Bar. garden, did one or two jobs in the box, devised a new towel rack inter alia. Botany class as usual. Long *auseinandersetzung* [confrontation] with Edge about the row between the R.C.S. and the Y.M.C.A. I think he took rather an unreasonable view and in any case got very excited. Supper, stroll, *Appell*, stroll, bed.

Oct. 10th Started embedding material 6 a.m. Lechmere 9–10. Struggled with some of Seward's ferns and Lechmere, Neville and I failed to identify two of them. Botany class as usual in course of which I developed a cold and felt rotten. Prowled about, Dodd to supper and put the embedding material in wax – went fairly well – only one careless mistake and not bad considering cold just coming on. So to bed and to Morley.

Oct. 11th Cold very much better, in fact almost gone this morning, but somehow the morning went without much being achieved. Gave Wolff order for Leitz. Afternoon Botany and a great inspection by a Swedish officer and an American journalist conducted by Von Borck, the young Graf [Count Schwerin's son], and Powell, the whole affair being stage managed by Benzene and the Fourier, – the latter was sent hustling off to the bookbinding dept to see that the *Herrn* [men] were at *arbeit* [work]! *D.T.* [*Daily Telegraph*] for a change – see an Osmaston[274] in the lost list. Dodd to supper, stroll in pouring rain, and to Morley.

[Insert: receipt for 1Mk for Hockey, 11th Oct. 1916]

Oct. 12th Sad news today that George [cousin – fn 31] has been killed. Of course, they're all cut up about it, and I feel terribly sorry for Aunt Kate. Then if you will go to war you've got to expect such consequences. Must try to write to Mary.[275] Spent all morning putting up our old floor board as to form a great luggage platform and very successful job it was too. Botany as usual. Doddering, Dodd to supper, and then to listen to quintette practice – mighty fine.

Oct. 13th Lechmere 9–10. Wrote p.c. to Mary and dispatched it by special interview with censor. Bulbs arrived from Barrs today, so planted them in usual array of tins and pots. Left the botany to Lechmere today and went to dress rehearsal of Dvorak quintette. Miscellaneous crowd of people there, including one of the English censors. Then walk, *D.T.*, Dodd to supper, and tried to do a little work at lecture diagrams.

Oct. 14th Up early and set material going in the embedding bath: only gave it 24 instead of 72 hours in the 56°C bath. Unfortunately, during breakfast it jammed and went out and the things got somewhat solidified. Played Hockey 9.30 – the most pitiful game I've ever played only ½ doz. people knew the rules of the game – anyhow had a rush about and felt no stiffness or anything – care of my morning run! Leitz sent in 4 litres absolute and 4 litres 70% [alcohol] this morning. Great triumph makes me jump for joy. Botany in afternoon and spent evening embedding the material – to bed mighty pleased with the alcohol success.

Oct. 15th Sunday: went up with S. to get a "dollop" of Kaiserliche marmalade at 7.15 am. Then quiet morning doing lecture diagrams, invigilated 12–1, read Morley – manufactured pie for supper. *Appell.* Lecture notes again. Dodd and Ponsonby to supper. Rather futile

---

[274] Probably Robert Shirley Osmaston, of the Royal Flying Corps who was killed in action on 24th Sep. 1916. Born in Limpsfield and listed on the Limpsfield village war memorial.

[275] Mary Gammell Stewart Davidson; George's sister.

discussion on difference between talent and genius. Letter – very friendly – from Biffen about my scholarship cash [see page 385].

Oct. 16th Lecture 9–10. Somehow wasted a lot of the morning. Deserted Lechmere and read Morley in cubby hole. Dodd and Bell to supper and wasted much time in continued futile discussion on talent v. genius. Hear that we are to get back the extra exchange which they pinched of our remittances – that means 17 Marks pocket money. The Y.M.C.A. have taken possession of S.W. corner room – much to J's annoyance. He was empowered to write a very stiff letter.

Oct. 17th Lechmere 9–10, during which poor old embedding bath regulator jammed and bust the thermometer. They have brought in one of the steam boilers today, and high time too. Played tennis 10–12. Botany in afternoon. Dante 5–6. Marshall to supper and evening doing lecture work. 125 Marks from Mrs. Mumby today. Ford in and yarned: Rüdiger sent for him for an account of the school and found out on questioning Powell that the *Kriegsministerium* [Ministry of War] has written to show what they, the military, have done for education. Only truthful answer would be *so wenig wie utglich* [as little as possible].

Oct. 18th Chilly and raw in morning. Started on a picture frame for "Chill October", then to work and finished lecture notes. Deserted Lechmere and walked round field in the sun. Then to work again, supper without Dodd, listened to Beethoven quartette – Harris playing very coldly and so to bed to read Neville's paper on Viticulture. Good.

Oct. 19th Chilly again but sun and beautifully warm later on, got rake and tidied up garden a bit, then to lecture diagrams. Botany class, tea, prowl, little work, Dodd to supper, buzz up and down to bed and to Morley.

Oct. 20th Lechmere 9–10 pm. Then Horticultural Society Committee at 10. Hockey at 2 – goodish game. Wrote letter home. Dodd as usual and then walk and to bed. Only read a short while – too cold on hands – there will be ten days before they get the boiler ready for use. Cross questioned Wimpfheimer about Hohenrein père et fils today and he thinks they've become naturalised – they just left without any explanation, farewells or anything. Had an inspection of the lab today by 4 officers (German) brought round by Benzene. Seemed intelligent and friendly: asked if microscopes had been lent by German students to which I replied "*Leider nicht*" [unfortunately not] which he took in quite the right spirit!

Oct. 21st Morning wrote letter. Botany in afternoon, beastly cold, quiet evening. Dodd and J. out having a great "hog" with the Silberleute [Silberman brothers]. I took courage and wrote home about J. today and trust it will have some effect. Given out today that 45-ers must hand in their papers and that those who desire to stay in Germany must make special application.

....

MSP to HBW [Note – this postcard wasn't received by HBW until Xmas day]:

Ruhleben, 21st Oct. 1916

Very many thanks for your letter of Sept. 16th. I expect you're back in London now and hard at work; I wonder how you find it. Here we are having the first snaps of winter and getting warm occupies much time. I play a good deal of hockey which is great fun, but most of my time is taken up with my Botany class. I am reading Morley's Gladstone, with Shelley as an antidote for the G.O.M's piety – I find this an excellent combination. Yes, we get a lot of music here, and some good chamber music too. Generally speaking, I find Brahms the most sympathetic to my temper. I shall look forward to hearing of your works. I hope your sister enjoys Bedales. Again many thanks, Best wishes, M.S.Pease

....

Oct. 22nd R.C.S. Committee 10.15 – dull and long. Cut invigilation and prepared lecture diagrams. To concert; quartette good but the rest dull. Jablonowski[276] sang "O Isis and Osiris" for 6th time! Given out at *Appell* for 45-ers to be photographed tomorrow. The C.O. brought round another visitor to the lab today, a Swiss person – much impressed by the *Sontag's ruhe* [Sunday rest].

Oct. 23rd Lecture 9–10. Bar. 10 in midst of cleaning, and rumour has it we are on tomorrow. Spent afternoon framing M.'s picture, or rather, giving a

---

[276] Mr B. (sometimes S.) Jablonowski, appears on concert programmes. The Camp Magazine Xmas 1916 refers to his 'magnificent voice'.

helping hand to S. in the job. Dodd to supper and quiet evening with Morley.

Oct. 24th "Spring" cleaning today. We didn't start till after breakfast and got comfortably finished by lunch when I had bath and complete change. Botany class; had interview with Blagden about impertinent note from Higgins about the installation and the so called "Research Department" – the thing calls for active *massnahmen* [measures]. Dodd to supper and then reading Morley. At 11 p.m., enter our old friend the drunk who kept up a constant flow of blasphemy till 4 a.m. during which none of us slept a wink. Resolution again to speak to Thorpe on the matter. Rumour that 45-ers are to go on Saturday.

Oct. 25th Very tired and sleepy and useless after sleepless night. Wrote letter to Biffen and D. about finances and dispatched them at censors. Dentist 10.30 – fairly severe but all over in one do. Too tired to work, so read Morley and walked about for rest of day. Got my great aluminium *topf* [pot] today.

Oct. 26th Saw Truelove[277] about Leitz order, and then to work on Cycads all morning and finished lecture notes. Botany in afternoon. Hort. Soc. Committee in the house of Lazarus. L. very friendly and deferring. Dodd to supper; had a bleeding nose and headache so took quiet evening with Morley in cubby hole. Hear that the cubby holes are to be warmed this year at our own expense!

Oct. 27th Lechmere 9–10. Spoke to L. and arranged to pay 50 Marks towards lighting expenses. Planted remaining bulbs, darned sweater, lunch, hockey 3.30. Dodd to supper and Ford in after bedtime, to tell of his Berlin experiences. Saw Birch[278] earlier in day about his 5 Marks per week, and arranged for him to take that; quite friendly.

Oct. 28th Set some material embedding in the high temperature incubator, as the proper bath was out of order. Saw Ford about Birch and payed B his

---

[277] Harold Edgar Truelove (1888–1966), an Oxford graduate in Modern Languages, son of Councilor Arthur Truelove of Sheffield. He was secretary of the Ruhleben Camp School and taught French.

[278] Birch seems to be an engineer/electrician who did paid work in the lab.

arrears. Class in afternoon. Dodd to supper, embedding material and so to *Appell* and bed and Morley.

Oct. 29th To the lab and finished off lecture diagrams. Bagged a box off Hatfield for our new shelves. Invigilated reading Morley. Buttonholed by Pritchard for Italian Circle – discussion on education, so went. Dull in the sense that set speeches were read and all the trite things said on Montessori. Then walk and to lecture work. Concert at 6 – really very good – old friend *Enfant Prodigue* and Mozart really wonderfully played by Bainton. Then late supper, Charlottenburg [latrines] and bed. Hatfield told me, by the way, that the 45-ers are "off." Letter from H.B.W. – writes in a good vigorous, energetic unsentimental style.

……………………

HBW to MSP (received Oct. 29th):

12 Beaufort House, Beaufort Street, Chelsea[279]

16th Oct. 1916

Dear Mr. Pease,

I really cannot stand the conversation of Father's friends a moment longer so I think I will write to you as an antidote! One of them (age over 45 of course!) is explaining to my brothers that young people really enjoy war even if they think they don't, and the other is conversing with Father about airy abstractions. Men seem to think that if you take a group of ordinary human beings and give them a name they suddenly assume peculiar characteristics; now it is – Greece wants, – Italy says etc etc. And of course they want and say something which no ordinary human being would dream of, and have given wonderful names to their wants into the bargain. And all the time the poor wretches only want to left in peace. I suppose the reason so many more women are reasonable, or at least frank about the war is that they are not so fond of making beautiful generalities.

Many thanks for your postcard. It was not just curiosity that made me ask your views, but from what Father said it seemed then that you might be home any day, and so be plunged suddenly from a circle where the subject, I realise, must be 'academic' into one where it is only too real and you might not be prepared for the special difficulties. How maddening it must be for an active person to be so completely shut off. I should almost have thought that to hear of our activities

---

[279] Wedgwood family home in London.

would make it worse. But I suppose it is better to be unhappy than to grow reconciled and dulled!

I have been working for the Federation for a month now. At first I thought I never could stand it. To live in London is so hateful. One side of one seems suppressed and starved. Also going round to strange factories is very alarming. What unthankfulness for one's blessings this must seem to you! Now however that I am getting to know the girls and to be "in the swim" it is not so bad and soon I shall be enjoying it.

Of course one comes up against the usual difficulties which one knew, in theory, to exist. – Much work for small results and worst of all, internal squabbles. It is depressing when the Unions waste their energy quarrelling among themselves. Also personally I feel very suspicious of the A.S.E.[280] *who are at present backing us. It looks as if they mean to scrap the women just as soon as they conveniently can – at present, for their own sake they must back us. Susan Lawrence says "do not be too feminist", but it is not that so much as it's being an example of selfishness and jealousy which may crop up and spoil things. Of course, really I don't know enough to talk, but one does feel so anxious, because if we are to win through the bad times after the war, people must stick together. That is what is so difficult to rub in to the girls one talks to. Their only question is "What can I get out of the Union?" It is awfully difficult to make them see that they are the Union and to rub in the idea of Fellowship. But it is work well worth doing! Miss Bondfield says too that there is an immense improvement since 20 years ago. There is plenty of humour in the work too. What do you think of this from the manager of a well known armament firm? – A deputation of girls (at 20s a week) ask him for a rise. After a long interview he closes it with the virtuously indignant remark "you girls seem to think of nothing but how to make money out of the war!"!!!!!! The other day I heard Miss Bondfield interviewing a manager. It was like watching a very exciting duel. He was a smooth tongued, heavy jawed Irishman, up to every dodge. He kept evading her and confusing the issue by totally irrelevant remarks and Miss B. kept leading him back unexpectedly. It was great fun seeing how soon one could guess what they were each going to lead up to. I nearly disgraced myself by shouting with laughter. It is not surprising though that girls will do anything rather than go on deputation to the manageress. That sort of thing needs a special course at the University. Last night I went down to the wilds of the West India docks – a weird place, pitch dark, with narrow streets and wharfs and masts and things sticking up, and one street crowded with Chinese sailors. Needless to say I*

---

[280] Amalgamated Society of Engineers?

prefer to bus all the way! But I much prefer that sort of place to the tidy munitions factories, filled with middle class women. Trade Union affairs in general are going very much better than you might imagine, and will be able I think to make themselves felt when the war ends.

Best wishes to the fossil ferns.

Yours sincerely,

Helen Wedgwood

....

Oct. 30th Lecture 9–10. Hockey 10.15. Got nose biffed at half time and poured torrents of blood, so had to come away. Rather interrupted and unsatisfactory afternoon. Got tickets for *Hindle Wakes*. Philips to tea, Dodd to supper and no end of a to do over a very soggy meat pudding which his man Brown made. Confirmed by Jones that the 45-ers are off.

[Insert: October accounts for Ruhleben Camp School]

Oct. 31st Saw Richardson who tells me Leitz order is in so to Lab where I found the Minot and all the other tackle. Lechmere showed me how to work it and we cut some sections of Lilium [lilies] and Pines – worked wonderfully and what is cheering is that the embedding seems well done. Botany class in afternoon; Dodd to supper, went and listened to septette rehearsal and then to bed. Jones has two interesting news items: (1) The Hall Control Committee resigned and Platford[281] and Redmayne installed instead (2) The military have agreed to supply extra coal for heating this year on two conditions (a) that the American Ambassador makes a written declaration that the original coal provided is sufficient and (b) that we pay for the extra ourselves! Ford came in and spoiled my reading – very friendly and talkative.

Nov. 1st Given out last night about the usual monthly silly inventory of government property. This morning, after *Appell* given out that the affair was off. First sensible thing that's happed for a long time. To the lab and worked the Minot. Birch pointed out that one of the wheels was slightly bent, owing to the thing not having been packed in a case. I instructed

---

281 John Harold Platford (1877–1966), a chartered accountant who was on the Finance Committee and Chair of the Canteen Committee.

Truelove to get the necessary spanner. Unsatisfactory afternoon, in which I smashed the tin opener trying to manufacture a bread crumber. Then to work on C&C'. Dodd left us in the lurch with a large supper, then more work and so to bed and Morley.

Nov. 2nd Long morning working up lecture. Field left open all day today. We get such obvious reforms by degrees! Botany in afternoon. Dodd as usual and quiet evening with Morley.

Nov. 3rd Lechmere 9–10. Then the infernal stocktaking business with hauling out mattresses and so forth, which occupied the rest of the morning. Pond expedition in afternoon and got some good algae but no spores on the Azolla, now turned bright red. Wrote letter home, and then to *Hindle Wakes* with Bell – not bad. B. into supper and so to bed.

[Insert: programme for *Hindle Wakes*, produced by Mr. C. J. Pearce]

Nov. 4th Poor game of hockey in morning. Then to Botany class, then letter writing, supper and bed. Finished Vol. I of Morley. Got back the filched exchange on my remittance of May 5th. Hear there is another great row brewing about an alleged stolen rug!

Nov. 5th Started on lecture notes – then to lab and L. showed me some staining technique. Invigilated and to lab again in afternoon. Ponsonby to supper and then finished letter home.

Nov. 6th Memorable day! [anniversary of his arrest]. Lecture 9–10 – rather pottered away the rest of morning, though I put in some time in the lab. The man Roberts into supper to discuss his record of study, but conversation was mostly on the morals of the peerage, a subject in which Dodd seems well up in. I hear there has been an attempt to "rag" the Maori show.

Nov. 7th Lechmere 9–10. Hopelessly ruined morning, hanging about at cashiers to sign that my balance on Sept. 30th was 94.40! Botany class in afternoon. Parcel from Neumeister. Dodd to supper and so to bed and Morley. The "rug" cloud has fizzled out. Appears the Graf took it in to his rooms with him and didn't leave it in the coach after all!

Nov. 8th Still beautifully mild, so they started our old boiler today in order to use up some of the coal before the frost sets in! Microtoming and hockey in the morning.

Nov. 9th Set to on the new shelving scheme, which kept me going all morning and then didn't get it quite finished. Botany class and then to French play – Ponsonby gave me a ticket.

[Insert: handwritten note: Dear Pease, My sins have found me out. At your expense I fear! I came to seek a match in your cubbyhole and fumbling in the dark tipped over your flask. After housemaid work with the handkerchief I have dried up the puddle on your desk but your notebook is sopped. Please forgive a penitent thief! Yours, John Balfour]

Nov. 10th Lechmere 9–10. Then continued and finished shelving. Botany class. Bulbs from M.C.S. Dodd to supper so to bed and Morley. Ascher has been put 9 days in the cellar and a month in cage for calling Rüdiger a *Kollosaler Schwein* [colossal pig] in a letter! Balfour pinched and broke my mother of pearl pen knife.

Nov. 11th The appalling news this evening is that the order has gone forth that we are to change with Bar. 6 "*und zwar*" [in fact] on Monday. They want to have the Jews in the middle of the camp under the eyes of the *wache* and hence the proposed change. All the usual alarms and scares. Went down and talked it over with Wechsler. The stink of the latrines is what terrifies me, but W. assures me it is not noticeable. More or less arranged to have their box in exchange. J. hustled around and drew up a petition; Saunders, Munro, and people all very excited. At *Appell* Thorpe made a lamentable speech on the matter. The devil is that the Graf has given the order and gone away for the weekend, not to be back till Tuesday. It looks very black. At bedtime Thorpe made another of his silly speeches saying everything that was possible was being done: Jones' account of the meeting of the captains and von Bork[?] was that Thorpe stood there trembling with fear ("piddling in his bags" was J's phrase) and that Powell and Ettinghausen[282] did the jawing.

---

282 Maurice Leon Ettinghausen (1883–1974), a Jewish internee and the camp's reference librarian. The son of German parents, he became a British citizen in 1894. Pre-war he was an antiquarian bookseller and newspaper correspondent and in 1914 he was living in Germany. After the war he

Nov. 12th Very unsettled day of claims and schemes. J. very much against the outlook of Wechslers' box so we went round, tried in vain to negotiate Lazarus' box; then after consideration we determined to fly high and put in a bid for the other "room" in Bar. 6 and got Thorpe to say he'd bear us in mind. Then to lecture work, invigilation and more work in afternoon. Didn't go to concert (Ballads) and had instead quiet evening with Morley. So to bed, perhaps our last in Bar. 11!

Nov. 13th To our great relief announced at 2 p.m. today that the proposed change is off! – at least as far as we are concerned, but I gather Bar. 6 is to be "*strafed*" [punished]. Rumour has it they are to go to Bar. 13[283] when the 45-ers leave. To bed in a much more peaceful frame of mind.

[Insert: mimeographed notice about cubby hole:

Cubby Hole No. Occupants: D.D. Jones, G.K. Logie, C.J. Masterman, M.S. Pease, T.H. Marshall, G.H. Morrison, used Mon. Tue. Wed. Thurs. Fri. Sat. Sun. (*In pencil:* Always)

Name of cubby-hole captain through whom future notices will be delivered and through whom requests, complaints, etc, are to be forwarded. (*In pencil:* None, but must be elected.)

Signed Leigh Henry and Horace G. Hunt (Cubby-holes Sub-Committee.)

This notice is NOT TO BE REMOVED.

Note in pencil: N.B. Please have times of use regularised in this book. It may be necessary to introduce new members during winter and more than six (if that number) cannot work here ALWAYS)]

Nov. 14th Lechmere off today on account of dresses for *Everyman*. Planted Peggy S's bulbs and brought in one or two of the other pots which had shot well. Then darning socks and so the morning went. Botany class, Doddering, supper, and then composed p.c. to Neumeister.

---

returned to England and continued collecting and selling antiquarian books, referring to himself as a bibliographer.

283 Barrack 13 originally housed the black and 'colonial' internees. Barrack 6 housed Jewish internees as well as new arrivals to the camp; it was subsequently cleared for use by the school and its residents dispersed to other barracks (see Ketchum, 1965, pp115-118).

Nov. 15th Set to and did a little microtoming, but without much success. Then hockey at 10.30 – played in the snow, but not a bad game. Botany as usual. Blagden back again. Went to Science Circle. Higgins on Valency. Ford in after bedtime to talk R.C.S. mongering.

Nov. 16th Lecture work in morning. Lechmere returned to botany class again, so got afternoon off. Ford and Blagden in to tea for a great discussion on R.C.S. business, especially re-creating a special dept. for the Higgins crowd. Then to Duncan Jones' *Everyman* – good, the dress effects particularly so. Bell to supper and so to *Appell* and bed.

[Insert: programme for *Everyman. A Moral Play*. Nov. 16, 17 and 18]

Nov. 17th Chilly. Lechmere 9–10, froze. Then dug up my roses and gave them to Cookson[284] for his bed by 3rd grandstand. Then to lab by appointment with Boole;[285] inspection by the C.O. with his daughter who looked at slides and expressed considerable interest. They stayed quite a long time and the C.O. stamped round and said "*Ja, wenn es nur geheizt wäre*!" [Yes, if only it were heated.] A sentiment I heartily agree with! Afternoon letter writing, Warkentin to supper and so to bed.

Nov. 18th Letter writing and line up for concert ticket. Botany class very frigid. Marshall to tea to meet the man Hughes who wants to lecture on the German empire: long talk – he's very difficult to shake off! Then to Dante – last canto of *Paradiso*. Late rushed supper. Dodd and S. at *Everyman*. Very cold and blowy – a snow and dust blizzard. Walk with J. and Ford and discussed R.C.S. business – Y.M.C.A. matter. The C.O. is much on the alert about the heating – been hustling old Benzene because the boiler by Bar. 6 not going yet. He was in our Bar. three times and the result is the boiler went all right. Fancy the old Baron doing that!

Nov. 19th Great luxury of getting up in a warm barrack and just as well too, as it was a morning of driving snow. Hair froze up solid on my way from baths to barrack! R.C.S. Committee 10 a.m. and great debate on inviting a

---

[284] Charles Wilmot Mawson Cookson (1888–1976), an engineer (car mechanic) before the war, he later became a journalist.

[285] Llewellyn Boole (1885–1935), a teacher who was visiting a German cousin in Cologne when war broke out in 1914. He played a prominent part in the running of the Camp School and was in charge of the French Department.

Bar. captain to sit on the R.C.S. Committee, or on Joint Committee. Jones and Patters in favour of latter but rest of committee voted for my amendment: J. very annoyed about it. Unfortunately Blagden was not there. I put on my great new yellow leather waistcoat today and found it a magnificent thing for "horizontal weather". Walked round the field with Dodd in driving snow, and to Cossart's concert in the evening – poor program, but well done for Ruhleben.

Nov. 20th Cold and snowy. Lecture 9–10. And then walked round field with Chadwick. Cleared up and bright blue sky like Switzerland. Interrupted afternoon, but quiet evening. Parcels started coming in again, but still no letters. The Grand Duke of Mecklenburg is coming to inspect the camp tomorrow, so there was a huge hustling round by Benzene – got squads of soldiers at work to clear up snow and so forth!

Nov. 21st The Duke of Mecklunberg-Strelitz arrived in great style and was conducted round the camp by whole bunch of officers of 1st and 2nd order. Lechmere interviewed by them in the lab. Did some staining, not much luck. Took Botany class in afternoon, quiet evening reading Morley.

Nov. 22nd Bishop of Europe[286] on a visit to the camp today and made a speech after midday. *Appell* only... didn't... [smudged page]. Pouring rain in torrents and mud galore! To Higgins on Valency at Science Circle. Started reading Montessori today.

Nov. 23rd Lecture work all morning. Saw Ford about Birch's going out to Berlin. Botany class in afternoon. Quiet evening reading Montessori and finished the Morley in bed. Hear that Morrison has had a nervous breakdown. Heard a good story from Bell. D.J. relating the Bishop's address in which he praised the wonderful spirit in Russia and gave as an example how in Moscow they took all German property, grand pianos and all and burnt it in the street!

Nov. 24th To Lechmere 9–10. Then odds and ends of jobs. Listened to sextette rehearsal in afternoon and to Bell's to supper to meet Jannasch[287]

---

[286] Bishop Herbert Bury, Bishop for Northern Europe. Published a book *My Visit to Ruhleben* in 1917.

[287] Hans Windekilde Jannasch (1883–1981), son of a Moravian missionary born in Labrador, Canada, who was teaching in Germany in 1914.

– discussed Bedales and he showed photo of the Landerziehungsheim[288] at Holzminden. Started Goethe's *Aus Meinem Leben.*

Nov. 25th Just two years today since we came to Ruhleben! Had my first serious accident in sport today, got a front tooth knocked out in hockey – got the ball slick in my mouth. I didn't hurt, I was too annoyed at losing a tooth to worry about that. Went straight to dentist, where I found Rutterford[289] unemployed, so I sat down and he set to work. Pulled off the broken piece, took out the nerve and patched up the stump. Said it could be crowned and gave me appointment for Thursday. A much more sympathetic and steady man than Moore.[290] Lip cut fairly badly, so that eating is difficult, and speaking is very trying – a ridiculous lisp. Got tickets for Dale's concert. Owing to great kick off by the Bishop only one pupil for Botany. Bishop came round the school and expressed interest. Very tired in the evening and to bed without reading.

Nov. 26th Not feeling quite O.K. even after a long sleep, so read Galsworthy's *Essays* all morning. Invigilated 12–1. To Dale's concert. Mighty fine – best we've had in Ruhleben, by a long chalk. Dodd and Marshall to supper and so to bed with a bit of a headache and tired.

[Insert: Ruhleben Musical Society Chamber Concert programme, including Brahms sextet (played by Peebles Conn, Marshall, Harris, Williams, St G Phillips and Schlesinger) – mentioned in p.c. to HBW on 1 Dec – and songs accompanied by B. J. Dale.]

Nov. 27th Lecture 9–10. Ridiculous performance – as I lisped worse than dear old Franklin! The Jews are having their "*Strafe*" [punishment] today being shifted into Bar. 13 and Bar. 13 distributed round the camp involving all sorts of shifts. The serious part of the affair is that the School gets into odium for having caused the shift, which is, of course, *rein aus der luft gegriffen* [purely out of thin air].

---

288 A progressive German boarding school, like Bedales.

289 Dr Percy Frederick Rutterford (1883–1957). Born in London, he trained there as a dentist. He married an American girl in Hamburg in 1911, so was presumably working there. After the war he returned to dentistry in England.

290 Henry Sumner Hyatt Moore (1891–?). A dentist, born in Germany and trained in USA. Practised in England after the war.

Nov. 28th Lechmere 9–10. Then read Coulter and Chamberlain. Botany class in afternoon. Confab with Ford, Bell, Jones and Blagden re R.C.S. situation with regard to Bar. 6. Then "supper" at 5.15. Blagden and Dodd in. R.C.S. Committee 6.15. Interrupted by departure ceremony of the Bishop but got finished before *Appell.* Walk up and down with Marshall and so to bed. Sent concert programmes to E.H.R.

Nov. 29th Did lecture notes in morning and domestic details in box in afternoon. To lecture by Hatfield on Freud at Science Circle. J. tells me there has been a very satisfactory interview with Powell about Bar. 6. Likely to get the whole premises.

Nov. 30th Had my interview with Rutterford this morning. He messed about with the tooth and measured up the vacancy for an ersatz tooth, but didn't do much else. Finished lecture work. To botany class: not much doing. Committee of R.H.S. 4 p.m. Mr. Lazarus very excited that I should get the proposed wire netting[291] moved back so as to exclude his *Wohnung* [lodgings]! Interrupted evening and so to bed and Goethe.

Dec. 1st [no entry]

....

MSP to HBW (received by HBW during Xmas week):

Ruhleben, 1st Dec. 1916

Very many thanks for yours of Oct 16th. The account of your work is most interesting. I know how discouraging it is at times, but the only thing is to stick to it; I am glad you are so sanguine for the future! We too, have our bickerings and jealousies, but here all is so small, petty, and irrelevant! The prospect of years of it doesn't fill one with joy! I follow eagerly the little scraps of news I get of what you and "they" are doing. My best wishes to "them". "Shop" still takes up most of my time, but I'm at present enjoying Goethe's autobiography and Dr Montessori's book, both full of interest. We've had some ripping music lately! Do you know the Brahms sextets? My best wishes and again very many thanks. Michael Pease

....

---

[291] According to Powell and Gribble (1919), a condition of having Barrack 6 for the school was that they had to wire off the compound surrounding the barrack and see it was locked at night, as it was very close to the outside wire fences.

Dec. 2nd Hockey at 9.30. Botany class in afternoon – only two turned up, which is disappointing – it is mainly on account of the cold, but the place is not nearly so bad now with the steam. Made lecture diagrams. Then letter writing till 7 and Dodd to supper. Had something which hopelessly upset me – sick as a cat about *Appell* time, and too ill to undress. However about 11 I got up, undressed and went to bed and all right next morning.

Dec. 3rd Fairly all right this morning, though not quite A1. Walked round field with Lloyd. R.C.S. Committee 10.30–12, preceded by photo of Cantabs organised by Sands [a science teacher in the camp school] – all sorts of funny people turned out. Cut invigilation. Lecture diagrams in afternoon, to concert in evening. Singing good, but instrumental bad. Ludlow made a complete mess of the *Kreuzer*. Dodd and supper and so to bed.

[Insert: p.c. message from Chairman A. C. Ford of the Camp School Office saying that books have arrived from Board of Education in London]

[Insert: programme for Sunday Concert 3rd Dec. conducted by Mr. E. L. Bainton]

Cambridge graduates at Ruhleben. Centre of back row: Douglas Jones; centre of front row: Michael Pease, Tom Marshall and Arthur Ponsonby

Dec. 4th Lecture at 9. Then found a whole lot of books had arrived for me from Board of Education. They were really ordered for the library but as they were sent to me personally, I put my name in them and put them in the library with the intention of pinching them after the war. Got into a row with Barrett[292] for cutting invigilation yesterday, but as I was giving some books, he only told me off mildly! Wrote out draft letter for Howat re Bar. 6 and gave it to him. Lot of bulbs came for R.H.S. and I gave Cooper a hand putting in some opposite the baths: his bed is full of couch [grass] so I prophesy hard times. To A.S.U. Schnitzler evening – quite well acted, but the man's cynicism passes understanding. Had Bell in to supper afterwards and we discussed them.

[Insert: programme for the A.S.U. Arthur Schnitzler evening – "Literature", a one act comedy]

Dec. 5th Two good bits of camp politics today! 1. Pritchard resigned from Bar. 10 captaincy about the memorial to King and Queen. Powell wanted to have space left for him to sign his name and "captain of the camp", and Pritchard had this deleted; hence row. Pritchard told off Powell and resigned. All the best people in the camp have been on the captain's body and then resigned! The other event is renewed activity of A.S.U. aggressive people: had a packed meeting of the Musical Society and deposed Bainton from his position as musical member of Entertainments Committee – but only by three votes. Great indignation by orchestra, who are not represented on the Musical Society, protest meeting at 2 p.m. and Johnson buzzing around all over himself at having a fight. If the A.S.U. are in for a fight with the orchestra and musicians, perhaps the R.C.S. will stand a better chance. To the dentist today and had stump of tooth ground away.

Dec. 6th Very poor game of hockey this morning. Otherwise read Montessori. Davies was good enough to put the microtome in order again this afternoon. Wimpfheimer in to tea who talked at length on finance and so forth – interesting. Then Nash and Dodd to supper – who talked at great length and persistence on his thesis about music, sex, and sentimentality.

---

[292] Possibly Robert Guy Lionel Barrett (1884–1974), living in Würzburg in 1914. In 1912 he had translated Rilkes *Das Marien-Leben* poems into English, and after the war translated *Alice in Wonderland* into German.

In many points his childishness simply takes my breath away! Strong rumour Bukarest [*sic*] has fallen.

Dec. 7th Worked on final lecture all morning, except when at dentist, who says he thinks other tooth has been killed by the shock. Botany in afternoon, and to *Pygmalion* in evening with Bell – good.

[Insert: programme for *Pygmalion,* produced by Archibald Welland]

Dec. 8th Lechmere got some steel filings in his eye, so not able to lecture today. Morning reading Montessori and darning. Afternoon ditto. Higgins and Blagden to supper – great do about Bar. 6 on – been sharing out the room, and going fairly amicably, though the A.S.U. has no end of a huge opinion of itself and the importance of its work.

Dec. 9th To dentist this morning and had a plaster cast for the tooth made. Then reading Montessori on the teaching of language – very suggestive. Botany in afternoon. Got my great rubber boots and wore them for the first time. *Nature* of Nov. 2nd has notice of R.C.S. program which I sent it earlier in the term.

Dec. 10th R.C.S. Committee 10–1 and 2–4.30 about new space arrangements. Rather afraid we were stampeded by Patters' vote and motion; declined to proceed with the scheme until amalgamation was effected. To concert – good, then Marshall to supper. New regulations about *Appell,* which is to take place at 11.15 a.m. of all rotten times.

[Insert: plan for the layout of the camp school]

[Insert: programme for Special Symphony Concert, Sunday 10th December. Conductor: Mr. E. L. Bainton]

Dec. 11th Lecture at 9 – v. cold and only about 15 turned up, owing, I suppose, to no *Appell*! Then spent the morning looking for fuses and ultimately borrowed a pair from Nebel. Didn't go to A.S.U. to hear Henry on Bocquet, and didn't miss much either. Saw Hatfield about belly stoves for cubby holes. Committee R.C.S. to consider letter about scheme: ultimately agreed to Ford's drafts, as against Jones'; and so to bed much in doubt if we have done the right thing. Finished Montessori.

Dec. 12th Perfect morning. Started reading the Darwin memorial volume.[293] To dentist in afternoon and got crown fixed, but neighbouring tooth is dead and has to be hollowed out.

Dec. 13th [no entry]

Dec. 14th Quiet morning – read Well's *Mr. Britling.*[294] Masterman in to tea to discuss A.S.U. situation and stayed to supper. Read *Mr. Britling* again and finished him off in bed – good reading as is all Wells. Drunks brought in who kept us awake all night – didn't sleep till 6 a.m.

[Insert: handwritten postcard from Y.M.C.A. Ruhleben office, 14th Dec.

Dear Mr. Pease, Just a note calling your attention to the three open discussions at our Xmas conference – the Social Problem, Business, National Temperament, regarded from the Christian standpoint. The discussions will be of the freest nature and if you are interested, you are cordially invited to attend and take part. The arrangements will be published by poster on Monday. Yours sincerely, Alex. K. Bodin, YMCA Secretary]

Dec. 15th The Barrack spent the day making an infernal row outside the cells – a sort of counter demonstration against the drunks. Last of Lechmere's Echinoderms today. Afternoon 1.30–5 at A.S.U. meeting. Sat with Jones and Masterman and very dull it was too. Patchett was clean off his head and did no end of harm. Ford made a bad beginning, by raising a hopelessly small point about the research chemists, who affiliated themselves to the A.S.U. – bless 'em I hope they appreciate the auspices! Unfortunately, I was drawn to ask why I was not included among the research workers and when Higgins asked what I had contributed I could say "please I paid 50 Marks towards the equipment." The amusing thing was, that in order to swell their importance they had a great beat up of circles and bragged no end in their report of the circles' work. Now when it came to the constitution question the circles demanded representation, and so persistently that the meeting was prolonged and not finished so the

---

[293] *Darwin and Modern Science; Essays in Commemoration of the Centenary of the Birth of Charles Darwin and of the Fiftieth Anniversary of the Publication of the Origin of Species.* Edited by A. C. Seward. Cambridge University Press, 1909.

[294] *Mr. Britling Sees It Through* is H.G. Wells's 'masterpiece of the wartime experience in England' published in 1916.

whole thing was adjourned. The meeting was obviously packed against us, with orders to shout. Owing to the adjournment Masterman didn't get an innings. In the meantime things have reached an impossible position with regard to the building, because the A.S.U. decline amalgamation, and the captains have acceded to our recommendations not to proceed till we have amalgamated. After supper my Bi departmental meeting. Edge, Hill, Lechmere, Neville and self there. Talked of things in general about Bi and I got elected to the R.C.S. Committee. I hear they have pursued Bainton and turned him off the R.C.S. Committee and we have Dale instead. In many ways that may be better, but I'm sorry for Bainton.

Dec. 16th Not much doing in the morning. Wrote p.c. to H.B.W. Botany class in afternoon consisted of Mr. Dodd solo, so I spent the time putting away the apparatus and tidying up. Then writing letter home and to Italian Circle – Cutayar on D'Annunzio. Dodd not in to supper – got *Urlaub* till 10 p.m., and so to bed and *Aus Meinem Leben* – the latter apt to be tedious in parts.

....

HBW to MSP: (receipt date unknown, but reply from MSP on 16 Dec. is below)

12 Beaufort House, Beaufort Street, Chelsea

Nov. 19th 1916

Dear Mr. Pease,

I positively look forward to the Ruhleben postcard, because you keep your end up so well. Father says that if you want any help with your Camp School or research work, you should write to Count Helmuth von Molkte, whom he knows, or to Prince Max of Baden who has the reputation of doing the decent thing by prisoners. But of course I don't know if you can write to 'vons' without having your head cut off. However to return to the postcards – you don't seem to realise that the possession of a friend in a German Camp enables one to speak with authority on the shortage of food stuffs in Germany and exactly what Hindenburg said to the Kaiser, – and you waste over a line, 15% at least, on thanks and good wishes! I want to know how you live, who your friends are, if you play scaat and "66" and whether "Entbehren sollst du, sollst entbehren" [Thou shalt forego, shalt do without] *is the length and breadth of your Faust, is whether you realise that when the clock went and struck he had discovered the merits and beauties of the Single*

Tax. Do you read it with a German 'Michael' dressed up as Margarete? Talking of Margarete reminds me of a 'funny story', such as you love! – A certain English M.P. lay wounded on the field of battle when he beheld a large German advancing towards him with a bayonet. Hastily recalling the lessons of his school days, the M.P. fixed a pathetically enquiring eye upon the enemy and murmured "Er Liebt mich?" "Liebt mich nicht?" [He loves me? Loves me not?], *ending, in tragic tones as the bayonet got very near, "Er liebt mich nicht!" The bayonet faltered, and the German flung himself on that M.P.'s neck, hailing him as a fellow disciple of the Master. – This is a true story –*

Do you lecture in that school, and what on, and is your audience appreciative? I hope you have other subjects (say cheese mites) besides fossil ferns which strike me as cold and unsympathetic at best, and besides must have a dangerous tendency to encourage Toryism. Don't you realise now what the pc has to say?

T.Uism is going beautifully, though I find it very different from the peaceful paths of science. – I arrange the socials and join in the dances – of course you know the importance of this side of T.Uism for females! I have discussed the "problem of the East End" with that delightful man Mr. Heath of Toynbee Hall,[295] *and endeavoured to explain to other settlement workers that Christians and T.Uism are not mutually exclusive. Life has of course its little ups and downs, as for instance when I have to attend simultaneously to two strikes at opposite ends of London. You find too that a strike is caused more often by a manager calling his workers 'hands' than by the sweating wages he pays. This shows a fine idealistic spirit and a realisation of the dignity of the individual, but is more difficult to deal with. – My real difficulty though lies not in the work or the play, but the pay. You see I work for nothing, because I can afford to, and because I doubt if I should get the work unless I did, but the paid organisers are inclined to regard me as a blackleg (<u>who</u> is worse than being a bluestocking.) What is the solution please? It is good work and I am getting on.*

Here is another – Josiah (known at Bedales as the Infant) has grown 6 ft, got into khaki and insists on falling in love. He is my youngest brother, and ought to know better. Now is it my duty to encourage him to go in and win or to adopt the maternal tone and turn his trousers into shorts? At what age may a Bedalian make a fool of himself? This is a serious question of practical politics, as practical as the great question of Shall We Make The Women Work which is now agitating the grey heads of the few males left in the country. If they do I am afraid my next

[295] A social reform 'settlement' in East London, of which John Heath was warden (1914–1917).

letter will be dated from Wormwood Scrubs, for as a convinced Anarchist I could never submit to State interference.

With best wishes,

Yours very sincerely,

Helen Bowen Wedgwood

....

MSP to HBW:

Ruhleben, Dec. 16th 1916

Your reproval of Nov. 19th received and I hasten to make amends. (1) There are extremely nice people here including several of my Cambridge friends: but the continual and inevitable presence of the none too clean sailor and stoker makes life very trying – my loathing of the profanum vulgus grows apace. (2) I'm hurt if you think I waste my time at cards – hockey and tennis are my recreations. (3) Faust part I is intelligible, but part II can mean anything you choose to read in to it. (4) I lecture in the school and only because it is appreciated. Next term I take sea weeds – I hope that sounds more liberal! (5) The case of the "infant" can only be judged on its merits – I've no general abstractions on the subject. (6) Many thanks for your father's advice: Prince Max has already visited us, and been most helpful. MS Pease

....

Dec. 17th Wrote letter home. Walked round field in awful slush with Bock:[296] quiet evening tearing up letters and reading.

[Insert: mimeographed note from Leigh Vaughan Henry and Horace G. Hunt (A.S.U. sub-committee) about heating the cubby holes]

Dec. 18th Frittered away the morning tiresomely with odd jobs – amongst others brought in the rest of the bulbs. After lunch set to to mend N's old mackintosh. Marshall came in and we discussed proposed R.C.S. constitution – we both criticised and after tea went down with Jones and Ford to the office and I proceeded to draft a new form on the council and executive scheme. Coming away from the office I ran full tilt into the new

---

[296] Charles Richard Bock (1879–1969). Born in Scotland, the son of German (Hamburg) parents who became British citizens in 1890. Bock worked in his father's export/shipping business before the war, and continued as a merchant after his release.

wire netting on my way towards Spandau [latrines]. Caught my face an awful whack on the barbed wire and came away with both eyes bleeding profusely. The lid of the left eye fairly badly cut with a barb, and also the brow of the right. Washed them well out, and tried to find Lambert[297] to see if it was serious – not I think. Couldn't find him so went and had supper with Ponsonby (by appointment) and then to Lambert. The *sanitäter* [medic] gave me some boric acid, said it was well cleaned out and told me to *melden* [report] myself next morning. Been a further meeting of joint committee today – Powell very on for the new building. In the London matric. exam that's going on, Patchett set in the English paper that famous notice about lining up [Sept 27th], to be put into correct and intelligible English.

Dec. 19th Spent all morning R.C.S. constitution mongering. Afternoon continued repairs on waterproof, saw Marshall and got amendments typed. Quiet evening reading *Aus Meinem Leben*. Doctor saw eye and said it was clean and going nicely. Sent off 3 standard xmas cards.

[Insert: medical appointment card]

Dec. 20th Morning dissipated sewing and drawing in midst of which Pender came in to see me with a brand new scheme for reorganising the R.C.S! Took it very politely and like a cabinet minister said it would receive my earnest attention. R.C.S. Committee 2.30–4.30. Made solemn protest against the theatre and defined the space we required. Synagogue discussed for long time. Science Circle 6.30, Chadwick on Planck's quantum theory. Then race up and down the front, but Patchett very heavily beclogged froze on to me and so we only waddled. So to bed and Goethe.

Dec. 21st Morning reading the Darwin memorial volume. Afternoon to Y.M.C.A. conference on social problems – a most dismal affair. Pearce in the chair and opened by a dreadful American who never got further than saying with a most awful twang, "now what is the Social Problem" this for

---

297 Stanley Harrison Lambert (1872–1950). Internee in charge of the Schonungs Barrack (invalids' and convalescents' barrack) located in Bar 19. He married in Gluckstadt, Germany in 1898, and on his daughter's baptism record (1909) he is listed as a commercial clerk, with addresses in Gluckstadt and Streatham, London.

half an hour. Situation rendered very piquant at one stage by Pearce declaring himself an atheist!

Dec. 22nd Morning rather wasted on odd jobs, but got in some time on Chamberlain's Histology. Got the Minot going, but she didn't ribbon perfectly. Worked away at it all evening. The young Graf and the Major had a great "pogrom" yesterday – went into Bar. 13 in a fuming state and ordered all the "snugs" and partitions to be pulled down and generally cursed the Jews up and down. This evening at the theatre the Graf was there with the young Graf, the Major and some of their women kind. The old Graf made his usual great Xmas speech – about all he'd done for us to "*mindern*" our "*Los*" [reduce our lot] and so forth – (fresh from the pogrom) and finally he hoped we'd soon be out and able to enjoy "*weibliche verkehr*" [female traffic] which was rather strong!

Dec. 23rd Morning reading, afternoon staining slides and then Bell and Silberman to supper.

Dec. 24th R.C.S. Committee 10–12 and 2–4.30. Constitution on agenda. I moved my amendments, supported by Jones, Marshall, Blagden and Wimpfheimer but violent attack led by Patchett supported by the commercial crowd and the backwoodsmen. Division taken after lunch, beaten by 4–7. Then Patchett's scheme discussed and beaten also – to my delight. Then rest of scheme adopted. Jones and I both very sick at the way the committee toothed [talked]. Scene between Jones and Patchett – Jones talked about the "folly of this committee" and P. said "the folly of some of its members, you mean" J – "yes" and then P. wanted an explanation and substantiation and so on: so Jones replied very coolly and effectively. P. very rude and overbearing. Apparently we missed an *Appell* and speech by the Graf announcing final agreement about the 45-ers, and the usual sentimental Xmas stunt. Hideous amount of drunkenness at night, though our Barrack was fairly quiet. Nebel and a friend, both dead drunk, came to pay Milner a visit, but mercifully they managed to negotiate the door and get out again after many good nights and best wishes!

Dec. 25th A wonderfully mild morning. Up early and watched a beautiful sunrise from the field. J and I about the only people out. Quiet morning and then worked in lab all day. Extraordinary proceeding to get drunk in the middle of the afternoon, but that seemed the fashion here. Had supper in Dodd's loft; included a roast goose which made much comment, and a bottle of very ersatz champagne – red in colour! Dodd went away to *Lazarett* to play to the sick, and so the party broke up and I went to cubby hole and wrote letters. At bedtime I took my lamp, Goethe, and overcoat and settled down in a chair in Dodd's loft – no earthly good going back to Barrack. Presently joined by Dodd and Marshall, and the latter ultimately stayed and slept there. Great stir in the loft adjoining as some drunks had broken in there to steal the beer that was stored there, and the police were rounding up stragglers. About quarter to eleven the door of the loft burst open and a drunk staggered in and asked if there was anything doing. I leapt up and he retreated out and stumbled down the stairs. I shut the door and Dodd joined me and we were just going back when several returned and demanded to be let in and then began to shove, pull and batter the door; we held firm and eventually they went off only to return again in 5 mins with reinforcements and loud curses and abuse. We returned fire and eventually one said "Well, who are you any way?" So Dodd replied "We're the musical crowd" – "God help us" was the reply and they crashed off down the stairs. We then sallied forth to survey – the place fairly quiet. Met Jones and returned to Barrack – very quiet except for Swale's box where Milner and Perrot were making considerable stir. Jones and S. also there but the party broke up and came to bed about midnight.

Dec. 26th According to all accounts the camp was in an awful state last night – not only sailors but people like Masterman and Farmer as drunk and noisy as lords. Went round and saw Dodd, none the worse for the night excitement, but developed flu in the course of the day. Quiet morning – afternoon in lab and in the evening, by invitation of Pritchard, to music in Dodd's loft. Quartettes by Mozart and Haydn and Fergusson sang. Long conversation with Bröse on maths, Bertrand Russell, and the shortcomings of English textbooks. Altogether a very pleasant evening lasting till about 10 pm.

Dec. 27th Spent most of morning getting my hair cut and the rest trying to find out if Olivier spelt his name with a 'y' or an 'i' and eventually plumped for 'i' and delivered the letter to censor. Rawson in to supper and long talk on all sorts of affairs. Pressed him to repeat the musical evening.

Dec. 28th Quiet morning reading Darwin volume – lab in afternoon. Marshall to supper and discussed R.C.S. politics.

[Insert: Herzliche Weihnachtsgrusse [Merry Xmas] card from the Neumeister family]

Dec. 29th Quiet morning. Marshall in at lunch time re R.C.S. politics – on for caucus meeting tomorrow. Played hockey 2 p.m. Wrote p.c. to Neumeister. Masterman in to supper and discussed reforms for R.C.S. Marshall told some wonderful stories about Powell – inter alia that at one stage he had asked money to be voted to him for bribery and corruption – and about the Graf, who went straight from the theatre where he made his pious speech to the soldier's *Schmaus* [banquet] and told them not to relax with us and to "remember that England was their *Hauptfeind* [main enemy]"

Dec. 30th Caucus at 9.30 – Wimpfheimer, Pritchard, Mackenzie, Blagden, Jones, Marshall and self present. After some discussion agreed to accept Masterman's plan of 5 members elected direct by general meeting. Went to find Ford, but found him in bed with flu. Came back to box to find invitation to "gala" performance of *Mikado* at 3.30 – first time I've been recognised as a "camp worker" – it's generally only the hewer of wood and drawers of water at 10 marks a week that get any privileges. However I went there, sat next to Patters (curious irony!) in a very good seat and had full view of the Americans who were seated at tables in the middle with the captains to entertain them, master Croad flirting vigorously with Embassy typists. Graf and officers, and Ambassador made up the company of the 1st class. Strange to find oneself in a crowd of real women, talking appalling American and perfumed to a degree. Even the prosaic Patters murmured to me how sad it was that there were so few pretty faces among them! Dodd in to supper after the show, walked up and down with Vincent and so to bed.

[Insert: letter from the Entertainments Committee about ticket allocation of *The Mikado*]

[Insert: ticket for a Gala Performance of *The Mikado*]

Dec. 31st Quiet morning. Invigilated 12–1, and then to lab. Supper at Dodd's; Ford and Philips there: small quantity of red wine provided, but quite enough to make Jones very excited and tell obscene stories about Byron. Dodd suddenly displayed a lamentable ignorance of the English romantic poems combined with a virtuous desire to know more by putting Ford and I through a great examination about Byron, Shelley, Keats and so on. J. called very vigorously for more wine and sent off Philips who searched in vain. I went off and finished my letter home and returned and slept in Dodd's loft on the floor, and very pleasant it was too – right under the window with the cool air blowing in. The camp was pandemonium – even at 4 a.m. when I sallied forth, there were still crowds singing "Are we downhearted". Walter Dodd[298] with difficulty fended Masterman, Fisher and co from visiting Arthur at about midnight; luckily – I shouldn't have liked to defend the loft against the Masterman crowd!

....

Marjory to MSP (letter 274, date of receipt unknown):

The Pendicle, Limpsfield, Surrey

4th December 1916

I have today sent you one of George's [fn 31] *blankets and two pairs of his socks and your pair of boots which I soaked well in Nicolas's military oil. Two other blankets have been sent to you from Edinburgh. I expect Xmas will have come and gone before this letter and the parcels reach you. I go on feeling how thankful I should be that N. is at the base and likely to be there for two months. Unless indeed he gets what he wants and is transferred to the R.F.C.*

I am writing this from my office and shortly going to the Parsons' to dinner and take midnight train to Wigan, breakfast there and then go to Leigh and reach the camp at 10am. I hope to catch up the Scotch express and get to Kinfauns at 9 pm tomorrow. It is a tiring journey but I think it is worth doing. I am going armed with a liver sausage, bought in Soho, flowers, jam, mince pies, chocolate, etc, etc. and I will send more at Xmas. Becher is, I think, still felling timber in Yorks. Who could ever have thought three years ago that I should be buying sausages etc for German prisoners and a football to send to Nicolas in France for his platoon!

I have had a very nice letter from Mrs. Jones. It seems she sends her son endless parcels of food and has had sent him boots and socks three months ago. It is too bad that Jones never gets them. I only hope that you will get all the parcels I and others have sent you during November. We don't feel at all happy about the new regulations for parcels. Everything must be got at shops and I can send you no more cakes, jam, apples, eggs. I do feel very sad about it. Sending your parcels was one of my few pleasures nowadays. Oh! How I hope it is not a severe winter. It will

---

[298] Arthur Dodd's brother, also a golfer.

add tenfold to your hardships. I see by the papers you have had a bishop! Not much your style nor mine!

I have asked Gertrude Ansell[299] *for Xmas and we shall probably have two Belgian soldiers who get a week's leave. You know you are never out of my thoughts and I long desperately for you.*

Every loving thought,

from your devoted mother.

....

[299] A suffragette, animal rights activist, and member of the Women's Social and Political Union.

1917 Diaries and Letters

Jan. 1st Got up at 7.45 am went down to box (all sound asleep) and to bath. Took tea up to Dodd's loft and had breakfast. Went back to box and brought S. up for breakfast; J still hopeless, very blue and the worse for last night. Took no lunch, and very ginger at tea. Appears he joined Masterman. However we had considerable fun in ragging him. I proved my fitness by playing hockey in the afternoon. From all accounts the pandemonium and scenes were beyond precedent in the history of Ruhleben: disgusting and inexcusable. To Dodd's loft in the evening. Marshall and Pauer[300] played Mozart Sonatas and later S. joined and they played a Beethoven trio – a very pleasant way of spending the evening, cf. the night before.

Jan. 2nd Day of pouring rain: enrolling at the school 9–11 and 2–4 – not much doing. Meeting at 4 p.m. of "cave" (Jones, Wimpfy, Pritchard, Mackenzie, Marshall, Blagden and self) and Ford and Patchett. Terrible two hours waste of time! Evening in lab.

Jan. 3rd Enrolling again, but I worked in the lab most of the time. 6.30 pm R.C.S. Committee – a lamentable scene. Ford at his worst and weakest in the chair – gave over completely to Patchett's scheme and wants the committee to adopt the plan – although on Sunday it had turned the scheme down! Marshall proved adept at polite obstruction – when P. saw he wasn't going to get his way by a snap vote he got very abusive, called Jones a consummate ass and generally slashed round. Ford just sat there blinking behind his spectacles and said nothing. Eventually the matter was "talked out" and no division was taken. Long talk outside the barrack with Marshall and Ford in which we all gave F. some good home truths!

Jan. 4th *Strafe Appell* [punishment roll call] this morning at 8 a.m. made an unusual *betrieb* [business] in the early hours. Hung about all morning for

---

[300] Possibly John Story Pauer (1891–?), son of the famous pianist Max Pauer. In a letter written in 1920 Michael mentions a meeting with his Ruhleben friend Pauer, son of Max Pauer. The *BBC Radio Times* 1 Aug 1941 says 'during the last war, interned in Berlin, he [the pianist John Pauer] formed an orchestra in the internment camp and conducted every Gilbert and Sullivan opera. After the war he became a professor at the Royal Academy of Music'. Records show a Waldemar Ernst Pauer (musician) at Ruhleben – did he change his name to John Story Pauer after the war? 'Story' was his mother's maiden name.

the Major to sign the alcohol *erlaubnisschein* [permit] and eventually gave it to Becker. 2 p.m. R.C.S. Committee. Blagden not there but we three sat tight and opposed Patters. Ford played us false – changed his mind and showed himself a complete Patchettite. Eventually lost by 6–3 – we tried to contest Bainton's vote, but in vain. Marshall in to tea and discussed things further. Then to Mozart evening in Dodd's loft to celebrate Pritchard's birthday: very nice indeed. Finally a caucus meeting in our box to decide on precise action and ticket, in event of victory.

Jan. 5th Spent morning whipping up. First saw Higgins – very reasonable and undertook to raise no cross-issues. Then to Heather [Spanish tutor] as per agreement, but found he'd already been hopelessly got at by the other side and started the old story of every up to date educational institute having a large body of governors and sub-committees – word for word from Patters. Saw Lloyd who consented to stand, and then rushed round whipping up all and sundry. Meeting at 2 p.m. – good crowd: all went well till point of confirming election pro forma. Duncan Jones wanted to know why he hadn't been summoned to meeting of English department – this resulted in motion and amendments and the like by MacKenzie and Wimpfheimer. Finally motion agreed to confirming all elections except Patchett's. Then we came to Patchett's motion about ⅔ majority – great set type-written speech. Wimpfy said that such a motion was out of order. Ford shilly shallied at his very worst, and said he didn't know. Mackenzie thanked the Prof. on behalf of the teachers for reading them an essay which he was sure was a pearl of English composition worthy of the head of the English dept. – roars of laughter. Pritchard pointed out that to be logical P.'s motion should require a ⅔ majority and so on ad infinitum. Finally Steer [Spanish tutor] moved that P.'s motion require a ⅔ majority – this was lost by 21 to 27 votes: then P.'s motion put and declared carried by Ford. Loud protests, after count the motion was lost by 45 to 37, so we scored first blood. P. was "*wütend*" [angry], said if the amendments were carried he knew ⅓ of teachers would resign. Jones on his feet at once and made him withdraw. Then Masterman moved his amendments in a short clear and able speech – seconded by Pritchard, not so good as usual. Jones in support and then we adjourned in good spirits – think we shall win easily. Ford came in, in a great state of distress, and we told him fairly frankly how things were, he so obviously doesn't mind which scheme gets through as long as he remains chairman. Masterman also came in in good spirits: later Dodd and Silberman came in and we talked of the possibilities of being taken out to work on the land – seemed to think that was very likely. Truelove came in and told me that with the alcohol *schein* [licence] getting into the *Zahlmeister's* [paymaster's] hands it has been turned down he simply wrote "*nicht lieferbar*" [not available] across it – damnable. Adjourned meeting for next day.

Jan. 6th Spent morning whipping up. At lunch time Masterman, Ford, and Patters seen in close confab. And it appears that Patters will climb down rather than be beaten again in a straight vote at the meeting. We agreed to insert a clause reviving my old pet, the Board of Studies,[301] for advisory purposes only. The funny thing was then when we got to the meeting, apparently Wolff and Bell had not been squared, and stuck to their guns, and insisted on the committee's silly-ass amendment being put. So after some delay the meeting started, and Masterman put his modified scheme. Then Ford, bound by sense of duty, immediately put the committee's amendment, and then Mack and Wimpfy were in their element, "was an amendment to amendment in order", "can the committee logically propose amendments to its own scheme?" and so on: after an hour the amendment was withdrawn and debate on Masterman's briefly resumed; Nash made a telling speech (after noodle) against, but all the other speeches were in favour: good speech by Marshall, and I briefly replied to a wild speech by one of the moral brigade. Division 53 for and 30 against – so much for the "wild goose scheme" brought forward by school boys. Then Masterman proposed Ford as chairman and election for committee resulted in Jones 58, Marshall 55, Lloyd 46, Bell and Wolff 39 each, Andrews 34. Andrews would have got in if only he had not been proposed and seconded by Hunt and Bröse. Bell elected on re-vote, both of them as sick as muck at doing so badly. Strange how completely they miscalculated the feeling of the teachers! Marshall, Masterman, and Pritchard all round to our box having mutual congratulations on victory: I was nicely thanked for my whipping up. Patchett, strange to say, very friendly. He froze on to me and walked up and down and gave me a fine jaw on not throwing up work in a fit of temper, and how we must all put in and work hard! Very satisfactory campaign.

---

[301] The Board of Studies comprised the Camp School department representatives, who had previously been on the R.C.S. Committee.

[Insert: draft constitutions for the A.S.U. and the school, amendments to the school draft constitution, and a R.C.S. finance report for Nov 1916]

Jan. 7th Enjoyed a nice quiet day after all the campaigning but Jones had a whole day of committees. Invigilated in library 12–1, and then by invitation to tea at Cookson's at 3.45, out of "*lauter freundlichkeit*" [sheer friendliness] apparently. Bell into supper and long talk, and so to bed and Goethe – latterly it's getting rather long winded and dreary.

Jan. 8th Somewhat interrupted morning – the *Appell* adds greatly to the waste of time. Afternoon in lab, distilled my precious xylol and saw Truelove who says it's no go with Leitz on that matter. Quiet evening reading Waggett's essay in the Darwin volume.

Jan. 9th Quiet morning interrupted only by the *Appell*. Afternoon microtoming. Darbishire to supper and coached him in our needs. Finished *Dichtung und Wahrheit* in bed.

Jan. 10th Finished the Darwin vol. at last, so now free to start on *Algae* – that is going to be rather a job! In the lab at the microtome. Started *Eugenie Grandet*[302] in bed.

Jan. 11th *Nichts von belang* [nothing of relevance]

[Insert: notice of meeting of Board of Studies for 12th Jan]

Jan. 12th Had first meeting of Board of Studies today at 2 p.m. Put Patchett in the chair, but nothing much happened; went away after an hour. 6.30 meeting of R.H.S. Committee – put in application for race course for cultivation purposes.

Jan. 13th Not much on. Interrupted morning and afternoon. Wrote letter home. P.C. from Johnson that all books [ordered] are prohibited.

....

HBW to MSP (date of receipt unknown):

12 Beaufort House, Beaufort Street, Chelsea

6th Dec. 1916

---

[302] Novel by Balzac.

Dear Mr. Pease,

You are probably staggering from the post office under a load of Xmas and New Year letters and parcels, but I should like to add my greeting to all the others and wish you as happy a Christmas and New Year as is possible. Also that by this time next year you may be running that experimental farm, and teaching both cabbages and agricultural labourers to rise above "their proper stations". After serious debate as to what to send you, the propagandist got the better of the humanitarian, and I decided on a book instead of a slab of Cambridge chocolate. I hope it isn't too great a disappointment. The book is a collection of parables by the American writer Bolton Hall, and I hope it has arrived. – Father and I find them invaluable for speeches. I recommend specially to your attention "The Rows of Belts", and the "Woodpeckers' Tree System", and the "Advance of Slavelization".

Talking of propaganda, I have somehow strayed into the dusty quarters of the Fabian Society and find myself set down to answer V.S.F. letters etc. How I got there is still a mystery, for I have long ago repudiated Sydney Webb and all his ways. I think it must be a subtle attempt to "permeate" me, but I do not catch germs easily! I have been hoping your Father would make a personal attempt at conversation, but I have not met him yet.

I have just started your Mother's fine book on Jaures.[303] *I always knew he was a dear, but that bit in page 37 about walking across the fields – "I have said to myself suddenly that it was the Earth that I was treading, that I was hers and she mine..." completely won my heart. – So many socialists seem unable to live away from asphalt – this is a special grievance with me at the moment, as two of them have just exhorted me (in terms worthy of John Knox) to renounce my ill-gotten income and retire to a tenement in Hoxton (anywhere but Hoxton!) So you see how active the younger members of C.U.F.S are to save the plutocrat from the burning. C.U.F.S by the way is still going strong, but I should like to point out to you, as a former president, that we are still paying off pre-war debts. – The president tells me that a desperate effort is to be made to retrieve its fortunes by means of a socialist play!*

You used to know my cousin Frances Cornford, didn't you? because we saw her the other day back at Conduit Head; also the two babies Helena and Rupert. It is lucky she has them, or she would find it very lonely at Cambridge as nearly all the

[303] Jean Jaurès, French Socialist leader and peacemaker, assassinated in 1914 – note this was written by a Margaret Pease, not Marjory.

people who used to turn up at her Friday evenings are dead or gone. Mr. Cornford is in munitions.[304]

My work is as usual. To anyone who suggests that T.U. organising is not a patriotic pastime I would point to the edifying spectacle of four extreme pacifists, perched on tables, beseeching and exhorting yelling crowds of munitions workers to return to work (their only idea when they have a grievance is to howl outside the manager's office). How is the school? I was told the other day that "Ruhleben is the only place in Europe where any serious mental work is being done", now doesn't that inspire you with a sense of your responsibilities?

I am getting rather bored with my own style of letter writing, and I expect you are too. What do you say to a series of letters modelled on various masters, beginning with Mme de Sevigny and ending with Lord Chesterfield. You might let me know what you like, the earnest, the frivolous, the sympathetic, the instructive etc. I would like to discourse on the problems of the moment – as "Did Lloyd George throw the inkpot at Asquith?" and "What is the price of caviar, and why?" but that must be left to "John Bull", and besides the censor wouldn't allow it. This at least I may say, with Gerald Massey: "The World is rolling Freedom's way And ripening with her sorrow! The powers of Hell are strong today Our Kingdom come tomorrow."

Yours very sincerely,

Helen Wedgwood

....

HBW to MSP:

Moddershall Oaks

Xmas Day 1916

Dear Mr. Pease,

Just a line to tell you that I have only today! got your pc of Oct 21st, as you may be wondering that I have not answered it. Poor Gladstone to be coupled with Shelley; how horrified he would be! We are a huge party here, and 4 Bedalians viz L. Bendit, J. Bekassy and my brother and sister (who has revelled in her 1st term). Tobogganing is the order of the day, Bekassy being particularly good at inventing breakneck devices. I suppose you are eating plum pudding and German sausages

---

[304] Francis Cornford – a classical scholar and poet. He was a Captain in the School of Musketry and Ministry of Munitions; husband to Frances [nee Darwin], also a poet.

and debating whether to write home letters in the comparative warmth of the loose box or get cold and wet going to the pantomime.

We have several children and therefore an excuse to be jolly in spite of things. And with the snowy frosty woods it is difficult to be anything else!

Best wishes H B Wedgwood

....

MSP to HBW:

Ruhleben, Jan. 13th 1917

Very many thanks for yours of Dec. 6th – and for your good wishes, especially that one about the farm. In fact, however, I am far more likely to find myself, for several years to come, hoeing ordinary cabbages on a German farm than nursing the superior cabbages on my own! I'm looking forward very much to your promised book: I appreciate in not sending the material: I'm sick to death with the hysterical howl about "poor starving prisoners". No, I enjoy your letters immensely, because they tell of activity. All my good relations write about food, or fatuous anecdotes, or gush pious wishes! Work rather at a standstill owing to absence of reagents, but otherwise I'm flourishing and find plenty to do in other directions. Very many thanks for your pc of Xmas day just received. Yours Michael Pease

....

Jan. 14th Blagden and I appeared before R.C.S. Committee to plead for science library, and B had sundry other points to mention. Shortly over. Skating on the pond this morning – a wonderful *Vergünstigung* [privilege]. Then at 2 p.m. statutory meeting of B.O.F. with R.C.S. Committee – not much doing – plan of distribution of space shown. 7.45 p.m. meeting of R.H.S. Paper by Cayley.[305]

Jan. 15th First day of term – but nothing doing in the Bi. Department. Skating still continued. Microtome afternoon and evening. Request for science reading room granted.

Jan. 16th *Nicht neues.*

Jan. 17th [no entry]

---

[305] William Cayley – a sailor from Cardiff.

Jan. 18th Adjourned to A.S.U. meeting in afternoon. We made no preparations, but just turned up to see what was going and vote for committee. Not many there: Wimpfy in great form and Henry, Bocquet and all that crowd as offensively rude as possible. On a vote for committee the old gang were returned plus Farmer and Winzer. The "trueblues" at the meeting voted for old gang only, and as our people scattered their votes, the new people were hopelessly beaten! However, we shall see what happens: the Bainton – Henry feud is now up under a new form viz. an attempt to smash Adler's concert by getting individual members of the orchestra to strike, little Harris very excited and on the rampage. Both sides nobbled Clarke[306] and Bainton refused to teach him harmony if he didn't play, and Conn refused to give him violin lessons if he did. My God, isn't it all mean, petty, spiteful and silly beyond words. Leitz order received – 6.50 for 100 ccs clove oil!

Jan. 19th Great do on about the so called music strike. At supper time Hatfield and Kapp came in in order to ask Jones to influence Marshall and get him to refuse to play. But Jones was very quiet and showed no signs of giving any help in that direction!

Jan. 20th French jaw with Bradney in morning and then sweating away at algae. Afternoon went down to lab to clear up and found everything simply frozen hard, temp about -3°C. So I went in for *energische massregln* [energetic measures], and lit a great fire of paper under the pipes till the steam trap was melted and then the steam started to gurgle through, though still beastly cold for a long time. Great excitement was a real fire this evening at 11 p.m. Just got to sleep when woken up by fire trumpet. Hurtled out of bed and dressed and went out only to find a few sparks flying out of the casino chimney: so returned to bed again. Just like them to rouse up the whole camp for a chimney mildly on fire. Needless to say none of the *vorschrifften* [regulations] that were so publicly placarded in the Barracks were carried out!

Jan. 21st Quiet morning – finished cleaning up lab in afternoon, Denholme helping, brought him back to tea and he told long yarns about the

---

[306] Alfred M Clarke, a violin student.

Stadtvogtei *gefängene* [captives]. Sent out cards scratching lecture until 1.30.

Jan. 22nd First lecture 1.30, but as I forgot about Chemi., I could only go until 2 p.m. Arranged lectures regularly for 7 p.m. on Saturdays. Went to A.S.U. show: good, best bit of women's acting I have seen at Ruhleben. Hall like an ice house. Amazing what an ignorant person Henry is. Talked about "Phlanax upon phlanax"! also "eepics" and "mediums"!

[Insert: programme for A.S.U's Ernst Hardt [German playwright] evening. Introduction by Leigh Henry, illustrated by acts from *Tantis der Narr* (produced by Leigh Henry and Joseph Stein)]

Jan. 23rd Went to committee of R.H.S. Seems that permission is practically granted for cultivation of race course plot, but at a rent of 100Marks a month. They are Jews the way they always make us pay. Dickson[307] put in charge of the whole scheme.

Jan. 24th Worked at Oltmanns in morning. Botany in afternoon. To Science Circle in evening, where I took chair for Lechmere – paper on microtoming. Main excitement was visit from Neumeister at 5 p.m. Very friendly and affectionate – came laden with good things. I gave him a tin of shortbread which he stowed away and I hope got though all right. Somehow ½ an hour went very quickly and we hardly got beyond the usual "*schöne Grüsse*" [best regards] to everyone concerned. Apparently he is the "*ausgeber*" [issuer] of "*Brotkarten*" [bread cards] in Jena and when I asked him if he didn't have difficulties with the exceptional cases, he made the wonderful Deutsch reply "*Es geht alles nach vorsdrift*" [Everything goes according to regulations]. He's very affectionate and faithful and would do more if he could!

Jan. 25th Not much doing – worked at Oltmanns and to R.H.S. meeting at 7 p.m. Butby on Vines. Much talk about those who have volunteered to go out to work: hear Henry has got the job of scenic director at Königliches Operahaus in Berlin. Much big swearing by Tom Sullivan and such true British sports about traitors!

---

[307] J. M. Dickson. An Edinburgh University graduate who taught agricultural chemistry and stock rearing in the Camp School biology department. He was also on the RHS committee.

Jan. 26th Worked at Oltmanns in morning after my French prowl with Bradney. Then to botany class, great crowd – all eight turned up. Letter writing in evening.

Jan. 27th Kaiser's *Geburtstag* [birthday] so usual great do on. *Gottesdienst* [church service] in the Y.M.C.A. with guard in full rig out and all the officers with coal skuttles and all great speeches and no end of a do. Camp took it in very good humour. Typical Deutsche *taktlosigkeit* [tactlessness] to make a great show off in a camp like this. Botany in afternoon and then my alga lecture at 7.

Jan. 28th Fairly peaceful day. Got hold of *Erewhon*[308] again and read it with great joy. Wrote letter in morning, walk round the field with Bell and Warkentin again. To Adler's concert – fairly hideous effort.

[Insert: programme for symphony concert conducted by F. Ch. Adler on Sunday 28th Jan]

Jan. 29th Got a great AmX[309] case of groceries from Selfridge today – oranges frozen hard. Scholes in to supper and long talk – he has completely lost his sense of duration and stayed till bedtime, thinking he'd only been with us half an hour. Very various accounts of Browning show.

Jan. 30th Lechmere rotten with flu and S[chlesinger] this evening also retired to bed with the same complaint. There are several of the *Zivildienstplicht* [voluntary service] people in camp now: their uniform consists of *Schwarz:Weiss:Rot* [Black:White:Red] arm band. They carry guns, but otherwise wear mufti. One of them out with a work gang started abusing the prisoners calling them *schweinhunde* and so on, and on return the matter was reported and old Benzene, I'm told, fairly told off the man. To Dante Circle 5–6. Dodd in Berlin, so quiet supper tête à tête with Jones.

Jan. 31st S. in bed not seriously ill but just rotten. Work as usual on Oltmann's in morning and class in afternoon. Letter from H.B.W. today. Complete failure of light today, owing to cable being broken, with result that (1) My incubators in lab froze up (2) abysmal darkness in the Barracks (3) water supply cut off (drainage pump worked by current) (4)

---

308 Novel by Samuel Butler.

309 American X (express) parcel - relief parcels dispatched via the American Express company.

accumulator can't be charged (5) private bogs shut up and (6) when I got to dentist by appointment he got me in the chair and everything ready and brace myself up for a drilling only to find no current to drive the motor!

[Insert: notice about fundraising concert for heating and lighting of hall]

[Insert: cash accounts for school for Aug–Dec 1916]

....

HBW to MSP (received Jan. 31st):

Moddershall Oaks, Stone, Staffs

Jan. 14th 1917

Dear Mr. Pease,

It is an immoral but a true fact that undeserved blessings are sweetest so I suppose that is why I enjoyed your postcards of Oct 21st and Dec 1st, for after my letter of Nov 19th I cannot be said to have deserved them (they both arrived in Xmas week). I am only worried though lest you should be a person with a sense of duty – a horrid Victorian thing – about answering letters, and should be sending me more than my share. – I am a casual person myself and anyhow, knowing you can only send 4 pcs a month I should quite understand if some letters went unanswered. – Please suppress any <u>conscience</u> on such matters. It was a relief to hear you play hockey – your other occupations sound so strenuous. Aren't you afraid of a reaction to ragtimes and shilling shockers when you get back? I haven't read Montessori – Rosamund (my sister) is the person for that, she considers herself an expert, having to a large extent brought up our small sisters. – Don't you hate 'systems' of education? and the Montessori one in particular sounds too elaborate to be natural. – Surely what children want is to be allowed to take their place as members of the community, with <u>real</u> work to do, like grown ups. Difficulties and getting tired are part of the fun. The jolliest and best education we had was our two years in S. Africa, everyone had to take their part there, and the grown ups were too busy to do much 'educating' beyond reading aloud. If I had children I would bring them up on a farm, with some real work, plenty of time to run loose on their own and reading aloud in the evening. The grown up's business is to tell stories, read aloud, and explain <u>when</u> asked. I think the atmosphere of a friendly and intellectual and physically 'alive' household should do the rest. One wants companionship with elders, not 'interference', and 'education' and 'developing' and 'moulding'. Parents seem to think their children are pots. (Sorry!

As the eldest of seven who liked to muddle along in our own way, and suffered from too much supervision and 'advice' this subject always rouses me.)

I haven't come across the Brahms sextets yet, but will look out for them, as we intend going to lots of concerts. The songs and Hungarian dances which are almost the only things I know of his are glorious.

In spite of your advice to stick to it, I am sorry to say that my career as a T.U. organiser, though brilliant, has been brief. I was literally homesick for science and the country, so as I can't at present go on the land I am going to work under Bateson[310] *at Merton – that is if he will keep me when he discovers how little I know. I feel an utter worm deserting the Federation when the work is so important and the workers so few, and they have been awfully nice to me too, but I just can't, so there it is. People and economics all day drive me crazy. My socialist friends anathematise me as a deserter, – I think I am. Working on the land would bring one into touch with people and provide a good basis for agitation, but I cannot persuade myself that playing round with fertilisation and heredity will assist the East End. Have you solved the difficulty about socialism and science? – You see it doesn't seem much good discovering things when it simply makes the rich richer and does no real good to the mass of the people. Research nowadays is like watering a dead plant. Besides, admirable as is the pursuit of knowledge, you don't study Plato in a burning city. And if scientists and people had turned their brains and energies onto solving human problems we might be saved from this hell. – It is humiliating to be like a beaver, irresistibly compelled to build dams even on dry land. – Of course I mean to keep in touch with the labour movement but science is exacting. Besides scientists are as superior and exclusive as priests, and upper class too. – My real friends are the Herald crowd and the Poplar jam workers, and I would stick the heads of Bateson and Doncaster*[311] *on a pike if it would help them. – However I will get onto the land one day.*

Best wishes for the New Year. Father is hopeful on the whole. Alas I cannot give you even scraps of news about 'them'. I wish we were more active, but all our best are gone. The spirit among us remains splendid. Thanks for your good wishes.

Yours very sincerely, Helen Wedgwood

---

[310] William Bateson F.R.S. (1861–1926), an eminent biologist and a pioneer in the science of genetics. Between 1900 and 1910 Bateson directed an informal 'school' of genetics at Cambridge. His group consisted mostly of women associated with Newnham College (where HBW studied). In 1910 Bateson became the first Director of the John Innes Horticultural Institute at Merton, Surrey. As a Cambridge scientist Pease also knew Bateson (letter in Appendix 2).

[311] Leonard Doncaster (1877–1920). Another Cambridge geneticist.

Feb. 1st Light came on at 6 p.m. today!

Feb. 2nd S. still in bed. Oltmanns in morning, class in afternoon. Dentist 4 p.m. – then theatre queue to change my tickets for Saturday matinee, supper and quiet evening with lecture notes.

Feb. 3rd Morning at Oltmanns. S. went to *Schonungsbaracke* [sanatorium] this morning – afraid it has gone to his chest a bit. Afternoon to matinee of German play. Very good, best acting I've seen in Ruhleben – Dumont makes a wonderful ♀[woman] and play itself good. Lecture at 7 – nice and warm and so to bed.

[Insert: programme for the German musical comedy *Das Konzert* by Hermann Bahr. Producer: Joseph Stein]

Feb. 4th -22°C today. Very bad night. Dick Halpin brought in drunk at 11 p.m. and shouted till 6.30 a.m. Stamp round the field with Jones and Blagden, cut invigilation on account of cold. Read Masterman's paper on party politics in 18th century – 2 excellent stories of Wilkes. Went to concert – well played but not the stuff I like. Bell in to supper afterwards and joined by Bradney, and discussed the relative morality of French and Germans towards ♀s [women]. S. still in bed but better.

[Insert: concert programme and lyrics for Feb. 4th "The Octra", vocalist F. W. Hughesdon]

Feb. 5th Camp fairly excited about the break off of diplomatic negotiations by U.S.A. Owing to breakdown of heating arrangements (-25°C last night) no Browning Show. Spent evening thawing pipes in the lab, which we succeeded in doing at 9.30.

Feb. 6th Cubby hole charcoal supply run out, so am frozen out of that haunt. The man Brown came round to photograph the Lab this morning and took two – very long exposures. Borrowed Dodd's skates and had my first shot on thin ice and didn't do brilliantly! Steam tap in our barrack broken down and the thing plugged up with a stopper. Milner was getting some water, and I came up to help, the plug flew out and a column of boiling water got me on the shin and did considerably damage: bound it up with lint and so on, but it smarted furiously. To concert at 6.30 – mighty fine. Enjoyed hearing the Grieg sonata again, and Fergusson's singing was superb: Little doctor[312] there; and so to bed mighty sore as to the shin!

[Insert: concert programme for Musical Society's "Musical Evening" held in the Loft, Bar. 1, by "kind permission of Mr. Arthur Dodd – please bring a small chair"]

Feb. 7th Leg not quite so irritable this morning and on examination it looked so very much better that I decided not to go to the doctor with it. More especially as I had an appointment with the dentist at 9.30. In course of morning made the discovery that some one had pinched my lecture note book, which did mightily annoy me. In course of afternoon, found Neville had carried it off so at ease again on that score. Went to see S in *Schonungsbaracke* and found him still in bed. 6.30 to Science Circle – Darbishire on sugar.

[Insert: dental treatment receipt for 12Mks]

Feb. 8th Spent morning, after French walk, darning and doing sundry domestic jobs. Sent off parcel of empty jam jars to Neumeister – a longish business. Wonderful sight to see the Jews "*schiebing*" [donating] foodstuffs and things, but the *Unteroffizier* [sergeant] was fairly sharp. Went to the repeat concert – great crowd. I sat in Dodd's den and listened through the wall.

Feb. 9th Did some darning and had a French lesson in the morning. Botany class in afternoon – clearing up the burnt aquarium. Roasted some of Dodd's coffee in the evening on our spirit stove.

Feb. 10th Quiet morning – Botany class in afternoon and lecture in evening. Thaw set in with a vengeance.

[Insert: German newspaper clipping: *Berliner Tageblatt* evening edition 10th February 1917 about food shortages]

---

[312] There are a several references to a 'little doctor' in the diaries; seems to be one of the German medics in the camp.

....

MSP to HBW:

Ruhleben, Feb. 10th 1917

Many thanks for yours of Jan. 14th. Very interested to hear of your new work. I wonder what in particular you are doing. Would you like to root out some of my seeds at Cambridge, and sow out some of my brassica hybrids? I look forward immensely to hearing how you are getting on. No, there's no contradiction between socialism and science, none – though you won't get much sympathy out of Bateson for socialism. I agree most emphatically with your observations on bringing up – but then you must have some "system" for the 99.9% who are born in the cities or of stupid parents. I hope you flourish. I am enjoying the cold enormously – only I long for my skis and for mountain tops. I've just been listening to one of the Grieg violin concertos – ripping! Best wishes M.S.Pease

....

Feb. 11th Spent most of the day writing letter home. Read "What the Public Wants" in bed.

Feb. 12th Great indignation today because of severe examination of parcels by military. Tins being opened and contents poured out.

[Insert: German newspaper clipping: *Berliner Tageblatt* morning edition 12th February 1917, again about food shortages]

Feb. 13th Quiet morning reading Oltmanns. Class in afternoon. Walk with J. and Marshall. Spent evening translating one of Dorothy Osborne's letters for French prose. S. out and about today but still sleeping in S.B. [*Schonungsbaracke*].

Feb. 14th Had my hair cut this morning – always a long and boring proceeding, but by dint of lining up before opening hours got done fairly soon. Domestic crisis precipitated by arrival of 3 enormous parcels of provisions from Selfridge, which it took me the rest of the morning to stow away. Also Bible from Grannie and *Raymond*[313] from the faithful Franklin[314]

---

[313] Possibly *Raymond or Life and Death* a biography of Bedalian Raymond Lodge, written by his father Sir Oliver Lodge after Raymond was killed in Flanders on 14th September 1915.

[314] Possibly Geoffrey Montagu Ernest Franklin (1890–1930) who was at Bedales with Michael.

– very pathetic considering the beastly way R. used to treat F. at school. Cookson in to supper and we talked Ruskin College.

[Insert: note from maternal grandmother "Michael Stewart Pease, with best wishes from M.G.D., Kinfauns Manse, Jan 1917. Proverbs III–5th.6th v. (Trust in the Lord with all your heart etc)"]

Feb. 15th The Havel has risen very high and as a result the pond now extends practically from one end of the racecourse to the other – quite a decent expanse of water. Spent evening translating D.O.'s letters into French and also made a beginning of a piece out of Dizzi. S. out and about again, came in and had tea.

Feb. 16th *Nichts neues.*

Feb. 17th S. returned to the box again – not looking up to much yet. Spent all day on lecture work and delivered same at 7 p.m. Pond floods increased enormously and people skating from the putting green right to the other end of race course.

Feb. 18th Quiet day doing French most of the time.

Feb. 19th Another eventless but interrupted day and not much work done. French all morning. Botany afternoon, Masterman to tea, and set Hill's seed testing class going and so to bed where I chortled over T.W.'s[315] article in the *Berliner.*

[Insert: German newspaper clipping, article by 'T.W.': *Berliner Tageblatt* 19th February 1917]

[2 days missing]

Feb. 22nd Bright and cold. Roberts to supper and then gave lecture to R.H.S. on pure lines. Started Rousseau's *Confessions*. Good so far.

Feb. 23rd French lesson in morning – translations from D.O.'s letters, Prescott, and Weldon. Wonderful afternoon – walked round field. Deutsche Zirkel [German Circle] at 7 to hear Bell on German Romanesque

---

[315] Theodore Wolff – chief editor of the *Berliner Tageblatt*. This article was making fun of the Prussian bureaucracy that was exacerbating the food shortages. The two early *BT* inserts on 10th and 12th of February were also about this topic.

architecture – dullish but cut short by *Appell.* Two escapes again – two boys going out for a night to Spandau – conversation (very lewd!) with soldier who was locking them up, our friend who plastered up the wall for us. Read Loti's *Egyptian essays* in bed – he's very sniffy about the English and, above all, about T. Cookson.

Feb. 24th Most of day putting lecture notes in order and then lecture in evening. Saw Wolff who says permission to get alcohol and xylol finally turned down but that von Borck had himself brought in a small flask of alcohol which he handed over, but he had evidently helped himself liberally to it on the way! However very decent of him to fag.

Feb. 25th Spent most of morning overhauling footgear and afternoon wrote letter home and evening to supper with Bell and long yarn: looked at his architecture books.

[2 days missing]

[Insert: "camp worker" invitation letter to the theatre]

[Insert: 7th Symphony Concert, Tuesday 27th February 1917, conducted by Quentin Morvaren]

Feb. 28th Usual sort of day. French in morning, botany afternoon – walk in field. French – supper – French and again French in bed – reading *Madame Chrysathemum.*

March 1st French lesson and then ditto by self. No botany in afternoon as there was the usual monthly stock-taking of government property. Ours was not tested but Bar. 2 seemed to be having a great do. Farmer and Hodgkinson into supper and longish yarn.

March 2nd [no entry]

March 3rd Most of day putting lecture notes in order and lecture at 7. Letter from home at last today. Yesterday got a p.c. from Ornstein telling me not to be alarmed if I saw a notice of Mother's death in the Daily News.

March 4th Went to R.C.S. Committee and raised points in connections with gardens, staff and our room 7a. Walk in afternoon with Warkentin.

March 5th Screamingly funny leader by T.W. in the B.T. [*Berliner Tageblatt*] about the Mexican blawage.[316] Very cold again -15°C – scratched class and walked myself warm instead. To concert – much better than last time. Did not sit out last two items as I had R.H.S. Committee. Books came today from Johnson: also parcel from Frau Becher containing cakes, eggs and apples – what about the blockade?

[Insert: clipping from the *Berliner Tageblatt* newspaper, 4th March 1917]

[Insert: 8th Symphony Concert, Monday 5th March 1917. Conductors: Bainton and Morvaren]

March 7th The beastliest day we've had this year. Cold N.E. wind and dust. Vaccinated[317] *barrackenweise* [barrack-wise] at 10.30 – surprising to see great healthy louts faint. Scratched botany class and walked round field in clouds of sand. Lined up for Danish bread. Read some Rousseau and Dickson in to supper, and yarned farming shop. So to bed, mighty cold, and read *Cyrano* till my arms froze.

March 8th [no entry]

March 9th Heavy fall of snow – hard work trudging round the field. French at 10. Botany class in afternoon. Cut a bunch of Polyanthus Narcissus for Mrs. Dodd. To work on lecture notes. Warkentin to supper and then to Deutsche Zirkel to hear Silberman on the present positing of German Art. Silberman is very conscious of his German half and took good care to abuse German painters and talk of *unsere* [our] great masters! Futile discussion, and so to bed – box very wet.

March 10th [no entry]

[Insert: agenda for joint meeting of School Committee and the Board of Studies, 11th March]

---

[316] Theodore Wolff's article was about the infamous 'Zimmerman Telegram' sent by the German Foreign Secretary to their Mexican Ambassador in January 1917. It proposed a German alliance with Mexico against the USA if the USA entered the war – in return Mexico would get back their 'lost territory' in Texas, New Mexico and Arizona. The telegram was intercepted by British Intelligence, decrypted and revealed to the USA, which encouraged them to declare war on Germany in April.

[317] Possibly against smallpox, as the disease was reportedly in Berlin at this time.

March 11th Quiet morning letter writing. Afternoon meeting of Board of Studies: dull and stuffy and Patchett opposing the new change tooth and nail. Carried by 11–3.

March 12th Domestic crisis today – 4 great AmX case arrived for me! Going to overflow into Dodd's loft.

[Insert: note from parcel office for 4 AmX cases]

March 13th Went to a mighty fine concert in Dodd's loft. Not such a crowd as last time. The Terzette was a jewel. They brought in more drunks this evening.

[Insert: programme for Ruhleben Musical Society evenings on March 13th and 15th]

[Insert: invitation to the Ruhleben Musical Society evening in the loft of Barrack 1, Tuesday March 13th]

March 14th A drunk in the bathhouse this morning. Just a heap of clothes, a pair of clogs sticking out and a dismal voice saying "I'll know when to get up when its daylight." Extra *Appell* this morning for said gentleman, who was reported absent. Awful lot of drinking going on last few days: more drunks again in the cells this evening and Dodd said that Simmons was bargaining with the Greayers [two brothers – William and Harry] of 12 bottles whisky at 25 Marks a time.

March 15th French walk with Bradney as usual. Finished French essay on Butler, afternoon started on lecture work. Sat in Dodd's cubby hole and listened to repeat concert – very good, better than last time. Walk up and down and so to bed and read *Le Crime de Sylvestre Bonnard.*

March 16th Very excited over good news from Petersburg,[318] one of the most really cheering events since we've come in here. French class in morning, botany in afternoon and at work on Oltmann's in the evening.

[318] Russia's February Revolution (so named because of the Julian calendar that Russians still used at the time) began with an International Women's Day demonstration in St. Petersburg on March 8th.

March 17th Heavy snow again this morning. Botany most of day and lecture in the evening. Some books came for me today, but were delivered over to censors. Heard the true story of Bolle's dismissal.

March 18th Went to Duncan Jones' *School for Scandal* – very good indeed. Asked to speak on co-education for the debating society.

[Insert: programme for *The School for Scandal* produced by C Duncan Jones]

March 19th French lesson and then put a few notes together for debate. I'm annoyed at having accepted. I don't like speaking on so serious a subject before so silly an audience.

March 20th Spent practically all day preparing debate speech – awful business to choose words and phrases which are not open to an indecent interpretation and calculated to call lewd laughter from the audience. However it came off all right, but not as well as I should have liked. I had not had just enough time for my final look over of notes, and I hesitated at points and forgot some of my epigrams. Ford opposed and spoke entirely as a schoolmaster, shirking the broader issues. Any how glad it's over, and it was at least good practice in composition and in speaking. Got £5 from home. Read Wedekind's *Musik* in bed

March 21st [no entry]

March 22nd French in morning – in fact, French nearly all day. Have relegated Rousseau to bed reading but I shall be surprised if I have patience to read him right through – just finished Pt I.

[2 days missing]

March 25th Wrote letter in morning, hockey afternoon, celebrated Schlesinger's 44th birthday in evening. Speed in to supper. S. has just bound my camp mags – mighty fine.

March 26th French lesson, odds and ends in morning. Botany in afternoon and to concert in evening – very good indeed though Harris played the Brahms sonata like a schoolgirl playing exercises. Heard "Oh Isis and Osiris" for the 7th and 8th time! Bell in to supper afterwards and much trouble with the accumulators, which seem to be running out.

[Insert: programme and lyric sheet for Chamber Concert, arranged by Mr. Leslie Harris]

March 27th Morning reading Rousseau – getting very fed up with him and his women. Botany in afternoon and to Musical Evening. S. came away saying he was too old for such music, so I said I supposed I was too young – anyhow none of it made any impression on me. I daresay I should have enjoyed the songs if B.[319] hadn't sung so rottenly. However the Debussy pieces weren't so utterly incomprehensible, quite the contrary.

[Insert: invitation and programme to the Ruhleben Musical Society evening in Barrack 1 Loft 'modern vocal and instrumental music']

March 28th [no entry]

[Insert: programme for French comedy *La Belle Overture*, 28th March 1917. Produced by Maurice Perrot]

March 29th French in morning. Botany in afternoon and French again in evening. Great floods again, found spreading all over field.

March 30th French in morning. Botany in afternoon. B. of S. meeting 4 to 4.30 p.m. – nothing doing. Dale to supper and talk on modern music.

March 31st Departmental meeting of Bi dept. today. Nothing much doing – only L, Hill and self there. Made out plans for our requirements in Room 7. Got letter from the botanical gardens agreeing to let us have flowers if we can send for them. Walk round the field and Franken[320] froze on to me: he was [present] through the Luttich[321] affaire and had rather an exciting time. Then to Historical Circle discussions on Patchett's paper. Desultory remarks by Rawson. Long reply by P. – great attack in clear close argued speech by Bell to which P. made no reply. Then a great exposition of

---

[319] Thomas Edward Bonhote (1885–1970), a professional opera singer. After graduating from Cambridge he went to Milan to study singing (*Hull Daily Mail*, 23rd November 1918). Like many others he was at the Bayreuth Festival when war broke out. After the war he continued as an opera singer, before becoming a Master at Westminster School in 1924.

[320] Johan Lambertus Machiel Franken (1882–1959), a South African, who read Law at Cambridge and was studying Roman Philology in Liege in 1914. He taught Dutch in the Camp School, and post-war he became Professor of French at Stellenbosch University, South Africa.

[321] The Battle of Liege [Luttich in German] – the German invasion of Belgium in August 1914.

Bergonism by Pritchard – which had not the remotest connection with the paper. Came away with Bell and laughed at the solemn Bergonists. They're putting up an enormous double wire netting screen about 30 feet high in the Bar. 6 compound to prevent communication with the house at the end of Bar. 7. As the old carpenter fellow said – *"Ich bin hier 2½ Jahre gewesen und jeden tag wirds toller!"* [I've been here 2½ years and every day it gets better!]

....

HBW to MSP (date of receipt unknown, but MSP replies on Apr. 9th):

12 Beaufort House, Beaufort Street, Chelsea

March 4th 1917

My dear Sir,

Your answers to our questions received with thanks, on the whole we think you are entitled to a first in your examinations. My Latin, I regret to say, has been neglected, but my brother informs me that "profanum vulgarus" is the classical equivalent for "b----y proletariat"

I do sympathise with you deeply; one can only pray that the war may end before the reaction transforms your mental outlook into that of a French Marquis of the 18th century.

I only hope it isn't as uncomfortable as the 5 months that my poor brother spent as a private, sleeping 24 in a room meant for 16, all windows shut and a drunk nearly every night. The only thing that can be said for it is that it increased his vocabulary and gave him a wholesome dislike for drink.

Goethe, I am sure, would be pained at your brief dismissal of Faust Part II; besides you shatter my illusion – I was expecting that you, at least, would have elucidated from it Goethe's conception of the perfect state.

But Goethe's genius is a myth – a knowledge of his works is not in the least assistance in struggling with the German of Correns[322] *"on Variegation". I am learning though to understand the feelings of a draper's assistant – (insufficiently described by H.G.Wells), for a fortnight I have been matching and comparing colours in Primula Sinesis (I expect you know it!) until my sleeping hours are pervaded by an awful policeman (embracing the qualities of Bateson and*

---

[322] Carl Correns – a German botanist and geneticist.

McTaggart) who arrests me under the Defence of the Realm Act and condemns me to be cut into sections for muddling up a pink and a magenta. The work at Merton is simply fascinating, and words will not describe the relief it is to deal with plants again – they are almost the only sane thing left in this world.

Talking of sanity reminds me that we went the other day to the first respectable meeting we have patronised since the war --- a suffrage meeting. We did not know ourselves in such good company, and nearly wept for joy at hearing once more the almost forgotten platitudes. It was a good meeting, and there is little doubt we shall get "our rights" at last (it is an ill war which blows nobody any good) --- but isn't it like their cheek to offer it to women over 30! Do you know Edward Carpenter's new book My Days and Dreams? The account of the beginnings of the modern 'movements' and of the people who led them are fascinating. Really things do seem to have got a move on in the last 20 years. But what an escape to have been born at the end of the century and not in the palmy years of Victorianism. Carpenter made me feel rather remorseful for not having better appreciated what the first comers had to go through, and from how much they saved us.

By an amusing coincidence Father was reading us in an old diary of his, written at the age of 20, an account of how he was sent by your father! to deliver a lecture on Municipal Bakeries to an East End socialist club. On turning up with an elaborate lecture compiled chiefly from the Encyclopaedia Britannica, he found 3 men playing cards, quite unaware of the existence of a meeting! So after calling for your father's blood, he consoled himself by delivering the lecture to Mother instead!

My sister and I spent a delightful weekend at Cambridge, seeing all our friends, and feeling as if we had never been away, as we discussed the various storms in the University teacup. You can guess round what they centred. Sing, Oh Muse, of the ever blossoming folly of Ridgeway and the Trinity Council, and of the joys of a "scrap" (unless like an unfortunate friend of mine you are in the position of being fought over.) For the rest, Cambridge is like a city worked in tapestry, always the same, -- the donkey man with the stools smiles as hopefully as ever, and the aged verger perambulates Silver Street on a tricycle. C.U.F.S. is becoming appallingly strenuous – said on good authority to be by a long way the most "live" society in Cambridge. Some of the members have even organised some of the girls at Saint's into a union. A total disregard of the chaperone rules on the part of the Newnham members has considerably facilitated the running of the society. I expect you remember the effect of 1 dozen Newnhamites walking in preceded by an aged don!

The H.P. Adamses[323] *with their room in Trinity Street were invaluable as a centre, but alas, owing to circumstances affecting a good number of our friends, they have gone; Mr. A. being among those to whom you sent your sympathy. You will see from all these that Cambridge life is as amusing as ever.*

With best wishes,

yours very sincerely,

Helen Bowen Wedgwood.

....

April 1st More or less quiet Sunday. Sad news today, G. K. Scott[324] killed in action on February 24th. To think of both he and Tommy O. gone – my God isn't it stupid and cruel and unnecessary. To the French play in the evening. Good of its sort, and well done but I couldn't keep my mind off poor Georgie Scott.

April 2nd Fairly quiet day. Played hockey in afternoon, very hot. Then to meeting of B. of S. with R.C.S. Committee – not much doing. Taken much against my will to cinema by Dodd to see the Mutt and Jeff[325] films that everyone is talking so much about. I was very glad to get out into the fresh air again.

[Insert: note requesting Pease go to Room 11a at 3 p.m. regarding Frau Joachim of Hamburg]

April 3rd Quiet morning – made inspection of R.H.S. digging operations – think they're going too deep. Pond very high again. Summoned to Rüdiger at 3 and on presenting myself told to come again at 4. R. at the cinema censoring the Somme film. When I got there he told me that Frau Joachim had written to have news of me, mentioning the Bekassy. I wasn't quick enough with my German to extract more, but he cross-questioned me on the Bekassy, and on myself fairly lengthily. The man Brown to supper – a very lengthy but quite good talker. Interviewed Franke in the new censors'

---

[323] Henry Packwood Adams was a conscientious objector who was imprisoned after refusing to undertake civil work (*menwhosaidno.org*).

[324] George Klaassen Scott, a Lieutenant in the Royal Engineers, who was killed by a shell in Belgium at the age of 24. An old Bedalian friend of Michael's. His brother, Tommy Oldrid Scott, had died at Bedales in April 1914 aged 18.

[325] Animated short silent films.

office in Bar. 1 and got off letter to Biffen, and cards to Peggy S and Johnson.

Preparing the vegetable garden

April 4th I suppose as a result of my conversation with Rüdiger I dreamt very vividly of poor Bekassy and of Tonika [his sister], just as in the old days. Great excitement today was we had a real damsel to tea – to whit the washing Fraulein: she waxed very enthusiastic over the "*Englischer keks*" [English biscuits]. Marshall and Masterman were also there. Walked round the field with former and discussed awkward situation caused by Jones insisting on resigning from R.C.S. Committee: Marshall to supper and then all to D.J.'s *Good Friday.* I couldn't stick it at all: it was well done, but the piece itself was bad – sentimental and melodramatic. Perhaps it's because I'm not of a religious turn of mind. The one healthy sentiment was that of the sentry who sneered at priests and preachers.

[Insert: programme for *Good Friday; a dramatic poem.* Produced by C. Duncan-Jones]

April 5th Nice warm day – put off French and went to rehearsal of Pauer's concert to hear the Brandenburg, but it wasn't played. Then sat in the sun and finished *Confessions de Rousseau*, for which the gods be praised. Played hockey in afternoon – without exception the poorest game I've ever struck. Little Williams to tea, and Whyte to supper.

April 6th Good Friday. Did French walk with Bradney as I had been too slack to prepare a composition. Botany in afternoon, then walk in field with Lochhead and Bell and quiet evening reading *Cyrano* (with dictionary). Started de Tocqueville *L'ancienne Régime* in bed. Letter from Peggy S. today telling of poor G.

April 7th First thing this morning helping with flower show. Not at all a bad display, but colour effects rather awful. Mainly hyacinth, and as the bulbs had been sent mixed and were planted 5 in a box some of the effects were awful. Had a talk with Marshall and Blagden about Jones' resignation and after "confab" with Pritchard and Masterman agreed to make strong speeches at meeting urging Jones to offer himself for re-election. J. seems to be wobbling himself now, because of threatened row between Ball and Wolf. Teachers meeting went off without event of interest. J. was persuaded and elected: Wolf stood and defeated. Couldn't take the amendments to constitution as only 74 people present and it was necessary to have 110. Helped clear up the flower show and wrote p.c. to Frau Joachim [see below].

....

MSP to Frau Joachim, Wittenberg Strasse 174, Hamburg:

Ruhleben, Apr. 7th 1917

Dear Madam, A few days ago I was informed by the authorities that you had been good enough to write to inquire after me, mentioning the Bekassys as mutual friends. May I say at once how much I appreciate your kindness in writing, and assure you that I am as well in mind & body as the circumstances permit? Am I right in supposing that you are related to the Fraulein Joachim (a connection of the Rollo Russells[326]) whose kindness to me in the early days of the camp I shall never forget? If you see, or are writing to our friends the Bekassys, I would be very grateful if you would convey to them my very best wishes. Again thanking you very much indeed, believe me, yours faithfully, Michael Pease

---

[326] (Francis Albert) Rollo Russell (a British meteorologist) who married Gertrude Ellen Cornelia Joachim of Haslemere, Surrey in 1891.

April 8th Quiet morning. To concert rehearsal and then darning. Invigilated and read Addison – reminded of old Grubb [Bedales schoolmaster]. Wrote letter home and then walked round field with Bell. Long talk on ♀ [women]: co-ed, suffrage, and prostitution. Then to concert. Very good – thoroughly enjoyed it thoroughly [*sic*]. Would have enjoyed it more if I hadn't sat next to that youth (forgotten his name) who was brought in here for keeping a mistress at the age of 16 and who was scented and perfumed to a degree and smoked cigarettes in my face the whole time. Any how the Brandenburg was fine, and the Liszt was the best I've ever heard of his – not saying much – *allerdings* [though indeed] Pritchard and Rawson walked out after Don Giovanni [overture] – like old Sedley Taylor![327] Supper party with Bell and Marshall and so to bed and *L'ancien Regime*.

[Insert: programme for the 9th Orchestral Concert (dir. W. Pauer, soloist Lindsay), Easter Sunday April 8th]

[Insert: invitation for *dîner amical* and *soirée artistique*, in the school handicraft shed, Lundi 9th Avril from Mr. H. A. Bell]

[Insert: request for voluntary food donations for the above, in French]

April 9th French prowl and then letter writing. Masterman in to tea and long talk on politics local and imperial. To French squash, though English spoken seemed to prevail. Sat between Nash and Blagden; very strange to be waited on again, by dapper persons in white jackets. Rather a long dinner, but the speechifying very amusing. A very lame and halting speech by Ford and then Butterscotch, rather long and platitudinous in awful Manchesterian French. But the fun came with Elies[328] in performing "The Allies". My God, if Rüdiger had stationed spies behind the curtains! Convinces me more than ever that it is the French who will be sticklers to any sort of reasonable peace. Bainton did very dainty execution on the piano and Morris was priceless with his songs of doubtful decency but otherwise the program was not much catch. After more fire eating by Elies,

---

[327] Professor of Music at Trinity College Cambridge in the 19th century. Wikipedia (2019) says he gave up his fellowship around 1869, renouncing theology in favour of academic freedom. He died in 1920.

[328] Pierre Elies (c.1876–?). Born in Paris, he is listed as a French teacher in Bristol in the 1911 census, and as a ship's steward from Avonmouth in the National Archives.

the Marseillaise and God Save the King, we broke up without disaster at 10.30 p.m. Enjoyed it more than I had anticipated!

[Insert: programme for a concert of French music (part of the Soirée). Reverse has menu for the French meal, including a *Ragoût Ruhlebenois*, and on reverse about 30 signatures]

....

Marjory Pease to HBW:

The Pendicle, Limpsfield, Surrey

17th May 1917

Dear Miss Wedgwood,

I have a letter from Michael written on April 9th in which he says "I have such a nice letter from Helen Wedgwood, and as she has written several very sympathetic letters she deserves [HBW has underlined this word, and in the margin wrote *'well dash my kittens!'*] *a message which I daresay you won't mind passing on". The message is as follows "Your letter of March 4th is very welcome indeed. Though many send me letters, so few write of things that interest me, or in a vein likely to appeal to a victim of concentration. I got two other letters by the same post as yours – one a treatise on Erasmus and the other told me to cheer up and recommended me novels for "a good nonsensical laugh", so you can imagine with what a sigh of relief I turned to yours and re-read it. My visions of tricycles and the aged don with the Newnham Brigade; how the thought that there are at least some sensible people left cheers one and gives me something to look forward to, when the fireworks are over and the diplomatists have saved all the necessary faces. Yes, aren't flowers fascinating and isn't the work interesting? It takes one right away from the petty personalities and mean motives to the area of wide issues and big fundamental truths. It prevents one from getting irritated with ones fellow creatures, a state of mind I should quickly get into if I lived in an eternal round of committees, organisings, schemes, meetings and political pamphlets. – I shall look forward to an autograph copy of your first paper! I've just come away from a very good concert; they did the Brandenburg concerto really very well for amateurs, also among other things the Overture to Don Giovanni. But for grandeur of expression, sincerity and depth of feeling, give me Brahms – only since I have been here have I realised what a power his music has to turn one's mind to great things. My best wishes to "them" and again very many thanks for writing."*

May I say how grateful I am to you for writing to my son? He is always so cheerful and plucky, but I often can hardly bear to think of what he must suffer in mind and spirit at being caged up in such hideous sordid surroundings in a perpetual crowd. I hope you have good accounts of your brother Charles. My younger boy met him at Oxford in September. Nicolas has been out in France since Oct. and his regiment (East Surrey) has been through some of this awful fighting. He was all right on the 11th and "trying to organise the remains of the battalion". With many thanks for writing to Ruhleben and hoping one day I may see you.

I am very sincerely,

Marjory Pease.

....

April 10th [no entry]

April 11th Heavy snow at *Appell* this morning, the latter aggravated by our barracking not "*stimming*" and two recounts were necessary. Afternoon got message from censor Franke, who wanted to see me on cabbage disease, but was late and only saw Forester. Started on Lamb's essay on pig for French translation – visions of T. W. Grubb's [Bedales] classroom!

April 12th Spent afternoon making out plan for garden in compound of R.C.S. and got Warner to approve it.

April 13th Got my letter to Frau Joachim returned,[329] as I had misread the address and turned Mittelweg into Wittenberg – good resolution to learn *Deutsche schrift* [German font]. Called up to censor Franke on the subject of finger and toe [clubroot] disease in cabbage and had some conversation on the subject.

April 14th Another summons to Rüdiger this afternoon – thought it was about my Joachim bungle, but found that there was an application in for release [see letter inserted after June 26th entry]. I was so taken unawares, that I didn't know what to say or to ask who had put it in. However, said I would go out, if I could go on with my research work. He was quite friendly – that is to say – neither rude nor very communicative. If I had been quicker with my German I could doubtless got more information out. Started on the R.C.S. compound job, not very promising.

---

[329] Which is presumably why we still have this postcard, written on 7th April.

April 15th Spent all morning on the R.C.S. job, invigilating in library. Afternoon at R.C.S. again and then to *Yeoman of the Guard* – rotten. The music was good but the acting was shocking and Polly's[330] Londonese [London accent] and Roker – Oh Lord! However talked shop with Willie, so it wasn't so bad! Bell in to supper and stayed up till 10 p.m.

[Insert: programme for *The Yeoman of the Guard*. Produced by John H. Corless]

April 16th On the R.C.S. job again all morning, sundry helpers, Blagden, Smith, Cookson. Afternoon to Schubert rehearsal, to censor with Joachim letter, to S.B. [*Schonungsbaracke*] for parcel of medicaments, Blagden to tea and long talk. Down to R.C.S. and helped to cart in lime, scene between Blagden and offensive soldier. Then to concert – very fine indeed. The Brahms and the Schubert were grand. Thynne[331] made very popular debut, though I didn't much care for his selection. Marshall in to supper.

[Insert: programme for chamber concert, Monday Apr. 16th 1917]

April 17th Spent all day on the R.C.S. job with a good squad of helpers, and really shifted things. Read A.E's book on Ireland – not much impressed.

April 18th [no entry]

April 19th Still on R.C.S. job. Went out with Warner in afternoon to investigate possibilities of getting soil. Very pleasant to go out for a stroll and walk over the wilderness by the canal where I was taken out to dig muck pits in the early days. The most interesting thing was that we met the Spandau munition strikers coming back from Berlin. Seemed to be making quite a holiday of it, all decked out in their best and with their women kind. Down at R.C.S. again: Higgins crowd finally evicted, but they dumped most of their stuff in the Bi. Dept. Great war on in parcel post office with Powell; J. in great style at having another tilt with J.P. [Powell]!

April 20th Got in a whole day on R.C.S. garden finally got the rubble off one plot and the whole dug up. Spent the evening reading Daudet's *Jack* – really

---

[330] A nickname for Ralph Archibald Welland (fn 157) according to Eric Swale's memoirs.

[331] Roger Charles Seymour Thynne (1885–1938) was in Munich at the outbreak of war. After the war he was secretary to the British Legation to the Vatican.

rather a boring book – sentimental and the psychology not really well drawn. However for the sake of Milner, I shall doubtless get through with it.

April 21st *Grosser Sieg* [great victory] over Ettinghausen today. Reference library been handed over to joint committee in spite of violent efforts and misstatements by E. Great rejoicing by J.

[Insert: camp messenger postcard, dated 21st April 1917 about three AmX cases, with handwritten note about some spare bricks that Michael can take for the lab.]

April 22nd Morning wrote letter home. Invigilated 12–1. Supper with Ponsonby and Cooper who, I find, knows the Allens and Newberrys and all the Glasgow crowd. Then to Dodd's loft and turned over music for trios – Dodd, Marshall, and Bainton. Then selections from the *Matthew Passion* and Brahms *Requiem* by Bainton on piano: mighty fine evening.

April 23rd The adjourned teachers meeting today at 2 p.m. and as there were only 65 (quorum required being 110) we passed nem. con. and special resolution moved by Jones, seconded by me, and supported by Wimpfy to go ahead with business. All resolutions agreed to without dissent and meeting adjourned at 2.45 p.m. Had great clear out of cubby hole with J. and Marshall, and took most of my "shop" books down to new science library – the latter promises to be a very nice place. Very fed up with Daudet's *Jack*.

April 24th D.J. came to see this evening and explained that he wanted to produce *Comus* here and would I do the dances! Accepted provisionally but the difficulty is the "*menschen* [people] material".

April 25th Saw Warner who has arranged with inspector for us to get the heap of stuff we had our eyes on. First lot of flowers came in from Engler[332] today. Spent afternoon fitting up science library with Hill. Jones had a great *auseinandersetzung* [confrontation] with Ettinghausen re the ref. library. Rather in dread about the Barrack cleaning to take place tomorrow.

---

[332] Adolf Engler (1844–1930). A botanist, professor at the University of Berlin and director of the Berlin-Dahlem Botanical Garden.

April 26th Awful day of cleaning out, but it was fine and bright and we got through without disaster though it's true we lost the bread board, and we all went to bed with sore throats. We had lunch chez Pritchard and I went to hear Bainton play through Lawes' music of *Comus* but I have my grave doubts on the subject of dances for the play. In all consciousness I'm too much of an amateur for such a job.

Spring clean of barracks, 1917

April 27th Woke up with a rotten cold which only got worse in the course of the day, the real old fashioned bunged up good for nothing cold. It rained too hard to go and fetch earth, so I was saved the disgrace of having to cry off on account of health. I read the book Green sent me about a stonemason (rotten but short) and finished Daudet's *Jack* – also rotten but very long. Like Dickens at his worst – sentimental to a degree. Went to bed early for the first time for years.

April 28th Still got this beastly cold hanging about, and as a result didn't do much all day. One or two jobs in school garden – grass seed arrived from Erfurt. School prospectus came in and I devoted happy ½ hour correcting all the typographical errors – hundreds of them, to say nothing of several very weak sentences. Borrowed *The New Machiavelli*[333] from Marshall and so to bed and read very late, feeling much better.

April 29th Very cold and dreary day, and cold still rotten. Read *New Machiavelli* most of morning. I read it last in the long vac. of 1911, lolling in the Fellows' Garden and all at one sitting. Invigilated 12–1. Went down and did up the path a bit at the school. Then to *Merry Wives* – really very well done; as Mistress P., Polly's Londonese and vulgarity didn't jar a bit.

[Insert: programme for *The Merry Wives of Windsor*, April 25th 1917. (Mistress Page played by the producer A. Welland)]

April 30th Spent morning at school doing filthiest job I've done for long – picking the last bit of the garden where the tar barrels had stood. Then in afternoon went out with Warner and a great gang to fetch in soil. Made three expeditions and landed one for the R.H.S. and the rest for the school. Interesting to be out and to see all the Polish girls working on the railway. Then to Russian evening – very able lecture by Mac and beautiful quartette by Borodin. The Scriabin pieces (played by Hewitt) were absolutely unintelligible to me. I couldn't even tell where one piece ended and the next began. Bell to supper and then to bed and Wells.

[Insert: programme for A.S.U. evening of Russian music (with lecture by Ernest MacMillan)]

May 1st Really beautiful day at last. Made a second great expedition for soil today and brought in 3 loads – one for R.H.S. There was a great giving away of food to the Polish girls on railway. To concert: 1st three items really good, excellently played, after which I walked out. I don't understand the temperament of a person who can take Schubert's Unfinished [Symphony] and Nell Gwynne's dances at the same sitting! Warkentin to supper, talk, walk, read, and to bed.

[Insert: programme for Symphony Concert, Tuesday May 1st, conductor Mr. Peebles Conn]

May 2nd Enrolling at R.C.S. again this morning and garden in afternoon. Huge squad helping shifting things round – beginning to take shape a bit

---

[333] Novel by H. G. Wells that draws on his own love affairs and satirises the Webbs.

now. Preparing lecture for tomorrow and so to bed and finished *Machiavelli*. It's good reading, like all Wells, but I think I realise more than ever the appalling bad taste in writing a book full of sneers at contemporary people.

May 3rd Lecture at 9 and then practical work – quite a good crowd, but rather an unprepared lecture. Then at work in garden till evening and after supper read – The Bible!

May 4th Worked away in school garden most of the day.

May 5th Called up to Rüdiger about release. Potsdam is no go, so I asked for a few days to think it over. It appears that Mrs. Russell [fn 247] has worked the thing. I feel very doubtful about the thing now; if there is not to be a general exodus, I think I will do as well to stay here. Finished off the hard work in the garden and now I must sow the grass. Ponsonby to supper. Wrote p.c. to A.M.T. and so to bed and read Bible. Wolf was in Rüdiger's queue and very inquisitive about my business!

May 6th Wrote letter in morning. Postponed French lesson 10.30 and invigilated 12–1. Finished letter in afternoon. To concert 6 p.m. – mighty fine – at least the first 3 items after which I went out. Philips to supper and so to bed and Bible. Finished Genesis and started Exodus – many visions of Kinfauns[334] days with my Grandfather called up!

[Insert: programme for Special Symphony Concert, Sunday May 6th, conductors Messrs J Peebles Conn and W Pauer]

May 7th In the lab all morning after French prowl at 8. To rehearsal of Borodin quartette at 1.30 and then to R.C.S. garden and sowed some of the grass seed. Sent off order for sundry things for garden from Haage and Schmidt. Went along and slipped into hall to hear the Borodin quartette again – hardly anyone there and it sounded fine in the empty hall, though I felt sorry for the performers.

May 8th Morning rather dissipated. Sowed rest of grass seeds in R.C.S. compound with Hill, and Hill to supper. Heard nightingale for first time from the R.C.S. balcony. Flowers came in from Dahlem.[335]

---

[334] Kinfauns Manse, Perthshire. Home of Michael's maternal grandparents.

[335] The Berlin-Dahlem Botanical Garden.

May 9th Bradney 8 a.m. Lechmere 9 and then more or less preparing lecture all day. Very fine and while out on field made good resolution to apply for *Urlaub* [leave] instead of *Entlassung* [release]. So to bed and finished Exodus.

May 10th Lecture in morning and then demonstrating. Went to Rüdiger in afternoon and communicated my decision not to go out, but at same time I asked for *urblaub* to Jena. He was not a bit rude, took it all down, and said *wollen wir mal sehen* [let's see]!

May 11th [no entry]

May 12th Very dusty – pottered round in school garden morning and read in afternoon. Bainton in to supper and then went up to Dodd's and they played trios with Marshall. The Tschaikowski [*sic*] is grand. They also did some Beethoven.

May 13th Still abominably dusty.

May 14th Magnificent thunderstorm this evening gave everything a grand soaking in the garden – still very hot though.

May 15th Spent nearly all morning in garden with Hill putting in seeds and so forth. Rest of day somewhat dissipated, but managed to read a good deal of de Tocqueville. And so to bed and read of Oz and his iron bedstead.

May 16th Bradney 8 a.m. Lechmere 9 a.m. and then looking through flowers from Berlin, lovely collection of flowering shrubs.

May 17th Lecture at 9 a.m. and during demonstration visit by a Danish red cross commission headed by a jolly little professor who introduced himself to me as Johanssen. Very friendly indeed when I told him I was a geneticist. I showed him all round the lab and finally went round the camp with him and talked shop and so forth. Did the usual rounds of kitchens, stage, cinema, and ended up at reference library. He was really a dear, so nice and kind, the way he patted me on the back and the encouraging things he said about our efforts really cheered me up enormously. Told me that Bedur[?] was captured in Egypt and escaped! Played tennis for first time with Bell and played hopelessly.

May 18th Not much on. Played tennis 5–6 with Bell, Wigg and Lochhead. Finished de Tocqueville and mighty pleased with it. Got A.M.X. case that had been under water!

May 19th Inspection this morning by a great bunch of Turkish people. Conversation with one in English, who said he was a Pembroke man and seemed surprised to find so many Cambridge men here. Plants from Haage and Schmidt arrived and I planted them out with Hill.

May 20th Got the microtome mounted and ready for action.

May 21st Bradney at 8. Then microtoming on and off all day. Filthy dust and wind. Started *Les Pensées de Pascal.*

May 22nd Worked with the microtome most of the day but knocked off after tea as eyes were getting sore. Walked round field with Bell and discussed *The New Machiavelli* and its genesis. In bed read article in *Fortnightly* by Gribble on Ruhleben[336] – very fatuous.

[3 days missing]

May 26th Lechmere at 9 a.m. Worked with microtome till tea. Tennis with Wigg. Geology Zabel,[337] supper, French 7.30 and then dipping into *Tristram Shandy* and wrote p.c. to H.B.W. [see page 201].

....

HBW to MSP (received late April/May):

Moddershall Oaks, Stone, Staffs.

Easter Sunday [April 8th] *1917*

Dear Mr. Pease,

---

[336] Francis Henry Gribble (1862–1946), author and internee who was released in Sep. 1915. On 3rd Jan. 1916 his 'Leaves from a Ruhleben notebook' was published in *The Fortnightly Review.* In 1919 he co-authored *The History of Ruhleben* with camp captain Joseph Powell.

[337] Charles Ferdinand Zabel (1887–1921). An Australian geologist of German descent, who was surveying manganese deposits in the Rhine at the outbreak of war. He was elected a Fellow of the Geological Society of London in 1919 in recognition of his services in lecturing in geology and mining at Ruhleben (*The West Australian*, 10 May 1919). He was working for the Portuguese Zambesi Mining Company after the war when he died of fever in Tete, Mozambique.

It is angelic of you to offer me your cabbage seed, but I'd be afraid of doing something wrong and being murdered when you got back. Besides, the food controller might get hold of them and insist on them being turned into soup. But alas, in any case I am leaving Merton for the present and starting as a labourer (at 18 shillings a week) so I shall have nowhere to grow them. Unless they are being spoilt and you would care for me to sow them at Merton, where one of the others might look after them, or at Cambridge, where I shall probably be every weekend. But you know, I know nothing, so if the seed is at all precious you had better not trust me.

Your February 10th p.c. has just come and I have not answered that of January 13th. Those tiresome war office people will only let one send books through a publisher, and as the one I had planned to send is published in America, I am afraid you won't get it just yet, – but do not despair!

You prophesy is ill omened, but I know my wish is much more likely to come true.

You ask for "activities" and it is <u>most</u> annoying what a lot there are to be discussed that must not be. Please go through them in your mind, and imagine the sort of letter this might be. What shall I tell you? How C.U.F.S. (flourishing as ever) is becoming too intellectual for words, and is holding a symposium on "socialism and foreign exchange" (to give the economists a chance of showing off); or how we hailed the Dawn in the East[338] *and father and G. Lansbury, united for the first time since the war by a common joy, roared from the same platform – to the scandalization of Father's new Tory friends who were really beginning to have hopes of him. It is good to find that things do happen in some parts of the world. I wish I could give you the spirit of that meeting. it was wonderful.*

Or in the scientific world there is the controversy between Bateson and Morgan[339] *on the true cause of coupling and the question of "Xing over". I object to Morgan's theories on pure artistic grounds. Also he will split his infinitives. Mr. Bateson is very nice the way he will argue out his theories and show one things however much of a beginner one may be. So many people won't be bothered. You are right about Bateson and socialism though! It was distinctly a shock to find myself among people who believed in an "efficient" and benevolent tyranny, and regard idealists and dreamers as undesirable mutations, quite unlikely (luckily) to survive! I have never heard anyone express such hatred of the Russians and Irish on these grounds --- but there, I am beginning to hold with the medieval view that*

[338] The 'February revolution' in Russia that saw the abdication of the Tsar and establishment of a provisional government.

[339] Thomas Hunt Morgan (1866–1945), an American evolutionary biologist and geneticist.

your true scientist has sold his soul to the devil. – Only I hope you won't grow into an "efficient" person who thinks Freedom an outworn superstition!

It must be perfectly maddening trying to do your work under such difficulties. I hope you are able to console yourself with the thought of the gentleman who used his furniture to fire his glass furnaces – or Priestley heating mercuric oxide with a candle! not to mention the traditional prisoner rearing a plant with his tears,--- only I never could see how anything but asparagus could thrive under such circumstances. Of course the modern gaol, as some of us know too well, is too abominably sanitary to afford even the consolation of a liverwort. (Do you remember Jim's prison in Huck Finn?) I just know how you must long for mountain tops and wind. Well "stick it!" as the burglar said to the C.O. in Pentonville.

With all good wishes,

Yours very sincerely

Helen Bowen Wedgwood

P.S. I wonder if you know Cecil von Hafen[340] *in Ruhleben? We used to know him quite well when he was a boy.*

....

MSP to HBW:

Ruhleben, May 26th 1917

Many thanks for yours of April 8th. How do you find your latest occupation and where are you? I hope you are really worth your 18 shillings, and vide GBS passion. I should prefer it, in many ways, to concentration, but personally I should draw the line at swineherding. Yes, Priestley wasn't the only one to heat his oxide with a candle, but I bet he didn't blow his glass with margarine. Now that it is warm I have got my cytology going again, but with many local difficulties to be overcome, so that it is vastly more of an amusing contest for me than a fruitful contribution to science. If you complain of the difficulties of writing, pray what am I to do within this narrow compass?? Yes, Russia is very interesting, quite the biggest event. Best wishes, M.S.P.

....

---

[340] Cecil Oscar von Hafen (1893–1974). Worked as an overseas representative for Josiah Wedgwood & Sons Ltd and was in Germany at the outbreak of war. Appears as an actor in some of the Ruhleben theatre programmes. Changed his name to 'Haven' after the war.

May 27th Odds and ends in the lab, much distressed to find all the dissecting instruments pinched. Afternoon still at lab, very hot and I started to get very stupid and clumsy so left off and went for a walk with Bell and discussed plans for reforming Cambridge and the selection of Rhodes scholars. After supper listened to Mozart wind quintette played on strings, Speed at the piano. While I was sitting there in an easy chair gazing out at the far pine woods and feeling quite sentimental over the slow movement, up comes old Schneider and wants to know how frogs copulate! Exchange my Pelerine [small cape] for a night gown with Kauffman.

[2 days missing]

May 30th Bradney at 8 then Lechmere at 9 and lined up to send off photos and miserable ones too. Too hot to do much in afternoon. Played tennis with Wigg 5–6. Marshall to supper and then at work on lecture. Watered gardens and so to bath, bed and Labiche[341] – the latter piffle and gave it up. Great binge on at Phoenix club – loathesome.

[2 days missing]

June 2nd Lechmere at 9 and then set to work microtoming – arranged for cart to go out and get soil for handicrafts garden, but this was prevented by violent thunderstorm, really phenomenal downpour. Parcel from Becher containing cakes, eggs and cigars! Staining on and off till 7 p.m. and then Examinations Subcommittee – got very annoyed with Ford's cotton woollyness. Eventually I was left to draft a statement of the irregularities that had been committed by the subcommittee with regard to the holdings of the examinations. So to bed, very tired and read the *Pensées of Pascal* which are most assuredly of the curate's egg type.

June 3rd Cutting in the morning, staining in afternoon. Then walk round with Bell. Set Lochhead going with Cystopus and then Dodd's loft to hear Mozart quintette again. Very nice.

[2 days missing]

---

[341] Eugene Labiche, French comic writer.

June 6th Great do today with *Appells*. We have to line up and walk out on to the field and be counted there twice daily. No mistake, they do chivvy us about! Lectured to Science Circle on sex limited inheritance, but no discussion owing to evening *Appell*. Lechmere lent me Pyke's book,[342] which I started reading.

June 7th Botany lecture and class all morning.

June 8th Great A.S.U. meeting in afternoon and Henry got dropped off committee, otherwise eventless. Event of the week is that Ettinghausen and Barrett have resigned from reference library and Rawson installed instead.

June 9th Wrote letter home in evening. Bentham and Hoskins came.

June 10th Spent day in R.C.S. garden stringing up creepers and sundry other things. Invigilated in library under new regime from 11.30–1. See in *Nature* that P.G. Bailey[343] has been killed.

June 11th Morning and afternoon in Lab – very hot. Lechmere has been sent for to Munich [University – where he had been studying in 1914] and doesn't know whether to go or no. Very nice if we could go together. Went to Chekov's *Seagull* – really don't know quite what to make of it.

[Insert: programme for A.S.U. Fourth Russian Evening – *The Seagull*, Monday June 11th 1917. Produced by Leigh Henry]

June 12th Very much set my heart on Munich, but I don't think L. wants to go – they treated him so badly there at the beginning of the war.

[2 days missing]

June 15th Hear today that F.O. has granted leave to have reagents sent to me – good work.

June 16th Sent off special card re reagents.

---

342 *To Ruhleben and Back* – Geoffrey Pyke's memoir on his time in the camp, published in 1916 after his escape.

343 Major Philip Gerald Bailey (1886–1917). Natural Sciences graduate of Clare College, Cambridge who took a diploma in Agriculture and did research into the inheritance of wool in sheep. Killed at Arras (the same campaign as Michael's uncle Oswald Allen Pease).

June 17th Stained sections in morning and spent rest of day reading lazily on 3rd grandstand. Mme de Staël is good, though there is too much which is merely descriptive.

June 18th Still very hot, played tennis in morning and got slight touch of sunstroke. At least I went blind and had to come off, and suffered from headache and slackness for rest of day.

June 19th All right again. Still very hot, lab impossible. Prepared lecture and made diagrams, but otherwise achieved very little.

[2 days missing]

June 22nd Got permit today to go to pond behind fortress [at the east end of the racecourse] so at 3 p.m. L and Neville and I sallied forth with a very weary soldier and went for a walk in the woods, for all the world like going out with a nursery maid. The ducks had eaten up most of the plants but we got a great store of animals including a gigantic freshwater muscle [*sic*]. Allowed to stay up till 11 p.m. tonight on account of the heat.

June 23rd I gather there's a great row brewing about the examination business. Apparently in the French essay exam several candidates committed gross indiscretions and wrote about "*sales boches*" [dirty Boches]. Matter came out in the censoring and got into Rüdiger's hands and the culprits got in the cells with a month's cage to follow. Meeting of Examination Committee called for next day.

June 24th Wrote letter home and worked in lab. Then to Examination Committee and decided to make excuses and try to get people off. I personally felt they deserved all they got for being such silly asses. Finished Mme de Staël (2nd half much poorer) and started on a book of African travel Zabel thrust on me. Camp magazine published today. Reference to Jones' famous jacket.

June 25th Cut some of the grass in the R.C.S. compound and resowed it. Hear that sentences of examinees have been reduced.

June 26th Another meeting re exams again today. Patchett and Ford were not granted an interview by the Major, and meeting decided to try again, Bell and I opposing any more badgering. What is due is an apology. Great news today, summoned up by Rüdiger and got 14 days *urlaub* to Jena!

Sounds incredible! Then straight away to R.H.S. Committee – not long but very stupid. Can't get over the Jena business.

[letter below – no addressee or addresser]

COPY

11th June, 1917.

In reply to enquiries and representations concerning Mr. Pease at Ruhleben I beg to report as follows :-

"Mr. Pease feels very well at Ruhleben and shows no symptons whatever of any illness. When asked if he felt the wish to be liberated he stated that he would like to continue his studies at Prof. Erwin's, of the Institute for "Vererbungslehre" (Department of the Agricultural Academy) at Potsdam. To let him go to Potsdam is however out of the question as Potsdam is forbidden area to aliens. Leave was given him to choose some other place of residence. He thanked for the kindness shown to him, but stated that he did not wish to be liberated at any other place. He added that he felt quite comfortable amongst his friends at Ruhleben, all the more, as he had opportunity to continue his studies there. He would be very grateful however for a short leave which he would like to spend with Mr. Neumeister, slater at Jena, whose son is a German soldier prisoner of war in England. The old man had repeatedly invited Pease to pay him a visit, particularly because his son in the prison camp in England was treated very well through the intervention of some of Pease's friends. A fortnight's leave has accordingly been given to Pease on the 28th ult."

June 27th Rather disjointed day finishing off things. Embedded material, wrote to Biffen were main efforts. Everyone very congratulatory and full of advice.

June 28th Flowers for lecture didn't arrive till 8.45 today so lecture was rather a scratch affair, but all the same did a record number of orders. Tackled the embedding for Lochhead, Neville and Smythe[?] and spent most of the day looking through my *Garde Robe* [wardrobe]. Tennis with Marshall 2 p.m., hopelessly beaten.

June 29th Really got to grips with the clothing and packing up question. Complicated by arrival of Selfridge cases. Bought a great green felt hat. Got money from cashiers. Afternoon to Zimmer 11 to find my *Schein* [licence/pass] is not yet signed and no chance of it being signed till the forenoon! Gallivanted all round the place to find a *"Kursbuch"* [railway guide] and eventually found one in the cash office, where they looked up trains for me and one of the chaps there offered to conduct me to the *anhalter bahnhof* [train station]. Wrote letter to H.B.W. and p.c. home.

[Insert: note: Michael S. Pease. *Ich bitte um erlaubnis, die folgenden nahrungsmittel nach Jena mit zu nehmen.* [I ask permission to take the following items to Jena]: *Kaffee, Kakao, Tee, Fett, Reis, Milch, margarine, Keks, Schokalade, Mehl* [coffee, cocoa, tea, fat, rice milk, margarine, biscuits, chocolate, flour] possibly signed by Rüdiger. 29 June 1917.

[no more diary entries until he returns to camp]

....

MSP to HBW:

Ruhleben, June 29th 1917 [letter received by HBW on Sept 4th]

Dear Miss Wedgwood,

A letter has long been due to you to make some attempt to express my thanks for all your kind and sympathetic letters. I know how busy you must be and I know how hard it is to do even a fraction of all one sets out to do. Therefore is my appreciation of your kindness all the greater.

I regret that we did not meet at Cambridge; we seem to have so many interests in common; and if we approach them from rather different standpoints, that would have made it the more interesting. Honestly, I can't remember meeting you at the Stewarts'; and, in any case, I always regret the ill grace with which I conducted myself on the occasion of the Morris dance society's constitutional revolution. Lord, how small and trivial that all seems now! But if you claim my friendship on the score of having met me at one of those "revolution" meetings, I apologise for my cussed behaviour.

I write to you just on the eve of leaving the camp for a fortnight's "holiday". I am going to Jena and I hope to indulge myself in peace and quiet, beautiful scenery and sweet woodland smells. Of course, I shan't really enjoy myself. Can anyone who has a brain to think and a heart to feel really enjoy himself now? It isn't Ruhleben I'm fed up with, it is the war. It is easy to keep up an outwardly cheerful disposition (I'm generally reckoned as one of the most imperturbably good tempered men in camp), but at heart I am as sad and sick as can be. To contemplate that so much good will and sacrifice, so much energy and talent, is being consecrated to death and destruction, to inflaming and perpetuating national jealousies and race hatred, reduces me to gloomy despair and confirms me in my pessimistic outlook on things social and political. I can't understand how reasonable people (e.g. my good dear parents) take it all lying down. Where has the spirit fled? Does no one read Shelley nowadays? Of course, there are a few bright spots – Russia for example. Even I, who have no implicit faith in Democracy as such, feel that any change there is for the better. Besides, the leaders seem to be a particularly level-headed lot, animated by the noblest ideals. Then again, the Suffrage is a great effort – but then women aren't any less stupid than men, so I don't anticipate startling political changes. They will surely be of a deeper and more far reaching nature than any Webbian Act of Parliament; there will be changes in man's attitude towards women. In the meantime, I congratulate you warmly on being put on the same level of intelligence as that monument of understanding and independent judgment, the British Elector.

No, I don't agree with you at all about Science and the Devil. That is one of the big mistakes the English have made. Surely research has in itself an intrinsic value, is for its own sake worth pursuing, as is art, or music, or literature? Surely the "goodness" of a thing is not necessarily measured by to the increment it adds to wages, returns, or something like that? And after all this, you may well ask what are my great researches worth? Frankly, very little. It is an awful business, struggling with a difficult technique, under particularly exasperating circumstances, e.g., frightful extremes of temperature, and minimal quantities of reagents. And then the whole thing is hopelessly interrupted, because instructing others makes considerable claims on my time. There are about a dozen who really care for Botany, as many again who merely dabble in it in order to amuse themselves. But it is worth doing for the few and I thoroughly enjoy it.

Apart from shop, I've been doing a little French; but so far am rather disappointed at its literature, both prose and verse. What a ridiculous thing an alexandrine [a poetic form] *is! I have just been reading Mme de Staël, who is good; but she devotes too much space to the merely descriptive. Of course, she surveyed Germany from the Court of Weimar at the height of its literary glory, not from the confines of a concentration camp.*

I wonder what sort of farm you're on and what you do. In spite of the hard work, I've no doubt you find it a pleasant change. I often wonder how the labourer with a lifetime of it ahead of him regards it – I don't think he regards it at all as a matter of fact. As a class, farmhands are about as unresponsive and unreflective as you make'em.

And now I'm afraid this is an awful ramble – I'm hanging about waiting for my "Schein" [ticket] *to arrive and hoping against hope that it will come in time to avoid my arriving in Jena at 1 a.m. Again very very many thanks, thanks which no mere words can express.*

Yours very sincerely

Michael Pease.

……………………

HBW to MSP:

Thorpe Grange,[344] *Farquhar Rod, Edgbaston, B'ham* [forwarded to Jena]

May 25th 1917

Dear Fellow Agriculturalist,

I write now as one cabbage grower to another. You may pride yourself on being in the higher walks of that profession, while I am merely a "hand", but do not forget that the industrious office boy may end up as a millionaire (vide Samuel Smiles). And I assure you I am most industrious, although I <u>am</u> only undergardener to an aunt, but "the duties are delightful and the privileges great". This is a picture of us in our potato field at home, just to show you that we do work – at least you can see <u>I</u> do, but Bekassy is obviously the lily-handed aristocrat giving tone to the group, while the Infant (rather a large one now) is too busy defying his country's invaders with a pitchfork to use for anything else [sadly this photo has not been found].

I've just this moment got a letter from your mother with your message. I do hope I shall meet her someday – Father knows her and has often spoken of her. – Besides she is "sound on the land question", isn't she?

Well, I won't recommend you novels – serious study I know is your line! So let me suggest Principles of Social Reconstruction (Russell) and Progress and Poverty (of

---

[344] Home of her uncle Arthur Felix Wedgwood & family. Felix was killed in France in March 1917 and Helen went to stay with his widow and children to help out.

course). Also you should read anything you can get about the various schemes for a League of Nations; it's a knotty subject and wants a lot of thinking about, especially if you regard all armed interference as bad, and sometimes I'm not at all sure whether an "enforced peace" of that kind wouldn't lead to worse things than the present system. Of course, there has got to be some sort of international system, but a lot of armed nations pledged to go to war under certain circumstances seems risky, and will besides make the task of those who want to do away with armaments altogether much harder. Of course, nothing really can be done while our present social system remains, but we do need to have the immediate fear of war removed. I hope this isn't too like "the treatise on Erasmus", but it has been bothering us a lot.

I was sure that you would like that about plants. So many of my otherwise sensible friends have threatened me with degeneration of the brain, and gradual loss of moral sense, culminating in a state of bovine indifference! – so if my letters become mere weather charts, may I at least furnish an Awful Warning, causing you to relinquish the idea of a farm for the more intellectual state of an office in the city (I don't think! as we say in the East End). I heard the Brandenburg for the first time the other day. It is splendid. It must make a difference to be able to get music.

I am just off to see some of the Quakers and other miscreants with whom I consort in the intervals of honest toil. All good wishes,

Yours,

Helen Wedgwood.

……………………

MSP to HBW [sent via L S Ornstein, Utrecht]:

bei Neumeisters, Lutherstrasse, Jena

July 13th 1917

Dear Miss Wedgwood,

I wrote to you just on the eve of my departure from camp, and so I write to you now just before I return to the city of futility and chatter to thank you very much for you letter of May 25th. It has been for me one of the most extraordinary feelings that I have ever experienced. To come out of a place of stink, and noise, and close companionship, where every aesthetic sense was jarred and grated all day, and suddenly to find myself before the appeal of beautiful scenery, solitude, and sweet woodland smells. It's no good to attempt to describe it; only those who've done a course (and a good long one) of concentration camps, can know what it's like. I dare say Bekassy knows! Remember me to him when you see him. I've been having the most deliciously lazy time, just drinking in the beautiful hills and sweet scent of pines; I've enjoyed myself much more than I thought I would. I was afraid I would be made painfully aware that I was in the enemy's country, but I have found myself received only with kindness and politeness everywhere, and only once was I treated to a discourse on who started the war. Yesterday I got a permit from the police and we did a great ausflug [excursion] *into the Thüringer Wald. Took the Munich express at midnight and at 2 a.m. we were right up in the heart of the Wald. By moonlight we climbed up onto the hills and watched the sun rise from the top. Then we rambled round all day and came back in the evening. My only objection to it was that it involved drinking an awful lot of beer, an unpleasant duty which, however, I can now perform with tolerable grace. Though my palate was thus revolted, you can imagine the feast my other senses enjoyed. I am staying with the parents of a German prisoner in England whom my mother has befriended. People in quite a humble way (small builders) but oh so kind, generous, and sympathetic. By the way, the arrival of the photo of you on the land caused great excitement and curiosity, involved me in a regular torrent of questions, direct and circumstantial! Well, I'm afraid this letter is all about ego. But for a fortnight ego has been indulging himself in selfish idleness and that reflects itself in his letters. Don't think that I ever forget the war; it darkens and saddens every moment like a dark cloud in the sky. Nor have I forgotten serious study; I've just been ordering books that ought to see me through for 18 months or 2 years at the Ruhleben pace of working. I notice you describe yourself merely as a gardener. I thought somehow you were doing the real thing out on the land, and I pictured you hoeing turmuts* [Wiltshire for turnip] *and foddering cattle. I was out visiting a biggish farm here (about 150 acres) the other day where all the work seemed to be done by girls and the farmer's wife who showed me round was a great expert at the beasts and the crops and the tillage. It interested me especially as it was the open field system brought up to date with modern machinery. We had to wander all over the place looking at strips of oat here and rye there, and so forth. The enclosed photo* [facing page] *shows me with parents and two prospective daughters-in-law on the kitchen balcony! Well, this time tomorrow I shall be just strolling up to the barbed wire in my best "go-to-town" get up and asking to be admitted again!*

Again, my very best thanks for your many letters to me: they have done so much to keep up my spirits and to spur me on to fresh efforts.

Yours very sincerely

Michael Pease

Michael with the Neumeister family at their home in Jena in 1917

July 19th Returned to camp on Sunday night the 15th to find everything in wild confusion owing to a fire which had broken out in the stables and had spread to adjoining barracks. Wind was in our favour otherwise whole place would have come down. It appears that it was the wildest scene of pandemonium and confusion, but no one was killed, though 4 horses and a cow succumbed. It was strange to walk through camp in Dodd's suit without being recognised by anyone! I found it very difficult getting into bed, nowhere to put clothes or anything, and bed was very unsympathetic and stuffy. Monday and Tuesday I felt very tired, dazed, and head aching all day, but Wednesday I pulled myself together and got more into my old ways. Played tennis 3–4 with Wigg. Thursday I had my usual Botany lecture. Class very much dwindled. I went in the afternoon to Rüdiger to see if the matter [permanent move to Jena] could be opened up again, and this he agreed to do. Quite nice and polite. Wrote p.c. to Frau Joachim.

July 20th Got my suit case today, but to my astonishment they confiscated all my great supply of manuscript paper! They also took out all my books and old letters, but I was to have these back when the censor had looked at them at 4 p.m. but when I returned there, censor hadn't been and nothing doing. Wrote letter home.

July 21st Nothing doing again at parcels post. Books came from Jena, and gift of *Shakespeare's England* from someone.

July 22nd [no entry]

July 23rd Usual miscellaneous day of interruptions. Wrote letter to Engler, got the pendant (10.50 Marks) for the flower girl and handed both to Wolf. Wrote p.c. to Neumeister. Am having another do now at the Old Testament – Samuel and thereabouts, all the part I got up for the higher certificate 10 years ago.

July 24th Got to work with the old microtome this afternoon and it cut quite tolerably. Tennis 2–3 and a bath always puts one in a good mood. Read Butler's *Life and Habit*, not very convincing.

July 25th Usual day of achieving nothing in particular. Did a little staining and prepared for lecture. Got my books and paper from the Parcels office, which did please me mightily. Got the library catalogue finished off, attended final geology lecture, filled the blackboard with diagrams, read a little more *Life and Habit* (Biol. was certainly not Butler's metier!), pined bitterly for Jena and so to bed and finished Samuel. Got my *wäsche* [laundry] and some peas from Neumeister today. Sent 50 Marks to Snamensky.

July 26th Got my final lecture over today – interest in systematic has very much dwindled even as I thought it would. R.H.S. Committee at 2. Tennis at 3. Examinations Committee at 6 and so the whole gone in usual interruptions.

July 27th [no entry]

July 28th Wrote letter home. Chose leather for [binding] Engler's Darwin and got that put in hand.[345] Got 52 Marks from Whyte for what I had to pay his swindling old landlord for his violin. So to bed and tried a little more French verse but it's awfully poor stuff.

---

[345] Thank-you note sent to MSP from Engler on 7 Nov 1917 (Appendix 2).

July 29th Very futile day. Rounded off *Life and Habit* and then invigilated 11.30–1 in new reference library – browsed through Dryden's works. Afternoon browsed through introduction of Driesch[346] and evening read *Die Ernte* [The Harvest], and in bed tried to do my duty by French verse but got terribly bored.

July 30th Got out and started *Memoirs* [of Napoleon] by de Bourienne.

[2 days missing]

Aug. 2nd Spent most of time this week setting Neville and co. going with microtome.

Aug. 3rd Bar. 6 garden to be photographed this morning at 8.30, so I hustled round and tidied up and then hung about till 9.30 or so and nothing happened [the photograph was taken eventually – see page 380]. Went up to flower show in Y.M.C.A. really quite good. Hill put out an instructive sheet to illustrate seed testing methods. Then returned to lab and chopped up sections. Mützenbecher in camp today. Geiger[347] is leaving us – we are supposed to have got a new Commandant whom M. says is a *sehr netter mensch* [very nice man].

[14 days missing]

....

HBW to MSP:

Barlaston Lea, Stoke-on-Trent [grandmother Wedgwood's home]

July 4th 1917 [her 22nd birthday]

Dear Sociologist,

Here is a question for your next study circle –"what is the psychological peculiarity which induces conservatism in gardeners?" – to me it is a mystery. To the normal man, nothing could be more conducive of red hot socialism, of the à la lantern order than hoeing in a blazing sun while the idle rich repose on deck

---

[346] Hans Driesch, a German biologist and philosopher.

[347] Dr Geiger, the Camp doctor who, though a good medic, hated the British and, according to Powell and Gribble (1919), treated his patients harshly.

chairs a few yards away in the shade. Sacrés aristos! And yet gardeners are a bulwark of the landed interest.

I wonder if you have got my very much belated Xmas present? After all, I couldn't send the one I wanted to so sent Russell's Principles of Social Reconstruction instead. I do hope you haven't already got it? I'm only in the middle of it as yet and am enjoying his dry humour immensely. His principle ambition at present, I am told, is to complete his education by a course in Wormwood Scrubs – I don't think he need lose hope!

Your remarks, and the example of my small cousins' education have inspired me to read a book on the Montessori system, and I retract some of my former ignorant cavils. She certainly seems to have hold of the right end of the stick. – Of course, the advantage of reading modern works on education is that one realises, as never before, what a wonderful person one must be to have turned out so well in spite of one's entirely wrong upbringing! – a comforting thought and calculated to put one on good terms with one's author. I can't quite lose my distrust of those artificial ways of educating the senses, though I long for sandpaper letters over which to run my fingers. Of course at present I know very little, but don't you think she takes too little account of imagination? Stories and books meant so much to us, and surely lack of imagination is the great fault in most people? I am always so sorry for children who know no stories and poems and have no idea of "pretending". They miss such a lot, both now and later. It is just as important to educate the imagination as the senses and both are mismanaged at present. I would like my children to be able to forget they are themselves and be something else. There is nothing so refreshing.

We spent a heavenly weekend at Cambridge – the bean fields were all out – I never knew their smell till my first summer there. But it is sad seeing one's friends scattering to the four quarters. Especially "our gang". – "We taught the art of writing things On men we still should like to throttle, And where to get the blood of Kings At only half-a-crown a bottle". And after that of course, the question of getting a living out of school teaching seems dull! – and if you hold unusual views now you can be terribly lonely.

I've been cultivating the society of the best Quakers in Birmingham. They really are splendid people. What we isolated people should have done without them at this time I don't know. It is fine too, to see how socialistic they are becoming. The Society has wakened up and will, I think, join forces with us after the war.

Farewell therefore, dear Friend, Let thee keep a cheerful spirit for the end will surely come. And so, all good wishes from

Helen Wedgwood.

....

MSP to HBW:

Ruhleben, Aug. 16th 1917

Many thanks for yours of July 4th. I'll let you know when the Russell turns up but I'm rather afraid the Censor may prick up his ears at the name. Very many thanks indeed for worrying about it. I hope the garden goes well: you've certainly had a phenomenal summer for your apprenticeship. With regard to your politico-horticultural poser may I ask, is there any evidence that gardeners are any more conservative than any other kind of flunky? Here I am back again in the old haunts: after a very unhappy 48 hours I picked up the old ropes again and now the beautiful hills and woods of Jena seem like a distant dream. Again many thanks and best wishes, M. S. Pease

....

HBW to MSP (date of receipt unknown)

Evesham.

July 24th 1917

Dear Mr. Pease,

Such a disappointment! Those Education people won't send the book after all (they've only just let me know) – passages in it which would not be good for the morals of our enemies!!! It is too stupid, especially as I happen to know that the book could be bought in Germany soon after publication! It is one I thought you would particularly like as, besides its own merits, it expresses very well, I think, the religion which the war has made so real for so many of us, and you would see what way our thoughts are tending.

It was nice to get your p.c. of May 26th. What an aristocrat you are to object to swine herding! Do you know of W. N. Ewer[348] *(writes poems in the Herald)? Well he is doing swine herding as "alternative service", and I am told by no means dislikes it. Pigs are nice companionable things, especially compared with oakum picking* [old rope, which prisoners had to untwist into many corkscrew strands], *or stone-breaking, or even shooting other people with a machine gun!*

---

[348] William Norman Ewer, a British journalist and Fabian socialist, remembered mostly now for a few lines of verse he wrote.

Poor man! I see you struggling to boil things in 'margarine-blown' flasks; and making your razors, as Jim in Huck Finn made his pens, out of brass candlesticks. And then probably, just as you have made a really efficient laboratory, the war will stop and you will have to leave it. Consider however, what an excellent effect learning to speak with pebbles in his mouth had on Demosthenes.

At present I'm spending a strenuous month on a market garden at Evesham (the job at my Aunt's was temporary). 18/- a week now seems wealth, as I only get 2d an hour for the first month, and the wages are never good, but I am only here for the month, in training. Market-gardening pervades the streets, literature and conversation of the place, and the town smells of young onions and strawberry jam on alternate days. Life is very amusing. There is a sense of delightful adventure at being plumped down in an utterly strange place, and as I started out with the determination to talk to any and every one, as the spirit moved me, I have been making all sorts of acquaintances. I take stray children to "the pictures", talk families and revolution with old women in the gardens (most intelligent old dears, – but a little vague as to what they wish to revolve about), and endeavour to instil Trade Union principles into the other girls; but they are hopeless and won't perceive the crime of under cutting other people. There are also a lot of German prisoners. Three work in our nursery. We see very little of them, and unfortunately my German does not rise easily beyond remarks on the weather. They have a good time, I think, as the foreman is a delightful Dutchman, and "the boss" is very nice to them. The other men appear friendly, but their only idea of speaking German is to shout in English, and wave their arms! It is particularly amusing to hear a conversation between a convalescing soldier and the Germans – the soldiers' knowledge of the language being extensive, but distinctly original!

This life suits me, and I find it much easier to get into touch with working people this way than as a propagandist from outside. I hope for a more or less permanent job in Staffordshire.

Best wishes to you,

Yours very sincerely

Helen Wedgwood

....

Marjory Pease to HBW c/o her father:

The Pendicle, Limpsfield, Surrey

3rd August 1917

Dear Mr. Wedgwood,

I have stupidly mislaid your daughter Helen's address and I am therefore writing to ask you to forward the enclosed. She had sent a photo of herself in "work on the land costume" to Michael and I want her to know it reached. Don't you think a desperate effort ought to be made now to compel our Government to accept the Germans "all for all" exchange of Civilian prisoners? I know you will do your utmost to bring this about.

In the most surprising way Michael got a fortnights "leave" and left Ruhleben on July 1st and spent his time with Germans in Jena who have a prisoner son here whom I look after. His description of German conditions varies considerably from that pictured to us by the Northcliffe Press!

Yours sincerely, Marjory Pease.

Dear Miss Wedgwood,

Just after I posted my card to you (and stupidly I did not keep your address) I got a letter from Michael written on July 12th–13th giving a description of a 30 mile walk begun at midnight through the Thuringia Forest in moonlight. In this letter he said "I had a letter yesterday from Helen Wedgwood enclosing a photo of herself 'on the land' and you may imagine the curiosity that that excited and the torrents of questions it called forth"! I think it is almost certain Michael has written to you from Jena but in case his letter doesn't reach you I thought I'd let you know he had got yours. He has written a letter to me every day from Jena. I am sure this fortnight spent with kind-hearted people in beautiful surroundings has done him endless good, but we must agitate for the "all for all exchange of Civilian Prisoners".

In haste, yours sincerely, Marjory Pease

....

Aug. 18th Fortnight's break owing to loss of fountain pen which distresses me mightily – just pinched from my cubby hole. Nothing much happened. Rumours and counter rumours of 45-ers. However, they are medically examining the 400: I'm afraid they wouldn't consider tortured aesthetic feeling sufficient excuse in my case, and as far as bodily fitness goes I should be the last to leave the camp. Up to Rüdiger yesterday who said it was no go to get out to Jena without some sort of a job. I broached the

Neumeisterian plan and he seemed to think that feasible. Letters from home again after a long pause. Grannie C.B. is dying[349] – I had always hoped I should have seen her again. They're getting my letters from Jena – they all seem [to be] coming through. Had an interview with Bolle re reagents but when I got back, found a letter saying there had been difficulties with C.P.W. [Central Prisoners of War] committee – damn them [correspondence in Appendix 3]. Got parcel containing shoes etc. Still reading de Bourienne. Much better in later chapters. Also read *Life of Carpenter* by himself, sent to me by the faithful Franklin.

Aug. 19th Quiet Sunday. Read Dietsche in morning, invigilated 11.30–1. Long walk and talk with Bell.

Aug. 20th Smitten with a great idea today to research on the cabbage white butterfly caterpillar for spermatogenesis. Rigged up a dissecting trough and got to work in the evening. Lechmere rather sniffy to begin with but once under way, mightily enthusiastic. Embedded a mass of material. If only the old reagents would come.

[7 days missing]

Aug. 28th Got advanced guard of Peieris [shrub] through and material looks thoroughly promising. Great do at *Appell* with "Barney" drunk as usual who made a dash for liberty and dodged round the grandstand and sent a soldier sprawling. Usual hideous scenes in the Barracks but they removed him to the *Wache* for the night. Had tea with Masterman and hatched a new scheme for independent member for Ref. Library on joint committee. Also discussed attitude towards the action of R.C.S. in dissolving the examinations committee. To Board of Studies meeting. Agreed to have no permanent chairman, but Blagden voted in pro-tem. Then Masterman launched his bolt about the examination subcommittee, and B. of S. agreed to make a protest. Then committee came in and the joint proceedings started by Masterman asking about the dissolution of the Examinations Subcommittee. Ford at his very worst when questions are being fired at him, on doubtfully correct proceedings. None of the committee is any good as a debater and really no defence was put up, though in my opinion the position was defendable. So ultimately the committee climbed down and

---

[349] Grannie Cote Bank (Susanna Pease) who died on 21st Sept 1917 (see letters on pages 329-334).

we were reappointed to finish off the work we were on, and also to report on future policy. Reagents have come today but have not yet been handed out: summoned up to parcels office to explain what I was having such dangerous things sent to me for, but I referred them to Bolle, whom I had already seen on the subject.

Aug. 29th Waited expectantly for my reagents, but no luck. Huge row brewing on the A.S.U. Committee owing to caddish treatment by old gang of Farmer. Examinations Committee meeting at 8.30 p.m. but spent two hours baiting Ford on points of order.

Aug. 30th Still no luck with reagents. Quartettes in the evening in Dodd's loft – mighty fine to get a little decent music now in the concertless days.

Aug. 31st Went to see Bolle today about reagents and he said he'd enquire. Played and lost in tennis tournament. Then to examination fray again. Got over our difficulty with regard to our *locus standi* after an hour's discussion and then got to work. However had to adjourn owing to bedtime. Patchett always runs a thing to death!

Sept. 1st Examinations Subcommittee at 8.30 a.m. and again at 9 p.m. Got everything ready and are only now awaiting report of London Matric Examinations. Still no reagents.

FIFTH DIARY

Sept. 2nd Sedan day[350] celebrated by flagwagging but no parade or speech making this year. Read *Ghosts* by request of Miller[351] who is going to lecture on the subject and wanted information on syphilis, which I gave him to the best of my ability. Otherwise I read *The Golden Bough* and had a day off committees!

Sept. 3rd Very grumpy over the reagents business. Went to see Bolle who said that the matter had now got into the hands of the *Kommandantur* [headquarters] who were going to send down a man to investigate. Lord what an existence it is always to be subject to this perpetual chicanerie.

---

[350] German national holiday, commemorating The Battle of Sedan (1870) which was held until 1918.

[351] Probably Hugh Miller, who was active in the Ruhleben Dramatic Society.

Sept. 4th Bolle true to his word! Summoned to lab. at 6 p.m. while making a tramp round the field. Found Bolle and strange man in mufty in possession. He was not introduced to me nor did he explain his mission but I twigged what he was. He didn't let on that he spoke English nor that he was a *Fachmann* [expert], so I dealt with him as best I could in my broken German. However bit by bit he showed himself to be well acquainted with everything. I showed him what there was and broached the question of my parcel. He said the xylol was all right, but was very doubtful about the alcohol, said I would booze it! Then we went down to chemie lab, asked to see Blagden. It seems that all orders from camp for material of a chemical nature goes to the *Kriegsministerium* [Ministry of War] and has to be O.K.ed by him. Took him to the A.S.U. dept. and there he interviewed Higgins. Truelove, Wolf, and Blagden turned up and we all talked and tried to convince him we were serious workers. I hammered away at the alcohol questions, but he seemed very sceptical! However, Bolle spoke good words for us. Final decision still unknown. Ended up the day with Examinations Subcommittee and finished vol. 2 of *Golden Bough* in bed.

Sept. 5th No chemicals turned up yet. Meeting re science library.

Sept. 6th Ditto. Quartette practice in Dodd's loft.

Sept. 7th Parcels given out today. There were 2, each sent off on July 6th. No alcohol or glycerine and only half the quantity of turps and of xylol. This perpetual chicanerie makes me wild. However, we had a great day clearing away old reagents and putting out a fresh set. Went to censors in afternoon but Bolle not there. Board of Studies meeting in evening.

Sept. 8th Busy day in the lab. Went to see Bolle about the reagents who says that Dr Burge has turned down the alcohol. I expostulated somewhat and he said he'd consult the doctor. Mercifully I've got enough alcohol to go on with. Tried using turpentine today for first time with mighty success. Played tennis 4–5 with Bell and then went to supper there. Discussed *Ghosts* and Spitzweg.[352] Then to lab and dissected caterpillars. Got a very marked preponderance of females, 6–1!! So to bed only to be interrupted by the usual drunks.

---

[352] Carl Spitzweg, a German romanticist painter.

Sept. 12th *Appell* today at 11 a.m. and those not already examined by the doctor were marched on to the field and inspected by the two doctors, with Rüdiger, the Major, Lambert, and Lawson hovering round. Kapp[353] pointed me out as the Herr Biologist and said I was looking very well! Went to see Bolle in the afternoon, who said all the chemicals were now at the doctors – good! Got the draft report of the R.H.S. to criticise – a most awful production, worse in composition than any of the captains' efforts and containing references to "experienced garden lovers"! – an expression open to quite another interpretation, especially in view of recent goings on! Saw Warner and told him straight out it wouldn't do, and he deferred very much to my criticisms and like the Kaiser, said it was really only a few rough notes to guide the committee. Finally to quartettes in Dodd's loft – little Williams in a great state of hurry.

Sept. 13th French as usual 7.30 a.m. Then saw Lambert re seeing Dr Kapp, but told to come at 10 a.m. Unfortunately had to go to R.H.S. Committee, which was a long and troublesome affaire. All the trouble arises from paying people – people ought to do things for love here not for cash. Got the report referred to a special committee to draw up. Anyhow it took all morning. Played tennis at 2 p.m. and then microtomed. To bed and to the *Golden Bough.*

Sept. 14th Spent all day over R.H.S. report and got about half through and delivered to typist. Went to see Kapp in morning about my alcohol and he assured me it would be all right, but if there was no particular hurry he would just let it take its turn. Got a great note from the F.O. about my reagents, so I wrote an acknowledgment to them. I see by their invoice that <u>all</u> the xylol and turpentine was delivered to me.

Sept. 15th Continued the R.H.S. report and finished that off in the morning. Letters from home saying that the scheme to get Walter N.[354] to Limpsfield is off – I feared it would be difficult with a soldier.

Sept. 16th Hear that Warner is as sick as muck about my alterations to his draft.

---

[353] Dr J. F. Kapp, one of the German doctors who, according to Powell and Gribble (1919), made life much better for invalids in the camp.

[354] Walter Neumeister – probably an invitation for leave in return for Michael's visit to Jena.

Michael at work in the biology laboratory

Camp school science department, September 1917. Middle row left to right: Pease, Lechmere, Blagden. Front row left hand side: Lochhead

Sept. 17th Meeting to consider my draft at 3 p.m., Warner absent in a huff! Several alterations made. Went to *Ghosts* with Bell. Very well done indeed, but poor discussion by Miller!

Sept. 18th Enrolling at the school, tiresome sort of a job and very exhausting. Spent evening with Harris retyping draft report.

Sept. 19th Second day enrolling. Birch got the new embedding bath fixed up, which looks mighty fine. Lambert rushed up to me and told me to come for my alcohol next day!

Sept. 20th Committee of R.H.S. Simon very critical of my draft; said it was too much like the old one and asked why I hadn't put the old one in the waste paper basket and started afresh – and that after I had taken such pains to spare Warner's feelings. Went away before end of meeting and got my absolute alcohol, so that matter is brought to a successful conclusion. Wonderful notice put up threatening the camp with all sorts of horrors if people continue to escape!

Sept. 21st Got to work directly after breakfast to make final corrections to R.H.S. report and got it "OKed" by Hill, Cooper, and Warner and so handed it over to typist. 10 a.m. meeting of B. of Studies at which I raised my pet point about departmental studies. More or less decided to order a microscope and got Higgins to make enquiries at Leitz. Harris has just got 6 days leave, so his concert is off. My joyous expectations of the Dvorak quintette have come to nought. Instead we mobilised a trio, S., Marshall, and Morvaren[355] – the 7th Beethoven is grand. And so to bed and read *Petit Bob* – not much good. Great box of pears from Neumeister.

Sept. 22nd Not much doing. Wrote p.c. to Neumeister.

Sept. 23rd Meeting of R.H.S. Committee 10 a.m. and awful "do" on. Warner had, in writing up the minutes left out the word "conflicting" in a resolution, there had been a great discussion about this resolution. He had taken the word as a vote of censure on himself and didn't like this to go into the official records, and so he just left it out. Of course everyone was up on his hind legs and after various explanations and long speeches, W.

[355] Quentin Stuart Morvaren MacLean (1896–1962), an organist, composer and teacher who was studying music in Leipzig at the outbreak of war. Known in the camp as Quentin Morvaren.

resigned and left the room. I was put in the chair and finished off the business. In many ways W.'s resignation is a great blow – but there was nothing else in the circumstances to be done – especially as it came out in discussion afterwards that he had said to Cayley that it would be all right, it would be read through quickly and no-one would notice! Then we had a subcommittee at 3 p.m. to read through a vast quantity of unsigned minutes! Then full committee at 7 p.m. Roberts[356] there and very concerned about W. Wanted him recalled, but as he got no support withdrew his motion. I was elected to take the chair at the annual meeting. Then a caucus meeting to decide officers. Went round and saw Simon, and then to Pritchard: P. will become president, but tells me Butterworth is going to take the chair!!! And so to bed with a splitting headache after a very hard day's work.

Sept. 24th Got hold of Butterworth first thing and explained the situation; quite agreeable to move adoption of report as a consolation prize. Got through meeting very well: kept the *"stimmung"* [tone] good all through. It was painful to have to explain the Warner incident but I was afterwards congratulated on it. Usual encounter with Wimpfy which I managed to keep in good humour. He got me out of the Chair at one point and then moved me back again. Then I got my own back by turning him down on many points! Ended up with moving from the Chair a vote of thanks to Warner – this on the wise instigation of MacKenzie. Elected top of the poll for Committee. Afternoon strolling round field and garden trying to take stock of things and in evening conference with Cooper and Howat re committee meeting. And so to bed not quite as tired and feeling that we've really got a stage forward.

Sept. 25th Wrote letter home in morning, rather late. Committee meeting in afternoon. Pritchard there and in great form and got through the business in great style. The only cantankerousness came from little Cooper.[357] Pritchard in to tea and Marshall in to supper and so to bed and finished *Petit Bob.*

---

[356] Leonard Plato Roberts (1879–1961), Vice-Chair of the RHS and keen rosarian. A handicrafts teacher, he was visiting Germany to see rose gardens when war broke out. He kept in touch with Michael after the war (letter in Appendix 1, page 368).

[357] Of the two Coopers in the Ruhleben Horticultural Society, Bert was shorter.

Sept. 26th *"Les habitants d'un certain box dans le camp parlent un jargon assez curieux, dout la singularité consiste dans l'emploi d'un galimatie d'expressions, tirées en partie de l'anglais et en partie de l'allemande ce qui n'enpêche pas leur conversation d'être généralement très banale"* [The inhabitants of a certain box in the camp speak a rather curious jargon, whose singularity consists in the use of a galaxy of expressions drawn partly from English and partly from German, although this does not prevent their conversation being generally very banal]. I found the above sentence in a French exercise book of Rawson's which he left lying on my place in the cubby hole, and the handwriting was either his or Pritchard's. Anyhow now we know the Pritchardian judgement on us. Thank goodness our conversation is spared the high flown verbiage of Bergson, mixed with Duncan-Jones' unctuous condemnations and Struckmeyer's[358] ultra patriotic sentiments!

Sept. 27th Had a conference with Roberts and Cooper about various R.H.S. business and particularly about public garden. Joined by Anderson who seems a very sound man. Dentist at 2.30 p.m. – not a long *"sitzung"* [session] but I thought Rutterford was not half as careful as Moore. Sent p.c. to order soap from Paris. Beautiful afternoon in field. Mobilised Pauer to play trios with S. and M. but not satisfactory – first M. got fed up, and then P. and instead of a soothing evening it was quite the reverse.

Sept. 28th Wrote up minutes of General Meeting of R.H.S. this morning. Microtome in afternoon, nice to be back at work again. Walk round field with Bell: talk with Cooper on camp gardens. Beethoven trios in the loft and so to bed.

Sept. 29th Work in morning, microtome afternoon and R.H.S. committee in evening. Pritchard very good in the chair, and in general the *stimmung* was very much better. All much annoyed at the report which Warner sent home off his own bat.

Sept. 30th Good day's work for once in a way!

....

---

[358] According to the Sherborne School lists, Otto Keith Struckmeyer (1896–1975) a student at Trinity College, was interned in Ruhleben with his schoolmate Arthur John Smyth. In 1938 he was Wiltshire's Director for Education and changed his name to Keith Struckmeyer Innes (*London Gazette*, 22 Mar 1938).

HBW to MSP (received September sometime?):

Moddershall Oaks, Stone, Staffs.

Aug. 20th 1917

Dear Mr. Pease,

It was so delightful to get your letter of July 13th and hear your news. Of course I haven't been interned, so perhaps I can't quite realise what you felt, but I can imagine a lot. It must have been the most wonderful thing in the world. I had just spent a long day alone in the Cotswolds, and up there it seemed unbearable that people should be shut up, and damnably silly to have crowded camps and towns when all the hills and sky are empty. So it was jolly to get your letter and know you had had a bit of it. But oh dear, how horrible going back must have been. And though imagination and memory will go a long way, they aren't really satisfying, are they?

If I had known the photo was "for enemy consumption" I would have sent a more industrious looking group. Thank you very much for yours. The old Frau looks a perfect dear. I use your letters extensively as evidence that Germans do not go round all day with the Hymn of Hate on their lips! Also I may say your account made me feel rather ashamed that I hadn't taken more pains to be nice to the German prisoners on the nurseries. I did try, but you know how difficult it is to think of opening remarks (especially if you can't remember your genders or irregular verbs), and I didn't see much of them during the short time I was there; so that great international subject, the Weather, was our principal topic. Both the foreman (a charming Dutchman) and "the boss" were very nice to them.

You can guess we are all much agitated about Stockholm,[359] *and everyone feels restlessly that events are in the air, but unfortunately everyone prophesies according to their wishes, without any regard for probabilities. I suppose the Revolution has had less effect in this country than in any other. But even here it is perfectly amazing to see the changes of attitude that have resulted from it. What used to be wild dreams now seem reasonable political aims; and it looks as if it would prove to be the final blow to the belief that "as things have been, they remain". I hope the Russian Revolutionaries who died know a little what they have done for us. I wonder what papers you get? It is fairly safe to believe anything in inverse ratio to what the Northcliffe press says about it!*

---

[359] Socialist conference in response to the Russian February conference; UK, French and US delegates were banned from travelling to it.

We are at home all together for a bit, with our usual large party of visitors. Perhaps you imagine us a serious and studious crowd, discussing the socialist state, or "pacifism in its economic aspect". – I am afraid you are a serious person yourself, – so I will not disillusion you, except by saying that in the last week I have been – a Russian Nihilist (masked), Mordecai, Noah, The River Nile, George Washington's cherry tree and Bluebeard. In the intervals I go round what garden there is with a professional air and an agricultural walk and give good advice, while the family listens in awed admiration.

I wish I could send you a bit of our wood – but as it is pouring with rain you might not be properly grateful. Good luck to the researches. Don't poison yourself or blow out an eye (Bekassy has just done his best to take off his hand with homemade gunpowder – to Rosamund's intense professional joy).

Yours very sincerely,

Helen Bowen Wedgwood

....

Oct. 1st [no entry]

Oct. 2nd An eventless birthday, which passed utterly unnoticed. The last birthday I was alive I cycled from Cambridge to home. Dodd wants "to learn science", so I started him off this evening with Thompson on astronomy – a lecture which was both facetious and philosophically unsound; however the former passages greatly amused Dodd.

Oct. 3rd [no entry]

Oct. 4th R.H.S. committee meeting this evening. Went off in great style, Benjy much less bumptious and got well snubbed.

[Insert: notice of R.H.S. Committee Meeting, 4 Oct. 1917 from Hon. Secy. Frederick G. Lane]

Oct. 5th Got my second *sendung* [shipment] of reagents via the A.M.X. today. Handed out by the doctor with no difficulty beyond waiting in the loathesome crowd at the *Schonungsbaracke*.

Oct. 6th Went to rehearsal this morning to hear Speed play the Beethoven Concerto – good. Lechmere 10–11, and took my first essay "class" at 11 a.m. To meeting of R.H.S. Committee at 7 p.m.

Oct. 7th Wrote letter home in morning and went to theatre in evening to *Candida.* Marshall as Marchbanks, very good indeed. The whole thing enterprisingly well done.

[Insert: programme for *Candida* by G. B. Shaw, produced by R. Llewellyn Brown]

Oct. 8th Looking through some of my slides on the immersion lens today – really very nice mitotic [cell division] figures, though no sign of sex chromosomes. There seem to be some quaint anomalies which much took Lechmere.

Oct. 9th Awful day of rain. Cut sections all afternoon, and went to concert in the evening. Mighty fine, and Speed got a huge ovation as his first public appearance.

[Insert: programme for Symphony Concert, Tuesday Oct. 9th. Conductor: J Peebles Conn]

Oct. 10th [no entry]

[Insert: programme for French play *La Charette Anglaise*, 10 Oct. 1917]

Oct. 11th Committee of R.H.S. went off swimmingly, though we didn't get through it all!

Oct. 12th Great joke is Ruhleben in the Reichstag. The *verbot* [prohibition] of the *B.T.* [*Berliner Tageblatt*] was discussed à propos of the so called "*Aufklärungsarbeit*" [educational work]! Anyhow it is rumoured that von Borck has got the sack over it, and the new officer that Powell was conducting round is his successor. We now have a 3rd *Appell* as a punishment for the repeated escapes!!

[Insert: programme for 1st Chamber Concert, Tuesday Oct. 23rd]

[Insert: memorandum from R.H.S. about purchase of vegetable seeds from England with the help of the Royal Horicultural Society, London, Oct. 31st]

[Insert: notice of R.H.S. meeting in the Science Lecture Room on Oct. 31st – Mr. Roylands Cooper talking on "The Immediate Work in the Camp Gardens", and notice of a Committee meeting in Barrack 6 Loft on Nov. 1st]

[Insert: letter from the Theatre Office, Oct 31st from Aubrey H Hersee (stage director) inviting all 31 Ruhleben play producers to have a group photo on Nov. 11th, 1917]

[Insert: programme for 2nd Chamber Concert, Tuesday Nov. 20th]

[Insert: programme for *Arms and the Man*, 21 Nov. 1917. Produced by T. W. Wilson]

[Insert: A.S.U. "Webster Evening" – Lecture by C. F. Winzer, illustrated by acts from *The Duchess of Malfi* and *The White Devil*, 26 Nov. 1917]

[Insert: programme for *Serata Musicale* concert by the Italian Circle, 16 Dec. 1917]

[Insert: A.S.U. Concert programme for 2nd Schumann–Liszt evening, Monday Dec. 17th 1917, arranged by Mr. E. H. Govett]

No more diary entries until January 1918, but the correspondence continues:

....

HBW to MSP:

Moddershall Oaks, Stone, Staffs.

Sept. 4th 1917

Dear Mr. Pease,

I've just got to my surprise and joy another letter from you, – June 29. It is all very well though for you to try to make up for having completely forgotten me at Cambridge by saying nice things about my letters. It won't wash! I am deeply hurt; but of course, I cannot wreak my vengeance on a captive, (especially if his dungeon is 500 miles or so away); but I assure you I shall prepare a fitting revenge for your return. Being only on the outer fringe of the Morris dancers I admit I contemplated the "revolution" with some amusement. But you won't get off by pleading that we only met once, for I went to nearly every party at Mrs. Stewart's that year, – besides C.U.F.S and Heretics, (and that awful man Ready's lecture), not to mention Mrs. Cornford's Friday evenings. – Cheer up, we only spoke two or three times, and my Proper Awe, as a fresher, made me far too nervous to mention Bedales or anything else (though I knew your Bedales nickname before I knew your real one). Besides you weren't exactly inconspicuous were you? So you should expect to be known by people you have never heard of. But you will never make a candidate for Parliament if you don't conceal your ignorance better. – You should see me acquiring the art under Father's able tuition –

What can one say about the war? All the world is off its head. We pacifists pride ourselves on keeping comparatively sane, but we aren't really. If we really used our imaginations we should go off our heads. At the least one would be impelled to go up and down the streets shouting to people to stop. But, like everyone else, one comes to take it almost as a matter of course; it remains only a dull ache in the background; and there is so much to do, and the sun shines, and one is fairly happy in spite of everything. It is awful how one gets used to things. By the way your mother has asked me to go and visit her when I go south. So I'm anticipating a lively time as she says she wants to "get to know my point of view". Is she very overwhelming in argument? It's awful to hold views like ours, – the moment you confess to them, everyone turns round on you and tells you to justify your position, – and it would take many fat volumes to do it adequately. In the future I mean to tell them to justify theirs first.

Yes, Research for research sake may be all very well. But Nero pursuing Art for Art sake, while Rome burnt, does not get much sympathy, and it seems to me that some people bury themselves in research to avoid more pressing and serious problems. But I have rather reacted from my too intellectual upbringing by going to the other extreme. Relations with people seem to be the one important thing and work seems important principally from its effect on the character of the worker. This makes actual achievement seem a small thing; – I wonder if that is a cowardly or a brave belief? The history of civilisation seems to me the history of people who have believed in work or knowledge or art for their own sakes, and never seriously bothered at all about people. So these other things which might be so splendid, have all been twisted wrong. Don't think that I don't sympathise with your research; because I do very much; but I should be sorry if you gave your whole life to it to the exclusion of, say, your socialism. I don't at all agree with you about French literature. I love the memoirs and letters, – Mme de Montpensier, Mme Roland, Mme De Sevigne; also Victor Hugo and many modern French writers; not to mention historians like Michelet and the chroniclers. Even those Alexandrians of which you complain have their charm, – only you must be in a powder and brocade mood!

Goodbye and good luck.

Yours Helen Wedgwood

P.S. Sorry this is such a meandering letter, but there was such a lot to answer in yours

....

MSP to HBW:

Ruhleben, Oct. 6th 1917

Very many thanks for yours of July 24th and of August 20th. Glad you got mine from Jena, but did you get one I sent from here on June 29th? Yes, I was afraid the English Censor wouldn't allow the Russell, but I too saw a copy in Berlin! Thank you all the same for the attempt! I have been frightfully busy and had no time for literary "frills" outside "shop"; it is important to get ahead with as much of the microscopic work as possible before the cold weather makes one's breath condense on the slides. Lately, I too have been doing Market Gardening – but as a "director"! The chamber concert season starts here next week, to my mighty content. My best wishes to you, my fellow gardener! Michael Pease.

....

HBW to MSP:

12 Beaufort House, Beaufort Street, London SW3

Oct. 12th 1917

Dear Mr. Pease,

Your p.c. of Aug 11 reached me safely in the wilds of S. Wales. Going back must have been dreadful, and internment is not the sort of thing that becomes less boring with time. There is nothing one can say is there? except "grin and bear it" – (a maxim most of our generation seems to spend its youth following) –. Don't let yourself get depressed thinking of the war. It can do no good. Think rather what a lot there will be do afterwards. Everything is in the melting pot and we shall have a chance few generations have had. Oh I know it is easy to talk, but we have got to keep ourselves hopeful, not to let all this unhappiness crush or deaden us. If only people will keep their spirits alive and their energies fresh we shall yet be able to make the world a decent place. So don't get dwelling on your "pessimistic outlook". Consider the war merely as the final smash up of the old system. The tragedy has affected us and our class more nearly and more spectacularly than the slums and factories did; but when an evil has a result as impossible to forget or hideous as this war, there is some hope of getting it set right. You hear all the worst where you are; you don't hear the talk, say, in railway carriages or see how the old standards are becoming more and more discredited. (This is what we really think, I'm not saying it to "cheer you up") # # # Here I pause to have a violent argument with a Scotch girl who believes in the divine right of Landlords; (as Bolton Hall[360] *says, "the fear of the landlord is the beginning of wisdom") # # #*

I am afraid you will form a very poor idea of my character when I tell you that I have changed my job again! It was due in this case to the intervention of Heaven, as I really was intending to continue my market gardening career, when a beautiful job under the Board of Woods and Forests dropped from the skies. So now I spend my days in larch woods, with four other very nice girls measuring samples and compiling statistics with a view to future afforestation – useful work, and interesting and one of the few good jobs that are not war work; also there are excellent prospects for us after the war.

It is a lovely life, though it is rather a drawback being so much in the wilds and out of touch with things. One feels such a worm to be enjoying oneself so and doing nothing. We move from Welsh farmhouse to farmhouse, and as our breeches and big boots save us from being considered mere ladies, it is easy talking to people, and I am acquiring a most professional air in discussing heads of sheep, different kinds of cheese, and the difficulties of ploughing on a steep slope. Our principal time for reading is the dinner hour, when I study the Herald or the Nation, or argue pacifism with W.H. Guillebaud (the economist's brother and our 'boss'). The others, I am sorry to say, are not as respectful to the Herald as they should be.

Sometimes we work in woods where prisoners are felling. Unfortunately it is "strengst verboten" to talk to them. They seem to be a cheerful lot, and it can't be a bad life, but it is hateful seeing men with a sentry always over them – every action to order. One can't get away from the war even in these Welsh hills.

I hope your opinion of French literature has improved. Have you tried Michelet's History of the French Revolution? It is splendid French and very good reading. Do you like Victor Hugo? Les Miserables is too long, but Quatre Vingt Treize is much shorter and very good. I am very fond of his poetry too. Do you know "Le Chasseur Noir" and "Les Lions"? A number of the old French rondels are charming also. But I shall become a catalogue if I go on.

The other night I had my first experience of air raids in London. I'm afraid I rather enjoyed it. There is a queer feeling of fellowship sitting in the dark on the landing with a dozen or so other unknown people, listening to a tremendous banging outside, with the bare possibility of being blown into the next world. The noise of the guns and the extraordinary whistling of the shells is wonderful, and there is just enough danger (about 1 in 200,000!) to give it spice. This is a heartless

---

[360] An American lawyer, author, and Georgist (a type of economic philosophy) activist.

way of looking at it, and I know it is a very different business in the crowded tenements of the E. End, where people are really frightened, and it comes night after night too. But it was such a surprise to find that a lot of noise and a little danger might be pleasant. One feels curiously irresponsible and ready for anything. Of course I only had 2 nights of it, and before bed time too!

Good luck to your researches, and all good wishes.

Yours very sincerely,

Helen Bowen Wedgwood

Here is a bit of Douglas fir. If you crush it, you can smell our woods

....

Otto Neumeister to Marjory Pease (received on 20th Nov. 1917):

Jena

Oct. 19th 1917

Dear Mrs. Pease,

From week to week I have been hoping to answer your two kind letters, to my wife of the 18th July and to me of the 9th August. Both letters have given us again a great joy: we saw from them that all news about our dear visitor "Mr. Michael" safely reached your hands and that you could form a picture of how Michael has been feeling with us. We always think with joy of Michael. He was so modest and kind and cheerfulness beamed from his eyes because for a few days he was removed from the monotonous camp life, we were very sorry that the time passed so quickly.

The reason for my long wait in replying was that I hoped to be able to communicate to you, dear Mrs. Pease, a still greater joy, and waited from day to day for a reply to my petition. After I received your kind letter of the 18th July I took steps to get Michael quite free so that he could live with us until the end of this most awful of all wars. Unfortunately up to today no decision has yet come in. I assume from this that my petition is being given consideration, otherwise I should have at once received a decision of refusal. The high authority will be first obtaining information about me and I hope that this has now been done. I shall as soon as I hear, let you know and if necessary I shall also, in spite of the short time at my disposal, journey myself to Berlin in order to put through what is necessary. We are bound to you in great thanks and you can, dear Mrs. Pease, reckon absolutely upon my gratitude: I shall leave nothing untried. You have spared my wife and me and Miss Frieda through your kind care towards our Walter, much grief and anxiety and we can only pray that God may reward you.

Through Prof. Ornstein I received news today of you and our Walter. We rejoice that Michael has written to Walter and could report to him how we are. We have learned with great joy from your kind communication, as the Prof. wrote to us, that you have received a letter from the Chief of the Prisoners Camp according to which he is troubling to bring our Walter to be interned in Holland, the greater my endeavour to exert everything to make possible also for Michael the transference to Jena. Please tell the Chief we shall always remember with gratitude his humane intention [note: neither of these schemes came to pass].

The last card we have had from Michael is of the 22nd September. I enclose it for you with this letter. We are always glad if we can have a few lines from our Walter. It is really touching how thankful your dear Michael is for every trouble. besides this he sent two cards [Ruhleben postcards], *one from his teaching college and the other from his Botanical Garden, I assume that you have received similar ones. On the 2nd of this month Michael had his birthday. We thought of sending him a parcel in order to give him special pleasure on this day. It is to be hoped that he received this on his day of joy. I have not yet written to him direct of my petition, the greater will then be the joy for him if my petition is considered. I hope for the best.*

Our best wishes accompany these lines, and send to you and your dear ones heartiest greetings,

from your grateful Otto Neumeister & Wife and Miss Frieda.

....

MSP to HBW:

Ruhleben, Oct. 20th 1917

Many thanks for yours of Sept 4th: glad you got mine of June 29 at last. Well, I decline to enter into controversies, political, literary, or philosophical on a p.c. I will take to heart your suggestions on French. Please don't be alarmed at my dear M [other]*: I love and admire her beyond words and we get on tremendously well together, though we hardly agree on a single point in political theory or in philosophy of life. Her specialty is immediate practice, not ultimate theories. I long to hear more of your agricultural ventures. Just been listening to Beethoven Trio No. 5 and a wonderful Dvorak quintet: dreaming away, in another world! Best wishes, MS Pease*

....

HBW to MSP:

12 Beaufort House, Beaufort Street, London SW3

Nov. 10th 1917

Dear Mr. Pease,

Many thanks for your postcard of Oct 6th. I am glad you saw the Russell. What did you think of it? Some chapters, particularly the first and the ones on War, Marriage and Education are very good, but "the State" I thought poor and inconclusive.

Is a 'director' of a market garden a swell term for foreman? We don't go in for frills of the kind; – "boss", "gov'ner" and "hand" are good enough for us. – But I bet you don't know what a "tusher" is?

We are still in Wales, at Llandovery, an absurd little Welsh town with 23 pubs, and about as many houses, – a townhall as large as all the rest, and – a Mayor!! He was elected on Saturday and went to chapel on Sunday in a scarlet robe preceded by a brass-band and the acclamations of the populace, and followed by gratified and superior chapel-goers. There is a great deal of truth in the Napoleon of Notting Hill.[361] *A Mayor gives the citizens a sense of civic responsibility, and an opportunity for making a noise, – both excellent. This one, we were informed in a speech by one of his supporters, is the best possible Mayor to have "as he has a large heart and a purse to match"!!*

This life is delightful. I do wish you could have seen the woods this autumn. (See Shelley and Swinburne). Of all parts of the day the evening is most pleasant, when one comes home through wet woods and gorgeous sunsets, to a good fire and <u>tea</u>! But the dinner hour is jolly too when we eat roasted potatoes and toasted sandwiches, round a log fire. Then it's "Have you got a Herald or Nation handy, Wedge? There doesn't seem to be a Daily Mail, and one must read something". – An excellent opportunity, for propaganda, you will observe. You should see our boots too! I am wearing the pair Father had in Gallipoli; – poor things, they aren't having a very peaceful old age.

Lately we have had added to our party a really very nice Eton boy, with a delightfully secure belief in the superiority of the "English Gentleman" (as raised at Eton) over everything else. He <u>was</u> so shocked when he heard I had spoken at

---

[361] G. K. Chesterton novel published in1904.

street corners. We are hoping to entrap him into reading the Labour Leader, – just to see his face. The other addition is a rather trying Scotchman, who thinks this isn't "women's work" – and we work a jolly sight harder than he does.

Perhaps you don't think that Aberystwyth is a centre of civilisation and 'Kultur'? I assure you it seems Paris and New York rolled into one after our stay in the "wild and woolly West". The above mentioned band has been our only dissipation for weeks.

I've been reading Dostoevsky's Idiot; it is splendid in parts, – but what a nightmare! Also Vol. I of Tolstoy's Diaries. They give a queer picture of him. What a fighter he was! This sounds funny from him though, doesn't it – "Resolve never to tolerate the least insult, but to make them pay double for it"!!! But through everything runs his savage hatred of shams. I don't think though it would be fair to read them unless one knew his life pretty well, and could realise, that, as he says himself, the Diaries give a very one-sided picture.

As you see, I have really nothing to tell you this letter, except to wish you well.

I hope the research work is satisfactory in spite of the cold. It would be rather impressive if you brought out a book, wouldn't it? I don't think a scientific work (except perhaps Raleigh's History of the World!) has been brought out under such circumstances.

So goodbye,

Yours Helen Wedgwood.

……………………

MSP to HBW:

Ruhleben, Dec. 15th 1917

I have thoroughly enjoyed the Russell now that I've had time to go through it properly. I agree wholeheartedly with the "direction", but not with every word. It is being much enjoyed by others here who can appreciate such things. K[aufmann]'s[362] *marginal notes are distressingly funny, because he keeps on missing the point! Very very many thanks for having mobilised it for me. I hope you flourish. I often think of you up in the wild Welsh hills I know so well. Here I have to make dream hills and woods do! But I've just been having the real thing in singing – I've been listening to some of the Mörike songs by Hugo Wolf. Do you*

---

[362] Georg von Kaufmann, whose son George Adams Kaufmann was at Cambridge in 1912 (and was President of the Cambridge University Socialist Society in 1915, succeeded by Helen in 1916).

know them? They are grand. Too cold for lab work now! My best wishes and again many thanks for the Russell. MS Pease

....

HBW to MSP:

Moddershall Oaks, Stone, Staffs.

Dec. 20th 1917

Dear Mr. Pease,

Mrs. Pease has sent me on a copy of your letter of Nov 4th. I am rather flabbergasted at the result of a casual remark of mine. I fear if the Daily Mail saw your letter it would proclaim me a bolo [Bolshevik] *of the deepest dye, and I hasten to disclaim any knowledge of the gentleman in the fur coat. As you must be wondering what on earth I was up to, I had better explain that when writing to the father of a boy we know I asked him to pass the book on to you, as I knew he had it. The results of my simple request seem to have been somewhat beyond my expectations! Did they bring you a gold and velum copy stamped with the German eagle? My correspondent, so far as I know, is in business in Galicia, and I haven't the least idea what his connection is with such exalted quarters. I am consumed with laughter every time I think of that book of all others being brought you by such hands* [Kaufmann]. *But I wish you would remember that censors are rather a large feature of modern life, – for all of us!*

I do hope it has been all right so far as you are concerned. I never dreamed of raising such a dust and I hope it hasn't bothered you, but has had a good effect.

We are sitting in a Temperance Hotel (of all places) in the rich and noble borough of Llanidloes. Yesterday we bicycled from Yspytty Ystwyth (nr Aberystwyth) 25 miles across the lower slopes of Plynlimon, over a wonderful barren pass between the Ystwyth and the Wye, – about 5 forlorn little farms the whole way.

Our principal topic of conversation at the moment is trains home, a most enthralling topic. It will seem very funny to be in England again and able to understand conversations.

I have a fearful lot of Christmas letters to write, so this is not a proper letter; but I thought I had better write to you and explain (I shall probably have to explain to DORA[363] *or some such person too).*

With best wishes for the New Year,

[363] Code word for the censors: Defense of the Realm Act.

Yours sincerely

Helen Wedgwood

....

[Insert: poster and programme for *The Gondoliers,* Gilbert and Sullivan. Xmas 1917. Produced by Fred Anderson and Harold F Hamlyn]

[Insert: M.S. Pease's menu for Christmas Day meal 1917, *Englaewoerlager Ruhleben.* Signed by F. Schlesinger, T. H. Marshall, Arthur E. Dodd, Douglas D. Jones and Walter E. Dodd]

[Insert: two unused satirical Ruhleben Christmas postcards]

1918 Diaries and Letters

Jan. 1st A New Year's resolution to start keeping my diary again; stopped partly out of slackness but also because Sharman adopted the habit of occupying my place in the cubby hole at the time of day at which I usually made my entries. New Year's Eve was spent in saying farewell to the various 45-ers.[364] Farewell meeting at R.H.S. Committee at which there was not much speechifying, some very genuine expressions of regret and good wishes. After supper some music in the loft. Marshall, Philips and Pauer played a Schumann trio and afterwards Marshall and P. a Bach sonata and then fairly quiet till nearly midnight when pandemonium started in the compound headed by a bagpipe and an enthusiastic band of Scots. About 2 a.m. things quieted down and it was possible to get to sleep. See Tom Eckersley[365] in the lost list today; I wonder if there will be a single friend left me after they've all finished? Ill luck that he should fall and not his worthless brother. Today I made my farewells to Pritchard; we shall all miss him very much. Allowed to stay up till 11 p.m., a *"vergünstigung"* [privilege] which the camp hardly appreciated and didn't make much use of after the revels the night before.

Jan. 2nd Quiet and eventless day. Worked on Driesch in the morning. Walk round the field with Masterman in the afternoon, more Driesch and so to bed.

Jan. 3rd Quiet morning with Driesch. Summoned to Censor in the afternoon who handed me another book, a Norman Angell[366] – from Kaufmann. The letter spoke also of one of Morel's,[367] but that was not forthcoming, so it will mean another visit to enquire. Dreamt vividly that Eleanor[368] had lost her husband and was trying to write a letter of condolence.

---

364 According to British newspapers, 360 prisoners over the age of 45 were released, including Prichard and Butterworth.

365 Bedalian/Trinity College friend Thomas Eckersley, who did survive the war, as did his brother.

366 Sir Ralph Norman Angell, journalist and author who became a Labour MP.

367 Possibly E. D. *Morel*, a French-born British journalist, author, pacifist, and politician.

368 Possibly Michael's cousin Eleanor Mary Pease, who married her 2nd cousin Gervase Lawson Ford in 1913.

Jan. 4th Quiet morning again, but furious snow blizzard in afternoon. This however gave opportunity for a solitary walk, so plunged out in the snow with Bell, but conversation was difficult! Wrote to Kaufmann and went to Censor, but Franke was there, who knew nothing of the missing book.

Jan. 5th Quiet day, reading with usual Ruhleben interruptions. Talk with Cooper about various R.H.S. matters.

Jan. 6th Thank goodness for another quiet day – really getting ahead with Driesch and see what he's driving at. Long walk and talk with Wechsler who told me about Zionism and Palestine.

Jan. 7th Driesch again in the morning. Went down to lab and found them putting up the double partitions without putting any stuffing in, so made them stop (for which they were very grumpy), and then mobilised waste paper in great quantity. Eventually they got the job finished and hope it will be satisfactory.

Jan. 9th Morning interview with Higgins' various private secretaries, re my business with the *Auskunft und Hilfsstelle*[369] [Information and Assistance]. Meeting of B. of S. with regard to lantern slides which are being offered to us by the famous *Aufklärungs Abteilung* [enlightenment department] of the war office. Decided to accept them on the understanding that we were in no way bound to go in for Deutsche propaganda! It's a very attractive catalogue. I suggested we should start with the series England *der Hauptfeind* [the main enemy]. Saw Higgins myself in afternoon – very *freundlich*! Saw Bolle re the missing book from Kaufmann. Seems that only one book came and that from Major Grabam[?]. Got finished with Driesch (which I found thoroughly interesting, though I don't know enough philosophy to be critical) and now we'll have a go at *L'évolution Créatrice*![370] To meeting of R.H.S. – Buckley on peaches – poorish paper but good *Stimmung* [atmosphere] and discussion. Having finished "*Le Blé qui leve*" a very rambling story (or rather stories), I turned to the Bible again and finished off Solomon.

---

[369] *Auskunft und Hilfsstelle für Deutsche im Ausland und Ausländer in Deutschland* – a Berlin-based charity founded in Oct 1914 by Frau Dr Elisabeth Rotten and Professor Friedrich Siegmund-Schultze, which helped civilian victims of the war. Higgins was their link in Ruhleben.

[370] *Creative Evolution*, by Henri Bergson.

Jan. 10th Quietish morning wrote letter to Dr Rotten.[371] Interrupted afternoon. Roupell at 4 p.m. (he's almost hopeless, I think) and R.H.S. committee at 7 p.m. Went off fairly well, slight *Zwischenfall* [incident] between Roberts and Buckley, but got over that by going on to the next business. I was put on the Constitution Committee in place of Pritchard. Then went and looked at the slide catalogue of the *Aufklärungs Abteilung* with a view to arranging courses for the R.H.S.

Jan. 11th Futile sort of day rather. Made a beginning with Bergson [*L'évolution Créatrice*]. Got skates, soap (second lot) and D'Arcy Thompson[372] today. Latter very attractive. Dentist at 11 a.m. who made several mildly unpleasant discoveries. Pottered about and sent off letter to Dr. Rotten. Then R[oupell] and Crossland at 4 p.m. (stick to my opinion of former). Then while I was dabbling through Weisman[373] in comes Corless to know if I'll give a lecture on syphilis, introductory to his performance of *Damaged Goods.*[374] I had to confess I didn't know the play but I undertook to read the play and do what I could. Lechmere was to have done it, but he's crocked. I hate doing things at short notice: one of my perpetual complaints against the A.S.U. Then Masterman to supper and to meeting of ref. library invigilators to discuss plan of campaign for ref. library general meeting next day. So to bed and read *Damaged Goods* – not great as a play, but a huge great puff by Bernard Shaw.

Jan. 12th I started the morning to search for Mr. Podsnap[375] for the quotation I heard Harold Wright cite long ago. Got him very quickly. Then finished reading Shaw's preface and got out more or less of a scheme for a 10 minutes jaw – it will probably fall out at about 20 mins. Failed to find a copy of *Quintessence of Ibsenism*[376] for a quotation about Ghosts. 1 p.m. the reference library meeting. Quite a big crowd there, came late myself. Thorpe in the chair and Jones speaking. Moved his resolution and after

---

[371] Dr Elisabeth Rotten, a Swiss national (and Quaker) raised in Germany, who ran the *Auskunft und Hilfsstelle* charity (fn 369). She helped source scientific equipment and other things for the school laboratories.

[372] *On Growth and Form*, published 1917.

[373] Possibly Prof August Weismann, a German evolutionary biologist with numerous publications.

[374] Translation of French play *Les Avariés* by Eugène Brieux, about a couple with syphilis.

[375] A character in Dickens' *Our Mutual Friend.*

[376] G. B. Shaw essay.

several speeches Ford got up and opposed. Danhorn supported Ford and got suppressed and eventually had to sit down. It was worth it just to see him squashed. Division at 2.30 p.m. on 2nd resolution 71–60 against Ford's amendment. Near go. Original resolution carried by 84–36. I hadn't expected so many people would turn up, and it was rather a near go. Farmer into tea. Then did some washing, and continued the syphilis paper after supper. Got a good passage out of Bertie Russell to end with.

Jan. 13th Most of the day doing the Brieux jaw – on and off. Letter from Elsie Rose! [Bedalian]

Jan. 14th Brieux jaw came off quite well, though I was much disturbed by Corless, who corrected from behind when I said that the play had not been licensed. As they didn't offer me a seat I came away afterwards. Was told the play was good, and was warmly congratulated afterward on my jaw inter alia by Bell, which pleased me as he is critical. I read the other plays (all but the last act of his *Trois Filles de M. Dupont*) good – but too didactic.

[Insert: R.C.S. Spring term 1918 membership card]

Jan. 15th Had a number of pretty compliments today on my paper. Got today from Baur[377] the *Zt. f Abst. v Vererbungslehre.*[378] Bell very bucked with the Russell and pointed out to me the similarity of Russell's line of thought to that of Fourier as expounded by Conrad.

....

MSP to HBW:

Ruhleben, Jan. 15th 1918

Very many thanks for yours of Nov 15th. I had a long and very friendly letter from Kaufmann the other day. I've been keeping his Russell ever so long, but so many people want to read it and make extracts! Thank you again ever ever so much for having mobilised it for me. I think the chapter on Education is the best. Been too cold for Lab. work, but I've done a lot of reading – nearly all shop unfortunately! I wonder what Wales is like in these days – I often think of my favourite crags up

---

[377] Erwin Baur, Professor of Botany (genetics) at the Institute of Agriculture, Potsdam [see below and Appendix 2 for correspondence].

[378] *Zeitschrift für inductive Abstammungs- und Vererbungslehre* [Journal of Inductive Science of Descent and Heredity], the world's first dedicated genetics journal, founded by Professor Baur in 1908.

there and wonder if your officials have been prancing over them, measuring them up for future forests! My best wishes, yours M.S. Pease

....

Jan. 16th Started work on abstracting from *Zt für Abstammungs u Vererbungslehre* and got a second lot today. Talked over the possibility of lantern slides with Lechmere. On the whole a quiet and profitable day.

Jan. 17th Very friendly letter from Baur and second instalment of *Abst. u Vererbungslehre.*

....

Erwin Baur to MSP:

Institute for Agriculture, Potsdam

11 January 1918

Dear Mr. Pease,

I thank you for your letter of 26th Nov. I apologise for the late reply, caused by the pressure of office work. It will be a pleasure for me to help you with the literature you asked for and the research material. I have put in a request at central command to allow you to visit me in the next few days in Potsdam or Berlin where I am giving lectures at the Institute of Agriculture on Thursdays from 4 to 6 pm. I also enclose the recent numbers of the Abst. u. Vererbungslehre. For any requests concerning literature please do not hesitate to contact me.

Yours faithfully,

Erwin Baur

....

Jan. 18th Quiet day reading shop. See my name up to repeat lecture on Monday!

Jan. 19th A very affectionate letter from Miss Taylor: quaint that she and Elsie Rose should suddenly have written again after years of silence! Wrote letter home.

Jan. 20th Very quiet day reading shop.

Jan. 21st Spent the morning re-writing part of my [syphilis] paper and delivered myself of same in the evening. House packed, so attractive is the unmentionable! Sat in the audience and saw the play. Then to supper and so to bed.

Jan. 22nd Got a note from Higgins saying leave had been granted for me to go out to see Baur on Thursday, and in course of morning got summons from Rüdiger. Occurred to me to ask to do things for the school (Wolf is in the bird cage for having lost his soldier), but didn't see R., I was just told leave had been given and to come tomorrow for time. Great domestic crisis today is 4 Selfridge parcels. Called up to censor and went in fear and trembling – thought it was my reference to the *Königliche Bibliothek* [Royal Library (Berlin)] business being turned down, but only to get the lost Morel book from Franke, who was very friendly and expressed surprise that such a book should have been published during the war, and announced his intention of purchasing a copy. Complimented on my paper by such various people as Wimpfy and Polly, Johnson and Truelove.

[Insert: letter from Higgins, p.p. *Auskunft und Hilfsstelle*
Dear Mr. Pease, I have to tell you from the Auskunft und Hilfsstelle, that Frl. Dr Rotten received your letter of Jan. 10. for which she sends many thanks. Also that on Jan. 11. Professor Baur applied for permission for you to visit him to the Kommandantur. This permission has been granted for Thursday Jan. 24. between four and six. If you do not hear anything about this from an official source, I should be much obliged to you if you would let me know so that a complaint can be lodged in the right quarters. Yours very sincerely, Eric Higgins, 21 Jan. 1918.]

Jan. 23rd Spent most of the morning trying to see Rüdiger with a view to going out earlier in the day for the R.C.S., but eventually, when I saw him, he was very curt, and said I had lots of time afterwards. Then spent hours in the afternoon sending off a parcel to Neumeister – pocket book and muffler for Frau N. Evening had a conference with Truelove and studied the map of Berlin with a view to getting "*orientiert*" with regard to the place.

Jan. 24th Most of the morning getting things ready for the great outing: got my hair cut, and after grave doubts decided that my beard would pass muster for Berlin. Eventually got dressed and sallied forth at 1 p.m. with an old soldier who had once before escorted me on a fishing expedition behind the fort. Trains were bung full and we had to walk almost to Westend before we got one. To make matters worse he was lame and couldn't pace out a bit. However we eventually got to Monbijouplatz having caught a glimpse of Unter den Linden, and the Siegesallee, and having come under the Brandenburger Tor. Dr. Rotten was a delightful little creature and I had one of the pleasantest ¼ hours I have ever had all these years. She is well *'orientiert'* [in the picture] with regard to this old camp. Then to the Landwirtschaftliche Hochschule [Agricultural College], which we reached at 3 punct and met Baur in the door. He was very friendly. In looks and build a little like Udny Yule,[379] full of energy and fairly hustled round. He got me out botanical material gassing hard the whole time. The sad news is that he has tried and failed to get me out. I gave him Grabau's card, but he didn't seem sanguine. He was very sure that the Hindenburg offensive was going to do the trick and prophesied peace this year. He is working on B. Oleracca and he's got a mean advantage over me! Eventually he had to go to his lecture, and so it was all over. I telephoned to Anderson and arranged to go and have tea there. Then I went to Leitz and enquired after my microscopes and to Renharts for skiving knives, but no luck. Leitz is a very swagger shop. Then we got to Anderson's and had a quiet hour's yarn – the stillness of a room is strange beyond description. Finally got back here at 9 p.m. after a very crowded train drive. Gave my old *Begleitung* [escort] his *bischen fett* [bit of fat (tip)] and so to bed.

Jan. 25th Rotten sort of day feeling thoroughly out of humour after having caught a glimpse of civilisation. Enrolling in the school. Bad news is that the censoring of letters is to be removed to Berlin, so wangling of extra letters is now out of the question!

Jan. 26th Still not feeling in a humour to start work. Walk round the field with Lochhead and Brahms quintette in evening. So to bed and read 'Spurell' – a rotten book.

Jan. 27th Kaiser's *Geburtstag* – so usual turn out of staff and a great speech by the Kommandant.

Jan. 28th First day of term, but without much effect in my department. The new censor arrangements are really very serious, as they put a stop to all extras except under really most pressing circumstances! Did a turn digging in the field in the afternoon; otherwise read journals. Finished

---

[379] Statistics lecturer at Cambridge.

"Spurell" – rotten beyond words. Held forth for 3rd time on Brieux for the A.S.U. – big crowd there again, but last time I hope and trust.

Jan. 29th Still very foggy. Finished off the *Zeit f. ind. Abs. u. Ver* today.

Jan. 30th Made a new start on *L'évolution Créatrice.* Went to hear Tchaikovsky trio in evening and took my essay class 7.30 p.m. No papers today on account of the strike. Rumours about the latter are prodigious.

Jan. 31st A few newspapers today with very *beruhigend* [soothing] articles about the strike. Read more Bergson – very attractive reading. Rehearsal of Brahms quintette in the evening. Wrote letter to Dr. Rotten, to bed and started *Our Mutual Friend*, with a good resolution to endure unto the end.

Feb. 1st Somewhat eventless day, *L'évolution Créatrice* in the morning. Had my first chemistry class in the afternoon, and turned over for the old Tchaikovsky again in the evening.

Feb. 2nd Got letter written home. Wrote half to Lesley S.

Feb. 3rd Screwed my skates on this afternoon and had my first try on very rough ice. Felt very weak, but didn't actually come down, though I ventured nothing to deserve a fall. Slides came in today from Berlin, but not yet censored. Got book of Cambridge pictures and Holmes' *What Is and What Might Be*[380] – a rather back number somehow in these days. Went to *Le monde ou l'on s'ennuie*[381] – best French play they've done here, but had a very rotten seat – I could have put my feet on the footlights.

[Insert: programme for *Le Monde ou l'on s'ennuie*, produced by H. Alf. Bell and M. Perrot]

Feb. 4th Turned out on the ice first thing. Very rough, but felt better on my legs. To rehearsal, after having sent off *Zeit. für Abst.* etc. Afternoon in lab dealing with sundry odds and ends, putting Minot in order. To censor – but no one in. Chemistry class but only Crosland there. Asked by Coller to hold forth at debating society on Endowment of Motherhood; but asked for 24 hours' grace to decide. Then thank goodness a quiet evening reading

---

[380] A book on education published in 1911.

[381] *The world where we are bored* by Edouard Pailleron, 1881.

Bergson and did a stroll after hours with Bell talking, general politics and Russell's views.

[Insert: letter from Higgins, 3. Feb. 1918
Dear Mr. Pease, In re your request to the Auskunft und Hilfsstelle, I have to tell you that the Zeitschrift für Pflanzenzuchtung is not to be had anywhere on loan. If the journal is likely to be of particular use to the botanists in the Camp the A & H will willingly subscribe to it and send it to us. Yours sincerely, Eric Higgins, p.p. Auskunft und Hilfsstelle]

Feb. 5th To rehearsal in morning after having lined up for tickets for real show. Got letter off via censor – triumph in these days of the *ver schärfste* [most severe] regime. Rather a rush round all day with this lantern business. Finally to concert at 6 p.m. Very good indeed, never heard this orchestra play better. Then to lantern lecture by Cooper on alpine plants. Quite a nice little crowd there, but unfortunately the Nernst lamp wouldn't work, so we only had the 75 c.p. neon lamp which wasn't nearly strong enough.

[Insert: programme for Symphony Concert, Tuesday 5th Feb. 1918. Conductor Mr. E. L. Bainton]

Feb. 6th Had a great field day in the lab and cleared up the library with a view to starting microtoming. Got D. Hill and Blackburn[382] started under the supervision of A. Hill. ~~Visit from little doctor in the lab.~~

Feb. 7th R.H.S. Committee in evening – rather a lot of talk. Simon in a rather cantankerous mood. Visit in the afternoon from the little doctor who was very friendly, wanted to examine some swine flesh for Trichinosis. He's a desperately affectionate party – *mein lieben Herr Doktor* every time.

Feb. 8th In the lab all morning. Rather a disjointed and interrupted afternoon. Quiet evening, and so to bed. I've really got waylaid in *Our Mutual Friend* – it's too boring for words. Like a weak ass, I gave into Coller and consented to hold forth for him.

---

[382] James Blackburn is listed as being on the RHS committee.

Feb. 9th Game of hockey in the morning – a poor game but good to have a run about. A beautiful afternoon, sat up in Dodd's loft by the open window to get the sun. Thynne was playing St. Saens concerto. Wrote p.c. home. Great domestic crisis today by arrival of 4 more A.M.X. parcels.

Feb. 10th Jones very excited over the new ref. library affair. Meeting of invigilators at 2.30 at which Filmore and Packe took the offensive over Jones' mild measures and demanded drastic action. Resolved to tear down notice of the J.C. [Joint Committee?] and send a deputation to captains. Came away with F.C.M. [Frank Clifford Milner] and discussed taking the offensive at the coming B. of S. meetings. Quiet evening with Bergson – the last part is to me quite unintelligible, but the first part, the more particularly biological part, will be worth going over.

Feb. 11th 9 a.m. R.H.S. business, then lined up for tickets, then played hockey, 2nd XI match against Bar. 10. Not bad game at all, played centre so had lots to do. Quiet afternoon, finished Bergson. Then class, then supper and then to concert. Don't like Short's playing.

[Insert: programme for the A.S.U. Two Brahms Evenings, arranged by Mr. E. H. Govett, First evening Monday 11th February – paper on Brahms followed by chamber music]

Feb. 12th Went and had my passport photograph taken (in company with a huge crowd of stiffs) and then Bergson. To bath in afternoon and quiet evening. Conference with Masterman about library business at B. of S. meeting. Had a conference with Roberts re. roses for garden, made out order in evening.

Feb. 13th B. of S. meeting at 9.30. I had a preliminary skirmish re the Wolfe business. Then Masterman asked innocently for a explanation of Marshall's resignation from the J.C. Long ramble by Ford, then explanation by T.H.M. [Marshall], then I spoke and M. and I and Ford kept it up. Finally M. moved vote of censure on Ford and Lloyd, seconded by me, and we mopped up the Celtic fringe and the Slavs and carried by 6–3. Then we had the formal business of the B. of S. and came away with M. who was in great spirits. Long afternoon and evening in Lab. looking through preps. Whyte round after dark to get me to sign a petition to the R.C.S. Committee to refrain from resigning till after a further meeting of the B. of S. This I refused to do and was glad to find afterwards that J.C.M. [Masterman] had also refused. Anyhow, we're giving old Ford some trouble.

Feb. 14th The vote of censure has made considerable stir in R.C.S. circles and quite a lot of the principals are to be seen in earnest conversation. Good day's work staining – struck some good lilium [lilies]. B. of S. meeting called for Sunday.

Feb. 15th Jones and J.C.M. called to the captains today and after a great speech by J. the "*Selbstbestimmungsrecht*" [right to self-determination] was granted. Now old Ford will look rather silly and goodness only knows what the B. of S. meeting on Sunday will do! R.H.S. meeting this morning re the manure question: a difficult point but for once we are all unanimous.

Feb. 16th Writing letter home and to Aunt Dora on and off all day. Quartettes in the evening – mighty cold – Mozart and Beethoven. Hauled up to the censor – Franke – today for statements I had made in my letter about the *Königliche Bibliothek* business – they denied all knowledge of the facts and asked me to substantiate them. This I undertook to do, so went round and saw Barrett who confirmed absolutely what I had said. The thing that really distresses me is that the said letters were written on Dec. 30th and Jan. 20th!

Feb. 17th Bergson for an hour and then the great B. of S. meeting. Blagden in the chair. Violent attack on me by Whyte. Resolution to rescind from a motion by Bock. We parried this for a long time, tried various amendments, and finally adjourned at 12.30 having staved off a division. At 2 p.m. library invigilators meeting. 3.30 resumed B. of S. meeting. Just before it, had a word with Bock. Masterman joined us and we agreed more or less on a compromise. Everyone was sick of the wrangle and the compromise was agreed on. The rescinding motion was not put and a mild vote of confidence in the committee was passed. I abstained from voting as I couldn't bring myself to express confidence in work panel. Coming away bumped into Barrett and went in and saw Ettinghausen and got details of the *Königliche Bibliothek* business. Made out memo which was confirmed by E and B. Finally ended up with an evening staining and so to bed and *Faust II* – which is about as unintelligible as the 2nd part of *L'évolution Créatrice.*

Feb. 18th Not much doing today. Yesterday's B. of S. meeting seems to have satisfied Ford and Lloyd. Got my *Königliche Bibliothek* memo and on my way to the censors with it ran into Franke, to whom I gave it on the spot. The serious drawback is that he was in a great hurry and I couldn't ask if my two letters had gone off.

Feb. 19th Lined up for concert tickets, then to dress rehearsal. Did some cutting in afternoon, saw Lechmere, (much better) and then to concert. Offered my second concert ticket to Wechsler, who accepted it as a gift (though I hadn't really intended it as such) and then when we came away he insisted on talking Bergson and psychology, though in fact I was feeling in a dreamy sort of mood with the *Siegfried Idyll* ringing through me.

[Insert: programme for Extra Symphony Concert, Tuesday 19th February. Conductor: Mr. E. L. Bainton]

Feb. 20th Quietish sort of morning after an hour's skating. Afternoon looked through slides and fixed lecture for Friday 3.30. During afternoon visitors brought round by Bolle. Finns – the first tangible results of the new Finnish republic! One was a Professor of Physiology at Helsingfors so quite intelligent. Came across a perfect gem of German composition on the acknowledgment card of the Royal Savoy Association.

[Insert: postcard: notification of a parcel from the Royal Savoy Association for the Relief of British Prisoners of War, London, dated 27 Nov. 1917]

Feb. 21st Bergson in the morning and lab. in afternoon. R.H.S. committee in evening. Badly turned down over suggestion to invite Dr. Rotten and Engler to the Flower Show. Cooper very sick over it, but I must say I didn't expect much else. The most extraordinary thing is a proposition made by Amelunxen that we should give him rice in exchange for manure!

Feb. 22nd Quiet sort of morning. Lantern slide lecture at 3.30, then did some washing, supper, and walk. Letter from Kaufmann who is very excited by Russell's[383] arrest.

Feb. 23rd Very quiet morning, afternoon in lab. Great *Appell* at 5 p.m. owing to escape of Ettlinger. Tale goes that he got wind of the fact that he was going to be arrested, so he just nipped out of the window, came along into the compound, tailed on to people going over to *Lazarett* and just

[383] Bertrand Russell was imprisoned for 6 months for criticising the US army.

disappeared, a very sporting effort. Notice put up about walks in Grünewald, but I don't much fancy going out 300 strong with a lot of stiffs who'll shout at every girl they pass.

Feb. 24th Quiet morning with invigilating. Lab in afternoon and Bergson in the evening.

Feb. 25th [no entry]

Feb. 26th Futile morning. Bath in afternoon. Saw Franke in the yard and offered him the Morel book, but he'd lost interest. Walk round the field with Bell. Bell to supper and then to lab and stained sections.

Feb. 27th Played hockey in morning and beat Bar. 7 thanks to Goodchild's[384] refereeing. Quiet afternoon staining and Bergson in the evening. Did as much of Bergson as I mean to do for the time being, as he's beginning to get quite incomprehensible. Scheidemann[385] today in the Reichstag said v. Kessel ought to be put in *schutzhaft* [protective custody]!

Feb. 28th First sitting of new constitution convention at 2 p.m. Hunt very active in protesting against the J.C. having been deprived of representation. Parlitt also very active. Cotterill put in the Chair. Adjourned after having elected a Standing Orders Sub-Committee. Lechmere out and around again. Sent off books to Kaufmann, and *Ernte* [harvest] to Frl. Frieda [Neumeister].

……………………

HBW to MSP (date of receipt unknown, but MSP replied in April):

Moddershall Oaks, Stone, Staffs.

21st Feb. 1918

Dear Mr. Pease,

I am afraid it is longer than usual since I wrote. Have you been wondering if DORA had got me at last, and having visions of me sewing mailbags? I regret that I cannot give any such good excuse, – it is merely that my faithless Father has

---

[384] George Spiers Goodchild, an artist who arrived in Germany to study 3 days before war was declared (*Western Daily Press*, 22 May 1920).

[385] Philipp Heinrich Scheidemann, a member of the German Social Democratic Party.

suddenly departed, leaving me the family, and all his correspondence to see to, a task which occupies most of my leisure moments. Besides when you have replied to half a dozen or so letters beginning "Dear Sir, Knowing your devotion to the cause of Liberty and Justice, may I beg you to protest against the Government prohibition of Typhoo Tipps Tea, as it is the only kind my digestion will allow me to take, ---" (this is authentic) one has no brains left for writing intelligently to anyone. I'm awfully glad you liked the book. Of course one never does agree with all BR says, but he is always delightfully stimulating. I should think old K's remarks would be perfectly shouting. Samuel Smiles or Theodora Wilson Wilson would be more in his line. It amuses me to think of the gospel being spread through Ruhleben!

I met your mother for the first time the other day. We didn't have very long, – just tea before her train left. My fears were quite unfounded, – after putting on my best hat to nerve myself for the meeting, I found her not at all alarming, but quite the contrary. It was very tantalising having such a short time, because you can't get to know a person. I wish I could tell you at all how she was, but it is difficult to tell when it is the first time of meeting. She seemed very pleased over your brother's M.C. [Military Cross, for actions in May 1917]*, but troubled at his running into danger to get it. I'm afraid she worries a good deal about the war. – Perhaps it is a pity everyone doesn't worry – most of us find it too easy to extract enjoyment out of everyday life though the world falls to pieces round us. I am hoping very much for the chance of spending a weekend with her. Think what a time we shall have exalting the Single Tax and trampling State Socialism in the dust. I'll hope to send you a fuller account then.*

We've been in Hampshire and Dorset since Christmas, – delightfully homelike after Wales, – I didn't know I was capable of such sentimental patriotism, but it is nice to hear the slow south-country speech and slow and simple minded people after the sharp Welsh with their subtle not to say cunning minds. I never did like Lloyd George!

We are learning to sympathise violently with the victims of "slumming" ladies. We had a philanthropic female today "oh, are you working on the land? Do you like it? Are your hours good? What lodgings have you?" etc. etc. Our replies however were chilling and she stopped short of asking how we spent our pay and whether we went to church. – We feel no such indignation with the old donkey man who gives us a broad grin and shouts "you'll get wet, my dear! Well, never mind, you're a good girl!"

I wonder how your researches are going? Badly I'm afraid in this weather.

I don't know the Mörike songs you speak of. I will look out for them – my musical education has been badly neglected. I've just been reading Anna Karenina. Don't you love Levin; and that description of the mowing; but I don't think the women are as well done as in War and Peace. The account of Vronsky's "code" too is delightful.

Goodbye and good luck

Yours Helen Wedgwood

....

March 1st Not much doing in morning. Wrote to J.C. re garden. Then afternoon Neville's lecture, tea at Ponsonby's and quiet evening reading D'Arcy Thompson. Gave up *Faust II* for bed reading – altogether too stiff and started *George Dandin*, to be prepared for Milner's play.

March 2nd Cold again. Wrote letter in morning. Lab afternoon reviewing.

March 3rd Quiet morning, invigilating, lab, and quiet evening. Seward material.

March 4th To *George Dandin* in the evening, good performance of a very mild play. Holland and 45-ers list up.

March 5th Excitement today is that they've been altering the 45-ers list. Bainton and Ford are on, the former a great loss to the camp. To concert, not bad. Thynne much better than I had anticipated though he lost his place in the 2nd movement. Old Prof. Kuno Meyer[386] burst in on me in the science library this afternoon looking for David Evans. So I trotted him round to the Celtic Dept.

[Insert: programme for Symphony Concert, Tuesday 5th March 1918. Conductor: Mr. J. Peebles Conn]

March 6th Quiet sort of day for me, though very exciting for those leaving. Saw Ford, Keel, Speed, and then farewell meeting with Simon, saw old Lazarus, and after many attempts found Bainton and said goodbye. The great excitement is that Rüdiger is said to be leaving.

---

[386] A German scholar, specialist in Celtic philology and literature. Friend of internee David Evans, who was head of Celtic studies in the camp.

March 7th 45-ers got off successfully: waved to them from the field as they passed at 3.30.

March 8th Quietish day, but R.H.S. committee in evening. Went off very well and after a little opposition from Buckley agreed to add Warner.

[Insert: notice and agenda for R.H.S. committee meeting on 8/3/18]

March 9th The Constituent Assembly[387] business at 6 p.m. – Hunt an infernal nuisance, but Mackenzie treated us to some gems from the captains' minutes. Higgins elected Captain of Bar. 7!

[Insert: notice and agenda for Constituent Assembly meeting, Saturday 9th March 1918]

March 10th Nothing much doing. Struck on some very good Nigella material showing excellent diakinesis. Rüdiger in camp again!

March 11th Went out to garden today and got a lot of material for fixing. Special meeting of R.H.S. in evening. Some mystery about one Campbell.[388]

[Insert: notice and agenda for R.H.S. special committee meeting on 11/3/18]

[4 days missing]

March 16th Been slack at writing up because the machine gun practice on the range just outside the camp makes work here almost impossible. Down at the school it's not so bad. Wed. and Thurs. I struck reduction divisions in Nigella and Tropaeolum [Nasturtium] – great days. Then the R.C.S. chairman business taken up a lot of time. Blagden of course was pre-eminently the man but he was so blaguarded [sic.] by Patchett and Wolfe that he declined to stand and that ass Lloyd let himself be put up instead. I think Blagden was wrong: he shouldn't have let himself be overcome by his sensitiveness, but should have fought it through. After several conferences with Masterman, Marshall and Jones at the eleventh hour we

---

[387] Criticisms against the existing camp administration, and Powell in particular, were growing in early 1918, leading for a call for a new, more democratic constitution.

[388] Possibly Oliver James Campbell (1888–1970) who, according to *The Ruhleben Story,* was a prominent member of the R.H.S.

persuaded Truelove to stand. Meeting this morning at 7.30 and Marshall got in by 37 to 36! If I hadn't converted Hill at the last moment we should have lost. Very glad to have put a spoke in Wolf's wheel and to have delivered a "*Schlappe*" [rout] to Lloyd for having allowed himself to become Wolf's catspaw. In the evening the constitution mongerie. Agreed to Mackenzie's proposal not to proceed till we had a guarantee from Powell that he would not oppose it before the legation or the military authorities. Lab visited this week by old Professor Traube – "*sehr auregend*" [adorable] – and also by Danish Red Cross, conducted round by Wolf who showed off 'his' school. Got *Entwicklungs Geschichte des Menschen*[389] as a gift via Dr Rotten from Hertwig himself and a note from him offering to do anything. Started to read Zsigmondy[390] on colloids.

[Insert: Camp Messenger Service card for the parcel office 16/3/18]

[Insert: notice of Constituent Assembly meeting Saturday 16 March 1918 – agenda item: Mr. W. F. MacKenzie's proposals]

March 17th Quietish sort of Sunday. 2.30 I went to stage for Coller to teach his crew 'Selinger's Round' [a folk dance] – quite like old times.

March 18th Spent the afternoon fixing up a Geisler pump and then fixed some moss sporangia.

March 19th Another Holland list up and great excitement.

March 20th [no entry]

March 21st The main excitement in camp for the last few days has been the Holland list game – i.e. having your name put on and then crossed off again. *Strafe* [punishment] officer round the lab today, and as he was about 7ft high he found the establishment '*etwas nieding*' [somewhat low]. R.H.S. meeting in the evening – went off fairly well.

[Insert: notice and agenda for R.H.S. committee meeting on 21/3/18]

---

[389] *Lehrbuch der Entwicklungsgeschichte des Menschen und Wirbelthiere* [Textbook of Developmental History of Humans and Vertebrates] by Oscar Hertwig, published Jena, 1886–1888.

[390] Richard Adolf Zsigmondy, an Austrian-Hungarian chemist known for his research in colloids.

March 22nd Hollanders finally went off in the afternoon and passed by at 9.15 p.m. with a huge cheer. Finished Zsigmondy and think I'll try Bayliss from cover to cover. Went to lecture by J.C.M. [Masterman] at Deutsches Zirkel on *Die Entstehung der Preussischen Wehrmacht* [The emergence of the Prussian army] – good.

March 23rd [no entry]

March 24th Played hockey in Oxford and Cambridge v. the rest. Good game but very dusty and got beaten 4–2.

[5 days missing]

March 30th Very little to report this week. Quietly working away with microtome and Bayliss. Camp is taking the German offensive on the whole very sensibly – surprisingly so. Had a great do today. Flower show – gave a hand at that. Then about 10 a.m. up turned Engler and two other Profs. (Diels and Gräbner) from Dahlem and I showed them the lab. Engler was very old – but decent and interested. The other two were very communicative and asked a lot about Cambridge and altogether took an intelligent interest in affairs. Then made sundry preparations to receive Dr Rotten in the library for the afternoon. Huge crowd turned up. Rotten, Kapp, Frau and Frl. K. Schumann and we gave them a very hurried tour in the lab. Kapp had patients at 5 p.m. so he couldn't stay and Frl Rotten couldn't be left with Schumann as the latter wasn't a full blooded officer! It was a great scramble and not the pleasant afternoon we had looked forward to. Then trotted round and helped clear up the flower show. Letter from Neumeisters (*père et fils*). Finally to bed and started Jean Paul.

March 31st To concert this evening, only stayed for the Mozart and Beethoven – good. Wrote letter home and to Seward.

[Insert: programme for Symphony Concert, Easter Sunday, March 31st 1918]

April 1st Went to hear Weber lecture on German opera – also good.

April 2nd Movement on foot to squash the silly note which the captains propose sending to the British Govt., whining for release. Very excited over leech sections, found a new organ we can't identify.

April 3rd Went to dress rehearsal of *Nan* in evening. Good – but I can't believe that the play is of permanent value. I dislike the plan of putting the mystic words of wisdom into the mouth of a madman. Played hockey in the morning and planted roses in the afternoon.

April 4th Spent most of day sitting in the garden and trying to prepare a lecture on adaptation. To R.H.S. meeting.

[Insert: notice and agenda for R.H.S. committee meeting on 4/4/18]

April 5th Great lecture came to nought as the current was not on. Roberts pruned roses for me.

April 6th Great day fixing fritillaries – goes to my heart to destroy flowers before they are out. Meeting of the Constituent Assembly was too awful for words.

[Insert: notice and agenda for Constituency Assembly meeting on 6/4/18]

April 7th Quiet Sabbath on the whole. Started reading Havelock Ellis. Went to R.C.S. Committee re extension.

April 8th Roughly speaking ditto.

April 9th Usual dismal round.

April 10th Got some mighty fine divs in pyrethrum. Hear there are great rows in A.S.U. camp – Pender and Higgins fallen out.

April 11th Got Bateson's *Problems of Genetics* today from the *Königliche Bibliothek* – a good effort – just in time for my lecture on adaptation. Pottered in the garden in the afternoon. Walk and talk with Bell in the afternoon.

April 12th Gave my lecture on adaptation. Exams Committee 10.30 a.m.

April 13th Rounded off letter home. Great gardening operation between the wires with a *Zivildienster* [conscientious objector] to guard us. To picture exhibition – rotten.

April 14th Tidied up garden in morning. Had first cut at celloidia [method of embedding] in the afternoon. Concert in evening – good in parts.

[Insert: programme for Chamber Concert, Sunday April 14th 1918]

General view of the east end of the camp with Spandau in the distance

The promenade, tennis courts, vegetable garden and pond

April 15th [no entry]

April 16th Held forth to Marshall's class on "The Poor Laws" – seemed all very ancient history. Webbs at Llanbedr and so on. Went off quite well, in spite of J.'s gloomy account of M.'s class.

April 17th Had first botany class today. Quite a big turn out, including Spong,[391] Balfour and Winzer's twin friend Thompson! Caucus of minority party re A.S.U. General Meeting at 2 p.m.

April 18th A.S.U. meeting very melancholy: every one of our people botched his part. Parlitt was aggressive when suavity was wanted: our elected Goliath Jefferson was a complete failure, and Ponsonby put the tin hat on it all – I left after that. Dannhorn elected president! No recrimination between Pender and Higgins. Long yarn with Lloyd, Blagden and Lechmere, re new premises.

April 19th Great event today. At 4.30 p.m. Bell came to pray me to move into their box to spare them from an intruder in the form of some new people coming into the camp. After considerable doubt, I agreed to do so, but remaining with old box for meals. R.H.S. committee at 7.30 and moved my bed at 9.30 and slept in my new abode after 3 years all but 3 days in Box 17. Gave up my cheque book by order today.

April 20th Spent most of the day fixing up various things in Bar. 3 [Box 10]. The new arrivals are passengers off the "Wolf"[392] – been 7 months or more on board.

April 21st Endless string of visitors to the lab.

April 22nd Holland list up today – Dodd on after all.

....

---

[391] James Leonard Spong (1879–1954). An engineer captured in Holland on his way home from working on a project. Imprisoned at first, he was transferred to Ruhleben in autumn 1915.

[392] Hilfskreuzer SMS Wolf, which landed at Kiel on 24 Feb. 1918 after 451 days at sea, with 467 prisoners (crew and passengers) aboard.

MSP to HBW:

Ruhleben, April 22nd 1918

Dear Miss Wedgwood,

I am a terrible sinner: it is ages since I wrote and your letters of Dec 20th and Feb 21st have lain for weeks unanswered. But I've been waiting for a chance to send you a letter instead of a pc. And now that the opportunity has occurred, I find it hard to say anything, because I've just heard from Kaufmann that your brother[393] *is reported missing. It is needless for me to waste words. One hopes for the best, but cannot help fearing the worst; and I know how sad and anxious it must be for you all. Anything that an outsider and stranger like myself might say would seem but affected sentiment, more especially since what I write now will only be read months later. Even though most of us have lost friends and relations – and I myself have lost several of my best Cambridge friends and my most intimate school friend*[394] *– yet one's woes somehow seem small when one thinks of the total of mess and desolation.*

Here things go on as ever, the weeks and years slip by and our petty daily events have little connection with the great outside world, except in so far as work is very dependent on the temperature. Are you still at work on your forestry? It must be a splendid occupation! Often have I thought of you and envied you with all my heart! Guillebaud is a decent sort isn't he? Remember me to him, if you are still working under him. I'm most awfully sorry I put my foot in it over the gentleman in the fur coat. Having myself been a prisoner for so long, I'm apt to regard everybody else as more or less free. I only hope nothing happened. DORA may be keeping it up against you and me (eventually). But after all, you can't be answerable to your friend's friends. It was indeed highly amusing receiving B.R. [Bertrand Russell] *from such quarters, but really the gent in question was capable of appreciating it himself – he had a keen sense of humour. I can't pass by the incident without again thanking you very much indeed for having secured it for me: it was thoroughly appreciated by many here. The 'direction' is right and as a piece of composition it is brilliant – far too much so for K[aufmann], to judge by the marginal notes. In writing he was lavish in his praises of it, yet apparently times out of number he had completely missed the point! However, I oughtn't to criticise him; it is awfully decent of him to worry about me.*

---

[393] Francis Charles Bowen Wedgwood, who was in the Royal Flying Corps.

[394] John Stewart Fothergill (1890–1916). John had become a farmer in New Zealand, and signed up on 13th Oct 1915 joining the New Zealand Rifle Brigade. He was killed on the Western Front near Armentières on 19th July 1916.

For many months back I'm afraid I've done practically nothing but 'shop', both in reading and practical work. Even though not working on any special line of research (beyond the purely local one of getting over special line of Ruhlebener difficulties) I find plenty to do in working up all sorts of odd things – Biology is a wonderful store of interest. For example, there are three leeches in the pond none of which is the <u>one</u> type given in <u>all</u> the text books. So we've just been sectioning the brutes on the microtome and trying to give them their proper names – and I think we've just succeeded. And now we're working out a new technique for cutting insects eggs; and so we go on with odds and ends, rather desultory and purposely, no doubt, when regarded in a general way by an active outsider and "realpolitiker" like yourself. But for us it occupies the time harmlessly, is mildly instructive, and keeps one's mind off world politics – a most irritating subject for a pawn, though no doubt highly interesting for the cynical onlooker.

We've had some very decent music this winter, but the exchange of 45ers has carried off many of our best performers. Perhaps you will hear Arthur Speed (pianist) in London – he is a treat, and if you hear Fergusson singing the songs of Hugo Wolf, you may be sure they are ones I've heard here. However in spite of departures, there have been some good items lately, e.g. Mozart's Kleine Nacht Musik, a Beethoven piano concerto and trio, and Bach Chaconne.

I'm very pleased with my bulbs in the school garden – my attempt at a college court and lawn! But Elizabeth is quite right – a garden can only be enjoyed in solitude or with one's kindred spirits. Elizabeth's dicta on gardening are generally right. Yet, even here, in spite of the destructive public, flowers are sweet sensible things. They come out fresh and bright, they try to look clean and smell sweet in spite of the filth in the camp and the folly in the world. In the autumn we fixed up two greenhouses with heating, so that all through the winter we've been able to grow all sorts of jolly things.

Now I'm afraid I've written a very prosy letter all about myself and my dismal and futile doings. But it's difficult to write at the best of times, and now I feel so distressed for you on account of your anxiety and uncertainty about your brother that I don't know whether it is fair of me to write to you at all at this juncture. Again let me thank you very much indeed for your letters to me: I enjoy all that you write because I know that we have some points of view in common. I long to hear from K. that he has news of your brother: I feel miserable for you.

My best wishes,

yours, Michael Pease

....

[2 days missing]

April 25th Hollanders went off this afternoon, said goodbye to Conn and sundry others. Farewell tea for Dodd.[395] Got timber from the carpenter and put Bell's bed on stilts. Local excitement is that Lechmere's eyepieces turned up. Very suspicious that Lange was the thief, because last night I was in the library between 7 and 8 p.m. all alone no one in outer lab. I heard a heavy footstep come up and go round the screen and then go out again. Ten minutes later same step and same movement, so I looked out and greeted Lange, who said he'd just brought up a pot for the lab!

April 26th Long and quiet – though somewhat interrupted day in the lab. Some good divs in fritillary. Cut my foot with sickle cutting the lawn, not seriously but got to be bandaged. Photos of lab taken in the morning. Letter from Neumeister.

April 27th School meeting at 2 p.m. – put up Zabel for committee and he nearly got in. If I'd only thought he would have scored so well I would have canvassed for him! Marshall becomes Secretary and Masterman and Bell on committee. 1.30 p.m. S.O. [Standing Orders] Sub-Committee of Constituent Assembly: went off all rightly, but the C.A. meeting itself went off too awfully for words. Cotterill is absolutely hopeless as a chairman and I haven't the patience to describe it all. Letter from home – hear that W.N. [Walter Neumeister] has got released – good. At R.C.S. meeting I had a regrettable *"zwischenfall"* [incident] with Scratchett [i.e. Patchett] – he is an old ass. I've no patience with people who fool[?] in public.

April 28th Finished re-reading several passages in *Problems of Genetics* and returned the book to Barrett. Invigilated. Wrote letter to Dad re the Dodd business. One of the new Russians to supper and then to concert – not good, though Lindsay played very well. Sitting just in front of the Major and family. Lechmere tells me that it is proposed to proceed against Lange as there seems fairly conclusive evidence of his thefts. I agreed to contribute my evidence on condition that it was not brought before the military

---

[395] Letter from Dodd to Michael's mother, written when he is in Holland on page 351.

authorities. Spoke to Jones about it who urged caution. Saw Douthwaite[396] and urged caution and an interview with Wimpfheimer before taking action. Flint[397] backed my view that it should not be made a matter of public prosecution. Hauled up before the school committee to discuss space requirements and stuck out as much as I decently could for the whole of Room 23 for science library.

April 29th The tragedy today is that Lange[398] committed suicide – at least in all probability it was a case of *felo de se*. I passed Flint early this morning and shouted "have you seen Wimpfy?" No, but they had reason to expect that Lange was suspicious and they were going to search at once – he, Douthwaite and Lechmere. I didn't worry and spent the morning pottering round the box in Bar. 3 inter alia putting up a washing line. At 2 p.m. we had a departmental meeting to discuss the space question after which Lechmere, just rushing off to a bath said, "We've searched and found everything. The poor boy had a terrible 10 minutes but confessed to everything". I thought nothing much at the time, made a mild resolution to go and look him up two days hence and cheer him up. Saw Truelove and agreed against taking any steps with regard to reporting the matter to Edinburgh[?]. Then went to censor and noticed an idle crowd round the surgery. Then to R.H.S. office and searched out the "*Akten*" [records] for letter to London and then Cooper came in and told me what had happened – that Lange had collapsed in the Charlottenburger latrine – heart failure. I at once said suicide. The irrevocable is difficult to realise. It is easy to be wise after the event. No one could have acted more gently than Lechmere, and no one could have let the matter slide. There is to be a p.m. of course, as at present it is only given out as heart failure. Long yarn with Higgins, Blagden and Lambert about it, and all agree that no one is to blame over it.

---

[396] Arthur Henry Douthwaite (1896–1974), a London medical student who was on holiday in Germany when war broke out. After the war he became a senior physician at Guy's Hospital. He married Olivia, sister of fellow inmate Albert Dannhorn (fn 208) in 1920.

[397] Gordon Bruce Flint (1894–1981), a medical student at Edinburgh University who was also holidaying in Germany when war broke out. He was in the Ruhleben medical corps with Douthwaite. After the war he worked at the Edinburgh Royal Infirmary.

[398] There is an entry in Berlin deaths (*www.ancestry.co.uk*) for a Herbert Lange, aged 19, who died at Ruhleben on 29th Apr 1918.

April 30th There seems no doubt that L. committed suicide – arsenic. It appears to be a purely pathological case of kleptomania; had been in prison before for similar offences, and had twice before attempted suicide. Curious, because he never appeared to me as morbid – quite the contrary always very keen and active, and withal clever and successful with his work. To the Constituent Assembly: longish debate by usual old bores. *Grosser Sieg* [great victory] of Jones 19–4 on his amendment against Shaw. Cocker and Pearce both quite lost their tempers, and the former and Thorpe left in a huff. Cotterill was much better, partly because nothing very difficult arose. Simmons tried the humorous with success.

....

MSP to HBW:

Ruhleben, April 30th 1918

Dear Miss Wedgwood, yesterday I got a letter from Herr von Kaufmann conveying the good news that your brother Charles is safe, "slightly wounded, otherwise well". He asked me to communicate this to you; but I fear the prisoners' post is desperately slow and in all probability you will have heard directly from your brother by now. In any case I should like to avail myself of the opportunity of saying how glad I am for him and for all of you that you are now out of your anxiety on that score. It must have been miserable! M.S.P.

....

May 1st Miserably cold May day. Saw Lechmere about the Lange business. Seems that the military do not admit that any death other than heart failure can occur in camp! Anyhow it saves the trouble of having the whole *Geschichte* [saga] gone into. His young brother seems quite unconcerned about it and cheerfully brought us round all his instruments and gear – as a matter of fact mostly <u>ours</u>! It is a great relief for us that the matter can really be treated as a case of mania. Devised the n+3rd scheme of dividing up the lab.

Long gap in diary as Michael again with Neumeisters in Jena from 8th May

....

HBW to MSP (letter forwarded from Ruhleben to c/o Neumeister, Lutherstrasse 24, Jena):

Moddershall Oaks, Stone, Staffs.

26th Apr. 1918

Dear Mr. Pease,

I really have been meaning to write to you for some time, but there has been such a lot to think about and do that all my correspondence is dreadfully in arrears and I have had to adopt the queue system. Father has just got home again, thank goodness, so I haven't got his letters to attend to.

Alas the forestry job is now a thing of the past, as I want to be near home – still I have earned my living for 8 months which makes one feel twice the woman one was, and one learns an awful lot that way – besides I used to have private doubts as to whether I was capable of subsisting by honest toil, and such doubts are most demoralising and do not conduce to that self-confidence inculcated by Mr. Pelman.[399] *The worst of honest toil is that it makes one less than ever at home in respectable society and, like the Irishman's amphibious beast, I "can't live in the water and die on land". And people treat you quite differently out of breeches to what they do in.*

My last lodging was in Branden where the Labourers' Union or some other poisonous agitators (you confined yourself principally to Essex didn't you?) must have been at work, as the lower orders seemed to be painfully lacking in reverence for our old institutions and we had to listen sympathetically to anything but respectful remarks about the local gentry "all dooks and earls they be". Two men whom we knew privately as "Goonflints" and "Lor lumme yes", were particularly emphatic and gave us a long recitation with chorus: – thus (Goonflints) "if one sacks you he tells all the others and you can't get a place in the county, unless it's your bit in the churchyard" etc etc (chorus) "Lor lumme, yes! might as well be dead."

Now my cousin[400] *and I are hoping to fulfil a long cherished dream of a cottage (in Hanley worse luck) from which to conduct agitation (she is T.U. organiser for the Potteries). I am to housekeep and cook and generally help paint the Potteries red, poor things (they much prefer black). We have a spare room and shall put an ad. in the Herald offering hospitality to all good rebels (with a note that no criticism of the cooking is allowed). This letter is all about myself but it is so depressing to think about big things now. We heard three weeks ago that my brother is missing*

---

[399] Selig Perlman? An economist and specialist in the US trade union movement.

[400] Phoebe Sylvia Wedgwood – daughter of Cecil Wedgwood (Helen's father's 1st cousin). Cecil was killed at The Somme in July 1916. Phoebe and Helen shared a house in Hanley for a few years.

and it drives it home worse than ever. He stands so much as a type of all the helpless victims of the ghastly folly. He only wanted to live in peace and paint. I know you've lost a number of your friends too – and you away from everyone – but at least you don't see all the heartless cant and armchair valour. The newspapers, cinemas and hoardings make one sick; and kindly people can be horribly heartless about things they don't see. – One gets so deadly tired. I could sleep a thousand years. –

This is not the way to write to a victim of internment, and I won't do it again. Things won't seem so bad when I've got back to work, and you must stick to your slides. After all, it is rather gorgeous to exist, isn't it?

Goodbye and best wishes,

Yours Helen Wedgwood

....

HBW to MSP:

Moddershall Oaks, Stone, Staffs.

May 16th 1918

Dear Mr. Pease,

My last letter has been on my conscience. I hope it didn't read as gloomy as I remember it. If so, please forgive. I have always quarrelled with people who insist on all occasions that life is not worth living and then calmly continue to live. Much better commit suicide decently or else keep their convictions to themselves – you see, I can be philosophical now, because we have heard that my brother is safe – a prisoner slightly wounded. It seems dreadfully selfish to find the whole world so much brighter because one's particular person is safe. It was so much horrider than I'd expected, and we felt sure he was killed – and now he is out of it till the end of the war. It seems too good to be true – when one thinks of all the other poor devils for whom it is not true. – The hardest thing of all to realise is that he has not believed himself dead for a month – while to us it is a resurrection!

I wonder how your researches go. I rather feel I ought to be sending you boxes of frogs (there are lots here) or collecting caterpillar eggs at various stages of development, even a tadpole might not be unacceptable. I'm afraid they won't let me send your reagents, but if you want anything dug out of the ground or extracted from nooks and corners, I'll do my best (n.b. imagine the censor investigating a box of live earwigs!)

My cousin and I get into our new house in the Potteries in a day or two. The furnishing has been fun, but goodness knows what the results will be, as she leans to early Victorian roses and I to Heals' hieroglyphs (I hope spelling is right, – Bekassy is responsible) and what happens when they meet in the same room? The china also caused some heart-burnings. I (economically) wanted "peasant art" ware but family pressure obliged us to have Wedgwood – and answered my protest that this was unsuitable to our station by saying that a Potteries tramp who was offered tea in anything else would be bitterly insulted. – Phoebe also suffers from fits of insanity; – her latest desire is to adopt a baby!! – but I'm eldest of seven and put my foot down hard. Life will be hectic enough without that.

Did you see they have got a 30/- minimum for a 54 hour week in Norfolk? The Wages Board did it, but of course it is really the Union – rather a score. I believe (heaven help the Labourer) I am to be on the Agr. Wages board here. Of course I don't believe in Wages Boards, but I suppose one may as well get what one can out of them. It will be fun trying to stand up to the farmers – you see they are always yelling for women and then pay them 18/- a week, which is ridiculous nowadays. # # # # The others have just come out and started talking psycho-analytically – this is not for my young and innocent ears, and besides it always ends in a free fight, and then where is the hapless neutral? Do you also read Freud and awful people like that? Not to <u>enjoy</u> them is considered hopelessly early Victorian.

I fly. Goodnight,

H B Wedgwood

....

MSP to HBW (sent via L S Ornstein in Utrecht):

bei Herr Neumeister, Jena

May 17th 1918

Dear Miss Wedgwood,

You'll be interested to hear I've got leave out of Ruhleben for 4 weeks! My friends here put in an application for me as their gardener, here I am tending the cabbages and potatoes and enjoying fresh air [photo on page 269] *and the peaceful solitude of the hills and woods. At first it was really overwhelming, to come out of the dusty and smelly old Lager* [camp], *and to find oneself once more in the country and everything in its full May glory. It's difficult for you who take wild nature for granted to realise what it means to one when one has been starved of it so long!*

I am very much relieved to hear that your brother is all right. "Just slight wounds on the lip" K. reports. K. asked me to write to you and tell you, and I sent a p.c.; but if I know anything of DORA's treatment of prisoners' post, it will come in a very bad last.

I had a long letter from K. the other day, full of his woes about his son – like all of us, he feels the separation very much – it doesn't grow any easier to bear as the years slip by! Anyhow he asks me "to take him into my confidence" and tell him "all about my life"! He writes extremely nicely of all you have done for his relations in England and says he's trying to get permission to visit Charles, but doesn't know yet where he is. You must be very thankful to know he is safe, and after all he'll only have 18 months, a mere nothing to hardy old prisoners like myself!

I find the garden here a very congenial occupation partly as I am in sole charge of it and organise it as I like, and partly because I am by habit very fond of plants, even material old vegetables! Intellectually I'm having a complete relaxation, I don't read anything in particular; sometimes just a few of my old favourite verses out of the Oxford Book. Even politics are rather at a discount now! I am quite happy to go up and sit down under the pine trees at dusk and watch the stars come out, all alone with the breeze and the fresh sweet woody smells. I'm afraid you'll think I've grown very silly! All I can say is, try a course of concentrated life for a year or so and see what it feels like to come out.

I'm staying with particularly nice people here, people in quite a small way, but kind and sympathetic beyond words. They are people with an intense interest in personal detail. They remembered the photograph you sent me last summer and were full of the most detailed enquiries about your doings, far more than was within my competence to answer.

Now I must go and water my cabbages. I'm having a battle royal with the turnip beetle – he seems to be a most aggressive gentlemen in these parts – attacks tomatoes voraciously. I sent you a letter about a month ago from Ruhleben, which I hope comes through. I look forward as ever to hear again from you.

My best wishes,

Michael Pease.

[Note to HBW written on the letter by Ornstein: "You can send letters to me, I shall forward them to Mr. Pease"]

....

Michael (rhs) with the Neumeisters on their allotment in 1918

....

MSP to HBW [sent via L S Ornstein, Utrecht]:

Bei Herr Neumeister, Jena

June 2nd 1918

Dear Miss Wedgwood,

I must just send you a few lines before I return to my old abode, as it may be years before I get the chance to write you a letter again, and I owe you so many for all the kind ones you have sent me.

You can well imagine what a grand time I've had here and how I've just revelled in the trees and hills and open air. One of the things that offends me most about camp is the perpetual smell of concentrated humanity: here everything seems so sweet and fresh and clean and the woods are one mass of lily of the valley. The wild roses now are beautiful – do you remember the roses on the Cam? I have done no reading worth speaking of while I've been here; I've just indulged myself in solitary rambling, and idling. My only regular activity has been tending the garden which has been a very congenial job. I've grown so in love with my cucumbers and tomatoes that I shall find it hard to part!

Very many thanks for your letter of Apr 26th, I'm sorry the forestry job is over – that must have been grand and I often envied you as I sat curled up in my little 'cubby hole', and "looked before and after and pined for what is not"! How's the Hanley lodging house getting on? Hanley doesn't appeal to me – it's too much like a concentration camp. I've had a great luck in the music line. I got in for four concerts of Beethoven Chamber music – heard my favourite trio (No. 7) excellently played. Three quartettes by the Dresden string quartette, performed simply pricelessly; a string quintette and a trio for flute, violin and viola (both new to me) and a number of songs. There was also a cello sonata which I had heard being practiced almost every day last winter in Ruhleben, and though the hall was hot to a degree I could only think of those cold musical evenings when people played in fur coats and mittens!

I've had a couple of long letters from K. He seems to have got into communication with your brother, although he doesn't yet know his whereabouts. I expect you have heard directly from him by now. I wonder what sort of a person K. is! I tried to size him up from his marginal comments in the B.R. – they were awfully funny in parts! He wrote to me at one time that he had had the book translated, but was hesitating to publish without the necessary permission. I urged him very much to publish without worrying – B.R. would be simply tickled to death at the idea!

Did you ever meet Paul Montague [fn 92], *I wonder? He was a particularly charming person, a Bedalian and a great friend of mine at Cambridge. Poor fellow, falling at Salonika.*[401] *What ghastly folly all this mess is. I'm afraid I get into a state of mingled resignation and bitterness over it. But what can one do, especially a prisoner?*

And now I want once more to thank you very very much for having written to me so often and so nicely all these years. Your letters have been a great joy to me and I look forward very much to meeting you again after the war – and then I won't treat you so badly as I appear to have done last time!

M. S. Pease

P.S. June 5th. I've just got an extension of my leave until further notice! M.S.P

....

MSP to HBW [sent via L S Ornstein, Utrecht]:

bei Herr Neumeister, Jena, Lutherstrasse 24

25th June 1918

Dear Miss Wedgwood,

---

[401] An acting Flight Commander, his plane went missing on Oct 29th 1917 after escorting bombers on a raid.

Just a line or two before I return to camp again the day after tomorrow, for it may be another year before I get the chance to write again! My last letter was written to you, just as I had got the news of my extension of leave. My friends had applied for 3 weeks extra, and when the answer came, 'until further notice' I rashly jumped to the conclusion they would let it run for a couple of months or so, then the other day I got a note saying that the 3 weeks asked for had been granted! However, I can't grumble: I've had a very good time and been exceptionally lucky fellow to get out at all. I've thoroughly enjoyed tending my friends' garden and will be sorry to leave the plants I have so carefully nursed. However I shall return to my Ruhleben garden and hope to find my roses in good trim there. However my Ruhleben garden suffers from abominable publicity. The offensive public has free access to it, and even if it is good enough to keep its clumsy feet off the border, it always flings its matches and cigarettes, and old paper all over the place – and withal it makes a noise and smells foul.

The great event here this weekend was the Max Reger Festival – 5 concerts in 2 days were a trifle bewildering. It was great luck to get in for it and to have the Berlin Philharmonic Orchestra and the Leipzig String Quartette brought to ones door. Some of the simpler chamber music compositions pleased me mightily, but the more profound and recent orchestral works were frankly too much for me – I got quite lost. He is undoubtedly a brilliant master of the art of composing delicate passages, especially dainty little fugues. The jewel of the whole festival was a little song 'A child's evening prayer' – the melody was nothing in particular, but the organ accompaniment was simply priceless; twinkling stars on a beautiful summer's evening and all that is sweet and innocent in a child's simple prayer. And then you look at the portrait of the composer – like a debauched edition of Cecil Chesterton; in fact he was an entirely impossible person in private life, and his early death was undoubtedly connected with his manner of living – at least so I'm told here.

I hope the Hanley scheme goes well and that you find satisfaction in it, and that people don't complain of your cooking. I and a barrister friend of mine [Douglas Jones] *cook for my party in Ruhleben, and although we criticise each other, the rest of the party are generally satisfied. I've just been buying enamel ware this morning to take back to camp to replace some of our gear that's got worn out after all these years!*

I hope very much to hear from you again shortly, but there has been a complete breakdown in the post for the last month. I hope you have good news of your brother; I have been hoping to hear from K. as to his whereabouts. And now you probably won't hear from me again for ever so long, or at least you may only get cards. But I trust you realise that our letters from Ruhleben are very limited.

Again thanking you very much for your letters and not least for the B.R. and looking forward to seeing you again sometime.

Yours Michael Pease

....

July 1st From May 8th to June 27th I was out of camp with Neumeisters. Returned here at 11 p.m. on June 27th [Thursday] and found Goodchild had been put in my bed, but Bell had hustled round and stowed in another bed, so I got somewhere to lie down. Bit by bit found things and made my bed. They gave me supper and I lay myself down tired. Next day was very exhausting because everyone talked and asked questions. Very disappointed in garden, obviously neglected by Hill, and everyone else says so. Lab on the other hand is excellent. Got boards and fixed up new shelves. Bed stands alone, which is a great comfort! R.H.S. Committee meeting: minutes *Geschichte* [saga] still going strong! Saturday [June 29th] still settling in – concert in evening. Sunday wrote letter home and inspected the R.H.S. premises and garden. Today devoted to my gardens and got things a bit ship shape.

[Insert: programme for a concert in The Music Loft, Saturday June 29th]

July 2nd Tidied up a bit in the garden and then got my old photos from Zimmer 11. To German P.P. for what I thought would be my valise only to find it was BR's [Bertrand Russell's] book from Kaufmann per registered post – got to be returned to Berlin to censor. Afternoon to Franke and sent off those photos of lab to Neumeister – long conversation and complimented on being clean shaven! Started microtome work in the evening.

July 3rd [no entry]

July 4th Got my suitcase today, but to my great annoyance find it had been raided on the way – soap, shoes, leather, candles, shirts, and so forth pinched. A literary thief too, for he took Meredith's poems and the Oxford book! However the *Unteroffizier* [sergeant] assured me that it had *keinen Zweck* to *reclamieren*, [no purpose to complain] so one has to grin and bear it. He's made a hopeless mess of my locks, but as Walley bros. have the "*grippe*" [flu] couldn't get it mended. Rather grumpy all day in consequence – Pritchard's articles came in.

July 5th Got the locks of my suitcase repaired and my clothes put away. Otherwise working at microtoming, mostly making a clean sweep of all the old reagents and putting out new ones, always a boring job. The "grippe" is the great joke in camp now – a mild form of flu.[402] Bell and Lochhead down, Jones sickening and in general the ranks are simply decimated.

July 6th Wrote letter to H.B.W. to get it off before I get the grippe. Got Russell's *Mysticism and Logic* today from Kaufmann. Goodchild now down, so I'm so far the only survivor in our box. Got some ripping preps of fritillary this afternoon.

....

MSP to HBW:

Ruhleben, July 5th 1918 [Friday]

Dear Miss Wedgwood,

As luck has it, I have the chance to send you a letter, and I hasten to avail myself of the opportunity. There is the complication that it must be written before Sunday, and I'm writing hurriedly before I develop a wild sort of flu, which is pretty prevalent in camp just now – my box-mates and mess mates and my lab staff are all down and I scarcely expect to survive many hours! So I write now in haste before I feel the first shivers! I wonder so much if you got 3 letters I sent to you from Jena. My mother has got hers, so I expect you'll get yours. It all seems like a dream now, a far off other existence, though it isn't really in fact so very much in the past. I didn't really find the coming back half as bad as I had anticipated: it was cool and wet and I took the precaution to return after dark. I'm very glad to get to work again on my cytology and as long as it doesn't get too hot I shall keep busy and not sigh unduly for hill tops or pine woods! Very many thanks for your letter of May 16th. – no please don't apologise for your gloomy tone – it must have been a beastly experience – I only wish I could think of Paul Montague resurrecting! Besides I'm an awful offender myself – but then after all the times are fairly gloomy and one only keeps cheerful by not dwelling on the big events and all the silly and heartless rot that people say and believe. To judge from press

---

[402] Spanish flu. Stibbe (2008) says there were 1565 cases of flu amongst camp population of 2336, but only 2 deaths, thanks to relatively good health and hygiene.

extracts, Mr. Billing seems to be the most serious topic at home, and if that doesn't make one gloomy and pessimistic, one can stand a good deal![403]

I can well imagine how relieved you must be at the good news of your brother, Kaufmann writes very confidently that he will be able to do all sorts of things for him, and I know he will do all he can. My young brother is wounded – not dangerously, but seriously enough to keep him out of it for some time, a mighty relief to my mother [see page 282]. *I know she has worried very much over him, and also, I'm afraid, over me – quite unnecessarily. My poor dear Mother, I'm afraid she still has some illusions, but not, I think, so many as she had a few years ago. I only wish that she and I saw more eye to eye in this hateful matter.*

No I haven't read Die Traumdeutung [The Interpretation of Dreams] – *though I went to a lecture here on Freud a year or so ago. I can't say I was attracted, though I made a resolution to read his works and find out for myself. I felt somehow (how shall I put it?) – he is too dominated by the Viennese atmosphere. At least that was the impression I got and the lecturer was a devoted admirer. However I heard the same chap hold forth on Butler (whom I do know something about) and I thought it a very inadequate account. By the way, what a rage Butler seems to be now – I only hope some people really take him to heart. But I distrust rages in general. When I first went up to Cambridge there was a great Nietzsche rage on and that had the most comical effects – all sorts of mild and meek specimens fancied themselves as 'supermen' and behaved accordingly. And I'm disposed to think that much of the fuss here over Reger is merely a fashionable rage: anyhow it struck me that the interval in the concerts was a very important item and the conversation seemed to be all about clothes and who was there!*

The enclosed photos [pages 275–276] *may amuse you. Owing to the low roof and uneven lighting it is a difficult subject to take, but they just serve to give you some idea. As a matter of fact we've had alterations and improvements since those pictures were taken. The Science depts of the school have still really got life in them, we are always on the expansion – we are the great annexationists – at the expense of the effete language depts. My biology crowd are still awfully keen and I thoroughly enjoy taking trouble with them – I really felt beastly selfish deserting them for so long. Now I'm back at the old round – hard at work on Fritillaries and I pray for a decent plague of cabbage caterpillars again this year – they are excellent material. The class is cutting up the frogs with great enthusiasm.*

---

[403] Noel Pemberton Billing MP, notorious during WW1 for his extreme right-wing views and his homophobic conspiracy theories, which eventually led to a sensational libel trial.

Apart from shop, I'm just going to read Lord Morley's[404] *Recollections and I'm learning the art of keeping bees, a side show which the Horticultural Society has started. Old K. has just sent me in B.R.'s Mysticism and Logic, which I see consists of reprints of old friends – but they are always excellent reading, especially in the light of one's last 4 years' experiences! I'm sure K. is an awfully decent sort – he was going to have come to see me in Jena. Again very many thanks for writing to me.*

My very best wishes.

Yours Michael Pease

....

A corner of the biology laboratory

[404] British Liberal statesman, writer and newspaper editor, author of the Gladstone biography.

The microtome and accessories

Corner of the science library

July 7th Invalids 3 deep in the box, none very serious. In general very rampant and all sorts of people dropping off. Read Russell in the morning – very good on mathematics. Microtome in the afternoon and evening.

END OF THE DIARIES

Perhaps Michael caught the "grippe" and lost the habit of keeping a diary. However his life in the camp appears to have continued much as usual. He would have been involved in the Natural Sciences Exhibition held in September 1918, when the school's science laboratories were opened to the whole camp and proved a great attraction.

[Inserts at the back of the diary: notice and agendas for R.H.S. committee meetings on 23rd July, 6th and 27th August, and programmes for chamber concerts on 27th August and 1st November 1918]

....

HBW to MSP:

Moddershall Oaks, Stone, Staffs.

August 5th 1918

Dear Mr. Pease,

It has been nice to get so many letters from you. The last two (June 20, 25) arrived particularly opportunely – the first when I was down with flu and wanted better and the second when my cousin had deserted me in our house for two nights. I am so sorry you are back in camp. If they'll only hurry up and ratify this agreement you may be home not so long hence. Your holiday must have been wonderful.

I do remember the roses on the Cam; they and the bryony and the beanfields are all intrinsically mixed up with my first summer in Cambridge – just before the war. It all seems now like a small illuminated painting very clear and remote; not real at all. All the same – although the sentiment is hackneyed it is a comfort to know they go on just the same.

What a lark if K published that book! If you are writing to him would you mention that I sent him 2 letters, but they were returned as they have to go through an agency now. He will be wondering why I have not written.

Hanley lodging house indeed! It's a beautiful house. We have the luck to be on the edge of a hill with a jolly churchyard in front and a view right across the valley behind. The Potteries have that advantage over most other industrial towns, –

there are not many parts from which you don't get a view of hills and woods. I am sure you would appreciate our house if you saw it; – cream walls and dark green paint and the right coloured curtains and cushions, – but mothers with their first babies aren't in it with us and that house! We are awfully happy there and are getting in touch with things in the Potteries. The people are very friendly and however ugly it is I feel more at home there than anywhere except Moddershall. Bad or good we belong to it. – I think we Staffordshire people pride ourselves on the fact that it takes a Staffordshire person to appreciate Staffordshire! In a little place too, a few determined people can do a good deal. For instance my two cousins[405] *(aged 24 and 23) summoned the women of the district to a housing conference with the result that housing has been the talk of the place for months. The local paper backed them and the town council will almost certainly move in the right direction. It is rather amusing raising a storm in the local teacup! My cooking goes very nicely thank you! In fact I am beginning rather to fancy myself in that line. Will you come to Hanley and hold a competition with me when you come back?*

My brother writes very cheerfully on the whole. He was at Karlsruhe, [in south-west Germany] *but is to be moved. For the first time in his life he has really got a chance to work at his painting which is his passion – he really is good, people say, in spite of having had practically no teaching. By the way I have just been answering a letter from a man who has served '2 years hard', – extraordinarily plucky too. I think it would send me off my head. I shall recommend the habit of writing to prisoners for those who wish to acquire a concise style – such a lot has to be got into a sheet!*

I never met Paul Montague, though I've heard Ivy Turner or Phyllis Lapthorn [Bedalians] *speak of him. I did not know he too was killed. What is one to do but "get into a state of mingled resignation and bitterness"? The only alternative seems to be to go mad or shoot oneself. And you get people even now talking about preparing for the next war!! Not to mention the "economic war". But I think when the young men come back they'll knock* <u>*that*</u> *on the head. What a joy it would be to hang some people – (a nice sentiment for a Tolstoyan, but at heart I fear I am a bloodthirsty Tricoteuse).*

I've just been reading the life of Francis Place, author of The People's Charter. He makes one feel a frightful slacker. "Went to bed about 2 or 3 but indulged myself by lying in bed in the morning till 7"! I am sorry though he did not love Cobbett,[406]

---

[405] Phoebe Sylvia Wedgwood (fn 400) and her sister Doris Audrey Wedgwood.

[406] William Cobbett, a Chartist. Michael read his *Rural Rides* in camp.

for whom I have a weakness. And they thought the millennium was coming in about 6 years!!,

With best wishes,

Yours

Helen Wedgwood

....

HBW to MSP:

Moddershall Oaks, Aug. 8th 1918

Just got your letter of July 6, a delightful surprise. Thanks awfully for the photos; they do help to give an idea of your life. I had no idea the place looked so businesslike; only I imagine the low roof must make it very hot in summer. I even managed to study the names of the books – with a magnifying glass!! I hope you escaped the flu or at any rate that it treated you kindly. It does make one feel so depressed. Did you get a letter I sent to you via Holland? My brother's address is not fixed yet. He has been all over the place. When I am scrubbing my kitchen floor I shall be able now to imagine you at one of those microscopes or slicing a wretched frog, (thank goodness my cousin is a vegetarian so I don't have to skin rabbits and things!) Good luck to your work. yrs HBW

....

HBW to MSP:

Moddershall Oaks, Stone, Staffs.

Aug. 30th 1918

Dear Citizen,

Having spent the afternoon talking red revolution with two elderly, and apparently respectable Potteries ladies (or rather having it talked to me) it seems somehow suitable to wind up the day by writing to you. I had resigned myself to not hearing from you for at least another year, when lo! your letter of July 5th, so "I think I will not hang myself today". (I hope you know your Chesterton).[407] *It has been jolly to get so many letters; they and the photos, which I admire immensely, have made it so much easier to imagine your life, and I do like to be able to imagine things properly. I am overcome with admiration of your labs. When Bekassy and Rosamund have finished their vast engineering works in triumph, I*

[407] From Chesterton's poem – 'A Ballade of Suicide'.

shall produce those photos and ***Crush*** *them – I don't know whether the chair in the library is yours, but it looks most professional and I imagine you just torn away from writing your great treatise on 'Dark Passages in the Family Life of Earwigius Squiggleosus' in that fat white exercise book. I even examined your shelves with a magnifying glass to admire your collection of books, but I couldn't read the ones with German titles. I couldn't quite make out all the Lab apparatus either, and I have a suspicion some of it was put there for effect, – but it would be ungenerous to inquire too closely. – When we photograph the inside of our house, I will send you one. I do hope the flu was not unkind to you. It gives an added gloom to existence which is quite unnecessary in these times.*

Please don't judge our most serious topics by the press! Those stunts have mostly no public opinion behind them at all.

I am so glad your brother is home for a bit. Every week makes a difference. Charles is at Danholm, Stralsund,[408] *having 'done' Germany pretty thoroughly in the interval. He seems to have got hold of some paints which is the chief thing with him.*

It is horrid disagreeing with one's people over the war. It is such a big thing and comes into everything; and it's so difficult not to get bitter with the other side – when one sees ones friends being gradually killed off. But afterwards I think it will be all right. I fancy people like my father and your mother will be quite 'sound' when it's over. By the way, people who ought to know, swear that even this county constituency here will go Labour after the war. They say the returned soldiers will go solid for Labour. Oh won't there be a clean sweep all over Europe. It would please you to hear the conversation of these good dames in the Potteries. Have I mentioned before that we had Mr. Outhwaite[409] *to tea (we're his constituency), likewise that the Editor of the local rag is going to drop in to one of our 'salons' – We're very nervous as to the right method of treating an editor. Do you "threaten its life with a railway-share" or "charm it with smiles and soap"?* [The Hunting of the Snark]. *It's most important to keep on the right side of him.*

For heaven's sake don't read Freud! At least not if you value your friend's peace of mind. One begins to relate (I admit it is an undesirable habit) an apparently harmless and innocent dream, and then perceives Rosamund fixing one with a coldly analytical gaze and probably drawing the most appalling deductions, and one's feelings are far worse than those of a microbe under a microscope.

---

[408] A small island on the German coast of the Baltic Sea.

[409] R L Outhwaite – a radical Liberal Party politician.

Good luck to the beekeeping. How the other Ruhlebenites will swear though! There can't be room to give them a wide berth. I've seen a feeling remark as it is in one of the magazines on the landgrabbingness of the Horticultural Society.

My cousin and I are become so enamoured of Hanley, or rather of No 16 that we can scarcely bear to tear ourselves away even for weekends. Do you use a haybox in your cooking? We've just started one, – a great saving. Phoebe is at the present at the T.U. Congress at Derby as Maggie Bondfield's ADC, so I'm consoling myself at home trying to write a novel. – We both retire into literature when the Industrial System becomes too much for us – so look out for the new Potteries School. I was ill-advised enough to go in for a hero instead of a heroine, and find him a most annoying young man, hopelessly uncertain about his own character. Also there are so many things one ought to have experienced as: – (a) gaol, (b) suburban society (c) a V.A.D.'s [Voluntary Aid Detachment] *life in a hospital; – you perceive it is a very modern novel.*

Father is saying "Go to bed. Go to bed" in a "soft undercurrent of sound", so I wish you a very good night, Sir,

from Helen Wedgwood.

....

MSP to HBW (received 10 Nov):

Ruhleben, Sept. 29th 1918

Very many thanks for your pc of Aug 6th and letter of Aug 30th. Very glad you got my letters and the photos. No, honestly there was no apparatus put there for effect, so you can enquire as much as you like! By the way, I never got the letter that you mentioned you had sent via Holland. Here things go on as usual and the months slip by and one grows much older. General meeting of our Horticultural Society just coming off, and I'm very busy with the Annual report. Much interested to hear of your literary venture – send me a copy, please do if Dora will pass it! Best wishes Michael Pease

....

Marjory Pease to MSP (letter 493):

The Pendicle, Limpsfield, Surrey

30th Sept. 1918

My dearest Michael,

I lunched with Mrs. Whyte at the Stories today and had a long Ruhleben talk. My latest news of you is your pc of August 18th, but Mrs. Whyte has not heard from Arnold for about 2 months. We talked much of you all and still cling to the hope that you will not have to spend a fifth winter in captivity. I have taken your library and lab photos to get them enlarged and if good, I'll send copies to Prof Seward for Cambridge lab and copies to Bedales.

Oct 1st, 2pm. Am writing this at Food Control offices at Oxted having just got back from Bletchingly and waiting for Brighton Train. I go on to Worthing to stay till early on Thursday with Nicolas.[410] *I shall find out from him how much longer he is likely to be there. I'm sure he is not fit for overseas yet. The local papers have got fine notices about him*[411] *and you are included in them all and everyone who congratulates me on Nicolas speaks most feelingly of what your return will mean to me. It is only when I get you back I will realise how I have suffered by this long weary separation extending over these 4 years. And you will be 28 tomorrow! I do think it is magnificent the way you have faced these years – you have "made history" as Prof Seward says.*

By the way no one here seems to know about the memoirs of the donor of mouth organs – are the Mendelsons mentioned in it? Do you ever see your old friend D.T. [*Daily Telegraph*] *now? I fancy not, but if he does turn up now and again you will find him quite an interesting companion.*

Worthing, Oct 2nd. I could not finish this yesterday and so continue today while waiting in my hotel for Nicolas. My bedroom faces the sea and as I lay in bed this morning I thought of you and your 5th birthday in a foreign land. I know you will be thinking much about me today but I know you think of me every day and now just as you are never out of my thoughts. One watches developments with anxious interest and a strong personal interest. This will reach you about Nov 15th I suppose, and goodness knows what may have happened by then. Will peace come as suddenly as war!

So far as Nicolas knows his plans he will be here till 20th Oct – then 3 weeks which will be spent in Bristol, Ireland and Kinfauns and then probably a month's Home Service before returning to [word erased by censor]. *We have had cold wet*

---

[410] Nicolas was wounded in a trench raid during the 2nd Battle of Dernancourt in May/June 1918, and after treatment in France and London he was sent to an Officer's Convalescent Hospital in Worthing, run by a Miss Cass.

[411] Nicolas received a Military Cross for his part in the Battle of Arras in May 1917, and a bar for the trench raid in 1918 (his personal account of this is in a memoir that he wrote for his children).

weather, but it has improved and here it is beautifully bright and sunny and warm and peaceful and Nicolas is in very great luck to be here.

May you be back to all of us who love you so dearly and who are so proud of you, long before your next birthday.

Your devoted Mother.

....

Marjory Pease to MSP (letter 498) sent to MSP, Baracke III Box 10, Ruhleben, and forwarded c/o Cyril F. A. King, Kings College Cambridge:

The Pendicle, Limpsfield, Surrey

15th Oct. 1918

My dearest Michael,

Your very welcome letter of Sep. 15th turned up this morning, also your most interesting 3 photos of the laboratory which are most valuable. What a shame to spoil your garden in Bar 6 with a lean-to shed. Such things are maddening. I wrote you a very hurried letter yesterday and forgot to number it – it was number 497. We go on waiting developments and working away as usual – I have had a long day in Staffhurst Wood starting school dinners and then home at 4 and out again round the Chart [Limpsfield]. *Your father stayed at home to receive the Cote Bank furniture which was expected here today, but though it is at the station it never turned up. I don't think anything very interesting is arriving – most of it goes to the cottage in the meantime.*

<u>*Oct 16th 10 p.m.*</u> *Busy day – War Pensions Committee in the morning and then afternoon in London at League – a visit from old Schmeisser who I fancy feels his position somewhat in spite of having 3 sons in the army. His eldest son has gone mad and is in an asylum – the reason being that he was rejected from the army for bad eyesight and this preyed on his mind!*

I told you R and R's [nephews Ralph and Reggie Davidson] *mother was very ill. She died on Sunday. Primrose is going to take Beatrice* [niece] *and Reggie will in the meantime stay on in Manchester, but the home will be broken up of course. The uncles have behaved in their usual selfish way, but I needn't elaborate on this.*

We go on from day to day wondering if it is to be peace or more war. I know how eagerly you will all watch the signs of the times. The thought of a 5th winter in captivity for you is almost more than I can bear. And yet what a splendid example you set us. I have a letter from Siward Horsley [Bedalian school friend] *who was pleased to get your messages. He is writing to you. What splendid photos there are of your lab. and how business like it all is. Schmeisser tells me the Daily Mail had a photo of you recently! I never saw it. What talks we'll have when you come back! How are you going to convey your possessions! I have sent Walter a violin case for travelling and today I have got a lot of music for him, so you see there is a considerable amount of flutter and preparation going on and I expect the Neumeister spirits are rising also and menus are being discussed.*[412]

Oct 17th 10 p.m. Your welcome letter of Sep. 1st arrived this morning – interested to hear about your flower show and all your other news including your visitors. Glad my parcels are arriving – I sent you off shallots today. I've made delicious pickled onions and long to send you some, but never mind you'll taste them here. Well Dora forbids me writing about the things that really matter!

Your devoted Mother

……………………

HBW to MSP (letter sent to Ruhleben, forwarded to Limpsfield, received by MSP on 8th Feb. 1919):

16 Wood Terrace, Shelton, Hanley, Staffs

Oct. 20th 1918

Dear Mr. Pease,

(I rather think that for the future I shall begin with "Dear Sir and Brother", a new and stinky form of address that I've just learnt from the Agr. Labourers' Union). I'm afraid it is some time since I wrote, – I allege in excuse pressure of Domestic and Public affairs! i.e. I have been (1) making jam (2) salting french beans, (3) knitting winter stockings (4) holding committees, (5) helping in charades at the Women's Co-op Guild, (6) making speeches, to anyone who will listen, (7) making myself sweet to Fathers' and the Outhwaites' constituents, and (8) reading William James' "Varieties of Religious Experience".[413] *There! if that list doesn't provide sufficient excuse nothing will. However, lest you should fear that the country is going to the dogs while I pause, I should mention that at this moment I am in an enormous armchair reading "Cecilia" (a nice antidote to an agitator's life)* [subtitled 'Memoirs of an Heiress', by Frances Burney]– *at least I would be reading it, if I weren't writing to you. I'm trying to imagine you equally lazy*

[412] From family letters written post-war, it appears that Walter was still being held in England in August 1919.

[413] Concerns the nature of religion and the neglect of science in the academic study of religion.

and comfortable, but I'm afraid the log fire is absent. It is rather difficult to talk about little things when you, even more than the rest of the world, must be watching events so anxiously. Perhaps by the time this reaches you, you may be packing up! One can't realise it and tries not to hope too much. Well, we shall have our work cut out when it is over – and I expect 'work' is what you'll enjoy after 4½ years internment. At least we rebels can't find life dull, or lonely for long.

Last night I made my debut at the local branch of the Agr. Lab. Union, which is going ahead everywhere like wildfire. I gave them a brief sketch of the history of the Agr. Labourer in England, – and if their blood didn't boil it wasn't the fault of the matter. It is very difficult to judge of the impression one has made on that sort of audience and I'm afraid it will take me a good deal of practice to know just how to appeal to them. I should like to hear someone good. For one thing one imagines them better educated than they are (there speaks the Cambridge Intellectual!) I imagine one should go in for concrete examples and parables. I shall be asking you to come and criticise one day, I warn you! I should like to learn to speak well.

Last week the local choirs performed the Elijah, – perfectly splendidly. Music is the thing we are proud of in this district. It was wonderful – only while I find I have rather an admiration for Elijah himself, I shall always think of him as a little man with a black moustache and eyeglasses!

The Women's Co-op Guild are in the throes of a concert, (I take the part of an aged labourer). We are all jolly and friendly and you'd be surprised what good actors those middle-aged matrons are, especially at 'patter' – and they do so thoroughly enjoy themselves!

We are beginning to feel quite important in the district – all the women representing different 'movements' get sent to us, and of course we hold forth on what the Potteries wants. As for my cousin, since a very suspicious (and very nice) potters official has deliberately addressed her as "comrade", she has scarcely deigned to speak to a "bourgeois".

I am afraid the cold weather will have put an end to your microscopic work, but I hope you have something else to absorb you.

With best wishes,

Yours H B Wedgwood

....

Marjory Pease to MSP (letter 501):

Limpsfield

Oct. 25th 1918 [Friday]

My dearest Michael,

Very glad to know by your p.c. of Sep 24th that you were well and getting my letters so surprisingly quickly as things go now a days. You must be very badly off for tweeds and flannel – I have got a beautiful piece of Harris tweed which I'm keeping here for you - I feel you are coming home soon and I sometimes even dare to put your room into shape and re-arrange furniture! How you and I will have to work to build up and to heal sores. I often wonder if you see the man who had mouth organs. I should think he ought to be more cheerful and better company now.

Nicolas comes home tomorrow, but I think he goes back again to Worthing and for this I am thankful. I have had sad news today. Mme Cattoir, the Belgian lady who lived nearly 4 years at Lombarden's and who went to France a month ago, died at Le Havre. She leaves 3 charming children. I was very very fond of her and we had made great plans for future meetings and for taking you to visit them.

Sunday 7a.m.

A little squirrel is eating our chestnuts as I write and the country is lovely with autumn tints in spite of much sodden weather. Nicolas arrived last night to stay till Tuesday and he returns to Worthing for fortnight - a boil on his neck gets this "extension" for which I am thankful. So now I think of going to Kinfauns on Nov 2nd, visiting Walter [Neumeister] *for certain and Becher perhaps. Your Grannie is a very old lady and my visit to her is very much overdue. I dreamt vividly of you last night, in a loft! It was the most vivid dream I've had of you. I feel certain you will soon be home – certainly in time for my election which is really seriously being considered.*

I can't really pad up my letter with trivialities when such momentous issues are in the balance. We are living through historic times with a vengeance, but what a price has been paid! What a toll of precious young lives – what desolation and misery – what a grey grey world. But those of us who are left must work with unabated vigour worthy of the spirit which prompted all these fine young men to lay down their lives for the right. The tragedy of it all. It will be a sad sad homecoming but what a welcome you will get from everyone who is left. You are never out of our thoughts -

your devoted Mother

Marjory Pease to MSP: (sent to MSP at Ruhleben, forwarded to c/o Cyril F. A. King, King's College, Cambridge, and then to Mount Pleasant, London)

Kinfauns Manse, Perthshire.

Nov. 5th 1918

My dearest Michael,

Just a line as you know how difficult it is to write letters here. I arrived at noon yesterday and found all well in their usual [sic]. *Grannie is wonderfully well – very anxious to send you a Xmas present, but this I have discouraged telling her to keep her gift and give it to you personally. As I have said before it is difficult to write a letter which will not reach you for a month. In a month or so much will have happened. Surely common sense will prevail and the shedding of more precious blood avoided! I have written to Herr Neumeister and I could truthfully give him a glowing account of Walter's health and appearance and also of the camp conditions.*

The country here is very beautiful. You must come up soon to see your grandmother once more. Nicolas still at Worthing. Your father writes that Mr. and Mrs. Arthur Dodd appeared quite unexpectedly on Sunday about 4 o'clock and stayed for tea! He walked down to the station with them for the 5.30 train. They are staying at Earls Court till the end of the war so I'll see them. Bad luck they should come when I was away. Did I tell you that Prof Seward wrote me a very enthusiastic letter thanking me for the enlarged photos of your lab? How splendid the University of Ruhleben is. So interested to read in Times of the exams. What a packing up you'll have! Well as I said before, letter writing is difficult in the face of present day events. Take care of yourself. You are very precious to me - your devoted Mother

....

HBW to MSP: (sent to MSP at Ruhleben, forwarded to The Pendicle, Limpsfield (7th Feb) and then to 5 St. Clements Gardens, Cambridge (8th Feb))

Moddershall Oaks, Stone, Staffs

11 Nov. 1918

Dear Mr. Pease,

Perhaps this won't reach you, – let us hope so, as you are not likely to deplore the reason! But I just must send a line tonight. I wonder did you get the news the same time as we did, only if you had as many false alarms first, I'm sorry for you. We were at The Ark [Moddershall Oaks] *and only guessed because we heard the bells 3 miles away making such a row, so we went up on the roof to listen, and sat in a row on the top, after running up the red flag. But one doesn't really feel much like flagwagging and cheering – and there wasn't really much of it, even in the Potteries, – except among the small boys who enjoyed themselves hugely marching up and down in procession with the lids of their mother's dustbins. Still, just for today one tries to forget how many things are far from what one would wish; and to feel that at least men are not being slaughtered every minute over there. – Otherwise, – well it's a dark and alarming world. I got your pc of Sept 22nd yesterday. – I expect you've grown rapidly younger in the last month, and that grey beard has had to retire hastily!*

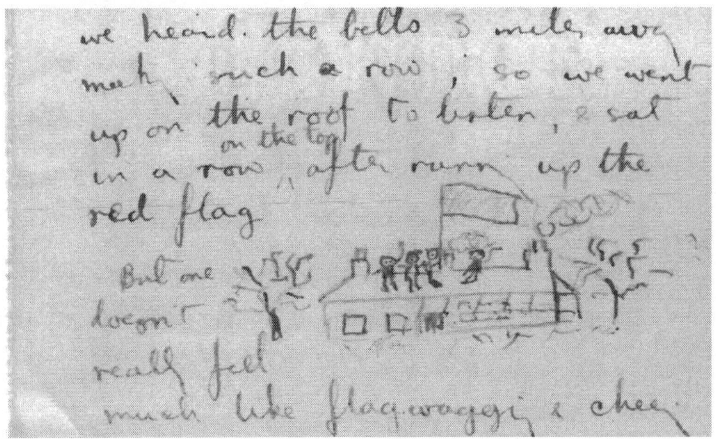

we heard the bells 3 miles away
mak[ing] such a row, so we went
up on the roof to listen, & sat
in a row on the top, after runn[ing] up the
red flag
But one
doesn't
really feel
much like flagwagging & chee[ring]

Extract from Helen's letter of 11th November 1918

No I'm quite sure Dora wouldn't pass my novel! How frightfully seditious we shall be able to be in our conversation when you get back; we'll have 4½ years suppressions to get off our minds. I wonder if you will be back for Christmas?

Well, in case you aren't this is to wish you and all good rebels luck in the building of the new World.

Yours

Helen Wedgwood

....

Otto Neumeister to MSP:

Jena, 12 November 1918

Dear Mr. Michael,

Very many thanks for your kind card of 10 Oct. We were indeed happy to know that our small gift/token gave you some pleasure. We, too, often like to think of the time you spent with us here, and now in the autumn the garden seems to be waiting for its knowledgeable gardener. I have communicated your kind regards and news of your dear mother to Frl. Zeiss. Last Saturday and the day before yesterday we received to our great joy two letters from your mother, and, enclosed, letters of our Walter that I am forwarding to you in this letter as we have a translation. Your mother writes that you have had an attack of this insidious influenza, I am really surprised by this as you lead a hard life inured to the surroundings. All the more we are glad to know that you have got over the disease without after effects. How full of occurrences these last few days have been! Before long priceless freedom will be awaiting you (Ihnen winkt die goldene freiheit) and most warmly do we congratulate you at this, but at the same time, I think of our Walter with sadness. Walter writes in his letter of 5 September: "I should like to mention once more that Michael's letter of 24 June gave me much pleasure. In every way it contains many satisfactory communications. Although I have never seen or spoken with him I have the feeling of knowing him just as he is. May it be possible that some time later we shall be able to talk together and exchange views. I am most heartily grateful for the great service he has repeatedly rendered me with his kind letters. He has communicated things of great interest to me and also to you. Therefore, I pray you, dear father, write to Michael if possible and tell him at the same time how sorry I am not to be able to write to him direct and why this is so." I comply most willingly with the request of my Walter and thank you, too, from my heart for your letters to him.

From the enclosed letters of your kind mother, you will see what continuous trouble she is taking to alleviate Walter's lot and you can imagine, too, how afflicted we are at the thought of our prisoners not being considered in the dispositions of the armistice.

I had purposed, in spite of the short time, to look you up and speak with you once more, but if you are lucky on being able to quit the camp in the next few days may I ask you to let me know so that I need not make the journey in vain. If I cannot speak with you, dear Mr. Michael, then our best wishes accompany you, may you have a happy journey, greet your kind parents from us and in particular your dear kind-hearted mother. We shall never forget and shall remember her always with gratitude for what she has done for our Walter during the years of his long captivity. Farewell, dear Mr. Michael, you too, we have learned to esteem, to honour and to love, in spite of all the misfortunes that this terrible war has brought on us there were lucid intervals so that we must not despair of humanity. I think back with joy on the days you spent under our roof. You were, and are to us a friend.

I hope it may be possible to speak with you again and send you warmest greetings.

Yours, Otto Neumeister

My wife, Frl. Frieda and Luci ask to be remembered to you likewise.

....

MSP to HBW:

On-board a Scandinavian-American-Line ship,[414] *North Sea* [postmarked Ripon, 28 Nov. 1918]

Nov. 26th 1918

Dear Miss Wedgwood,

Just a line to let you know I'm now all but home again. We sighted May Island [in the outer Firth of Forth] *an hour or so ago and are now coasting down to Hull, which we hope to reach at 6am tomorrow. I shall look forward very much to seeing you sometime or other and expressing my thanks for your many kindnesses to me during my internment. As soon as I find how things are at home – I feel dreadfully vague about my future movements – we must try and fix something up. Of course, I know you are always very busy and now you will have your brother back again, so I quite realise how many claims you have on your time.*

We came through Stralsund on Saturday morning and I thought of your brother. However, one of the men on the railway whom I asked, said that the officer's camp had been "schon aufgehort" [already ceased] *so I suppose your brother is back before us. It was very pretty: it was a beautiful morning, the sun just rising and shining on the old red brick buildings as we crossed over the ferry to Rügen. Well,*

[414] Ruhleben was the first camp to be emptied under the 'Danish Scheme' devised by Captain Charles Cabry Dix, the naval attaché at the British legation in Copenhagen, who sketched out an idea on Nov 1st that British POWs could be brought out of the Baltic ports with the help of Red Cross agencies and Danish shipping. The first ships left Copenhagen on 21 November for Sassnitz (on Rügen Island) to pick up the Ruhleben inmates, and on return to Copenhagen the POWs were transferred to the trans-Atlantic liner 'Frederik VIII' to sail to Hull, landing on the 27th November. They were then taken to a reception centre at Ripon Camp for a 3 day de-brief before being sent home.

I'll tell you all about it sometime, so I won't bore you with any more written stuff now. Perhaps you'll pay old Cambridge a visit at the end of term.

Again many thanks and looking forward to meeting you sometime soon.

Very sincerely yours,

Michael Pease

……………………

MSP to HBW:

Limpsfield,

Surrey,

Nov. 31st 1918 [sic]

Dear Miss Wedgwood,

Many thanks for your lines of welcome. It is splendid to think of seeing you so soon: I will do as you suggest – 1917 Club[415] *3p.m. on Thursday next. I don't know the club or Gerrard Street but I suppose I can find my way there, and not being a member I shall just ask for you and see what happens. I do hope your 'flu isn't serious, but I know well what 'grippe' can be. I'm surprised that your brother is not back. It was a very reliable looking railway official at Stralsund that assured me that the officers' camp had been broken up.*

Well, I won't write more now but will look forward to Thursday next.

Very Sincerely Yours

Michael Pease

P.S. I am going to Cambridge on Tuesday, so if you want to catch me, write to Trinity College. If I don't hear to the contrary I shall turn up at the 1917 Club as agreed. MSP

……………………

[415] A club for socialists at 4 Gerrard Street, Soho, founded by Leonard Wolf.

Epilogue

After Michael's return to England the correspondence between him and Helen continued with increasing frequency and passion as the friendship blossomed into love. Helen and Michael were married at Chelsea Registry Office on 24th February 1920. Helen's father, Josiah Wedgwood, an MP who had recently defected from the Liberal to the Labour Party, celebrated this union between two political families in a letter to Michael's father: *'I am so glad our descendants have decided to marry. Nothing could have pleased me better – good stock, good brains and good ideals. I do not forget that I came to you – a boy of twenty – to get my first dose of political work; and I like to think that our joint stock will go on with the work'.*

After a lengthy search Michael found a plot of land in Girton, a few miles north-west of Cambridge, where they built Reynolds Close – the family home to the end of their days. True to Helen's wishes they had lots of children – four girls and two boys – who had 'plenty of time to run loose on their own' (*HBW to MSP, 14th Jan 1917*). Sadly, their fourth child died from complications following scarlet fever, aged 5½yrs.

Michael initially returned to the research post held open for him at the School of Agriculture in Cambridge, and was also appointed a Lecturer in Agricultural Botany. In 1920 he joined the Small Animal Breeding Station as assistant to Professor Reginald Crandall Punnett, where they created the first chicken breeds – the Cambar and the Legbar – that could be sexed at hatching (no mean feat). He spent the majority of his working life researching the genetics of small animals and poultry, and his last job was as a Senior Principal Scientific Officer at the Poultry Genetics Station.

Michael, despite his avowed dislike of meetings, remained a committee man through and through. He joined the Girton Parish Council in 1925, became Chair in 1937, and remained in that post for over 25 years. He became a member of Chesterton Rural Council in 1928, and a member of Cambridgeshire County Council in 1958. He was one of the founders of the National Association of Parish Councils, and was Chair of its Cambridgeshire branch. Another post he held was secretary of the Cambridgeshire Federation of Labour Parties. In June 1966 (six weeks before he died) he was awarded an OBE for political and public services in Cambridgeshire.

Helen was no less active in local politics: she was President of the Cambridgeshire Divisional Labour Party in the early 1930s, became a County Councillor in 1937, and was heavily involved in the Cambridgeshire Federation of Labour Parties. She was also notable as an early woman magistrate and had the distinction of being the first Labour woman Justice of the Peace for Cambridgeshire, appointed in January 1925. In this she followed in the footsteps of her mother-in-law Marjory, who was appointed one of the country's first female magistrates in July 1920.

The Pease family at Reynolds Close, Girton in 1939

Michael's experiences in Ruhleben remained part of his life, and he kept in touch with other other internees both through personal contacts with the friends he made there, and through the annual reunions. Soon after the outset of World War II, he entrusted his youngest children, Fabian and Dora, into the care of his Canadian Ruhleben friend, Winthrop Pickard Bell, then living in Nova Scotia.

He also continued his friendship with the Neumeister family, with regular correspondence and a number of family holidays in Jena, until the Iron Curtain made travel impossible. Michael died in 1966, but Helen remained in contact with the family and heard of Walter's death in June 1978.

In 1976–77 Helen loaned the contents of the Ruhleben chest to the Imperial War Museum who microfilmed the collection for their archives. She also recorded some oral history tapes on her wartime experiences for them, which can be found at: https://www.iwm.org.uk/collections/item/object/80000815.

In addition she was contacted in 1977 by Peter Liddle from the Faculty of Humanities at Sunderland Polytechnic, who was creating an archive of personal experiences in the Great War. He made copies of the Ruhleben papers which are now held in the University of Leeds Special Collection (https://archiveshub.jisc.ac.uk/).

Helen died at Reynolds Close in 1981.

Postscript from Fabian Pease:

I not only learned about my father's time in Ruhleben from him, but took advantage of some of the items he had brought home with him. These included a large transformer the prisoners had built so they could run their electric lights without batteries. They had discovered that a power line ran underneath one of their buildings, and by sticking pins through the insulation were able to extract the power (at 240 volts) and transform it down to power their low voltage bulbs. He was quite pleased when, some 35 years later, I used the same transformer to charge the accumulators that I needed for my home-built radios.

My earliest recollections are of life at Reynolds Close before we were evacuated to Canada in June 1940. Already we had two refugees living with us. One was Nicolas Perez Sama (an engineer from Spain), who drew cartoons of us, including one of me conversing with the moon at Christmas. Sama, as we called him, left for Canada in March 1940. The other was Gerda Senser, a refugee from Berlin, who lived at Reynolds Close employed as a home-help until after the war ended. Our parents believed strongly that you should look after those less fortunate than ourselves.

Our parents were very busy during the war years and their activities are well recorded in the book *Girton's War* by D. R. de Lacey. Our father clearly was the local leader, a role he kept after the war as Chairman of the Girton Parish Council but also because he was the person people came to when they needed help; often to find somewhere to live but for many other reasons as well. Our mother was active as a magistrate and also served on the Cambridgeshire County Council. So both were kept busy with local government affairs and were stalwarts of the local Labour Party.

By 1955 they felt financially secure enough to buy a car and learn to drive. It turned out that my father didn't need to take a driving test because he had purchased a license in 1919 (before the days of driving tests) from the Surrey County Council so he could borrow his brother's motor bike. This irritated my mother significantly because she felt she was the better driver; but she eventually passed her test. The following year they added the extension onto Reynolds Close.

About 1960 Dad retired. Although I helped him occasionally on the University Farm I know little about his professional accomplishments. I've a feeling that his civic activities kept him from immersing himself completely in his scientific work and so he never made a big name for himself there. After retirement, to keep fully active, he ran for, and was elected to, the County Council representing Papworth and nearby villages. One of my last recollections of him talking about Ruhleben (in about 1964) was his commenting how attendance at the annual Ruhleben Alumni dinner had dwindled so much. But the main message I learned from my time at Reynolds Close was the obligation of those better off to take care of those less fortunate.

Appendix 1. Additional personal letters

....

Dr L S Ornstein to Edward Reynolds Pease [ERP]:

Helpman, BIJ Groningen, Holland

7th Nov. 1914

Dear Mr. Pease,

I have not yet heard whether my card to the parents of the Belgian officer have reached them. But I think the chance is very small. The German authorities have refused last days to pass the post of our Ministry of Foreign Affairs and their attitude in Belgium is terrible. But I will try what I can if I hear that my card cannot pass. What a pity that your son now is imprisoned, I often think of him when I speak with the interned soldiers here.

With kind regards, truly yours

Ornstein.

....

Dr L S Ornstein to Marjory Gammell Pease [MGP]:

Helpman, BIJ Groningen, Holland

14th Nov. 1914

Dear Mrs. Pease,

The letter announcing you that your son is imprisoned will have reached you now. I have yet now little success with the letter to Mr. S [?]. The post to Belgium is refused by Germany. I have now written to the ambassador of Belgium and to a friend (Dutchman) working at a manufacturer in Germany for it seems that post can be sent from Germany to Brussels. As soon as I know something I shall write it you for your poor Belgian officer.

With kind regards, truly yours,

Ornstein

....

Mary Gammell Davidson (maternal grandmother) to MSP:

Kinfauns Manse, Perthshire

14th Dec. 1914

My dear Michael,

I valued much your kind letter of Oct. from Jena – and you are constantly in my thoughts. I have not written to you for letters are not always delivered, but your mother is very good and keeps me informed as far as she can about you in this trying time – I feel for you being deprived of your interesting work at Cambridge – but hope there is a good time coming for you, and for your dear parents – I am glad they have Nickie [Nicolas] with them from time to time. Your mother kindly gave me a weekend in November and we had 4 very peaceful days together here. She resting and chatting with me. She looked very well in spite of all she does for the good of others – of course this is only what we should all try to do – but not to all [illegible] to work more than strength can stand. Here all goes on peacefully. Uncle Roger and Aunt Janet[416] busy in the Parish and other work. Alastair[417] doing well at Fettes and Jack[418] at Perth Academy. I, still able to move about and read and knit a little, but I feel my age bringing increasing weakness. I have many comforts here and thank God for his many blessings – I like to hear you speak of the early days you spent at Kinfauns – many a change since then – I hope before long you may revisit the old place. Christmas is at hand again, and my love and best wishes go with this for you now and always and may the promise given of "Peace on Earth and good will to all men" soon be fulfilled. I am glad you have books to read now and hope among them is a Bible. I know now much help and comfort in all our trials are to be found in it.

We have boisterous rainy weather, little frost or snow as yet – days very dark – goodbye now and with much love and kind wishes, your affectionate Grannie,

Mary G Davidson

....

Postcard to MSP from the family:

Cote Bank, Westbury-on-Trym, Bristol

Easter 1915

Good wishes from

S. A. Pease, Charlie P. Sanger, Rose E. Pease, Alfred Depreter [visitor], Winifred Pease, J. Gerald Pease, Margret Pease, Tony [Clark], Daphne [Sanger], John A.

---

[416] Her son Reverend Roger Stewart Davidson, Minister of Kinfauns and his wife.

[417] Grandson Roger Alistair McLaren Davidson, elder son of Roger and Janet.

[418] Grandson John Harcourt Stewart Davidson, younger son of Roger and Janet.

Clark, Marian F. Pease, C. Arthington Pease, Purefoy Pease, Monica Pease, Blanche Sandemont and Angela Sandemont [two young refugees?]

....

Tonika Görgey[419] *to MSP:*

Budapest

14th Oct. 1915

Dear Pease,

Many thanks for your kind words – it is so good to feel that although my poor brother had drifted so very far from all of you during this dreadful year, yet he is not forgotten by his friends; it is so dreadful to think that a life like his should have had to end in such a way! My husband[420] is at home after 14 months at the front with a luckily only slight wound – hence my delay in thanking you for your card. I hope you are as well as can be expected under the circumstances!

Yours ever sincerely, Tonika Görgey

....

Susanna Ann Pease (SAP – paternal grandmother) to MSP. [Note: her writing is particularly hard to decipher.]

Cote Bank, Westbury-on-Trym, Bristol

[Undated – possibly 1915]

My dear Michael,

I am thinking it is long since I wrote to you but that is not that I forget you but for I do not think there is a day that I do not think of you and pray that you may be kept in the patience and wisdom with which you seem able to meet conditions of captivity. I feel much of my eldest [illegible] grandson for the way in which you have made the best of your limitations and have used your time profitably both for yourself and others. It is an exceptional opportunity for influencing others – I do not mean so much educationally but as we are always influencing for good [illegible] evil those around us.

---

[419] Antonia Görgey, née Bekassy, an old Bedalian friend, sister to Ferenc and János Bekassy.

[420] Jòzsef Görgey, officer in a Hussar regiment.

We had a week ago a 24 hours very welcome visit from Nicolas who looks well and cheerful – he has seen very little fighting as you probably know, and is not at all in love with war. I was able to join the party at tea on the lawn that p.m.

We are having lovely weather now – a fortnight to [illegible] since we had any appreciable rain. We have ten [illegible] who come to our field, more than ever since the [illegible] had a wet p.m. It has been much colder and unsettled on the east of the Island judging by letters from Limpsfield and Letchworth.

If you come across Ponsonby [fn 68] will you tell him how very much we enjoyed a visit from his mother a little while ago. It was a very quiet visit but she just wanted to rest and she was delightful [illegible] at [illegible] times we have seen something of his brother Wynfrid who is at Clifton College. [illegible] continues to make [illegible] quiet and [illegible] thus do not seem to be very many of acquaintance, who are not intimate friends, we see very little.

Gervase Ford is in France with the Friends' Ambulance Unit and Eleanor finds it difficult to get much help in the house – I only hope she will not get over worked. She has 2 paying guests so is not lonely and she has a most charming little blue eyed golden haired [illegible] little Cara and they are very short of hands [writing crosses over first page so very illegible]. I am much better than at [illegible] time but a cold has kept me in my room this [illegible]. We expect J. Hogg soon for a visit. How gratifying the notes of your [illegible] in the Lit. Sup. of the [illegible].

Your very loving g. mother SAP.

P.S. I hope you and Ponsonby have received the gingerbread cakes I have sent.

……………………

ERP to MSP:

The Pendicle, Limpsfield, Surrey

5th Nov. 1915

My dear Michael,

Your letter to your mother of October 16th has come today and we are much interested to hear of your doings. I taught myself Italian when I was much younger than you, but what I read was Dante, *The Inferno* and *Purgatory*, which is extremely worth doing. I don't know if by classics like Chaucer, you include these? Surely not. Dante, by general consent, is one of the half dozen greatest poets, and Chaucer isn't. Tasso and Petrarch I did not take to. If at my age I started a new language – which is faintly possible – I should do Icelandic. There is this about Russian – that now's your chance. It is a job to be undertaken when one has time. As to money, your mother will write. I've just made up my accounts and find allowing you the usual sum, I still have some at your credit: so I think the B of A [Board of Agriculture] can await your return. But of course we don't take account of small items. I have plenty: ask for whatever you want, and we can settle up, if need be when the good time comes.

I've cut down the thorn and laburnum in the scullery bed and am digging it over. The clearance of that dark corner is a great improvement. I'm also making splints, so I am busy, though I don't go to town much. The Webb–Shaw[421] lectures are a great success. Every seat was sold for the first, and we shall make a big profit. My book[422] is really finished and has been read by the Webbs, who are complimentary. Shaw has it now. Another copy is at the publishers, but they have not replied on it yet. I am not however anxious, as if they refuse, it will be published all the same.

Don't be down hearted. The world is not so mad as you suppose. You hear all the silly things said here as we hear all the nonsense talked in Germany. In fact, people are less absurd than before. Most people are working together sensibly and cordially, (like your mother and the Jew) who before were separated by unreasonable dislikes.

Affectionately,

Edw. R. Pease.

....

SAP to MSP:

Cote Bank, Westbury-on-Trym, Bristol

6th Dec. 1915

My dear Michael,

It is a great satisfaction to us to hear of you from time to time through your parents as they are able generally to give as good news of you as one could expect under the circumstances. I hope the comforts with which your mother provided for you reached you and have prevented your suffering from the severe cold which came rather early and lasted longer than I think is usual in Nov. This is what [illegible] of such weather is common in that month. Quite mild now. From what we hear of you I picture you as wisely and bravely

---

421 Fabians Bernard Shaw, Sydney & Beatrice Webb.

422 History of the Fabian Society, published in 1916.

making the best of things, and determining that the time of captivity shall not be wasted in useless repinings. I like to think that this spirit may be, no doubt is, such a help to your associates. There is such a great deal in your lot that all would like to know but [illegible] that. For much hereafter we must try to wait in patience.

As Christmas comes the longing for home and family must be hard to bear and perhaps the greatest trial of all must be the uncertainty where it will all end. Then again there is nothing for it but patience. There is too the great comfort that what you have to bear you have in no way brought on yourself. I think your parents all wonderfully uncomplaining too.

There seems scarcely any family news. Willie [son William Benson Pease] and family have again fled to California from the cold of a B.C. [British Columbia] winter – they are at La Jolla. Nancy wrote of July sunshine and writing out of doors in thin clothing. They are by the sea, the place seems delightful. The girls attend Chapeloak College nearby where they attend diligently to their studies. Willie has a small motor which Dolly [daughter Dora] drives. And the Oswalds [son Oswald Allen Pease[423] and family] have a motor boat. They have moved to a place "?upian Landing" at some distance from Kelowna [in B.C.]. Willie is better than he was at one time but still has frequent headaches. We do not expect a large party at Christmas, which is just as well as we are in no mood for festivities except for Children and the Poor.

It is a great comfort that there is so little, one may perhaps say no destitution in England for the present. With much love from us all dear Michael, your very affectionate grandmother

S.A. Pease

....

MSP to MGP:

Ruhleben, 18th Dec. 1915

A printed Ruhleben Xmas postcard: "Ruhleben bei Spandau. With heartiest Xmas and New Year's Wishes"

....

To Helen Bowen Wedgwood from her mother Ethel:

---

[423] Oswald signed up with the Canadian Overseas Expeditionary Force in December 1915 and was killed in France in 1917.

Borden Wood,[424] Liphook, Hampshire

31st Jan. 1916

Dearest Daughter,

It is indeed good – and you will be able to go on – as his [Michael's] letter opens up points and is the letter of a hard thinking keen man. Personally I should tell him there is a change of heart. It would be strange if there weren't – and to believe in it helps it on – no doubt it is rather paralysing to the new spirit being born – luxury has dropped off – and service is the rule not the exception. If you go on telling people they will resort to the old selfishness after the war, you hinder and don't help with the new birth. However you will know what to say. The mother is evidently a good mother of a fine son – and I congratulate you on your friendship. Winifred is sending you an effusion on 'nurses' I believe. It was very good to hear from you – your loving M

....

ERP to MSP:

The Pendicle, Limpsfield, Surrey

30th March 1916

My dear Michael,

We were very glad to get your letter the other day, and fuller news than you can send on postcards. Your mother writes you all the regular news. So I will scribble a little about my doings. I am feeling more at loose ends than for long; for my book [*History of the Fabian Society*] is really done now. I made the index last Sunday and have only to revise it in proof, a ten minute job. I have spent a lot of time over it, because Webb and Shaw amended, or corrected, or amplified every page of the manuscript, and besides, Wallas, Oliver, Ensor, Mrs. Shaw, Mrs. Webb, and Sanders read and made suggestions. All these had to be considered, and embodied, or rejected. Then I had to negotiate for a dozen portraits, and so on and so on. All the readers so far have been congratulatory. Shaw has written two memoranda in his own name on particular points. The book will not, I expect, be published till after Easter. I have sold 100 copies in advance to Fabians, the Fabian Society has bought 500 – and I hope to sell more. Fifield has sold a thousand to America. It is not, of course, a good time to publish, but the book will go on selling for some time. It

---

[424] Home of Mr and Mrs Edmund Lamb – close family friends. Their daughter Winifred was the same age as Helen and also went to Newnham College.

is difficult to say whether it will sell: but anyway it is done. I am still busy over the Fabian Society, and our year ends tomorrow in a flush of cash. Various causes have contributed, but for the first time for years, I have to scheme to hide away our abundance! Of course, for one thing, I am working the show as honorary secretary, though the executive insisted on paying me £5 a month for expenses.

We've had the most extraordinary season. December, January and February so warm that we had tea in the verandah more than once. March a perpetual frost and snow and rain, ending in a blizzard two days ago. Literally, vegetation has not moved in a month. Some plums were out at the end of February, in the hedge. There are none out now.

The roses were all out but luckily I have not pruned them. I put in a few potatoes last Sunday, but otherwise I have hardly gardened all month.

Your mother has doubtless told you that my mother is rather seriously ill. A series of little illnesses since Xmas have left her with a weak heart, and at 89 this is dangerous. Very likely her splendid constitution will pull her through. But I fear she can never recover her old robust health.

I suppose you know that I sent a parcel of books to one Brown (I think) who wrote on behalf of your camp debating society. I'm afraid they were not much good, but they were all I could send. We are starting to publish again. We stopped for fear of financial difficulties, but now these are over we have a stock of things in hand. I'll send you a copy of my book when it is out. You are constantly in our thoughts. That you know.

Your affectionate father,

Edw. R. Pease

....

SAP to MSP:

Cote Bank, Westbury-on-Trym, Bristol

28th April 1916

My dear Michael,

It is a long time since I wrote to you and you are so often, so lovingly in my thoughts that I will no longer delay to tell you in this. I have no material for a letter of any interest, you must just know that I do not forget you. You are remembered perhaps more than you suppose as is shown by many interested enquiries.

My life since the beginning of the year has been spent almost entirely in my room whether from influenza or old age or a combination of the two I hardly know. The winter with its long succession of cold winds a longer continuance of snow storms than I ever can remember, has dealt rather horribly with some of us old people.

Our cousin Priscilla Fry has been ill almost as long as I have and my brother Edward has had a serious lung attack which causes [illegible] very weak [illegible] (physically not at all mentally) has caused much anxiety which is now much improved. It was very disappointing to me to be in my room after the first day of a visit from Eleanor Ford[425] and her little Cara, such a very bright attractive little girl of whom Eleanor has a right to be proud as she has done everything for her from the time of her recovering from a long illness after the baby's birth [on 29th Dec. 1914]. Eleanor had had so little experience that it is really very clever of her to have managed baby so very successfully.

We have had another [illegible] fine Easter week tho' unfortunately Monday was the poorest day of it. We have not had much of a holiday party, just Charlie,[426] Dora and Arthington are with us now. Peggie [Arthington's wife] who has been much better lately is staying at Limpsfield.

With much love dear Michael and wishing I could send you a better letter worth your time reading.

Your loving grandmother,

S.A.Pease

....

ERP to MSP:

The Pendicle, Limpsfield, Surrey

4th May 1916

My Dear Michael,

I'm sending you a copy of my book. I have only got two yet, and it is not to be published until the 10th. I hope it will interest you. The Fabians have bought (individually) nearly 200 copies and the publisher has sold 100 to the trade as well as a thousand to America. How many more are sold remains to be seen, but some at any rate will sell for years.

---

[425] Step-granddaughter Eleanor Mary Ford (nee Pease).

[426] Charles Sanger - daughter Dora's husband.

Summer has come directly after winter, and things are coming on with a rush. Your mother has told you no doubt how gorgeous your polyanthus seedlings have been. I failed again with the wallflower, why I know not. Last year your nitrate made the plants too big. This year they are all too scrubby. A lot were killed with clubroot which pervades a corner of the plot above the henhouse. The bitter spring cold has quite destroyed many tulips, which are not even attempting to flower. Apples will be a poor crop, plums we may get some. Other fruit promises well. The garden keeps in fair order, though I am in town five days a week, besides the arsenal on Sunday evenings. Did you hear of the sad end of our cashier, Brimley,[427] who disappeared as soon as I took up the work, having stolen something like £200. A month ago he committed suicide, and at the inquest it was reported that he objected to conscription (which he did because he could not leave the country!) and was a studious high-toned youth, vegetarian, one mealer, etc. All lies. He stole in order to live luxuriously and spend money at music halls! What weird people there are! A whole life for a competent young man is worth more than £200. It is easy to understand people stealing who are terribly hard up, (ailing wife, business) or who are suddenly in a hole (betting or gambling), but to steal systematically in order to belong to three of four clubs and eat 2/6 dinners and dress rather well would be incredible were it not the fact.

Well, we think of you constantly and hope for the joyful day of your return.

Your affectionate father,

Edw. R. Pease

....

ERP to MSP:

The Pendicle, Limpsfield, Surrey

1st June 1916

My dear Michael,

It is some time since I wrote to you, but your mother keeps you supplied with nearly all our news. We sent you my book which I hope will reach you safely. It is being excellently reviewed. Two columns in the *Times Lit. Supp.* today. A column or more in *The Westminster, Star, Daily News, Daily Chronicle, Mail, Guardian, New Witness* etc, all very polite. It is not selling very fast, but that was to be expected.

---

[427] Harold John Brimley.

We thought of you yesterday and wondered how your play went off. Did you get the church wardens [tobacco pipes] in time? They were a most puzzling thing to get at a moment's notice. I tried at twenty tobacconists, 4 slum shops, and all in vain. At last I discovered the name of a dealer in Finsbury. When I presented myself, it was a wholesale place, and they utterly declined to sell a dozen. Then I explained why I wanted them. As soon as I came to the word Ruhleben, the chief beamed at once "I'll give them to you with pleasure. What size would you like? Fetch the gentleman a box at once." He had, it seems, a friend who had been released and who had a son there still, so I got your pipes all in a beautiful box, for nothing.

The garden is at its best, as usual. Wallflowers, for some reason, probably the cold spring, were an utter failure, and so were many tulips, cut by the late snow and frost. The May tulips have been fine and are hardly over yet. We have promise of a great crop of strawberries, and, notwithstanding quite a number of bullfinches, a fair crop of plums. Apples are very uneven, but there is no blight this year, and I hope for a crop on some trees. The hay is both heavy and early, and already the garden seems choked up with it. Daylight saving (summertime) is a great invention and has doubtless come to stay. It will enable me to keep the garden in order, notwithstanding regular work in town. "Nature" is literally the only objector known to me, except for a few old farmers. I had a note from my mother today asking for some news of you. She has recovered slowly but has really recovered, it seems, from her illness, though she has not been downstairs yet. The doctor fears the stairs for her. Uncle Edward [Fry] is also better, but in a very weak state. He can't be far short of 80.

Your affectionate father,

Edw. R. Pease

....

Isabella Ormston Ford [cousin; fn 37] to MSP:

5 Hyde Park Mansions, London

2nd July 1916

Dear Michael,

I went down to Steep a short time ago and stayed at Mrs. Russell's, and went on the Sunday to Bedales to that kind of service. I felt much excited because I know you and Alixes Florence and others who were educated there. It poured with rain, which resounded on the roof, and the wind howled – we are having rather a horrid Summer so far and are worried over the hay – but it was all very interesting to me and it made me feel rather religious for once. I saw and talked with your friend Mr. Bellot, is that his name? And Mr. Becassy at the Russells'. Enquiries after you were <u>many</u> and very warm. Little Margaret Russell, Mrs. Russell, Mr. Powell, Badley etc – all talked of you. I told them of your postcard. There is a growing number who are in the same galerie as you and J and Bessie [pacifists?]. It is all this which has drawn me into that part, though we don't all agree. I am finding few new friends, and alas losing old ones – we all are. That is life. I do so hope you are well and finding things tolerable. Do you remember your Shelley? I don't believe you do! The end of "*Prometheus Unbound*" is a text for these days. We are all well – very busy – that society you referred to in your postcard goes well. A couple of Sundays ago I was at a fine[?] meeting on a hillside by a moor – a stream rushing along in the ravine below. About a thousand people there and all so interesting. That was in Yorkshire, of course, not London. I do earnestly hope you will keep of the same cool and sane mind as now – when you return – I do hope for that.

Thank you for your kind message in your mother's letter. But I shall understand, and have faith, if you send me none. I only wish I could be of any use to you at all out there. Remember, we are all right, over here.

Goodbye. Bessie [her sister] is here and sends much love too.

Yours affectionately,

I.O.Ford.

....

ERP to MSP:

The Pendicle, Limpsfield, Surrey

19th July 1916

My dear Michael,

It is a long time since I wrote to you. Summertime, a splendid institution, now grumbled at exclusively by "*Nature*", makes it light till 10 o'clock and that does not conduce to writing, especially in this extraordinary summer when the lawn wants mowing once a week and weeds in soil continuously damp flourish exceedingly. I am glad you like my book. Split infinitives are barred by pedants. I split them when I think fit. Shaw, I notice, splits more freely than I do. My book has been splendidly reviewed, in all sorts of papers. So far, about 550 copies have been sold by Fifield and the F.S. [Fabian Society] which is not great. We have had the best crop of strawberries on record and it is not done yet.

Some have moulded of course, but we have had crowds. Peas now are so abundant that a daily jay makes little impression on them! Today has been summer, literally for the first time since May or early June. I shall leave off the last of my winter clothes! There has been no great amount of rain, but grey sky and some rain every day. My snapdragons, of which I had a lot of fine seedlings, have all died of some disease. I planted out a lot in the winter and scarcely one has survived.

We have the summer school [Fabian Society annual event] at Sedbergh in the hills 10 miles south of Kendal and I am going there for the first week on Aug 5th. It is close to the farm of Barbara[428] and I expect I shall put in a day there. We have only taken a girls school for 5 weeks. I am sending you a copy of Shaw's new book, which I hope you will care for. I had bought another for myself and then the author sent me one! I think much of it excellent, though I have not read all. I have not referred to all your own news. We are always eager for it. But your mother answers you fully.

Affectionately,

Edw. R. Pease

....

MGP to Josiah Clement Wedgwood M.P. (HBW's father):

The Pendicle, Limpsfield, Surrey

11th Aug. 1916

Dear Commander Wedgwood

I am so grateful to you for your kind letter and for the very prompt and practical steps you have taken to urge the govt. to clear out <u>all</u> Germans <u>now</u>. I know you carry great weight in the House and your question will help matters greatly. I have a letter from Michael written on July 16th. He never under any circumstances would whine and he always could make the best of things for my sake, but I know how he suffers mentally and he once said "the hideousness of the place was enough to drive one mad". Please do ask your daughter to write to him again. Her letter gave him real pleasure. He told me that she seemed to realise exactly how he felt.

With heartfelt thanks,

---

[428] His half-niece Margaret Barbara Harvey (nee Pease) who farmed with her husband near Low Bentham.

Yrs sincerely

Marjory Pease

....

ERP to MSP:

The Pendicle, Limpsfield, Surrey

18th Aug. 1916

My dear Michael,

I will write you a letter about my own affairs, as usual. Your mother keeps you posted on family doings. Our summer school was at Sedbergh in the hills 10 miles east of Kendal, I was there for ten days from August 5th. It is very much country, but not at all equal to the lakes. Great bare hills running up to 2300 feet, but all grass: no rocks, no ferns, no streams to speak of, not much heather. We had quite a pleasant party and a week of gorgeous weather. I played tennis, which I have hardly done in your life-time! For a few days a Miss Wiskemann, a Bedalian, was there, asking cordially after you. Also a Miss Culpin, who has a nephew in the camp, same name. She had a card from him while I was there. She lent me several numbers of the R Paper [Ruhleben Camp Magazine]. Are you not going to send us the numbers with your articles? I proposed to visit Barbara but they were so busy haymaking that I was by no means encouraged to come. Glad you have seen B[ernstein] again. I sent him a copy of my book via a Danish professor. Who replied thanking me for the gift! and I had to write telling him to send it on. It sells steadily and is still being reviewed, e.g. by J.R.M. [James Ramsay MacDonald] in the *Socialist Review.*

After a month of sunshine we have floods of rain and damp skies. I'm hoping to get some order in the garden before we go to Ireland on Monday. One is more in the mood for holidays than for a long time past, but I never enjoy them in prospect. We shall have a sprinkling of plums and a few apples, including the big Bramley which is loaded: but there is hardly a Pippin in the whole orchard. I've been too busy this year to keep things in good condition, though daylight saving has helped.

The only thing I have been reading up is Scientific Management (of industry) which is an American invention hardly heard of before the war. It is quite interesting and important, but overrated by the inventors. But my recent experience as a manual worker in a workshop has shown me what room there is for it even in the most famous establishments. I lectured on it at Sedbergh.

The F.S. goes on gaily and we get a surprising quantity of money. We are arranging six "pay" lectures for November which will probably go off well.

Affectionately

Edw. R. Pease

P.S. Don't hesitate to ask for books, money, or whatever you want. We are always anxious to send whatever we can.

....

ERP to MSP:

The Pendicle, Limpsfield, Surrey

24th Sep. 1916 – Sunday

My dear Michael,

I received your letter some time ago and sent it on to Olivier for his reply. I have heard nothing till he came in this afternoon. He says this break will be treated as a blank. The B of Agriculture will pay you what they promised in due course. Anything paid now will be deducted from the balance. We have already sent you the money. I told Olivier he could let me have it, as I fancy you will prefer to feel that it's completely your own. But you need not worry over money. I don't know how your account with me stands, because I only write up my accounts once a year, in November. But however it stands does not matter.

We have plenty for our needs, and we would sooner spend on you than on anything else. A man came into the office and in conversation enquired tenderly of you: his name is Frank Rönnfeldt (Swedish). I think he was a Bedalian and he is now in some government service. The F.S. is rather booming. The Summer School has been a great success with £80 or more profit. The Autumn lectures by the Webbs, GBS, Wallas and Clutton Brook are going off like hot cakes. We have sold £80 of tickets though the prospectus is not yet issued! Sales of literature are precisely three times last year, excluding my book! So I am pretty busy and shall not be able to take any more days off I expect. I was at Cote Bank last weekend. Grannie is really very bright and well. She still does not walk up or down stairs, but that is rather a precautionary measure. Your Uncle Ormston was there, after a good many months at the YMCA huts in France. The others as usual. Your Uncle Arthington's translation of the Odyssey has just been published and is really excellent. Your mother has told you of our Irish visit and I can't recollect if I have done so too. AE[?] who dined at Uncle J's [Jonathan Hogg] is a delightful person. Some day you will doubtless meet him though his line is cooperation and not biology. A beautiful weekend at last, there are fewer weeds in the garden than 48 hours ago. The two "sham Bramleys" and the large Bramley are loaded and though there is little else, we shall have enough apples for a long time.

Affectionately,

Edw. R. Pease

P.S. The *D.T.* [*Daily Telegraph*] had two long articles on Ruhleben, and your name was given twice as a leading educationalist.

....

MGP to MSP (letter 255):

The Pendicle, Limpsfield, Surrey

2nd Oct. 1916

Dearest Michael,

You have been much in my thoughts today and I know you have been thinking of us and of the birthdays you used to spend here years ago. This is the 3rd birthday you have spent away from me, may it be the last that finds you in a foreign country is my fervent desire and hope!

It is so nice having Nicolas at home and helping to do things as in the old days. But he won't be here long and of course we are saddened with the loss of dear George [nephew George Davidson]. He was a wonderfully beautiful character. I hope Kate [his widowed mother] will come here and perhaps settle with us for the winter. Her sister is with her now and the girls. Nicolas and I have been in London today and lunched with Winifred [sister-in-law] and her girls. She was very full of enquiries after you. On Thursday we go to Brighton to lunch with the Prince and we hope to see Mrs. Ritchie too. By the way McDonald the dentist was full of minute enquiries after you, Nicolas says. I am glad to say Nicolas requires next to no dentistry and this after 14 months without a visit to the dentist. I have got Geddes' book from Franklin and will send it to you on Friday along with two copies of *Nature*.

3rd October. We are having wet days again, but not cold. I have tried to get the aluminium saucepan with the frying pan lid, but so far have failed to find one the right size. I shall try Selfridge. I am glad you are able to do some cooking. I must send you more variety of stores now. I saw Margery Olivier yesterday – just back from Aviemore where she had been for 3 weeks with Alixes Florence. She is full of admiration for Scotland and the Scotch and especially the soldier spirit among them which had come as a revelation to her. I sent the R.C.S. prospectus to the Oliviers as they are all really interested in you and your works. By the way, what a fine fellow Aubrey is – I mean his mind. It is quite surprising considering his upbringing!

I do indeed think of your mind and spirit and do not I realise painfully what living in sordid, hideous surroundings means to you! But you will not be dragged down. You will rise above these material things and help yourself and others to face and conquer adversity.

I wish you could feel you could send a message to Nicolas for his birthday. You can hardly imagine what it means to a refined super sensitive boy to do what he has done and is doing.

Now this must go. I see by the papers that 25 men are returning from Ruhleben – invalids I suppose – but perhaps I may get news of you from them.

Many loving thoughts from your devoted mother.

Marjory Pease

P.S. Very grateful letter from W. Neumeister who greatly enjoyed a melon and other fruit I sent him.

....

ERP to MSP:

The Pendicle, Limpsfield, Surrey

6th Oct. 1916

My dear Michael,

I hope you have got the £20 we sent you before this. It went via Switzerland. The B. of Ag. has paid me the amount on your account so it is your own money. But cash is plentiful just now. I've got an unexpected £80 from Uncle Joe [Joseph Storrs Fry], the last, apparently. But I had not anticipated it. The odd thing is that everyone seems to have lots of money. Last year we thought our autumn lectures an unparalleled success: this year I've sold already £230 of tickets and there are still three weeks before the first lecture. It is a long way ahead of last year's takings – it is a good course, GBS (2), Webb, Mrs. Webb, Wallas and Clutton Brook, who has in the last year or two become a great man. The result is that I am very busy at the office, and can't get days off for the garden. Nicolas and I have spent most of the day picking the big Bramley, a bumper crop. There are no eating apples, but we shall have far more cookers than we want. It keeps very wet in this part of England, with the result that leaves fall early and fruit ripens early. It is odd, but by my observation, the fact. Some years I have left Bramleys to the end of October. Today they are overripe, and the pears were half blown down by a mild gale, though as a rule they are weeks later. I met Miss Bodkin at your mother's Rural Conference on Wednesday, and she enquired tenderly after you. I have corresponded with her for years, but never saw her before, and always supposed her to be an elderly party of 50 or so. In fact, she is very much otherwise. My book still gets reviews occasionally. J.A. Hobson wrote two or three columns on it (or rather on the F.S.) in *The Nation*. It was not signed, but I knew it was his because of his talk about Democracy. I dined with him at the N.L.C. [National Liberal Club] the other day and he enquired after you appropriately. The government has annexed the N.L.C. and the club is moving today into the Westminster Palace Hotel, which will suit me excellently. Did I tell you that Arthington's translation of the Odyssey has been published? I think it is really very well done.

Affectionately,

Edw. R. Pease

……………………

SAP to MSP:

Cote Bank, Westbury-on-Trym, Bristol

8th Nov. 1916

My dear Michael,

It is long since I wrote to you which is not because I do not think very often of you but you know how many letters I have to write and what news there is to tell you probably [illegible] this your mother [illegible].

I hope that a box of chocolates may have shown that I was not oblivious of your birthday and my good wishes hardly need expressing.

My dear brother Edward[429] had his 89th birthday on the 4th. He is as strong in mind I believe as ever tho' physically very feeble not from any organic trouble but from great muscular weakness making him very helpless. He can get into the garden in a chair and is I think generally free from pain but the helplessness can [illegible] himself, must be very trying.

Oswald is now in England in camp at [words erased by censor] having come over in the Mauritania. He expects a 6 days leave and I hope we shall see him here in a few days.

---

[429] Sir Edward Fry (1827-1918) a judge in the British Court of Appeal and an arbitrator on the Permanent Court of Arbitration.

The account in the *Telegraph* a few weeks ago of the Camp School at Ruhleben interested us extremely and your father has allowed us to see the photos and illustrated prospectus all of which have seemed to make your life more vividly realised by us. I think what you and others have done to prevent the time of your captivity from being a wasted one is really splendid and I feel proud of your part in this and in the cheerlfulness and courage with which you accept the situation. This must I am sure be a great help to the community and you may be gaining in this little dreamt of situation experience which may be of some greater use when the days of freedom come than had you been meeting people in your profession in the ordinary circumstances of life.

With much love and every good wish my dear Michael

Your affectionate Grandmother

S.A.Pease

....

ERP to MSP:

The Pendicle, Limpsfield, Surrey

18th Dec. 1916

My dear Michael,

I was glad to get your letter a short time ago and your mother has had others since. I am very glad your microtome is a success. It is a sort of thing quite outside my experience. As to money, according to my books, there was a balance in your favour of £22.15.10 on October 21st. I sent you £5 recently and will send as much more as you can spend. I am glad you are reading, or have read, Morley's *Gladstone*. I can't help admiring the man immensely. He had his limitations, as we all have, but considering that he started mature life in the 1830s he was wonderfully up to date in the 90s. I've recently read *Beaconsfield* as far as published; he had plenty of faults anyhow! I wonder if you have read Naumann's *Mitteleuropa* [Central Europe] I have recently done so in an English translation. It is really a remarkable book, and indicates German national policy – which I understand it represents – in a way wholly different from the press snippets we get here. I've just started on Goch's *History and Historians of the 19th Century*, why I don't precisely know, but I like a good solid book off my own line at times. I'm less busy now. The immensely successful lectures are concluded and we are now trying to devise ways of spending the money. One way or another we are almost too well off. I shall take a long Xmas, for the garden. The autumn has been so wet that everything has got neglected. We were very lucky in our apples: we can't hear of anybody in the district who had any at all. I dare say your mother has told you that the Pember Reeveses[430] are staying at the Chart: he is ill and spends long weekends in the country. He is a remarkably good talker, I have rarely met a better.

At last there seems to be a break in the clouds. People I see do not appear to expect much. I admit I have been too optimistic in the past. Still I can't help hoping that the end is in sight. Today the German letter[431] has reached London. Tomorrow I suppose we shall know its contents. I'm reading Wells' *Mr. Britling*. I wonder if you have it at R? It is just an elaborate statement of his views from day to day about the war: nothing to me very novel, or very clever, but interesting rather as a record than anything else.

Ever affectionate,

Edw. R. Pease

....

SAP to MSP:

Cote Bank, Westbury-on-Trym, Bristol

Dec. 29th 1916

My dear Michael,

I want just to assure you of being [illegible] of you and of my very best wishes for the year so soon to begin. One cannot forbear to hope that before it ends it may see you reunited with your [illegible] dear people and I feel I should like to live to see you again [illegible] as it may be. I hope you have not been suffering frightfully from the cold. Today a west wind and driving rain is due – ending a long period of [illegible] and most dangerously slippery road.

In Leeds the roads have been terrible and both [illegible] and Emily Ford [Isabella Ford's sister] have had falls in consequence, neither I think [illegible] a slight concussion left Emily a [illegible].

As I have other letters to write you will excuse dear Michael the brief assurance of the constant loving remembrances of your affectionate g.mother

S. A. Pease

---

[430] William Pember Reeves was Director of the London School of Economics. His wife, Maud, was a member of the Fabian Society.

[431] Germany offered to enter into Peace negotiations, with a return to the pre-war national boundaries, excepting Poland and Lithuania which would remain as German Kingdoms.

We have not had a large Cote party. The Sangers and Arthington are with us and we hope for Peggie every day.

Postscript from Dora:

Dearest Michael. I think so much of you, tho' I have written so little to you not once since the summer – but your name is as often on my lips as any ones. My work makes me think especially of you – both the work for the interned men in England and the other things I am doing. It has been a very very busy autumn – now we are taking a 10 days' rest at Cote Bank. Your loving Aunt Dora

....

Excerpt from the *Labour Leader*, 11th Jan. 1917:

"Among the contributions received at the I.L.P. [Independent Labour Party] Office last week was £2 to the Special Effort Fund from Mr. Michael S. Pease (son of E. R. Pease, secretary to the Fabian Society), a member of the party who is interned at Ruhleben".

....

ERP to MSP:

The Pendicle, Limpsfield, Surrey

22nd Jan. 1917

My dear Michael,

I write occasionally to assure you that you are constantly in my thoughts, though your mother with her unfailing output of letters tells you all our news. She is dining at the Thompsons tonight, for a War Committee which however has very little to do, except organising potato patches which at the moment are all the go. Even the Government is alarmed lest the patriotic populace plants so many potatoes that the autumn will bring a hopeless glut.

I was very glad to hear you had been reading *Mr. Britling*. I read it recently, with much appreciation. I have sometimes thought that you did not quite understand how most people felt in England. You can take Mr. B. for the gospel truth. It is precisely what I, and many of my set as far as I can judge, think and feel. To me, roughly speaking, there was not a new idea in the book: merely a fine literary expression of one's own thoughts and feelings. Of course I can't guarantee every detail. There were towards the end I think, a few ideas fresh to me: there may be sentiments, though I can't recollect them, with which I do not agree. – I had a little chat with Lord Haldane[432] this morning, the first time for 20 years and more. He came into the shop (which you have never seen) to buy my book when I was there. He is to lecture to us on Feb 9th, and we are a little alarmed because the present form of W.S.P.U. [Women's Social and Political Union] madness – the W.S.P.U. is a mere remnant now – is to attend his meetings and shout traitor. The Labour Party Conference begins tomorrow – for the first time since the beginning of things I shall not be there. I could no doubt have gone but I am out of the swim now, and had no particular wish to spend a week in Manchester. The Socialists have an election for the first time, and the I.L.P. will have to decide between Webb, and Fairchild of the B.S.P. [British Socialist Party; forerunner of the British Communist Party] – I can hardly believe they will go for the latter. They have 30 out of 43 votes. I do not suppose anything startling will happen. The Labour Party occupies a big place in the Government now, but so far the Government has done well, and I do not think it is unpopular even in highly Liberal quarters. It has created the Ministry for Labour which we have demanded for a decade, and its only weak point so far revealed is in its literary power!

Ever affectionately,

Edw. R. Pease

....

Siward Horsley[433] to MSP:

356 Dickenson Road, Manchester

18th Feb. 1917

My dear Tuskey [Michael's school nickname]

I feel a great sinner for not writing to you before but will try and make amends from now on. I hear you are a Prof. and all that sort of thing, I hope the Univ Cantab will recognise your new found dignity when you come back. The war has dealt very kindly I think with all our little circle and as far as I know they are all well and flourishing. The prophet, of course, is a great man these days, a mine of totally unreliable information "on the highest authority". He doesn't

---

[432] Lord Chancellor 1912-1915, but was forced to resign because of alleged German sympathies. He helped found the London School of Economics.

[433] Siward Myles Horsley, an old Bedalian friend. A 2nd Lieutenant in the Gordon Highlanders, who relinquished his commission in Nov 1915 on account of ill-health after being wounded. Became a science master at Bedales after the war, but died in 1920.

write much nowadays but what he does is quite good; it is also whispered that he is in love – but tell it not abroad for I do not really believe it. Jarry[434] the Bold has got the Military Cross – nobody seems to know what for; I feel certain it was for rushing round somewhere at top speed. He probably did 10 laps of the trenches "to keep fit" as he used to do at Oxford and the authorities were so surprised to see anybody running that they decorated him on the spot. Nobody seems to know where Pauly[435] is. There were rumours that he was (a) ship's carpenter (b) second class stoker on the Victory or some such preposterous post; for myself, I believe he is probably Deputy-Assistant General of Entertainment etc.

Me you behold as the complete Manchester man. It is a low hole and the fogs here this winter have been something poisonous. Still we put in some good skating – the thermometer went down to zero t'other day, which wasn't bad for these Islands. However it's all cleared off now and the sun is out quite warm and bright as I hope it will be with you when you get this.

I suppose you know that George Hicks[436] and Ethel Trubshawe are married and possessed of a daughter. A very fine child (so they say) – at any rate it does all the usual tricks and the fond parents imagine that it can already say "damn" or something very like it.

There's not a great deal that we can say without incurring some officials' displeasure and so I will shut up, but I just wanted to write and say that I hope you aren't too awfully bored and feeling "out of it" for we all think of you and look forward to seeing you again soon.

From Siward Horsley

....

ERP to MSP:

The Pendicle, Limpsfield, Surrey

26th Feb. 1917

My dear Michael,

---

[434] Dmitri Jarintzoff (fn 111), an old Bedalian (killed by a sniper on the Western Front in France on October 8th 1917).

[435] Paul Denys Montague (fn 92), another old Bedalian (killed in a dog fight over the sea near Salonica, October 1917).

[436] Another old Bedalian, as was his wife.

I've been thinking of you even more than usual today, because I've spent the afternoon at the Ruhleben prisoners release demonstration. It has been a terrible affair, a howling waste of misrepresentation, political rancour, exaggeration and sentiment, only relieved by a charming little speech by Sir Timothy Eden. Gribble also spoke harmlessly and Israel Cohen very much otherwise [all three ex-Ruhlebenites]. Lord Beresford and Joynson-Hicks were the worst offenders. Bishop Bury was unctuous, and Lord Henry B[entik] inarticulate as usual, but quite in good taste.

I have written to thank Sir T. Eden (I had forgotten that your mother had already corresponded with him), and perhaps shall hear from him. Well, I hope the frost has gone with you too, though I dare say you hate the mud. At last there is a touch of Spring, and the snowdrops are appearing quite a month late. The frost was not severe, though long here. And I dug up the grass all around the plum tree you last planted, as a potato ground. I've always meant to take in that part, as we want more room for vegetables. Have you seen, I wonder, that Ll. George has decreed a minimum wage of 25/- for agricultural labourers in return for a fixed price for wheat? Rents too are to be unalterable, and cottage rents are already fixed. So we are getting on. But the political escapades of the premier are astonishing. His latest is to appoint a committee to reconstruct the empire after the war. He is chairman and the committee consists of a few M.P.s (Leslie Scott and Hills) two Labour M.P.s (Clynes and Thomas) Mrs. Tennant and Mrs. S.W. [Beatrice Webb] and so on. Apparently they are to do the work that might be expected of the cabinet. He would not have S.W. and said he could get brains without his manners through Mrs. S.W! It is a queer world, e.g. partly through economics and partly through my working for a nominal salary the F.S. is richer than in the whole course of its career! I shall have to hide away £400 or £500 excess of income over expenditure! And that in addition to the estate (£175) of a Scotch member killed last August, who left us all his property. War must be destructive of wealth, but its present effect seems to be the contrary. – We had Lord Haldane to lecture on education the other day: we were rather in alarm, as wild women pursue him to shout traitor. Happily they were all kept out, and the people were perfectly polite. He is a very attractive person and spoke delightfully. I have not spoken to him for some 20 years.

Ever affectionately,

Edw. R. Pease

....

Appendix 1

Postcard from Cyril Asher[437] *to Marjory Pease:*

Pension Hesperis, Davos Platz, Switzerland

24th Feb. 1917

Dear Mrs. Pease,

Just a few lines to inform you that I received a nice parcel from Mrs. Mumby. The things she sent me were perfectly to my taste and I wrote her to that effect. I again take the opportunity to thank you for your great kindness. You will be pleased to hear that I received a good report from the doctor a few days ago and am feeling very well at present.

Yours sincerely,

....

ERP to MSP:

The Pendicle, Limpsfield, Surrey

29th March 1917

My dear Michael,

I often wonder how much news you get of the doings in the world. This has been a really wonderful month. The downfall of the Tzardom is the biggest event of the age, in some senses. It seems to have been very well managed. The Socialists are the danger: they want too much and too soon. I sent a resolution I drafted for the Fabian Society to the President of the Duma a few days ago. As for the retreat from the Somme, that is an occurrence which seems to please all parties, a singular phenomenon in war. For us, the more the better. Bagdad pleases only one side which is a pity, and today we hear – for the first time – that the British are embarking on a new Crusade, and are not very far from Jerusalem! At home the event is Mr. Asquith's conversion to W. Suffrage, and the definite settlement – for the moment – of that problem.

The never-ending winter is wearing slowly away. We had snow today, with a S.W. wind! Snowdrops are over: crocuses are well out, but not a daffodil yet in flower. Frost has killed most of the wallflowers; and the gorse on the common is sad to see. It has been too cold and wet to plant much: but I shall I hope get in a lot at Easter. – The dismissal of S.O. [Sydney Olivier] is personally unfortunate. I am told that the Premier made up his mind to get an expert, and

---

[437] A former Ruhlebenite who was released in 1916 due to ill-health – destitute, according to the National Archive records.

proposed two whom Prothero[438] rejected. Finally he selected Hall,[439] and one can't but admit that no one in England is so good an authority. S.O. is still at his office – I had a note from him a few days ago – and of course he is not retiring: they will find him some other job, possibly the Governorship of a German Colony! I met Major Gillespie the other day who asked after you. I forget if you know him. He has been at the front from the first till recently when he returned on sick leave. I don't think the new committee for governing the Empire has got to work yet. Mrs. Tennant has refused a seat and Marion Phillips[440] gets her place! – I find I have cleared £50 from my book up to date: not bad, quite as much as I expected. There will be more, of course, but not much. I still get occasional notices, in such things as Italian monthlies. For all the war, books still sell. Allen and Unwin who now publish for the Fabian Society and its Research Department, sent me £195 for about 6 months sales of our stuff. Don't fail to let me know about money. You can have as much as you want. I hope you don't miss the Americans much. That by the way is an event of this wonderful month which I forgot.

Ever affectionate

Edw. R. Pease

....

MGP to MSP (letter 312):

The Pendicle, Limpsfield, Surrey

3rd April 1917

Dearest Michael,

Still no news of you and I gather from information I got in town today that no one has had letters later than the 18th Feb. I can only hope you are getting my letters and weekly parcel from Selfridge and Uncle Jonathan's bread from Copenhagen. I cannot think why letters are stopped. Mrs. Mumby was going to send you handkerchiefs and I hope they may have reached you by now. I am longing to send you your Lovat flannel suit. I wonder what you are thinking of the country where Mrs. Martin White is abiding. I am looking forward to seeing her letters. Did I tell you that Reggie's going to Canada is deferred and he is going off felling timber which will be excellent practice for his future. He and

---

[438] Rowland Prothero, President of the Board of Agriculture from 1916 to 1919.

[439] Sir Daniel Hall 1864-1942, British agricultural educationalist and researcher.

[440] LSE graduate and Fabian Society member

Ralph[441] are coming here on the 5th. Ralph is to work by day on Miss McAndrew's farm and sleep here. I wish I could get up any enthusiasm or affection for these boys, but they are frightfully colourless – so different from Mary and Betty and poor George.[442] How I grieve for that boy and many others and how thankful I am that Nicolas so far has been spared to me. I am feeling that now he is in comparative safety, though only for a short time, but I am glad he has lived to read President Wilson's epoch making speech.

April 4th.

I had tea with Aunt Kate and Mary[443] at Selfridges today and we talked much of you. Mrs. Harris has just been talking of you over the phone. Warwick is home for 10 days leave. Stuart Cooper is back with a sceptic toe and is in hospital in London. He has been on the Somme since November and his mother says he looks much better than when he went out.

I wonder if your polyanthus narcissus are as fine as mine. I hope so. Your purple and white crocuses are very fine and greatly admired. Poor things, they have been repeatedly buried in snow and tonight it is freezing hard. I don't think I told you that on Monday your Father and I entertained to tea the step-son of the Mendelson's friend who once gave you a mouth organ. We had as you imagine a very interesting talk.

I had a p.c. from Isabella Ford giving a great account of the Albert Hall Russian meeting. She said Stepniak's[444] name was cheered to the echo. As you may imagine we are all delighted at the Votes for Women triumph and I feel sure women M.P.s will soon be amongst us and everyone will wonder why the suffrage didn't come years ago!

April 5th.

Reggie and Ralph arrive this afternoon. I am just off to R.D.C. [Rural District Council]. Lovely spring morning at last. No letters from you yet.

Your devoted Mother.

....

ERP to MSP:

---

[441] Marjory's nephews Reginald and Ralph Davidson, two of her brother Andrew's children.

[442] Another nephew, George William Smyttan Davidson (fn 31) killed at the Somme, and his sisters Mary and Betty.

[443] Marjory's sister-in-law, wife of William (who died in 1906), and niece – see previous footnote.

[444] Sergius Stepniak – a Russian revolutionary who fled to London from Russia in 1882.

Appendix 1

The Pendicle, Limpsfield, Surrey

26th April 1917

My dear Michael,

Your letter gave me much pleasure, though of course your constant letters to your mother give me all your news. It came after a long pause and we are still hoping for more recent news. It is good to hear you have so much to do: that seems to me the secret of happiness, and in truth I sometimes think with regret that when peace comes, my Fabian work will cease. As you may observe all men of your age, or nearly all are in a sense marking time. Those in the army complain of the futility of it, even when they are most convinced they are doing the right thing. In that respect you are on the whole in a better case than the rest.

I have been reading Israel Cohen's book about Ruhleben – which is excellent. From his speech, as I wrote you, I formed a low opinion of him. His book is free from all the faults I disliked, and is a well-written apparently fair account of the Camp and its doings.

Your mother will write about pure alcohol and xylol: she has the matter in hand. Our authorities here are terrible. Today we hear they have stopped all books sent to prisoners, and your *Natures* have come back. We may find some way to get them though, as we do not know yet why they are returned [note: at the top of this letter is "P.S. 27/4/17. I find there is a list of authorised agents through whom we can send"].

As for the garden, such a spring has never been known in my recollection. Till a week ago we had snow and frost and bitter winds every day and the S.W. wind was as cold as the N.E. A week's sunshine, though often with night frosts, and some cold days has brought out daffodils, and pasane flowers and primroses. But not a pea is showing, or a potato, or any sort of blossom on the trees. By the way fruit flower is supposed to depend on well-ripened wood. No wood could be more ripened than that of last year, when there was hardly any sunshine, and yet the apples are full of buds and so are the plums. As no weeds are showing yet I've got things into fair order. Daylight saving has been in operation for some weeks and it is light till nearly 9 summertime.

I am well pleased with the Food-production Bill, and have been wrangling with J.R.M. [J. Ramsay MacDonald] over it at the House of Commons, on the Workers' National Committee. He objects, but he always objects to Wages Boards. The Bill fixes a minimum price for wheat for some years, the state to pay, if the average price is below 60/-, 55/- and so on according to the year. It is a debatable proposition, but on the whole I am in favour. In return rents are not to be raised: wages are to be 25/- at least, and a Wages Board to fix rates etc: and the state has power to take over under-cultivated land. In the house yesterday Runciman[445] opposed and got 27 supporters! On the whole the Government is doing well, but I can't tell how long it will last.

I read Rousseau many years ago and do not recollect very much of it. French History is always said to be good. I've rather taken to History in my old age. I've got Freeman's *Sicily*[446] in hand, a tremendously long and rather too learned book. Norse history rather attracts me, and there was a Norman period in Sicily of which I know nothing. Sanders[447] has gone to Russia, in charge of Thorne, O'Grady and a lot of Frenchmen.[448] Today I have been seeing a Russian Naval Officer, of a ship arrived in Plymouth, which started before the Revolution and learned of it here. All but 5 approved. He is trying to adapt Trade Unionism to the Russian Navy! Isn't that Russian?

Affectionately

Edw. R. Pease

P.S. I agree about Raymond. For some reason physicists are no good at psychics, e.g. Lodge, Crooks, and I think there are others.

....

ERP to MSP:

The Pendicle, Limpsfield, Surrey

16th May 1917

My dear Michael,

It is pleasant at last to get more news of you; and in this spring weather I think of you, if possible, more often than ever. It has been an extraordinary season. Till the middle of April constant snow and frost: and rain or snow every day. Since then a perpetual drought, with usually hot weather and sometimes cold. The lawn is as hard and dry and almost as brown as at midsummer, and the flowers last no time. Apples and plums came out almost together, and the

---

[445] Liberal MP Walter Runciman, 1st Viscount Runciman of Doxford.

[446] *The History of Sicily from the Earliest Times* by Edward Augustus Freeman (published 1891).

[447] William Stephen Sanders, secretary to the Fabian Society 1913–1920, though ERP was still acting secretary in 1915–1919.

[448] A Franco-British socialist delegation to keep Russian comrades fighting in the war – written about in *Memoirs of a British Agent* by R H Bruce Lockhart.

latter are nearly over. There is a grand show of blossom, which shows that blossom does not depend on well-ripened wood, for last year was the worst for ripening in my gardening recollection. We have not any frost, and so I hope we may get a crop, and I hope too, and almost believe, that you will be home to eat of it. Seeds seem to come up without rain. Most of mine have had none, and they are all showing excellently.

I am hoping at last to get you out xylol and alcohol. I had a very satisfactory talk at the Board of Education, in the Davies[449] Ruhleben book room. A man there rang up the censor, and then the War Office, and then the Foreign Office, and the result was that they would probably grant a request in writing from me. In politics there is not much I can write of. The Franchise Bill has been introduced today and is only opposed by a few such as Lord Claude Hamilton. There is little doubt that Women's Suffrage will get through at last. I had a talk this afternoon with Mrs. W[ebb] who told me – very confidentially – of great schemes for carrying through her M. Rep.[450] plans with the help of Lord G. H. [George Hamilton] with whom she had made it up. This of course is part of the Reconstruction Committee work which is going ahead, and concerns the Ministry of Health, one of the new and excellent Government plans. Of course it may not come off, but Lloyd George is out after grandiose schemes and there is no reason why he should not back it. Lord Rhondda[451] is not unlikely to help. I saw him at a small deputation some weeks ago, and liked the look of him very much. He was D. A. Thomas who was nearly drowned in the Lusitania. He is now at the L.G.B. [Local Government Board].

I am interested in and agree with all you say about Raymond. I'm just arranging the Summer School to be held this year at the Huxley School[452] at Godalming. I shall have to give a Sunday sermon, not much in my line, and I think I shall discourse on the Duty of Unbelief. Dr Clifford (Kingdon, not John) wrote some stuff on the point when I was your age. Wells is the latest convert to fancy religion: he has discovered God, as he discovered philosophy, and the Working Classes, and has written a book to inform the world of it!

Affectionately, Edw. R. Pease

---

[449] Alfred Thomas Davies ran the 'British Prisoners of War Book Scheme (Educational)' established in 1914 to create a library for internees at Ruhleben, and sent several hundred books to the camp. The scheme eventually expanded to include all British war prisoners.

[450] The 1909 Minority Report calling for the breakup of the Poor Law, headed by Beatrice Webb.

[451] Liberal MP David Alfred Thomas, 1st Viscount Rhondda.

[452] Possibly Prior's Field School – a girls school founded by Julia Huxley, first wife of Leonard Huxley.

P.S. 17/5/17. Rain at last!

....

ERP to MSP:

The Pendicle, Limpsfield, Surrey

8th May 1917

My dear Michael,

At last I have got a permit from the Foreign Office to send you xylol, alcohol and everything else you want [see Appendix 3]. There may be other difficulties. But the order has been definitely issued that you are to be supplied every six weeks with the quantity Biffen[453] recommends. The Education Office is to be thanked in the main.

We are happy with Nicky at home. The relief from anxiety is immense. But he goes off in two days.

What a queer world we now live in! We decided recently to send West[454] to Petrograd in response to an invitation from the Duma. Today he tells me that, finding a difficulty in getting a passport from the Russian Consul, the Foreign Office gave him a letter to the Russian Embassy who instantly gave him a diplomatic passport usually reserved for high functionaries! Whatever else the Russian Revolution has achieved, it has rendered our set almost the biggest factors in the game for the moment.

I gather you have had a drought as we have here. One result is that caterpillars are innumerable and the fruit crop is seriously damaged. The blossom was superb, but it remains to be seen what the crop will turn out. It has been the hottest May for 60 years, and the flowers fly over. I shall net the strawberries tomorrow: there will be a grand crop, if the rain comes, and it looks like it.

I'm busy arranging the Summer School, which is to be at the Huxley School at Godalming this year, a new experiment so near London. Apparently it is popular. Railway facilities are few and expensive still. We are not raising our

---

[453] Sir Rowland Biffen, Professor of Agricultural Botany at Cambridge and director of the Plant Breeding Institute.

[454] Julius West, a poet, historian and clerk for the Fabian Society, was the son of the Russian émigré Semon Rappoport. He stayed in Russia for seven months reporting on the October revolution and its aftermath, but was plagued by ill-health and increasingly hostile secret police. He escaped across the Baltic in February 1918 and died within a year from influenza.

prices on last year, for various reasons, and so we are offering a cheap holiday at a fixed figure. Result a rush of orders already.

Do you recollect the little plot of columbine you sowed just before you left? For various reasons they grew very slowly and only now at last are they making a show in the big bed near the kitchen window. We still talk of tree cutting, but I shall wait till you return before doing anything drastic.

Ever affectionately,

Edw. R. Pease

....

Invalid Comforts Fund for Prisoners of War,

19 Second Avenue, Hove

16 June 1917

To: Michael Pease Esq.

Baracke 11, Box 17, Ruhleben

Dear Sir,

I am informed by your Mother that you are in need of Anti Vermin paste and powder.

Under the regulations of the Central Prisoners of War Committee, I am not allowed to send individual parcels, but despatch fortnightly consignments of Invalid Comforts to Ruhleben, addressed to Captain Powell, for distribution among the men there.

In our last consignment, a certain quantity of Anti Vermin paste and powder was included for general use, so if you will apply to Captain Powell, I expect he will be able to give you some from that consignment, and thus save delay. In the next consignment which goes I will include some clearly marked with your name.

Yours faithfully,

Muriel Bromley Davenport[455]

....

---

[455] Mrs. Davenport founded the Hove Hospital Supply Depot and was created a Commander of the Order of the British Empire for her work.

ERP to MSP:

The Pendicle, Limpsfield, Surrey

4th July 1917

My dear Michael,

I have thought of you more than usual all through this gorgeous summer of perpetual sunshine. The rain has come at last, and today is quite dank and chilly. It is just in time for planting greens: too late to prolong the strawberries, of which however we have had an excellent crop. Caterpillars – a novel plague – half destroyed the apples all over the country. We shall have enough, but by no means the gorgeous crop which the flower promised. But plums are abundant.

I had a letter a day or so ago from the Thurloe Place[456] people saying they were sending your chemicals. So I hope they will arrive at last. You are to have supplies of alcohol and xylol every six weeks.

I've been thinking a lot about the Russian revolution of late. It is a bigger affair than at first appeared. The people in power, and likely to remain, are socialists, and the first effect on us is that we have all become more than ever, a power in the land. The F. S. sent West to Russia, and his observations on the situation are telegraphed home to *The Times* as important foreign news! That however is only the beginning. If the Russians carry the business through decently – as the French did not in 1789–94, the rest of the world is not going to stand still and look at it. I say nothing of other countries, but I know that we shall follow suit, not necessarily with a Republic, but with a very big dose of Socialism. Thirty years of slow progress had indicated that progress would continue slow, and so it would, (though gradually accelerating), but for the war. We have learned a lot, not only the indispensability of the working classes – we shall have no more of the kind rich providing employment – but also their power. I know you sniff at the Labour Party – but it is not for nothing that the Labour Party is half governing the country. Hardly a day passes, so to speak, without another announcement of a Trade Union leader in office. Though in fact they are all used up now. Clynes and Walsh, who have just joined the Government, are about the last, so far as I know, except Goldstone, who could take the job. Yes the world will be a very much better place when you are my age.

Affectionately, Edw. R. Pease

---

[456] Headquarters of the Central Prisoners of War Committee, formed at the end of 1916 to replace the ad-hoc humanitarian aid being sent to Ruhleben and other POW camps.

....

ERP to MSP:

Cote Bank, Westbury-on-Trym, Bristol

Monday 16th July 1917

My dear Michael,

I came here on Friday because your Granny is very ill. In fact she is dying and the only wonder is that she still lives. The doctor on Saturday said 48 hours was the outside. It is old age – she is 87 – but heart weakness is the form of it. It is all wonderfully peaceful. She knows her end is near, but how near, perhaps, she does not know. But there is no indication of death. Religion has always been a part of her life, and it is now no less and no more than before. There are no prayers, no Bible-reading, no goodbyes, no mention of death. At times she is bright and chatty as of old, and likes to hear *Uncle Tom's Cabin* read, and to laugh over old humour. Today she drops asleep every few minutes and sustained talk is impossible. They say she greatly wished to see you again, but she has not said so to me. Ormston [step-son] was here on Saturday: Gerald [son] came for Sunday. Dora and Katharine [daughter and step-daughter] are settled here. Johnny [Jonathan Hogg, step-son-in-law] comes over from Dublin tomorrow, but he may be too late. Oddly enough she desires to be cremated: this must take place in London, and there will be a Quaker burial of the ashes afterwards. Cote Bank looks beautiful in the midsummer sun. It will probably be kept on till after the war, so I hope you will come here again. It will be a great break up. One can hardly be very sad. At 87 life must end somehow soon, and this end could hardly be easier. Oddly enough I have never seen a death bed before. Certainly in this it is dropping asleep.

Your Mother got your card with instructions as to the chemicals you wanted, and I wrote at once to the Foreign Office to vary the order accordingly [see Appendix 3]. You had never before said to me exactly what you required, and Biffen's list was different from what you sent. I have had no reply yet, but I expect they will do as you desire.

The war seems far away from this peaceful country. I still hope that the end is coming, but I confess I have had many vain hopes!

Affectionately, Edw. R. Pease

....

Appendix 1

Marian F Pease (Michael's Aunt) to MSP:

Cote Bank, Westbury-on-Trym, Bristol

24th July 1917

My dear Michael,

Your Mother has most kindly let us have a sight of your letters from Jena and it has been such a pleasure to Grannie and to us all to hear of your enjoyment there. How I wish we could still think of you there. I am so glad I know the place and can well imagine you in those charming woods. I stayed many years ago for 6 months at a school for mentally defective children above the town. I went for one of Prof Rein's[457] courses on education during the university vacation and I have a vivid recollection of the view from a terrace in front of the school.

You will have heard from your Mother how ill dear Grannie is – we are just quietly now waiting for the end. It is not easy to believe it is so near as the Doctor expects [she eventually died on 21st Sept]. She is still so entirely herself, talking this morning with Arthington [her son] about the relation of Christianity to war, without the slightest confusion of mind. She knows that the end is near and awaits the future with complete calm, and the hopefulness which her long life of faith in the distinct ordering of the universe has given her. It seems difficult to face life without her and I am very, very sorry that she will not have her wish – often repeated – to see you again, fulfilled. She sits in an armchair in her room by the wide open window in the western sunshine looking out on the familiar view – with her face still full of expression and her eyes full of light. Up to a day or two ago she has been full of her natural humour, smiling over the old folios [Quaker tracts]. Your father has been here for nearly a week. We have been very glad to have him especially as we have seen so little of him since the war. We so, so wish Nicky had been able to run down when he was at home on leave and that we had been able to see your mother. She is making such a brave fight with her anxieties for you both and I am sure she must need a rest. Mother was so much interested in what you say about the awful wear of prison life. It made her dictate to Dora [her daughter] her view about imprisonment as a punishment. How little we could have imagined 3 years ago when we were all sitting chatting in the verandah, the experiences which you and Nicky would have to go through. She felt hopeful, and so do I, that all you are enduring in prison and all so many young men I know (Friends

[457] Professor Wilhelm Rein, University of Jena, follower of the 'Herbartianism' system of education.

[Quakers]) are now enduring in prison will help to a more rational vein of punishment. But all this makes her wish again that she could have seen you. I can't help hoping that you would have found much [illegible] and sympathy to your view of the war. She has been so splendidly staunch to her life long view about that. I shall miss her sorely. For Dora, I and Arthington are [illegible] sympathisers in such views. But I believe there will be lots of men coming back when it is over determined that Europe[?] shall be a very different place in the future. If only Russia will keep firm. It is awfully anxious work there.

Goodbye my dear boy,

your affectionate aunt,

Marian F. Pease.

....

Bedales, Petersfield, Hants

30th July 1917

Old Bedalian Meeting

Heartiest greetings from us all

B[ryson] Bellot, N[oel] Olivier, L[eslie] Bickmore, Annie Patrick [a housekeeper at Bedales], L[ucy] C[aroline] Thorp [a matron at Bedales], Gertrude Herzfeld, Ivy Turner, Florence Schuster, Donald Kinnell, D[ouglas] R[ayner] Hantree, J[ohn] Robbins, K[onni] Zilliacus, Margaret Russell, Peggy Scott, H[ugh] H[Hale] Bellot, L[aurin] Zilliacus, Oswald Byrom Powell [a teacher and one of the school's founders].

....

Isabella Ford to MSP:

Adel Grange, Leeds, Yorkshire

Sunday 5th August 1917

My dear Michael,

Your postcard of 23rd June has just come. Don't be depressed about the poor old world. You needn't be for there seems to be coming a better spirit – the good work is beginning to tell. (I wish it spread to my pen! It won't write – wretch).

This is a lovely hot day and Bessie [sister] and I are sitting in own verandah – do you remember it? – writing, and oh how I wish you were here. I am hurrying because I shall scramble through lunch and go off to an open air women's meeting at a place outside Leeds – we can't get enough weekdays and Sundays now, to hold all these meetings! You see women are naturally persistent and they are showing it now increasingly.

Of course the Suffrage is got in a clumsy way as you say – but what else can you expect now! You know Havelock Ellis[458] says somewhere that women are the organisers of the world, and must be so in the future, the men will do science and inventions and railways and art etc, but <u>we</u> shall be the managers. Amen I say. Nothing in the world is worth getting at such a price as all this business is – that's my view.

Cheer up my dear little cousin – yours cheerfully and our love to you,

I. O. Ford

....

ERP to MSP:

Cote Bank, Westbury-on-Trym, Bristol

21st Aug. 1917

My dear Michael,

I have come here for two days to visit your Grandmother, and find her wonderfully better than when I left a month ago. She no longer requires oxygen, sleeps well, and talks better. It is I suppose, impossible for her to recover, but her heart which is the weak spot is actually stronger, and the dropsy which oppressed her is relieved.

I was very glad to get your letter from Jena. I have not read Bergson,[459] though I suppose I ought to have done so. I don't see much stuff in it.

I had quite a good time at the Summer School, and lectured, not on unbelief, but on Socialism. It is said that strangers come to learn about socialism, and nobody tells them anything. So the Directors are ordered to speak on the topic. We had a lecture on 'How I escaped from Ruhleben' from a friend[460] of yours, who came for a couple of days. Shaw made himself very agreeable, and talked a lot of nonsense as he usually does nowadays. The thing is a huge success, crowded the whole time. Your criticism of Wells is quite sound. It was just what

---

[458] An English physician, writer, and social reformer who studied human sexuality.

[459] A prominent French philosopher.

[460] Geoffrey Pyke, who gave a talk on *My Escape from Ruhleben* (his book) at the Fabian Summer School in Godalming (*Surrey Advertiser*, 13 Aug 1917).

we found in the great fight. He had no new ideas to speak of. We were to do immense things but he did not know how, except of trying obvious methods which we had abandoned because they had proved failures.

I'm interested in Biffen on S.O. [Sydney Olivier] – I am afraid he is correct. His new job is just marking time, as I understand it.

I hope you are feeling a bit more kindly towards Henderson.[461] He has played straight and honestly and I am sure his was the right policy. I suppose it is being "turned down" this afternoon and in any case it could not have come off. I was appointed a Stockholm delegate,[462] but in any case I shall not go now as the Fabian delegation is cut down to two.

We have had a considerable plum crop this year, a lot of those coalhouse plums which were superb in 1914; a fair apple crop; potatoes finer than I ever recollect; lots of peas – the Dunbars shot 24 jays! But there are some left. So I have plenty to do.

Ever affectionately

Edw. R. Pease

……………………

ERP to MSP:

The Pendicle, Limpsfield, Surrey

20th Sept. 1917

My dear Michael,

It is some time since I last wrote: I think my last was when I was at Cote Bank – your Grandmother really seems to be recovering [she died the next day]. We only hear of her occasionally now.

I always think much of you when I garden, and I have been doing a lot of late, as things are slack at the office, and I only go up 2 or 3 days a week. The damsons have needed a lot of picking: they are not done yet; I intended to complete this afternoon, but the wind was high, and the tree tops are not agreeable in a gale. The fowlhouse door apple which you wanted to slay has been great this year, loaded with the biggest apples I have ever had, which roast superbly. There are heaps of Coxes, no Blenheims, only a third of a crop

---

[461] Arthur Henderson, leader of the Labour Party August 1914 – October 1917. His proposal for an international conference on the war was rejected by the rest of the cabinet.

[462] Socialist Peace conference to try and end the war, which the Americans vetoed.

of Bramleys, and better Peasgoods than I ever recollect. Pears are a complete failure. The frequent rain of the last month has made everything rank and sodden.

The F. S. is extraordinarily flourishing: never in its whole history has it had such piles of money. Whichever we touch turns to gold. The Summer School was crowded from start to finish. G.B.S. stayed there all the time. Result, a clear profit which may be £250. Now we are starting our autumn lectures. Last year we made a record success: this year our sales are double those of same date.

Summertime has ended and the days are short: so I can do some reading. I'm starting on Freeman's *Norman Conquest*. Meanwhile I have to read things to review in Fabian News, which are generally dull, though Dr Brend's "Health and the state", which criticises current views of infant mortality is rather good. This afternoon I have been to a District Council Conference on the drainage scheme, which is to include only about 5 houses. They want us to voluntarily contribute. I have promised £50. Keen refuses to pay a penny. It is worth £50 to me to get rid of that pump and all it involves. Also it ends the lawsuit. But it is not certain that it will come off.

Ever affectionately,

Edw. R. Pease

....

ERP to MSP:

The Pendicle, Limpsfield, Surrey

27th Sept. 1917

My dear Michael,

Your mother has doubtless told you already that your grandmother died somewhat suddenly a week ago. She had got decidedly better, but a slight attack of Bronchitis came on and she died quite peacefully in less than 24 hours. I went to Cote Bank on Monday. There was a funeral service at Redland Meeting at 10; at her express desire, her body was taken to Golders Green [crematorium] whither Ormston, Gerald and I accompanied it. There was no service there. The ashes were interred at Lawrence Weston[463] yesterday.

---

[463]The Friends Burial Ground at Lawrence Weston, Henbury.

Your postcard, very nicely expressed, arrived on the Thursday morning, just before the attack came on, and was read to your Grandmother and gave her much pleasure.

She has left a large number of small legacies, £30 to you, which is a special one. The other grandchildren I think get £10 each.

Probably Cote Bank will go on for 6 months. Already a purchaser is in the field. The furniture and things have all to be distributed. Is there anything you would specially like? You can have it for the asking, in reason. It will be a great business to wind it all up.

Of course we come in for a lot of money, though it is not easy to say how much in these times. I expect it will be £10,000, but it may be only £8,000. The estate will have to be kept open for years, probably after my death, and we must put some younger people into it, probably you for example. One sum cannot be divided till after the deaths of May and Rosa.

I've been at home today, a gorgeous day of midsummer heat, picking Coxes, of which there is a splendid crop. Apples are rather early. That cankered tree by the henhouse door produced several which weighed 17oz! They don't keep, but they cook superbly.

Mrs. Jenner [Marjory's washer-woman] has just been here to discuss her nomination for the Central Agricultural Wages Board. The Government could not get a woman and applied through Mallon to your mother for a suggestion. Exactly what the Central Board does, I forget, but it is very important, and Mrs. Jenner is getting on in the world! We persuaded her to accept. As she chars for S.O., he knows her too, and is writing to the President to recommend her.

I went to tea with Tom's[464] wife after Golders Green. She was supposed to be below par, but the story is not true; very elegant, very pretty, perfect manners, probably no brains, but that he does not demand, I expect. He is in the R.F.C., just made lieutenant, but has a permanent inspection job, and lives in Hampstead.

Ever affectionate, Edw. R. Pease

....

Marian F Pease to MSP

Cote Bank, Westbury-on-Trym, Bristol

---

[464] Nephew Thomas Ormston Cave Pease, who married Lucy Woodmansey in 1915.

30th Sept. 1917

My dear Michael,

Your card to me came just about 24 hours before dear Grannie died. We were scarcely anxious about her though (the cold seemed passing off) and I took your card up after breakfast and read it to her. She was sitting in her chair and was pleased and cheerful though I noticed when she spoke that she was hoarse – the beginning of the bronchitis which proved too much for the heart. On Tuesday – she died on Friday – she was very well, she was speaking of her wish to see the end of the war and I know that part of that wish was that she might see you again, though personal hopes and fears played little part in her desires and her longing for peace was something very fundamental. We read at the funeral service the chapter in the Epistle of John (cap. 4) about love being the basis of all true life – it was her favourite chapter, and she based her life on that principle. When she was so ill in July, she dictated a little paper on prison reform; a matter very near her heart. We have had it printed and I will get your mother to send it to you, if it can be sent. Your courage in making the best of your life at Ruhleben was a great satisfaction to her. She often spoke of it. I hope to write again soon. I wanted you just to know that she had the pleasure of hearing your expression of love and admiration. She was wonderfully humble – in spite of the adoring love by which she was surrounded. Her face and especially her eyes were most beautiful almost up to the end.

We have no fixed plans yet about Cote Bank,

your loving aunt, Marian F. Pease.

....

Isabella Ormston Ford (fn 37) to MSP:

Adel Grange, Leeds

8th Oct. 1917

My dear, dear Michael

We have all three [Isabella and her 2 sisters] been thinking about you so specially much because of your (and our) loss. There never was anyone quite like your grandmother. One could tell her anything whether she approved or not and what a splendid faculty that means – such a broad-minded outlook and understanding, she was always so comforting and so sunny – I loved her so deeply and that makes me understand how you must feel dear little Michael – there you are far away in that weary old camp – and we are so sorry. But be cheered up – things are changing. This old world moves slowly but it moves now. People are becoming more human here – I cannot say more – but be cheered, do keep well, we are holding on and feeling encouraged. We are all well and so busy, busier than ever. Such fine meetings we are having. I used to write and tell Aunt Pease about them – she was so keen.

I won't write more now – but I will write soon.

Your loving and ancient cousin,

I.O.Ford.

Love from us all and we are so sorry for you in your trouble dear child.

....

ERP to MSP:

The Pendicle, Limpsfield, Surrey

15th Oct. 1917

My dear Michael,

I have just come back from a weekend at Cote Bank. You will like to hear about things there. May and Rosa have now decided to stay on till next summer. So the great and sad break-up of our old home is deferred. They were alone. The big house seems rather empty, and the garden, only half kept up, rather desolate. But the trees are as grand as ever, and I was glad to see the kingfisher once more at the pond. Ultimately Rosa will take a house in Clifton where May will have two rooms. May will buy a cottage in a Somerset village. Of course it might be long before we can sell the old place, but one can't tell. I spent much time reading records of the family since 1750 or so, both Fry and Pease, written some 20 years ago by my mother. There is a lot of silver to be divided, much of which came from the 18th century ancestors, and bears their initials. I wonder if there are any Cote Bank books you desire? I want Calkins' *American Indians* and should like Morris's *Birds,*[465] but others may want the latter. The books as a whole are terribly useless, but there may be a few I shall care for and can secure. We shall no doubt have some of the family oak. Victorian furniture I do not greatly care for. May and Rosa, who are setting up house, will take what they require first.

Autumn is settling in early. I have picked nearly all the apples: Bramleys only a small crop; Coxes super-abundant; Blenheims, three trees with 1 each! I find the soft apples which weighed over 1lb are Warner's King. The Peasgood

---

[465] *A History of British Birds* by Reverend Francis Orpen Morris, in 6 volumes.

Nonsuch were particularly fine and numerous. Pears, generally abundant, especially so at Cote Bank, were a failure here.

Did you ever hear of a biologist named Bonhote,[466] who has studied the genetics of rats, pigeons etc? I never met him, but have known his wife for some years. I am reading his *Vigour and Heredity* which however does not greatly impress me so far; save in so far as it goes for the extreme Mendelians.[467] He is running something for the Egyptian Government now.

Affectionately, Edw. R. Pease

....

ERP to MSP:

The Pendicle, Limpsfield, Surrey

25th Nov. 1917

My dear Michael,

We have had two long letters from you in the last few days, and we are hoping you may be getting back to Jena. I will get the B. of Ag. Journal sent you. We did not know that you cared for it, and one can't send anything anyhow now. I will tell the Board of Education to send it. I am ordering the Christian Science Sentinel to desist – I see it is a Boston paper.

The Labour Party reorganisation is merely the result of the alternative vote which destroys all the old policy. They will run 300 or 500 candidates, organise in every constituency and make a local, in place of a Trade Union Socialist, basis. The results are on the knees of the Gods. But North Salford is astonishing. Tillett,[468] who has many faults, beat the coalition man hollow, on a policy of Labour, socialism, and fight-to-a-finish. As for the Labour Party, they may not be very great, but what will you have? If you reject all politicians as unfit to govern, the only inference is that you yourself are the only fit person, in your own opinion. I know you don't think this, but surely it is a mistake to regard all men as incapable.

---

[466] John James Lewis Bonhote, an English ornithologist.

[467] Gregor Johann Mendel (1822-1884), a scientist who established many of the rules of heredity and modern genetics.

[468] Benjamin Tillett was a member of the Fabian Society and the Labour Party MP for Salford North from 1917 to 1924.

There is not much to report on the garden. I am busy in it because the days are short and there is always lots to do. The medlar crop is peculiarly abundant, fine, and well-ripening. Other crops are all harvested and getting eaten.

Nothing much is happening about Cote Bank yet, and the wills etc have not yet been proved. The effect of war finance has been to reduce the value of gilt-edged securities exactly 20%: they were 25 years purchase (4%) and are now 20 years (5%). I doubt Cote Bank will be sold for building; it is more likely to find a purchaser as a residential estate. I may be going there early in December, and will look out for Buffon and Sowerby. But nothing will be done for months I expect. I am sending you another £10 as requested, and am glad you are getting a good microscope.

I was reading Bonhote when I last wrote: by no means conclusive, but interesting as recording all sorts of gaps which I think Mendelians usually ignore. – The Gradan[?] business is odd, and we can't understand it. Well, good luck to you.

Affectionately, Edw. R. Pease

……………………

ERP to MSP:

The Pendicle, Limpsfield, Surrey

4th March 1918

My dear Michael,

It is long since I wrote to you but I do not seem to have much to say. I confess my cheerful views of the end of the war have all been wrong, and I've had to give up prophecy. But dreary as the process is, costly in life and happiness, and money, it is achieving a lot for this country, as it has achieved a lot for Russia, and will for all other countries. The Persian Wars were the making of Greece: the Franco-German War created modern Germany this was has already created a new Russia, and will create a new England.

This afternoon I have been sitting on a list of 31 Fabian candidates for Parliament, all Labour of course, half a dozen officers naval and military, aristocrats and authors, all sorts. The election is put off till October, when the new register with 6 million women and 2 million men comes into force.

The L.P. now definitely socialist: they have adopted a programme which embodies Socialism. But nowadays nobody notices that. Socialism is taken for granted.

I've been working away at the garden as usual, and have had two fine months, as a whole, tho' just now the weather has turned cold. The season was very early and the hedge plums are in flower, snowdrops over and daffodils just coming out. I've mown the lawn, in Feb., a thing I never recollect doing before. We have had no bullfinches and fruit-buds look fine.

Nothing much has happened about Cote Bank and the estate. I expect your little legacy will be paid soon. Your Aunts talk of buying a house at Almondsbury, 8 miles from Bristol, beyond Brentry, a lovely district. Property sells well, as everybody seems to grow richer – rich and poor alike. I suppose it must be fictitious, but the fact remains. For example the Fabian Society never in all its career had so much cash in hand as it has at this moment.

I went to hear Litvinoff lecture the other day, but he had nothing much to say. West is still in Petrograd. I heard from him on Jan 19th when things were pretty bad, tho' he was not so down on the Bolshevists as some people are.

Ever your affectionate father,

Edw. R. Pease

....

MGP to MSP (letter 427):

The Pendicle, Limpsfield, Surrey

31st March 1918, 11p.m.

My dearest Michael,

Your p.c. of Feb 9th is still my last news of you. It is very trying to have letters hung up like this – you may be writing asking me to send you things and it all means such a dreadful delay. We were much relieved by having 2 p.c.s and a letter from Nicolas yesterday and a p.c. this morning. Again good luck has attended him and we hope now he is back at base for a rest. It is 7 weeks today since Mary and I started him from Victoria – what an age it seems!

I had a visit from Mrs. Lock yesterday who had had a very vivid dream about you and thought you were home. Coppard was full of enquiries for you. Today we had Mrs. Reeves and Amber to tea. Gertrude Ansell [fn 299] is a very pleasant inmate. She looks well in spite of continuous hard work in Ministry of Munitions.

March is going out like a lion and your beautiful blue and white hyacinths have suffered by the gale. I gave Mrs. Reeves a large bunch of ones which had snapped across.

I long for more recent news of you. I am seeing Mr. Mackness[469] on Wednesday and hope for news from him. Ones thoughts are full of the dreadful battle in France and the terrible sufferings of the dying and maimed and the agony of those at home waiting for news. It is all too dreadful. Four years ago could any of us in England dreamt of such an awful development of 'civilisation'. I think constantly of you and know how you suffer.

Your devoted Mother

....

MGP to MSP (letter 428):

The Pendicle, Limpsfield, Surrey

2nd April 1918, 9:30p.m.

My dearest Michael,

Your p.c. of Feb 9th is still my latest news of you. I only hope you get my letters with less delay. Easter has come and gone and we begin London again tomorrow. Gertrude Ansell is a delightful visitor and I think the change did her a very great deal of good. She went off with a beautiful bunch of lilies out of the ghetto, which lies empty as the Dunbars (who now live at Eastbourne) tell me to go and pick flowers. After some days of intense anxiety we hear from Nicolas whose wonderful luck has still followed him and he is well on Easter Sunday and we think may be out of things for a few weeks – at least we hope so, but one never knows.

April 3rd Mack came to see me today and brought with him Mrs. Latham whose husband[470] you know. I took them to tea at Army and Navy Stores where we met Miss Sellers and we talked – well you know how we talked about the man who gave you a mouth organ and about his colleagues – not in very flattering terms I'm afraid! It seems Mack saw something of our Squire in 1914 and I am hoping to arrange a meeting later.

Our league's annual meeting is on "the part time food producer" which I mean to make a success. Did I tell you Walter [Neumeister] is at work in the North? He was just leaving Leigh as he wrote on March 26th and in great good spirits. He was much delighted with a book of English literature which arrived on 16th

---

[469] Geoffrey Marlow Mackness (1868–1942), a classics graduate of St Andrews, was initially held in Sennelager Camp. He was released from Ruhleben on 6th March 1918.

[470] Probably internee Charles Latham (1890-1926), who according to the *Ruhleben Story* became a member of the International Labour Office when it was created in 1919.

March from M. S. Pease and he wondered who M. S. Pease was! I talked much about your various works today as you may imagine and I seemed to see and hear you.

April 4th. Finishing this from Selfridges where I am ordering your weekly parcel. I have just got a pair of rope soled canvas shoes here which I will send off via T.P. [Thurloe Place] with ½ doz tennis balls. I have an account from Johnsons for books which I hope reach you all right. How I admire your grit and pluck! I know so well what it means to face life under your conditions. Who ever dreamt 4 years ago what you and Nicolas would have to face. Nicolas has developed so marvelously and is evidently very highly thought of. In some way we don't know why, he was at the last moment sent off on some special work and was not with his division on 24th, where it suffered heavily fighting 8 to 1 – Poor Malcolm Carter[471] has fallen. His poor mother! I am extraordinarily well though I work every day and all day and you and Nicolas are never out of my thoughts.

Your loving Mother.

....

MGP to MSP (letter 429):

The Pendicle, Limpsfield, Surrey

5th April 1918

My dearest Michael,

Still nothing from you since your p.c. of Feb 9th but I know you were well on March 7th and for this I can be thankful. These spring days with birds and flowers make me think more than ever of you. The blackthorn is so beautiful. I always think of the donkey and pony cart expeditions with Hinder and Eleanor in Staffhurst Wood at this season. All those days seem like a dream of a previous existence now.

Saturday 6th April. Regular typical April day. Been to see Mrs. Harris who has gone very run down. She has never got over poor Trev's death and no wonder. She is awfully plucky, but life can never be the same to any mother who loses her boy. Joan is working hard and doing splendidly at her medicine, but is very little here. She more or less "keeps company" with Warwick, but of course

---

[471] A Bedalian who went missing in action on 23rd March 1918 in The Somme, at the beginning of the German Spring Offensive.

don't refer to this. I hope he is good enough for her. He is invalided out of the army and is working at Cambridge I think.

In my last letter I told you of poor Malcolm Carter and now we see Bellot minor [Bryson Bellot] died after an operation in hospital in France. I have written to Hale, but what can one say! Nicolas was all right on April 2nd for which I am profoundly thankful. Some good stroke of luck attended him – but one can't help passing many anxious days and nights. I often think of all "Mack" told me. – The Frys have been at Clifton and say May and Rosa [Michael's aunts] can think and talk of nothing but "Harts" (their new house) where they go in August. Curious isn't it in times like this to get absorbed in that. I am doing a certain amount of speaking once again and am on various reconstruction committees. One is determined to clutch on to any good which arises out of this terrible war. I do hope I'll soon have a letter from you. You are probably asking me to get sundry things for you which you doubtless need badly. I do hope you get my weekly parcels and that the contents I send arrive in good order. I could send you such much nicer parcels if I could pack them myself. I hope the soap reaches you. No scarcity of it here! There is such a wonderful crop of fruit blossom of all sorts this year, but of course things are much too far forward.

April 7th. Post just in, bringing your letter of 16th Feb with letter to Dora [Michael's aunt] attached. Will write later, only do believe me when I ask you not to hastily conclude Dora's views are more in accordance with your own than mine. Try and picture Dora and me and our circumstances. Does Dora suffer as I do? She knows nothing about War or Peace.

Your devoted Mother

....

MGP to MSP (letter 430):

The Pendicle, Limpsfield, Surrey

Sunday 7th April 1918

My dearest Michael,

Your letter of Feb 16th has turned up this morning and I acknowledged it on a letter I posted immediately after receiving it. I have now been writing to Dora and sending her on her part of the letter. Such a typical April day with such wonderful clouds and gleams. I have been in the Ghetto picking such beautifully sweet smelling lilies for sick people. I am taking some to Miss

Greeney[?] tomorrow. I have been wondering if you have got at all a good show of bulbs.

Glad books from Denny reached you. I sent you the Turgenev (though I haven't read it) and Aunt May sent you the Lester, and J.B.C. [uncle John Bright Clark] Mrs. Jarry's book. By the way I believe Dora and most of her "set" have had their eyes very considerably opened by recent doings in Fanny's native land.[472] You cannot know the truth, the whole truth and nothing but the truth. How can you? Meanwhile hang on to the faith in which you were brought up, and believe your mother. It would be comic, were not all the circumstances so tragic, the efforts that the once time high and mighty are now making to do what I have always done in regard to the daily round.

April 8th. I have written to Paul Cooper for advice about the morocco skins as I don't know where to buy them. I foresee a tremendous fight with T.P. and perhaps I'll start off by enlisting the B. of Educ. Yes the Neumeisters were delighted with your Xmas presents. What a curious person Mrs. R. is. I will give her your message. Of course you can't possibly ask the Neumeisters to extend hospitality to Tom Marshall [Ruhleben friend]!

A cake has arrived today from Aunt Nancy [wife of Michael's uncle Willie, who lived in Canada] for Nicolas and she wants to send one to you! How wild these T.P. regulations make me! Why can't I send you cake and marmalade from home.

April 9th. 7 a.m. How the birds sing! Nature is regardless of mankind and his works! Tomorrow Ralph [nephew] arrives from Reigate for 3 weeks and the prospect does not elate me. I struggle to do my duty by him but oh! the contrast between having him and having you and Nicolas! Ralph is to go into wireless telegraphy and goes to London for this, but he is to continue to board at Reigate and have a season ticket. Reggie [Ralph's brother] is with his mother and working at munitions and I presume getting good pay as his mother has ceased begging from me.

By the way I hope I have been able to do a very good turn for "Mack" and through Mr. Lloyd-Greame [M.P. later Lord Salisbury] got him into an excellent berth. Lloyd-Greame felt he must do his utmost for a man who had suffered so unjustly all these years. Mack met the Squire and I think the latter thanks God he was spared what Mack has endured.

Your devoted Mother

---

[472] Probably Marjory's friend Fanny Stepniak (fn 17), so she means Russia.

Letter just in from Nicolas, all right 5th. For this I am thankful.

....

MGP to MSP (letter 431):

The Pendicle, Limpsfield, Surrey

10th April 1918

My dearest Michael,

November fogs are upon us and it is now cold and drizzling rain. My usual London day and I came back to find Ralph here from Reigate for 3 weeks. He looks well and has grown a lot but still is very quiet. It is difficult for me to keep him going when I am out so much, but I'll get him employed in digging cottage gardens.

I am of course very anxious about Nicolas but he is very good in writing and he was all right on the 7th. I need hardly say I don't read newspapers and their ghastly descriptions. One's own imagination is sufficient to cope with.

11th April. I am writing this from my office having handed in rope soled shoes with loofah soles at Thurloe Place and left an order for hard court tennis balls to be sent to you. Paul Cooper is in pursuit of morocco skins for you. I have sent you the usual weekly parcel which I hope travels all right and reaches you intact. I wish you would criticise the food supplies and make suggestions. I could send you much more variety if I could do the parcel myself. We are busy here in the office with arrangements for annual meeting [of the National Land and Home League]. Mr. F. D. Acland [Liberal MP] and Prof. Dunstan[?] are to be our principal speakers. Did I tell you I had such a nice kind letter from Nancy who is very anxious to send you a cake!

I have never seen a more splendid crop of plum blossom than this year, and pear and apple too is most abundant. T.P. send us copies of your letter and card acknowledging re-agents. I am so thankful you get these all right.

Read much love between these senile lines from your devoted Mother

....

MGP to MSP (letter 432):

The Pendicle, Limpsfield, Surrey

13th April 1918

My dearest Michael,

Your letter of 19th Feb still my latest, but having heard first hand of you on March 7th I wait patiently for news. I am now wrangling with that precious T.P. about sending you tennis balls (6)! They say they must see a letter from you asking for them! I am replying that the war may be over before I get a reply written to me by you.

14th April – A bitter N.E. wind like January. Such a contrast to 3 weeks ago when fires were abandoned and the sun drove us from the verandah.

Ralph is very docile and obedient, but very lacking in any initiative. I try to plan out his days and send him to dig in the garden of Leaming's old house which is now inhabited by Belgians. There is a Belgian boy of 15 who is good company for Ralph when I am out so much.

I have letters from Peggy Scott and Bellot [Bedalians] and Mrs. Carter. I wonder if my letters reach you. I wonder if Mrs. Mumby sent you handkerchiefs – I hear that Betty Shawcross is threatened with lung trouble. I fancy she has never got over poor Trevor's death. Oh! How I long to have you back but there will be, alas, many blanks among your generation and other generations too and I know how you will mourn Cote Bank. Your Grandmother [Davidson] will be 89 on the 18th. She keeps wonderfully well and no sign of senile decay. My dear dear Michael I know full well how you must suffer and I know how often your thoughts are with us and I know you know how anxious I am about Nicolas.

All good wishes from your devoted Mother.

....

MGP to MSP (letter 433):

The Pendicle, Limpsfield, Surrey

16th April 1918

My dearest Michael,

We woke up this morning to find the ground white with snow and all the flowers frosted. I fear the plum crop will have suffered and other things as well. It is curious being back to winter after so much beautiful warm weather. I've been back at the Workhouse and then Food Control Committee where Mr. Page from the Chair uttered platitudes. Sybil Pye promises to find out about morroco skins. Meanwhile T.P. and I are wrangling over tennis balls! Your letter of 19th Feb. is my latest, so if I take a very long time to execute any commissions it is only because letters are delayed.

I am thankful to have a line from Nicolas. He has been made adjutant at a re-inforcement camp, but whether this is a permanent or only a temporary post I don't know. He writes most cheerfully and naturally is pleased at his rapid promotion. I long to have him back and his time for Home Service is now due, but I am not counting on having him yet a while. I have been busy as usual over N.L.&H.L. annual meeting which takes place tomorrow. I have had to prepare carefully the speech of a certain noble Lord [Henry Bentinck].

By the way neither you nor I have written much about the women's votes but that doesn't mean we don't think of it a great deal. It seems curious that the vote should have been given almost unanimously to women in the midst of this awful war. The great argument the antis used to have was "women can't fight". I constantly think of you and can picture you fairly well now. I hope you get my weekly parcels?

Your devoted Mother

....

MGP to MSP (letter 434):

The Pendicle, Limpsfield, Surrey

18th April 1918

My dearest Michael,

Your welcome p.c. of March 23nd actually arrived this morning. My previous letter was written on Feb 16th (no. 187) so 188 and 189 have yet to turn up.

In addition to getting your p.c. we have today seen Mr. Keel [repatriated from Ruhleben in March 1918] and had a lot of interesting talk which I need not repeat in a censored letter. I fear your music will have suffered by recent departures but I know you won't grudge your fellow sufferers their freedom.

I saw Lord H. yesterday and he had been hearing about you and about all your public spirited work.

20th April. I work late and early and I don't like sending you "tired" letters. I keep extremely well and fit. I have Ralph on my hands for his 3 weeks holidays and of course this is rather a tax and strain. He is quite a good boy but I'm afraid he is a very very poor substitute for you and Nicolas.

Weather has turned very cold and we have snow again. One can hardly bear to think of the wounded in this weather added to the other tortures. Nicolas has been moved on to his Battalion again and I am in constant anxiety. His letters are so bright and I try to be as brave as he is.

My dear Michael, I never cease thinking of you and I know how you suffer. I know the passionate longings you have and I know what you must suffer in spirit in these awful times.

I have a letter from Mme. Jarintzoff which I'll quote in my next. She has I suppose had a letter from you as she sends you messages. She has taken up the Oliver Lodge line and feels she is in close touch with Jarry.[473] Poor woman.

Ever loving thoughts from your devoted Mother

....

MGP to MSP (letter 435):

The Pendicle, Limpsfield, Surrey

21st April 1918, Sunday 10 p.m.

My dearest Michael,

Here we are back to snow and sleet and it feels far more like January than April. Your p.c. of 23nd March is quite recent news of you! I hope you haven't got it equally bad – I realise now after Sunday talks what the Ruhleben cold is like.

Your grandmother was 88 on the 18th. She is wonderful for her years. I shall go up again before very long to see her, but not while Nicolas is in such danger.

22nd April. Nicolas is all right on 18th and one realises by his letters how far ahead of me he is. He has entirely sunk himself for the common good – I can't claim to have got that length – I want my sons back again. I want them to live for their country.

I fancy you have written to Mme. Jarintzoff. She sends me a p.c. saying she is keeping some of Jarry's things for you but they are too precious to risk sending to Ruhleben. She has evidently taken up the Oliver Lodge line and is publishing a book about Jarry and the intercourse she has with him now. She writes "I did not answer your or Michael's letters because there is no corresponding note in my heart for any painful or gloomy sympathy. I am full of happiness of my new natural-as-daylight happiness. Explaining in a letter would mean no end of time". Well, one is only thankful she has found something to make life tolerable. Personally I have felt Jarry's death very keenly. I think of him as a bright little boy.

---

[473] Lodge's son Raymond and Jarry [fn 434], both Bedalians, were killed in the war; Lodge then turned to spiritualism and wrote a book about his son.

I am hoping for some of your missing letters. I want news of all your works. I am trying to get Bd. of Educ. to forward the morocco skins.

Your loving Mother

....

MGP to MSP (letter 436):

The Pendicle, Limpsfield, Surrey

24th April 1918, 9.30 p.m.

My dearest Michael,

Your very welcome letter of 31st March arrived this morning. It is very nice to be getting such recent news of you but 4 of your letters and cards are still missing. I hope they turn up as quite apart from wishing to know all your "news", I am most anxious to get any little commissions you wish executed. I hope Mrs. Spencer Mumby's handkerchiefs reached you long ago. I have just written to Prof. Seward and sent him on your letter which I had read with great interest. It is curious to read of your visitors. I presume your original work is the reason for the changed attitude. I am so thankful I worried through the re-agents. I had not heard of Miss Sargant's[?] death. I believe Alexis has gone off on a very mad tack.

I have been thinking much of you during these weeks and felt sure you would feel with me in my constant anxiety about Nicolas. Fighting has begun again just where he is and one can do nothing but wait and watch for news. Teddy Scott (Mabel's husband) who was missing on March 21st is now reported a prisoner of war and we hope Malcolm Carter may also turn up and many others. The Whiteheads have lost their younger boy flying and poor Paul Montague who also was in the flying corps has been killed at Salonika. I know you will feel his loss very very keenly – following poor Jarry's. It is terrible to think of your generation from whom we hoped so much, being sacrificed. I know how Mr. Badley [head of Bedales School] will feel all the casualties to Bedalians, boys he had trained and influenced to work for the common weal [good]. Who could have dreamt in the old days that this terrible state of things was what your generation had to face, and that my generation had to look on powerlessly.

April 25th A letter from Walter [Neumeister] who is now at Lancaster and greatly enjoying his work there. I must get Mr. Lindley to translate it for me. I have got Ralph on my hands till the 30th and I am taking him up to town today for clothes etc.

April 27th I failed to finish this yesterday. I have quite unexpectedly got Eleanor McD on my hands, as well as Ralph, so Jane rather rushed. Nicolas was all right on the 21st, but I just go on from day to day making no plans and living from hour to hour, and working at full steam all the time.

I have at last got permission to send you 2 morocco skins via Thurloe Place and Sybil Pye is getting them for me. At the same time I'll send you some leather for mending shoes and I hope soon to send you the canvas shoes.

I have been thinking very much of your letter to Prof. Seward and your work and your visitors. I fancy they came to you just as Montague Fordham[474] came to me in the early days of the Land Club! I think it is magnificent of you to do original work in the midst of such surroundings and I feel equally proud of both my dear and precious sons.

Your ever devoted Mother.

....

MGP to MSP (letter 437):

The Pendicle, Limpsfield, Surrey

30th April 1918

My dearest Michael,

I have posted you on a letter from Lesley Sambrook [Bedales]. I have such a nice letter from Prof. Seward who says "I was delighted to receive your son's most interesting letter which you kindly forwarded". He and I are in complete agreement in attributing to your visitors the Montague Fordham motive. Do you remember the daily visits here which Fordham used to pay at a certain stage! We do feel awfully proud of the work you are doing under such trying conditions. I have to steel my heart and keep myself from thinking of what your work at Cambridge "might have been" if the war lords had not let lose hell.

After some rather anxious days I have a few lines from Nicolas who is all right on the 27th. I have just been doing him up his weekly parcel of gingerbread etc.

Eleanor is here till the 6th of May. We talk much of you and she and I look at all your plants which now you have not seen for nearly 4 years.

Ralph went off today after 3 weeks stay here. He is a good looking boy but stupid and a weak character.

---

[474] An agriculturalist and advocate of rural reform.

A letter from Mrs. Spencer Mumby who has failed to get handkerchiefs sent to you from Switzerland. So I have to fall back on Thurloe Place and will try to send some with the morocco skins.

London 1st May. Did I tell you I hear from Walter that he is out and at work near Lancaster? He enjoys the change of scenery and the friendly children and others.

"Cote Bank" is full of moving to the new abode. I may go down there for a couple of days to pick out some furniture and souvenirs for you, but the final break up is deferred till August.

All loving thoughts from your devoted Mother

....

Arthur Edgar Dodd to Marjory Pease (received 17th May):

Holland

30th April 1918

Dear Mrs. Pease,

I have had the good fortune to be amongst those exchanged from Ruhleben to Holland and hasten to let you know that Michael was in the best of health and spirits when I left a few days ago. I was fortunate enough to come a good deal in contact with him and received very many kindnesses at his hands. He has faced the discomforts and monotony of the Ruhleben life better than anyone I know and his energy and strength of character to make the best of a deplorable sort of existence was a lesson to a great many of us. His friend and box mate Douglas Jones was also an intimate friend of mine and they kindly allowed me to have my evening meal with them and I have no hesitation in attributing my good health to the splendid meals they prepared. Even the life of an interned civilian living in a horse box for 3½ years had some few if not many redeeming features and I shall always look back on the splendid fellows one met there – whose spirit is not to be broken – as the bright spot in a dark period. They gave us a great send off as our train left the siding outside the camp and I'm sure there was not one of us whose joy at leaving the barbed wire was not considerably diminished by the thought of those cheering fellows behind the big gates. My sisters have several times written to me of your great kindness at the time when they had difficulty in getting our parcels through, and both my brother [Walter] (who is still in Ruhleben) and I are really indebted to you for all the trouble you took. I have spent my time during the first three days of freedom in going on long walks in the country and I can hardly appreciate yet the joy of it all. I have very nice rooms in a hotel together with half a dozen other 'Ruhlebenites' and we are just settling down. Yesterday however we received a great shock when we were told that we were to be sent to camp near the German frontier. This coming after the conviction that we had finished with camps was as I say a pretty unpleasant pill to swallow, but I am hoping that we have misunderstood the authorities.

I sincerely hope you and Mr. Pease are keeping well in this trying time and beg to remain with sincerest regards and thanks,

yours very truly

Arthur E. Dodd

....

MGP to MSP (letter 438):

The Pendicle, Limpsfield, Surrey

2nd May 1918

My dearest Michael,

I had rather a rush of a day in London and come back to the usual pile of work here. The evenings are lengthening out and one is tempted to spend them in the garden. The apple blossom is just bursting. Eleanor McD. is a great lover of this place and she says the air here braces her up. She is a very pleasant inmate. I hope to have Miss Gruner here for June and July – living in the cottage. I wonder if you are working in your garden and I wonder if you miss Mr. Pritchard and others – but I know you won't grudge them their freedom. May the day not be far distant when you are free too.

A few lines from Nicolas this morning written on the 28th. He still keeps all right in a miraculous way and I am almost beginning to think I may perhaps have him home on leave before so very long. But I don't dare to let myself count on this. All the trivial things I write about to you seem heartless and futile, but as you know one of the great hardships of these long 3 years and 9 months is the impossibility of putting ones real feelings in written censored words. But I cling to the conviction that you and I see eye to eye in all the great happenings, though our surroundings have been so absolutely different. And I live in hopes of seeing both my sons accomplishing much useful and abiding constructive work. Think kindly and tenderly of Nicolas. Think what an ordeal that sensitive, shy reserved boy has had to face. The words of one of his wounded sergeants singing Nicolas' praise always ring in my ears.

Every loving wish from your devoted Mother

....

MGP to MSP (letter 439):

The Pendicle, Limpsfield, Surrey

4th May 1918

My dearest Michael,

I thought much of you today as I cycled through Staffhurst Wood and I talked much of you as I sat in the Days' cottage and tried to console them about Alfred who is a prisoner in Germany since March 24th. They had just had a card from him and I have been writing to him tonight. He is at Limburg. I am arranging for him to get parcels of food. The four Days are all fighting – one in Salonika, one in Palestine and 2 in France. I do my utmost to get the biggest possible pensions and allowances for all soldiers dependents.

Eleanor and I have been walking in the Ghetto and pulling flowers! There are some exquisite auriculas and as the place is up for sale I mean to transplant some of them here!

I have just been writing to Mrs. Spencer Mumby and sending her a cheque for Asher who writes me very grateful letters. He says he is getting better and that the operation has been successful.

<u>Sunday.</u> The Carlile's successor [Colonel Maurice Hankey (fn 34)], who as perhaps you realise is a very important person nowadays, has just come back from a few days in France where he saw Nicolas last Thursday! It was quite thrilling to get such recent news. How one longs to have this awful strain ended – I am feeling hopeful that the end will soon come.

The morocco skins have come and as I have got a permit I hope you will eventually get them. I am trying to send handkerchiefs also and canvas shoes. My last news of you is your letter of March 31st. I am afraid the parcels for Ruhleben are being delayed again.

We talk of you so often (Eleanor and I) and of the old days.

Your loving Mother

....

MGP to MSP (letter 440):

The Pendicle, Limpsfield, Surrey

7th May 1918

My dearest Michael,

A p.c. addressed by you and signed by you dated March 6th came this morning acknowledging candles. I hope the Mars oil and bath towel also arrived all right? I do hope a letter soon comes as March 31st is still my latest news. A pouring wet day but so mild – one can almost see the beeches coming into leaf. I had my Merle Common day and the woods seemed full of nightingales and other birds.

I have just been going round the garden and looking at all your plants. The May tulips are just coming out. I have got some gorgeous auriculas from next door. I wish you could see them and smell them. I have a letter from Nicolas this morning – very excited about seeing Sir M. H. in France! Leave is now due, so perhaps N may be home again once more.

I had an interesting day yesterday, lunching with the Vicar of Kingswood and then holding forth at a Christian Social Union on Housing. I afterwards went on to Mrs. Nuttall and spent 4 hours with her hearing much about her distinguished friend and neighbour. Many questions were asked about you and great interest expressed in your work. Did I tell you the President of our League is very interested in all you are doing and had heard about it from others.

By the way, your grandmother's £30 legacy has been paid into your bank. Did you ever get the microscope? Your father is sending you £5 tomorrow. I fear many requests never reach us when there are so many missing letters.

Loving thoughts from your devoted Mother

....

MGP to MSP (letter 441):

The Pendicle, Limpsfield, Surrey

9th May 1918

My dearest Michael,

At last your letter (no. 190) written on March 16th turns up with about ⅓ of a page blackened out. The censor seems to object to descriptions of the wood beneath the Headland Cottages with bluebells! But he kindly lets me see that you had got a parcel with 6 candles. Yes I got your letters 180 and 183. The latter had some lines blackened out. I am amused to hear they are taking to blackening my harmless, colourless domestic drivel.

Tomorrow I encounter T.P. – always a trying ordeal as I find great difficulty to refrain from lashing out and saying what I think and what they deserve. I have got two nice pieces of morocco – one green and one brown. I got Sybil Pye to order them. I am also sending candles, brown canvas shoes, 3 handkerchiefs and leather for soling shoes. I hope all these things reach you.

We are having beautiful weather now and the country is looking lovely with the young fresh green and the apple blossom just coming out, but one cannot enjoy it. Ones thoughts are for ever in France and the happenings there. Indeed I do know how you will mourn poor Jarry and now Paul Montague gone too – I find I have to steel myself – one is so powerless. In case my previous letter didn't reach I repeat that Mrs. Jarry has gone off on the Oliver Lodge line – she is publishing a memoir of Jarry.

My last news of N. is 3rd May. I rather think he may not be in this present fighting, but one never knows. How his nerves have stood these years of war I know not. I am awfully glad you are "researching" so successfully. What a welcome you'll get from Prof. Biffen and others here. Hold out a little bit longer – the end cannot be far off now.

Did I tell you Miss Gruner is coming to live in our cottage for 3 months. She will do lots of little things for me and she is a great gardener and will cope with the weeds and help over fruit bottling and jam making.

I know how much and how often your thoughts are here with us, and I do know only too well how you have suffered during these long ghastly years. What a wicked shame to think of a handful of people having had the power of plunging the world into such misery! To think of the numbers of "just" who are sacrificed for the "unjust". How I long for you – but it cannot be long now till I see you and that thought gives me courage.

Your devoted Mother

....

MGP to MSP (letter 442):

The Pendicle, Limpsfield, Surrey

11th May 1918

My dearest Michael,

Your p.c. (193) of April 7th came this morning. I can't think why my letters don't reach you. I send 3 or 4 every week. And I fear my parcels also are very irregular and the parcels are more significant than the letters. A few lines from Nicolas comes this evening written on the 6th.

Such a lovely day! I cycled to Blindley Heath to see Mrs. Ackerman, my colleague on the R.D.C. She has a lovely house with such beautiful furniture and pictures. I cycled through Broadham Green, Tanridge and Crowhurst and thought of the days when I used to drive you and Nicolas to Godstone Station in the old Bedales days. The lanes are beautiful and full of birds and flowers and the skies full of swallows and aeroplanes. Yesterday I went to a very interesting little show of wounded soldiers' handicrafts. May Morris opened it and Paul Cooper and Mr. Okey and others were there. The speaker was remarkably good and inspiring.

Sunday the 12th A gorgeous May morning but I can no more enjoy its loveliness. I work, work, work away, and go to see people and thus the days pass – Nearly 4 years of this sort of existence now. I have had a very sad letter from Paul Montague's mother who sends very touching references to you and hopes you will come to see her one day. I often think how Mr. Badley must grieve for those fine young men whom he trained so carefully, and yet though they had lived 1000 years could they have risen to nobler self-sacrifice, but the human is strong in me and I want them to live not to die for their country.

Your devoted Mother

....

MGP to MSP (letter 443):

The Pendicle, Limpsfield, Surrey

18th May 1918

My dearest Michael,

Your letter (194) written on April 13th turned up last night, surprisingly quickly, and I also had a very kind and interesting letter from Dodd from Holland. It was very good of him to write. It was written just a few days after he had left you. I can't think why it took so long. I wrote to him last night. Such beautiful weather – like a gorgeous June evening only more beautiful because the air full of sweetness from lilacs and hawthorns. I have been in the ghetto getting sweet smelling azaleas and rhododendrons and the nightingales are singing, but one enjoys nothing. I think of Nicolas and the horrors he so pluckily faces. The Mendelsons used to say that the Russian nightingale had far more notes than the English one. I hope your nightingale stayed.

I am so thankful you've got a garden! Mr. Dodd remarked on the excellence of your evening meal so the thought I put into your parcels is not wasted. Do continue to keep well and fit!

Mrs. Donaldson will knit you stockings but I do not propose to send them or a nice pair of brown leather shoes to you, and I will keep the blue gray Harris tweed too! I hope the big garden boots have reached you? Aunt May sent you Lister,[475] Mrs. Green Holmes and I sent you the Cambridge pictures, also Turgenev.

I am thinking of organising the Ruhleben men's wives and mother's for a definite line of action. I tried (but failed) to get Walter moved to Greenhurst (near Hurst Green) where his fellow countrymen who are working on the land are luxuriously accommodated. You remember the house between Mr. Barry's and The Halt? I have written to Uncle John and Uncle Jonathan and I'll write to Peggy Scott and Neumeister tomorrow. I'm hoping Nicolas will soon get leave. It is due now, and oh how badly he must need a rest [Nicolas was wounded shortly after she wrote this letter and invalided back to England; see page 282].

Your loving Mother

....

Siward Horsley to MSP:

The King's Head Hotel, Thirlspot, Cumberland

21st June 1918

My dear Tuskey,

I was very glad to get your P.C. about 10 days ago and will try and answer it without being too indiscreet. At the moment Oswald[476] and I are walking for a week or so in the Lakes. He has a few days leave so I cut the last week of the Oxford term & came up with him. I didn't know whether you knew I am out of the army. That first winter in France brought back my old trouble and I had to give it up. So I've been back at Oxford, trying to pick up the broken threads of chemistry from where I left 'em in 1914, for the last 6 months – a bit of a job. Old Oxford is very changed, of course – about 18 men in St John's all crocks or allies, and other colleges in proportions – but I think the spirit of the place is still there, though perhaps a bit dormant, and of course the cadets of whom there are lots keep the place from looking deserted – the river is positively dangerous with these budding oarsmen and why half of them aren't drowned I don't know.

---

[475] Arthur Lister, or his daughter Gulielma, botanists and experts on Mycetozoa (slime moulds).

[476] Siward's brother (another old Bedalian) Captain Oswald Horsley, a Captain in the Gordon Highlanders and a test pilot with the R.A.F. experimental squadron. He was killed in a flying accident on 18th Aug 1918 when his plane fell out of the sky at Aborfield, near Farnborough.

This country is as charming as ever. We started from Windermere, came across Coniston Old Man and Hard Knott to Eskdale; had a great batus in the old wallow, [bath in the mud?] got vilely soaked in Langdale and called on the Miss Badleys[477] looking two of the worst tramps you could wish for. However they didn't seem to see anything strange and we got a very good tea. Today we went across under Fairfield to Ullswater and back across Helvellyn. Just as we got up to the 2500 foot mark at the beginning of Striding Edge the cloud came down so we sat under a wall and waited for the clouds to roll by. After an hour they were thicker than ever and it was raining with some vim so we had to carry on! The last bit was quite exciting because the path has been rather abolished by a cloud burst and left a rotten looking scree. As we were struggling up this there was a deuce of a fuss somewhere higher up and a good few tons of rock came down past us. We couldn't see anything in the mist and it was quite like old times in the trenches. I'm going down to Bedales for the last 3 weeks of term to do a bit of reading and perhaps play a little croquet. Oswald will, I hope, be close enough over at Farnborough testing new planes. The school is going on very well I think considering the difficulties of getting staff and the boys leaving so young. As to various people – I saw Bellot [fn 67] last weekend. He came down to Oxford and we played around and went over to Henley together the next day to see Sylvia Mundy who's no end of an expert milkmaid and carter on a farm there.

I'm afraid most of the news is pretty bad. Young Bellot died of appendicitis, which he got in the trenches, last March, and Malcolm Carter was killed in this last offensive [March 1918] and also poor George Murray [April 1918]. He'd only been married to Margaret Molteno about 2 months [Oswald Horsley was their best man]. She's being jolly decent about it; is working down at Bedales now along with Mrs. Flinson[?] helping her with the babies, and I believe is going to found a Scholarship for Bedalians at Trinity in memory of him.

Also, Tuskey, poor Pauly [Paul Denys Montague] has gone. He was in the flying corps out at Salonika and some time at the end of last October, he was reported "missing" after a raid, and some 4 months later reported "killed". It was a good straight end and he was doing very well as a flyer – but it is beastly sad.[478] Only, I don't think it's all in vain. It seems to me that feeling, in England at any rate,

---

[477] The sisters of John Haden Badley - Head of Bedales School.

[478] Further information on former pupils who died in the war can be found on the Bedales School website at https://www.bedales.org.uk/home/history-bedales/ww1, which currently lists 66 pupils and staff who lost their lives.

is so much cleaner[?] – that we are opening our eyes so much more to ideals, and that the old ideas of crush and grab are going under.

There are three good things this war has done:

1) It has filled everybody with a loathing of war and a great desire to find some real basis for a decent friendly peace.

2) It has brought women up almost to their proper level, economically and politically.

3) It has given the great mass of people a taste of high wages and independence and the self-reliance that men learn in the army that is going to bear fruit very abundantly in the future.

I don't say the results are worth the price – but it is something to feel that these friends of ours have not died in vain. I hope most sincerely that you are keeping fit and that you had a jolly time on leave, and that we shall soon meet again.

Yours Siward Horsley

P.S. The latest people to get married are Peter Eckersley, L[aunceroy] A[rthur] Newnham, Lucy Thompson and Connie Scott (Trig's [George Klaassen Scott's] sister)

P.P.S. We have moved and our new address is 10 York House, Church Street, Kensington, London

....

ERP to MSP:

The Pendicle, Limpsfield, Surrey

23rd June 1918

My dear Michael,

Your letter about the money paid by Dodd reached me a few days ago, and I have written to Dodd to say I will pay him at once in full, or as he pleases. I have been selling some Fry stock, of which I had too much, and also my cottages at Westbury, and I have plenty of money in hand; also money in the form of securities has come from my mother's estates. I was concerned at your letter to Biffen. As I understand it, the B. of A. will pay up in due course. Any way, please don't stint yourself in any respect. We have plenty for our needs, and strange to say, I have done very well with certain investments,[479] though of course the value of most stocks has fallen owing to the rise in the rate of interest. But the yield remains, but for tax, which is heavy. However, with new money coming in, we feel rich in spite of taxes and prices. What we have will come to you and Nicolas. So please spend whatever you want to, and we will pay. – Much of your letter was blacked out in Germany: and I think one letter to me is missing. I wrote to you asking about certain parcels of chemicals supposed to be sent you in the autumn, and have had no reply. Thurloe Place said I was not to pay till I heard you had received them, and I have not yet heard. I dare say your mother has told you that I spent two utterly helpless days in bed with a scratch on the cornea of an eye: result that I could move neither eye, and could scarcely manage to eat. On the third day I was suddenly well! A most curious accident.

Strawberries are excellent, and in full blast. Gooseberries too a bumper crop. Small fruit promises well, but we have only damsons out of the big promise of plums, and hardly any apples. However garden stuff promises well, and the flowers as a rule have been excellent.

I am a delegate to the Labour Party Conference this week (the date is altered to the summer) but I do not expect I shall attend very much. I have not been at the office since Monday – my accident was on Tuesday, and this is Sunday – and I shall have a lot of arrears there; and Nicky to visit also. This constituency now runs to Croydon and Reigate is cut off. I started a L.P. here on Thursday, and spent the day in bed. The preliminary meeting was rather a fiasco, and I don't suppose a candidate will be run. You have a vote for Cambridge University on payment of £1. You had better claim it. I will send your form. J. C. Squire is the Labour Candidate! Women graduates also have votes.

Your affectionate father, Edw. R. Pease

....

L S Ornstein to MSP (sent to c/o Otto Neumeister in Jena, but forwarded on to Ruhleben on 3rd July 1918):

Utrecht, van Speyckstraat 17,

23rd June 1918

Dear Mr. Pease,

---

[479] Edward worked as, and in partnership with, a London stockbroker from 1880–1886.

Today I have received your kind letter. I am glad that I can do something for you and for Herr Neumeister. Your letters arrive most in groups of four or three. Till now I have received from 1 to 19 except 17, and several letters for friends which I have forwarded.

It must be very fine for you to be out of the camp, it is very nice that Mr. Neumeister has obtained that favour for you. I have tried to send him tobacco as he asked me but it was impossible. I will [illegible] however again perhaps I will be happier then. I send you a photograph of our child and we two, it is much better than the card which I have sent to Mr. Neumeister after your first leave of Ruhleben, after you had indicated me that the Neumeisters like such photographs. Perhaps you will give this photograph to the Neumeisters.

I hope that soon you will have the occasion to see your mother again, that peace comes for the world, of course for our class much is to have for many money but the workman suffers much.

Scientific work gets more and more sufficient what belongs experimental work at last for instruments and materials are hardly to have. At the other side a great part of our students is mobilised and it is difficult to have assistants, for the young man who have finished their studies and who are free can get so much employment that they don't stay longer at the university. I will be very interested to get the photographs of your Ruhleben laboratory.

With kind regards truly yours,

Ornstein.

I am glad that I can do something for you in forwarding your letters. Many kind regards to the Neumeister family.

Photograph enclosed:

The Ornstein Family, 1918

....

Cyril Asher to Marjory Pease:

Gilserwiessan[?], Flums-Kleinberg, Switzerland.

7th July 1918

Dear Mrs. Pease,

Have just received a card from your son. He begs me to inform you that he has received your message. His leave had been extended for a further 3 weeks you will be pleased to hear, and he returned to Ruhleben on the 27th of June. He also begs me to tell you, that Neumeisters have received your letter dated May 19th.

I shall probably be returning to Davos at the end of the month. The weather has been awfully bad these last few weeks. Yesterday and today however, it has been very fine, and I hope it will continue so.

There is great excitement at Ruhleben at the prospect of an early exchange. Hope they will not be disappointed this time. Great that your son [Nicolas] is recovering rapidly from his wound.

Yours sincerely,

Cyril Asher

....

Bedales

29th July 1918

Dear Pease,

Just a line of greeting from the O.B. [Old Bedalian] Meeting, which is just over. Though many of the signatures will convey little to you, they will at least show that a good number were here and that we have not forgotten those who are moped up elsewhere and unable to come. In spite of everything it has been a good meeting. Lovely weather and a first rate concert.

Signed by 52 ex-pupils and staff

....

ERP to MSP:

The Pendicle, Limpsfield, Surrey

5th August 1918 (Bank Holiday)

My dear Michael,

Your two letters from Jena reached me recently. I am always glad of your letters, though of course I share those to your mother. I had hoped for 4 long days in the garden, but the weather is excessively damp; today a misty rain which makes gardening impossible.

I went to Cote Bank a week ago to wind up affairs, that is, to divide the furniture, silver and crockery. I get a Charles II oak chair, the cherub bed, my father's writing table and a lot of other things: a silver salver, perhaps 150 years old, is the chief silver item; an interesting but not very useful possession. Your aunts move to Harts[480] in a fortnight. It is a most charming house, a little like a small scale Cote Bank, with a delightful garden, a gorgeous view, a big orchard, attractive fields 20 acres in all. Cote Bank will be shut up, and it is impossible to say when it will be sold. It was looking beautiful in the hot summer days, but already is rather derelict.

Your story of German blackbirds is very strange. Here the summer fruit is done, and plums are coming in, quite a sprinkling. Apples are proving a little better, but only 3 trees have a crop.

I am off to a place near Dartmouth for a week or so, to direct the Fabian Summer School, in 3 or 4 days. It is at a requisitioned boarding house, on the coast, and so on a small scale, only 30 people. We could not undertake catering in these complex times. I don't think I've seen the sea, to speak of, since St Cast[481] days.

When you come back, which now we hope will be relatively soon, I think we will cut down the sycamore. It is not needed for shade, now the chestnut is so big, and it darkens much space. The removal of the pump is a great improvement. I've planted the space with sprouting broccoli, but the rhubarb must be moved, and a flower garden created. I can only just keep the garden going, but I shall have lots of time when the war is over.

Dodd wrote he did not want the money immediately and he had not settled the exchange with you. I had told him he could have it, all or any, as he directed.

It has been very pleasant to think of you at Jena. You laugh at my prophecies, which have mostly been wrong. Still there seems to be more hope of your release than ever before, and indeed the wretched war looks like coming towards an end at last.

---

[480] Harts House, Almondsbury, Gloucestershire.

[481] A place in Brittany where the family often holidayed before the war.

Your loving Father, Edw. R. Pease

P.S. Yours from R[uhleben] just arrived

....

ERP to MSP:

The Pendicle, Limpsfield, Surrey

21st August 1918

My dear Michael,

I've returned from my usual Summer School week, this time at a Veg. Boarding House near Dartmouth. We took 30 places, in order to avoid the trouble of catering, and are holding the School on a small scale. I had a very fine time. I don't think I have seen the sea properly since our old St. Cast days, and I've been hungry for it for years. The house was right on a promontory, and from some rooms one could chuck a stone into the sea at all states of the tide. The builder, an old sea captain, had cut steps down the rocks, almost cliffs, in all directions. We had our own quite private bathing cove, and close by a quite big beach to which we alone had the right of access. The shore was steep, a fine shingle or coarse sand, and one was out of depth in 3 or 4 yards. I had 8 cloudless days, bathing once or twice every day. The garden was full of semi-tropical things, and alive with countless butterflies. The food was not bad, notwithstanding the shortage of cheese, eggs, cream etc, and fruit, which vegs. rejoice in. It was even anti fish! I had to give 2 lectures, which I did badly. I am getting too old to lecture, and shall give it up. – On my way back I stayed a weekend at Cote Bank – it is now vacated. The vans arrived as I left. But of course it is not sold yet, and may not be for years. We found a lot of curious old letters from the Aldam family, which is extinct, though some Pease relations assumed the name. They were addressed to Oliver Cromwell, and George Fox. Most of the furniture is distributed amongst the family and our share will arrive in a month or two. There will be a sale of things nobody wants. We get the oak Chas II chair, a Whitelock [ancestor] oak chest, 18th Century, and other things.

I took Bertrand Russell's *Principals of Social Reconstruction* to read, and we had a lecture on "The greatest living thinker" by an admirer who happily described the book as a facile solution of difficult questions. I don't think the world is anything like so silly and reactionary as B.R. depicts it. Like so many philosophers, he has made a sad mess of his own domestic life, and supposes other people are as incompetent as himself. But it is well written and suggestive. It is however much easier to say what ought to be done than to think out how to do it.

Someday we will all go to Penlee, the Dartmouth place, for a holiday. The only drawback is a smooth southern sea, and no sea fauna, why I don't know. I never saw a place so barren of seaweed and beasts: one star fish and 2 polyps was the total. But I found one beautiful flower new to me, Grumwell, a sort of borage; did you ever see it? Now I am busy over the garden, overgrown with 10 days neglect.

Affectionately, Edw. R. Pease

....

No date given, no name, just initials, but possibly from an old Bedalian friend

Tuesday morning

Mrs. Erskine has just forwarded me a letter from our Tor written on 26 January from the 23rd B.G. Hospital Amara. Much of it is taken up with thanks for a letter and parcel she sent him but he says that they were "so busy that we scarcely have any time even for sleep! And in the most of this time of unrest Turkie was tactless enough to wing me in the right hand, thereby doing no small damage and breaking 3 bones and since then I have been travelling slowly down river and have had an operation which has kept me in bed for some days where I still am. When I am considered fit enough to travel they are to send me on to Basra and thence probably to India as it will be a long time before it heals. Now I am comfortably settled in a soft bed with all the literature and eatables that I could wish for. Please excuse a very short letter for I am not yet very much use at writing with my left hand and a letter means a lot of labour still. However, I am quickly learning." It's wonderfully well written considering and it's nice to have heard from himself after 14 January. You have probably got one by the same mail and perhaps it will get here tonight. The pc from Noel[482] enclosed came this morning. Poor Mr. Fortune died this morning at 8.30 this morning. He had been so much better and stronger lately till he took this illness. A thaw of sorts this morning. Hope to get back to work tomorrow,

Yours, E.B.

....

---

[482] Probably Noel Olivier, a Bedalian and daughter of Sir Sydney Olivier (fn 15).

Mrs. Eduard Bernstein to MSP [sent to Michael at Ruhleben while he is waiting for repatriation to England]:

Schöneberg, Berlin

Nov. 1918

Dear Mr. Pease,

Many, many thanks for all the good things you bought yesterday, they are real delicacies for the time being. I am a little ashamed to send now again my maid for more, but as you have been kind enough to ask me to do so, I cannot help to make use of your kindness. I believe we will have for a long time very bad times to pass in my fatherland. I send our portierfrau [concierge] with my maid because she does not know the way properly.

Mr. Bernstein is sending you his photo and his Berliner Arbeiterbewegung [labour movement] as a little remembrance and both of us hope to see you very soon in England. We are looking forward to this time.

May I ask you to take the little book "Erinnerungen" [memories] to our son, till now we could not give it to him but with your books it will easily go over. The address is c/o E. B. Schnaffer, 117 Corringham Road, Golders Green, London. If you will be kind enough to bring to our children there our love we will be very grateful.

If we don't see you on Sunday next Mr. Bernstein and I wish you a very good journey and hope to have soon good news from you and your parents.

Yours sincerely Ed and R[egina] Bernstein

....

Grant Lochhead [fn 48] to MSP:

Macdonald College, Ste. Anne de Bellevue, Quebec, Canada

26th Dec. 1918

Dear Pease:–

At last I am back in 'Amurika' and have just been enjoying a quiet Xmas for a change after the hilarious ones I indulged in in old Barrack 3. I left on the 10th Dec from Euston on the boat-train for Liverpool which took us to the side of the "Melita". She sailed that afternoon at 5 and made a very creditable trip for this time of year. We had a very good passage indeed although the ocean was somewhat bumpy the first 2 or 3 days out. Fortunately I did not get sick, although the first day out I did consider it prudent to take but one meal – but I lost nothing and lived very comfortably for the remainder of the voyage.

Poor old Warkentin [fn 109] had a thoroughly miserable time most of the way across, but I rather think he enjoyed being sick. He managed to get up when we got in sight of land after he had spent 5 or 6 days in his bed. We reached St John on Wednesday noon (18th) rather sooner than was expected. My mother was there to meet me, or rather I was there to meet her for she only got in about 4 in the afternoon. We went up to Fredericton [capital of New Brunswick] that night and spent a couple of days there before coming up to Montreal, where we arrived Saturday morning. My father was there to meet us and insisted upon getting me a few respectable clothes for I did look a bit Ruhlebenesque on my arrival.

Since getting home I have been trying to get accustomed to the new environment (including the snow) and have been busy relating "*Greueltaten*" [atrocities] to open-mouthed auditors. Most people assure me I have not altered very much during my absence except for one thing – namely, that I have acquired an English accent; that is certainly amusing. I was aware that I had picked up a choice assortment of expletives from our sea-faring comrades but sweetly ignorant of the fact that I had got hold of an "accent". However.

I have been wondering whether Bell sailed on the 21st as he had been intending to – or whether Lloyd George had found him too important to let go and had persuaded him to join the Coalition Cabinet.

How is D'Albert?[483] If he is still within hailing distance please give him my best. I expect I shall be working for a time at least on the bacteriological dept. here. It will certainly do to get started on anyway. I shall probably have to start in at the beginning of the year. The labs are extremely well equipped with everything in the way of apparatus etc. I have often wondered whether we shall ever see our books that we left behind in the Y.M. Latest reports in the papers indicate that there may still be trouble before peace is signed. It is about time that somebody did away with Liebknecht[484] altogether. Still perhaps when everything is quiet once again we may see some of our belongings. I had no trouble with the mike [microscope/microtome?] at all – except the nuisance of

[483] Wolfgang Eugen d'Albert, son of the famous pianist and composer Eugen d'Albert, who taught Italian in the Camp School with Lochhead.

[484] Karl Liebknecht, a German socialist and one of the founders of the German Communist Party. He was executed on 15 Jan 1919.

looking after it – but did not have to undo the cover I so carefully sewed on in Ruhleben.

With regard to the cash which you so generously lent me I am sending you a money-order with this letter. For the last 200 marks you gave me they handed out only £6.8.0 in London which seems shockingly little: I don't know the value of the first 100 marks you gave so am just presuming it valued at the same rate. Therefore I am enclosing order for £9.12.0. If this is not right be sure to let me know as I am not an expert on the English coinage system.

I do hope you still will find time to give us news of yourself occasionally and you may be sure I shall be very glad to hear from you. In closing – my warmest thanks not only for having helped me out of my "financial embarrassment" but also for your kindness in so many ways during our stay "there".

Best of wishes,

Sincerely,

Grant Lochhead

....

Leonard Plato Roberts (fn 356) to MSP:

Westhill Lodge, Westcott, Dorking, Surrey

28th December 1920

Dear Pease,

Many thanks for your kind card of the 24th received this morning, also for the card you sent while on your Honeymoon, it was nice of you to think of me, especially during such a time. Regarding your wife's Christmas gift to you [birth of their daughter Noel Joanna on 24th Dec], I don't know whether to offer congratulations or not. Of course it's the orthodox thing to do, and I expect you're as pleased as pleased can be. It's a sure thing I wish you every joy, and you will have a very interesting new study of your beloved science. You see we've never had any offspring so can only imagine the pleasures of parenthood. I'm very interested in your gardening operations, and I do admire your manure heap, in fact I'm quite jealous.

I suppose nothing has been done, relating to the winding up of the Ruhleben H[orticultural] S[ociety]. So far I've heard nothing from the President nor any other Officer of the Society. David Wright wrote, asking if the society was active, as he wished to resume his membership. I proposed him for the Royal Horticultural Society, and he is now a fellow. Hill and Redmayne called here in the Autumn. They told me they had both seen you. Caffrey, the camp dentist has commenced business at 11 Coleherne Terrace, Richmond Road, Earl's Court SW5.

I spent a fortnight with Wyllie[485] in Scotland last August. He took me 1,000 miles in his side car, it was a glorious reunion. Our mess had our Annual at the Strand Palace Hotel on the 20th November. Pressman, Nash, Harris and Francke were there, unfortunately Redmayne contracted the 'flu just at that time, so he was the only one absent.

How are your roses doing? The prices are worse than ever now, I expect you've noticed that though. Owing to the extra work entailed in getting back into a normal state, my garden has gone to rack and ruin. I'm afraid I shall never have the time to get it right again. Nevertheless I find pig keeping a very useful adjunct to a rose garden, to say nothing of the delicious home cured bacon.

We both of us hope sincerely, that your wife and daughter will thrive exceedingly, and send our heartiest good wishes for this and all seasons, to you and yours, and with kindest regards from yours very sincerely

Leonard P. Roberts [Vice-Chair of the R.H.S.]

....

Extract of a letter from Douglas Doyle Jones to HBW:

Valley Farm, Higham, Colchester

2nd January 1978

My dear Helen,

Thank you so much for your Christmas greetings. I was very pleased to get news from you and especially to learn that it was good.

. . .

I too have had some intercourse with the Imp. War Museum and another one a rival in Sunderland. I have recently presented to the London one a little book of poems which I transcribed in illuminated lettering and illustrated in the camp and had bound in the book binding dept of the Camp School in the skin of a rat – which I had given to the people I was staying with in Germany in 1914 and which had been returned to me by their son as he has no family or

---

[485] George Alexander Moncur Wyllie (1893–1932), a committee member of the Ruhleben Horticultural Society.

relatives and wanted the book preserved. I had last seem him in 1914 but somehow or other he managed to find me after 63 years! And now he wants to come and see me in the summer. But with my immobility it is rather difficult...

. . .

Yours ever, Douglas

....

Appendix 2. Correspondence with the academic community

Correspondence with Professor Albert Charles Seward

Professor of Botany at Cambridge and Master of Downing College

....

The Master's Lodge, Downing College, Cambridge

April 22nd 1935

Dear Pease,

It occurs to me that the enclosed letters may be of interest to you as records of days which now seem remote. I found them on going through old war things; and I am trying to put into order a lot of miscellaneous savings from old days.

Yours sincerely

A. C. Seward

....

Ruhleben, December 27th 1915

Dear Prof. Seward,

As I daresay you may have heard, there has been started here in Ruhleben a so-called "Camp School"; in this organisation Dr Lechmere and I are conducting the Biology Section. Since last spring we have been giving lectures on Zoology and Botany to a class of some 12 serious students plus a variable number of "time-killers". We have at last had space allotted to us where we can erect a bench and set up microscopes (of which we have several in camp) and we have permission to get in reagents necessary for practical work. Dr Lechmere has got in a quantity of spirit material from Prof Tubeuf[486] in München [Munich], but, as there are some serious omissions, and as we do not

[486] Carl Freiherr von Tubeuf: Pioneer in the biological control of plant diseases and Professor of Forestry Science at the University of Munich from 1902 to 1933. Lechmere was working in his laboratory in Munich in 1914 when war broke out. Tubeuf arranged for Lechmere's release to serve as his assistant but Lechmere chose to remain interned with his countrymen (see diary entry for 11th June 1917). Tubeuf provided microscopes and other equipment for the camp school laboratory (*Ottawa Naturalist*, Vol. 32, November 1918).

like to ask again in that quarter, I am taking the liberty of writing to ask you whether your department could spare us a small quantity of sundry preserved material. We should be extremely grateful to you, if you could arrange this for us; we have a sufficient number of students whose seriousness and perseverance in face of difficulties encourages us to go on and do all in our power to make the best of the time spent here. Last summer we collected and preserved all that was of interest that we could lay hands on in camp. We got permission to search an adjoining pond, whence we got a goodly supply of the chief types of green algae. For ordinary flowering plants, conifers and mosses we are well supplied, as is also the case with the ubiquitous moulds and bacteria. It is the more out of the way specimens that we are completely without, and the following is a list of what we should really like. We only want quite a small piece of each, suitable for cutting, and they could all be put together – good practice for us to sort them out! I think they would travel quite safely in a couple of small bottles. Here is the list:

Fucus, Halidra, Cytocyrus (to show receptacles), Batradiospernum, Gracilaria, a Lichen (any bit suitable for cutting), Polyprus (and wood attached), one of the Uridineae (to illustrate the different phases), Peziza, Isoetes, Selaginella (any sort), Marchantia (or some other liverwort), Lycopodium (selago, clavatum, squarrosum), Equisetum Silvestre, Equisetum Palustre (in any quantity. We have E. Arvense), Angiopteris (frond), Botrychium, Ophioglossum, Cycas Revoluta, Encepharlatos (fronds). Water ferns I know are not plentiful, but they are awfully thrilling things, and we should much appreciate a bit of Pilularia, if possible. We are getting a microtome, but, as there seem to be insuperable difficulties in the way of setting up an embedding plant, I wonder if you could send us some odd bits of embedded Lidium or something like that suitable for making a start on cytology [study of cells].

I am afraid this is a most formidable list – I only hope it is not asking too much of your department.[487]

As you may well imagine, the Cambridge of the good old days is ever in my mind, and it is difficult to picture the change. I hope you all keep well and flourish. With kindest regards to Mrs. Seward and to all of you,

Yours sincerely, Michael Pease

……………………

---

[487] Nearly all of the list have a tick after each item, so Professor Seward must have provided most things.

Ruhleben, Jan. 25th 1916

Dear Prof. Seward

We were overjoyed to get the great bottle of Botanical material, which turned up yesterday, perfectly safely. I haven't had time to open it up and sort it out yet, but Dr Lechmere and I have turned it over and over, and eyed it eagerly from the outside. We are extremely grateful to you and your department coming to the rescue and helping us with the Ruhleben Camp School. The help which we get from folk at home and the response with which we meet among our fellow prisoners here are enormous encouragement to us to persevere in our educational experiments. In the biology department there are some very promising students. I've fitted up a very nice bench and with our six microscopes; we take 20 people in 3 relays. Your material will be invaluable, and both of us send our most grateful thanks to you.

I think we're fairly near solving the embedding problem by using a Dewar flask and an electrical thermostat. If we can manage this we shall try our luck with some Cytology.

I won't trespass on your valuable time and more, except to thank you again very much indeed. With kind regard to Mrs. Seward, and best wishes to all of you.

Yours sincerely, Michael Pease

....

The Lodge, Downing College, Cambridge

Feb. 17th 1916

Dear Pease,

I am very glad that the material reached you safely and that it is likely to be helpful in your teaching. Please remember me to Lechmere. I did not know that he was with you until I received your letter. The plants were looked at and packed by Morgan with Schulz[?] attendant so I am passing on a good proportion of your thanks to him. If you get stuck for want of anything let me know and I will do what I can.

My wife and the family join with me in kind remembrances and fond wishes.

I am yours sincerely

A. C. Seward

....

Ruhleben, March 17th 1916

Dear Prof. Seward,

After receiving your kind letter, we are venturing to take advantage of your generous offer by asking for some more material for our practical Botany class. We have been tremendously struck by the enthusiasm of the students and we feel that they really deserve to have the opportunity of doing the course fairly thoroughly. The laboratory is now excellently fitted up; we have seven first class microscopes – so we just manage to take our class of 21 in 3 relays.

We have not been through all your first jar yet, but the material so far examined has been excellent and I don't know what we should have done without it. I enclose on a separate sheet a list of the specimens we are taking the liberty of asking from your department. They are mostly Algae and Fungi; species that don't usually grow in concentration camps. I'm afraid I haven't thanked you nearly enough for what you have already sent, and I hope you will forgive our asking for more – it looks awfully greedy. I daresay you can realise what it is for us in these circumstances to have this little outlet for our energy.

I was terribly distressed to hear of poor Marsh's [fn 172] death. Mr. Tansley's [fn 173] note in *Nature* was my first intimation of it. The loss of such kindred spirits will indeed make it a sad home coming.

Yours sincerely,

Michael Pease

....

Ruhleben, April 18th 1916

Dear Prof. Seward,

Thank you very much indeed for the jar of Botanical specimens which arrived safely yesterday. They are excellent; and we are very deeply indebted to you for the interest which you have taken in the Biological work here, and for the trouble it has caused you. The class continues to flourish, and displays great enthusiasm, and is a great joy to Dr Lechmere and myself. The lab is quite one of the show spots in camp now!

We have an embedding bath in course of construction, and are in great hopes of setting some cytology going. In the meantime the Pond is a great source of joy: I had no idea "running down" Desmids[488] and the like was so exciting! We're getting a huge collection!

I'm afraid I haven't half thanked you enough for your two gifts. For they alone have made our course possible. You can well imagine the limitations of a camp "compound" flora. Please thank who ever packed up the specimens: they have in both cases arrived in excellent condition.

I hear you have Violet Scott[489] coming to look after your gardens. That will be excellent: I hope she stops the encroachment on Downing College park!

I hope you all flourish, in spite of the rush of these times. Please give my kind regards to Mrs. Seward and my best wishes to you all. Again with very many thanks,

Yours sincerely

Michael Pease

....

The Lodge, Downing College, Cambridge

July 16th 1916

Dear Pease,

I was glad to hear of the specimens being received safely though that is now old news.

I wonder how you are getting on: if you require more material I will try and supply what I can. I wish you would send me a list of the courses that are being given to the camp: you did send one sometime ago and I probably lent it to a man and he has not returned it. I should much appreciate another. Our Long Vacation is rather desolate, practically no undergraduates except a few medical students. Remember me please to Lechmere. I hope both you and he are flourishing though you must long for a wider field of activity.

With kind regards,

yours sincerely

A. C. Seward

....

Ruhleben, August 2nd 1916

---

[488] Single-celled green algae which can only be found in fresh water.

[489] Violet Gertrude Scott - an old Bedalian, sister of George, Tommy (fn 324) and Peggy (fn 22).

Dear Prof. Seward,

I am once more taking the liberty of writing to you for some more botanical material for the Ruhleben Camp School. I'm afraid I'm a terrible Oliver Twist. Your two previous gifts have supplied us with many months' work; but, so far from being satisfied, we are only too anxious to go and do more! Hence my boldness in bothering you again.

Since Easter I've been taking the class through mosses and ferns. I got in from a florist all the types I wanted as far as morphology and anatomy were concerned; unfortunately, in many cases the structure of the sporangia had to be taken on trust. I wonder if you could come to the rescue once more, and be good enough to let us have some fragments of the fertile fronds of the ferns on the enclosed list? We should be most awfully grateful.

This Autumn I want to take a course in gymnosperms.[490] Inside the camp I can get pines and thuia [thuja], but for the rest I must turn elsewhere. Hence this formidable list which I venture to send to you, containing the common or garden Juniper and such varieties as Taxodium and Epedra, which latter I put on in fear and trembling! However if you could just send us what you happen to have at hand, we should be extremely grateful. Very small pieces are quite sufficient – we've taught the class to be economical, both in material and reagents.

Lechmere and I are flourishing and finding the Bi. section of the R.C.S. and our little lab. a great occupation and source of joy. He has been lecturing on Vermes[491] for a year, but practical is impossible in zoology. The Botany class consists of 21 persons, nearly all really keen workers, putting in 3–6 hour practical work daily: much more satisfactory than the discouraging type of languid youth – not unknown to the Cambridge demonstrator – who limits his time by the marker's pencil! I've got a very miniature glasshouse and we've been growing water ferns in an adjoining pond, to which Lechmere and I have leave of access. Very bucked to get Azolla [aquatic fern] to produce spores. We're trying to set some cytology going; but there are awful difficulties in getting the necessary resistance wire to construct an electrical embedding bath.

I expect this will reach you while on holiday. Somehow, after these years of imprisonment one has forgotten about summer holidays and going away for a

---

[490] Flowerless plants that produce cones and seeds, like yews and conifers.

[491] A now obsolete taxon used by Carl Linnaeus and Jean-Baptiste Lamarck for non-arthropod invertebrate animals, like worms, molluscs, corals etc.

rest and change of air! Hence my oversight in leaving this till so late; but possibly somebody may still be at the Botany School who could attend to the matter. If not, we can easily turn to other things – we've no statutes here to tie us down to definite terminal dates. Our only enemy is the cold weather.

I hope you are all keeping well and standing the strain of these busy times – I can well imagine the rush of work you must be living in. Please give my kind regards to Mrs. Seward and my best wishes to you all.

I am afraid I have not thanked you nearly enough for all you have already sent nor offered adequate apologies for my temerity in asking for more. I can only hope that you will forgive my short comings under both heads, and rest assured of our extreme gratitude to you for the very great assistance that you have rendered our somewhat unique educational venture in this camp.

Again with very many thanks

Yours sincerely

Michael Pease

P.S. By one of those amazing coincidences that occasionally turns up, I had no sooner finished writing this letter, when your kind letter of the 16th ult came in. Very many thanks for your offer, which I am afraid I had anticipated! I enclose the two prospectuses you ask for. MSP.

....

Downing College Lodge, Cambridge

Sep. 3rd 1916

My dear Pease,

Morgan has packed and sent to you such of the material asked for as we could find but I fear there are several omissions as some of the plants are not easy to get and we had none or only very little.

I am very glad to know that the course prospers and that you and Lechmere are flourishing: the botany must be a great boon both to you and to the students. I have had no real holiday this year but tomorrow I go to the British assoc. meeting for a few days.

If more needs arise let me know and I will do my best.

With kind regards

I am sincerely

A.C. Seward

....

Ruhleben, Sep. 22nd 1916

Dear Prof. Seward,

Thank you very much indeed for your letter and for the great pot of material which arrived in perfect condition yesterday: my thanks too to Morgan for packing it up so carefully. We have not had time yet to break the seal and sort out the material; but we have feasted our eyes by peering in at the contents of the jar. It will set up the class in great style for many months. It is extremely good of you to send it and it is difficult to express to you how much your kindness and very practical help is appreciated by all of us concerned with Botany here.

Apart from the class work we are getting a stage nearer doing some cytology. Lechmere has fixed up an electrically heated and controlled embedding bath and I am about to indulge myself in a Microtome – I think a Minot model by Leitz. The only serious difficulty we are faced with now is the scarcity of alcohol.

The picture of the lab which I send you [reproduced in the school prospectus for Autumn Term 1916] is not only a very poor view of the premises, but is also hopelessly faked – there ought to be a window where those empty shelves are! As you may judge, we suffer from extremes of temperature; but the lighting is surprisingly good. The class continues to grow both in numbers and in interest, and is a great source of pleasure and satisfaction to Lechmere and myself.

I hope you have had pleasant holidays and all return refreshed and prepared for the strains of term. Please thank Margery[492] very much for the greeting sent to me by the Old Bedalians, and to which she contributed. With my warmest regards to Mrs. Seward, my best wishes to you all, and again very many thanks for all your help with our work here,

Yours very sincerely,

Michael Pease

....

Ruhleben, Nov. 5th 1917

Dear Prof. Seward,

---

[492] Prof Seward's daughter, who went to Bedales School.

I am afraid I am writing once more to bother you for some botanical material for our work here. I have found someone here who is willing (and competent) to take a course on plant diseases, and it is a matter of providing spirit material for the practical work. You have been good enough to come to our rescue here in previous years, and therefore I am taking the liberty of trading once more on your kindness by asking you if you could get us a jar of diverse and sundry specimens. I had, as a matter of fact, written to Prof. Biffen [see correspondence below] in June last on the matter; but, as I have heard nothing, either the letter went astray or he has been too busy to attend to it. Lechmere also wrote to Prof. Tubeuf some time ago, but without producing any result. Therefore, as a last resort, I am writing to you, though I know only too well how many claims you already have on your time and attention. Perhaps if Mr. Brookes is still with you, he could put together some material. Large quantities are not necessary; but, as we have years of time, the class would be able to deal with a great diversity of stuff. If there are any difficulties with the Central Prisoners of War Committee in the matter, will you please write to my mother (Limpsfield, Surrey) who is an expert in dealing with that committee. I shall refrain from entering into a dissertation on the C.P. of W. committee, as I want to leave a few lines for general news!

We've been making great improvements in the Bi. lab. and have now a small library (over 600 vols) attached. We have at last managed to construct a really satisfactory electrically driven thermostat, specially designed to meet the appalling extremes of temperature in our lab. The Minot microtome has been doing valiant service and I'm much attached to it. Lechmere is working on the

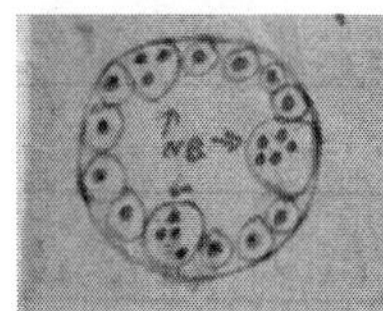

embryology of the common water snail and I'm trying to work out the spermatogenesis in the cabbage white butterfly, Pieris Brassicae. But one is miserably cut off from literature and authority when one starts on anything approaching research here. However the material is interesting and it's good practice for me. We keep on finding polynucleate spermatocytes (6, 7 or 8 nuclei where normally there is only one) and we don't know what to make of it. As we have no references here, I think I'll make some decent drawings and write to Doncaster[493] about it. I am getting a new microscope, which will, I hope, be a great joy to me. Do you know the Leitz Binocular with single objective model? It strikes me as a most attractive instrument. Steady work is very difficult here. The interruptions are awful and

[493] Prof Leonard Doncaster F.R.S., an English geneticist and a lecturer on zoology.

never enjoying any solitude is frightfully wearing. However, I personally manage to keep surprisingly good tempered through it all.

I've been very busy in the School garden this week. We are the proud possessors of the only lawn in camp; it is true is it not yet as good as a Cambridge Lawn, but I tend it carefully and try to make the place look like an ancient college court!

Barrack 6 (Camp School) garden, August 1917

I've just started reading a book of Hertwig's – *Das Werden der Organismen*[494] – which attracted great attention in the press here, but so far I haven't found anything new in it, but I must give it a fair chance. I've just sent for D'Arcy Thompson *On Growth and Form*[495] which sounds most attractive.

Well I'm afraid this is all very much about ego. I see *Nature* regularly, so I am more or less familiar with your activities at least in so far as they appear in its columns.

By the way, one very important matter on which I wanted to ask your advice. I have under my charge a youth aged 20 who wishes to study medicine at

---

[494] *The Origin of Organisms – a Refutation of Darwin's Theory of Chance*, published in 1916.

[495] Published in 1917. Its thesis was that biologists over-emphasised evolution and under-emphasised physical laws and mechanics as the determinants of the forms of living organisms.

Cambridge. He starts from scratch; is, I think only fairly clever (by no means brilliant). Now the question is, is there a tolerable chance of Greek being dropped for the Previous after the war? Would you advise him to chance it and work up his other subjects without overloading his program with Greek, which I know he'd find a bore? Of course if there is no chance of a change, he would be better to start his Greek now and let it slowly sink in. I should be most awfully obliged if you could advise me on this point.

I hope Mrs. Seward and all of you keep well and flourishing. Please give my kind regards to Mrs. Seward and remember me to your daughters. Like yourself, I expect they are all frightfully busy now. Again thanking you very much for all you have done in the past for us here, and with apologies for bothering you once more,

Yours sincerely

Michael Pease

....

Botany School, Cambridge

Dec. 11th 1917

Dear Pease,

I was very glad to have your letter and to hear that your class is still at work. I wrote to Newby[?] to ask him about material and we are now sending you such as we can share; I hope it will reach you and in good condition. Biffen I know has been here and is very busy so I did not ask him. If we have any difficulty with the box I will write as you suggest to Mrs. Pease. It is I think quite wonderful what you have been able to accomplish considering the conditions under which you live and work as regards lack of scientific periodicals, etc.

I was glad to have the proof[?] which is a particularly interesting record of Ruhleben. As regards Greek in the letter – so: my own view is that compulsory Greek will be given up after the war or it is just possible before the end of the war. I shall assume that it will go after the war and <u>very</u> soon after. Your friend need not – at least so I think but cannot speak with absolute certainty – get up Greek.

Let me know if the material reaches you.

With my best wishes,

Yours sincerely,

A.C. Seward

Correspondence from Professor Rowland Harry Biffen

Professor of Agricultural Botany at Cambridge and Director of the Plant Breeding Institute 1912–1936 (Michael's boss). Only letters from Biffen are available.

....

Royal Agricultural Society of England,

School of Agriculture, Cambridge

April 18th 1915

My dear Pease,

I have just got your letter. We will try to self-pollinate all of the parent plants and all the F1s.

If the weather keeps fine we shall probably manage to do it – if not I'm pretty sure that we shall only make half a job of it.

Parsons has worked through most of the F2s. I put in a day or two with him – just to get him more or less familiar with the work. The main outlines of the inheritance of most of the characters seems fairly simple. There is not as much of the "more or less" business as I anticipated. Even the lobing of the leaves is fairly clear. Colour is a bit difficult though, for many of the plants have the merest trace of purple. At first sight they are green but one finds colour in the midribs and so on. We've noted them down separately though.

The kohl-rabis look distinctly promising.

The tricarpellary broccolis stood the winter wonderfully well. We ought to get plenty of seed from them.

I'm not looking forward to sorting out the F2 of the broccoli crosses though. I once had the best part of an acre of them and made an awful hash of them. I got absolutely different counts each time I went over them!

The wheat crosses are doing very well in spite of all the wet. We have a lot of interesting stuff amongst them – but a lot of it has to wait over till next season. We couldn't finish the sorting in time. The barley is just coming up. Likewise the oats.

I have less time than ever for research now, thanks to the fact that I have to do all of my own demonstrating.

Your scholarship will be renewed all right. The Board [of Agriculture] are going on the principal that the scholarships are given for three years of research work and as you are not doing much in that line at present the time won't count.

We are just getting the laboratories ready for next term. Most of the senior staff are back now and I'm to send you all sorts of good wishes from them.

Yours,

R. H. Biffen

....

School of Agriculture, Cambridge

Dec. 13th 1915

My dear Pease,

You'll think it's about time I let you know how things were going in the Department! I'm a good correspondent – occasionally.

We managed to get a certain amount of seed from your plants though not as much as I hoped for. There was only time to put bags on the inflorescences [flower heads] and we couldn't do much in the way of artificial pollination. Some set freely enough but others were practically sterile. It isn't sown yet for I thought Hewitt was hardly competent to sort out the progeny and I've had to keep Armstrong on at the cereal crops. However it looks as if I might put it in in the spring. We had a good cereal harvest and I've put a new wheat and barley on the market as the result. There are several more growing on too – and some very promising F3s.

We ripened off a crop of maize too, wonderful to relate. Take it all round things are going very well. And now I've the usual report to write for the benefit of both houses of parliament. They must be mighty fond of reading reports from the number they seem to require. But they stipulate that no words of more than two syllables shall be used unless it's absolutely unavoidable – so probably they don't learn over-much from them.

Just had a long screed from Backhouse[496] on rust-resistance. He's getting some very pretty results out of it. Engledow[497] is out in India but I've no news of Trought.[498]

---

[496] William Ormston Backhouse, Michael's 3rd cousin, who worked at the Plant Breeding Institute.

[497] Frank Leonard Engledow, an agricultural botanist who worked for Biffen at the Plant Breeding Institute. Enlisted in the The Queen's Own Royal West Kent Regiment and served in India and Mesopotamia.

All good wishes from us both,

R. H. Biffen

....

School of Agriculture, Cambridge

Feb. 4th 1916

My dear Pease,

You seem to be running quite a Biological section at Ruhleben. I can't see how you would rig up a thermostat for embedding work, and I don't know of any make that could be sent through the post. To be satisfactory they want to be made on a large scale and filled with toluene. The ordinary mercury ones are not much use. You will have to learn the gentle art of cutting hand sections! I had to in my student days before microtomes were as common as they are now. If there's botanical material we can send for your classes let us know.

I'm rejoicing in your Roman hyacinths. We've given them a miss for several years owing to disease in the purchased bulbs. But there's any amount of flower stuff in the garden now. The mild weather has brought things on in an extraordinary fashion. We've even roses showing colour on the walls of the house. You are misinformed as to turnips! It's true we've dug up part of the lawn but the new space is devoted to roses. Madame [his wife] has the National Amateur Trophy in view much to my amusement. However she is shaping well for it and grows far better stuff than most people. If you imagine from this that the greenhouse is used for seedling roses you won't be very far out. Further, the motor house [garage?] contains much artificial manure and the paths are cut to pieces by Hewitt wheeling wads of "farmyard" to the beds for mulching. No we don't want any turnips thank you.

That Frenchman's broccoli is a first. It gives a tricarpellary pod now and then but you've got to hunt for them. But it's a rare good brocc. and there's any amount of seed saved. We are going to grow a plot for home consumption. Some of the heads last autumn must have weighed about seven pounds each and they were of excellent quality.

March 4th 1916 – Interval of a month. Not because I've been lazy but because I've been gadding about all over the country in the interval between lectures – inspecting endless samples of oats, barley etc. which the farmers are giving

---

[498] Trevor Trought, a botanist and graduate of St John's College, Cambridge, who also served with the West Kent Regiment.

their friends in the ruined areas of France. And I've seen many things which as Pepys used to say "pleased me mightily". Meanwhile we've had a healthy change in the weather, some frost and a heavy fall of snow. It seems to have come just in time to keep the fruit back sufficiently. The pear buds were plumping out too much and they've had a warning – without coming to any harm.

Dawson has been going to send that forestry syllabus you want but it hasn't reached me yet. I must go and dig it out of him.

We've got the end of term in sight – thank goodness. The whole place is very quiet now-a-days and it would be good for research if one hadn't so many jobs to attend to.

I heard from Engledow a week or so ago – he's in Rawal Pindi. Parsons is just home from Servia, very fit and quite cheerful; I've not head from Parker of late but his wife sends good news of him occasionally. Trought doesn't write but Pyke is bubbling with information. That's most of the news for a bit!

Yours sincerely

R. H. Biffen

....

School of Agriculture, Cambridge

Oct. 2nd 1916

My dear Pease,

I have been longer than I meant to be replying to your letter. As usual you will say! I gather that the problem of your microscope is fixed up satisfactorily now though. The Board are apparently willing to pay a part of your scholarship over to you, but it will come out of the sum due for the other year you still have to run. So don't draw too heavily on it! If it can be managed I shall try to sow the seed from your F1s and the first crossed seeds so that you will have material to go on with straight away when things become normal again.

We've had a fairly good year on the farm. Our crops were all well over the average and I've sold all the wheat for seed and already see a market for all the barley for the same purpose. But the harvest was a dragging affair and took a long time to get up satisfactorily. Now I want to break up some grassland or better still get some more arable. With a bigger area I think we could make the Institute practically self-supporting.

I've had to drop most of the frills in the way of research this season and grind away at purely economic stuff. However it's been enjoyable and the results are useful. The millers' problem of yield v strength seems solved for we've grown a huge crop of really strong stuff. The best parts of the yield must have been over 64 bushels per acre. It's a good corner to have turned. We are also getting on with the oats but so far I can't work up much enthusiasm for them.

Sad to say the roses were rather neglected this year. The missus has been out on the drug-giving ticket, investigating the possibilities of growing Hyoscyamus [henbanes] and Atropha [spurges?] with the result that the garden has been kept tidy but nothing special in the way of cultivation done. But there are symptoms – in the shape of long lists and plans for new beds – of a serious recrudescence in the immediate future.

Yes, we got a holiday all right though I didn't expect to. We stopped at the head of Dovedale and did a certain amount of walking, sketching and loafing – chiefly the later. But we didn't motor and I sadly missed the old bus. It suits my nomadic habits which always break out after a long spell in this part of the world!

Just got to get ready for an audit of the accounts so I'll dry up now and write later.

Yours sincerely

R. H. Biffen

....

School of Agriculture, Cambridge

May 15th 1917

Dear Pease,

Your letter has just come in. I didn't manage to get the seed sown this spring for our ordinary planting took too much time thanks to shortness of labour. But I must have a shot at it in the autumn if it can possibly be managed. It will be difficult, for the harvest will be a biggish job and, as far as I can see, I shall be away from Cambridge most of the time. I'll go up to the farm one day this week and sort out some of the seed for you. I haven't been there for a month! But I hear that things are going well and that the crops are better than usual. We've had an awful winter – cold drying winds and an inadequate covering of snow. The wheat looked miserable and at one time I thought we should lose a third of the crop. However it pulled round in an amazing fashion and if the season is anything like normal we shall get an over-average yield. The spring corn went in a bit late but it's caught up all right and looks well.

You must have had a cheerful winter of it. I can't fancy playing round with a microtome under such conditions!

So our government agricultural policy has penetrated to Ruhleben. It's a big thing and the extraordinary part of it all is that it's working. I didn't think the farmers could possibly tackle it but they just grunted and went at the job for all they were worth. They are breaking any amount of land up round here – some of it – along the edge of the fens, extraordinarily good stuff. Even Hatley Wilds [about 3km west of Wimpole Hall] is coming under the plough. I don't know whether you ever saw this district. It's the stiffest boulder clay I know and absolutely derelict. But the old stagers tell stories of the wheat it used to grow in the Crimea days and I fancy they are right. We shall know soon. I've fairly enjoyed the hustle but it's been somewhat of a change thinking in thousands of tons of wheat rather than in tiny packets. One of my mad-cap dreams has always been to double the wheat area in the country and now I fancy it's been done permanently.

[Sir Sydney] Olivier was no good at this sort of job. He was a past master of the old policy of sitting still and letting things slide so he had to give way to someone with a drive on. Now the place fairly hums.

I saw in one of the gardening papers that you'd started a Horticultural Society. It's a good idea. I wish I could pack my garden over to you by way of a nucleus for it. Just now it is glorious with alpine plants, the winter seems to have suited them for they are flourishing riotously. My pet gentians are sheer joy. We used to think a half dozen blooms of G. Verna were miraculous and now each plant is smothered with them. We've extended the garden a bit – taken in another quarter of an acre – and made a moraine. It looks a bit raw at present and will for a bit I suppose but one's got to put up with that if one wants to grow "niffy" things.

I'll see what can be done about the xylol.[499] I'm not very hopeful though for it's been exported in a more energetic form than we usually use it in for some time now! But there are still a few c.c. in the lab. and no one here uses it at present.

greetings from all of us –

Yours sincerely

R. H. Biffen

……………………

[499] See Appendix 3 for getting chemicals to Ruhleben.

RHB to Edward Reynolds Pease:

School of Agriculture, Cambridge

May 25th 1917

Dear Mr. Pease,

I do not know what quantities of absolute alcohol and xylol are contained in the tins supplied by Burroughs and Wellcome. You should aim at sending out about half a litre of each, and the same quantity of glycerin and of turpentine. This will probably last for some six weeks – judging from the rate of consumption here.

The wax referred to is paraffin wax. You should send out one pound of hard wax and a half pound of soft. This can be obtained from Townson and Mercer, 34 Camomile Street, E.C. These quantities will probably satisfy all needs for a twelve-month.

I hope you will be able to get them through to Ruhleben.

Yours very truly

R. H. Biffen

....

138 Huntingdon Road, Cambridge. [RHB's home address]

Jan. 6th 1918

My dear Pease,

I expect that you have been cussing me all ends up for not writing before this. Your letter took a long time in coming and then as luck would have it I was away and out of reach of posts.

Since then I've told myself a dozen times that next Sunday I would reply, somehow or other, but this is the first Sunday I've had energy enough to do so.

I'm afraid I let you down very badly over the fungus material you wanted for your classes. It was beyond me though. The laboratory stocks of a good many types were exhausted and there has been no chance to replace them; then we were practically out of tubes and last and worst my only lab-boy was a new importation fresh from an elementary school and thick in the head at that. I half thought of sending you some material of a species of Urophlyctis [plant pathogen] to work at but it struck me that the Ruhleben library would not be equal to the scanty literature on the group.

To make amends I am gradually getting together for you some F1 and some heterozygous [having two different forms of a gene] barleys which you can plant out and amuse yourself with as they come into flower. The splitters are drawn from F2 and F3 cultures and should be interesting. I only managed to make a start on them last week but I fancy I can see a few days leisure ahead now and I want to go for them strenuously.

It has been a busy time here this last six months or so. We have been stimulating agriculture a little and really got a move on the farmers now. We have bust up most of the grassland in the district and got it down to corn. You will not recognise agriculture when you get back. It has suddenly jumped from the horse to the motor age and every blessed type of petrol and paraffin engine has been called in to do the work. Even the redoubtable Henry Ford has forgotten his peace propaganda and turned out a plough which bids fair to rival his "flying bedstead" car. It is a fine thing, very cheap and capable of fifty acres a week under good conditions. On top of all this we went allotment mad and the movement turned out extraordinarily well. The season suited garden stuff wonderfully and every blessed man who ran an allotment is now wondering what to do with the produce. The boys from the various labs cultivated all the spare ground up to the Downing fence and made a wonderful job of it.

It was a real delight to get round amongst them when they were at work. If you had only seen Shrubbs, Stoakley and a few of the older ones demonstrating the best methods of putting the turf underneath to the younger fry you would have enjoyed life. They all became profound believers in deep cultivation and the smaller the boy the deeper he dug himself in.

I spent most of the late summer and early autumn scouring the country for pure stocks of wheat for distribution. I have always wanted to really see the crop and this time I did.[500] For a whole month we averaged over seventy miles a day on the roads and found time to inspect something like eight thousand acres. I am keen on driving but for the first time in my life I had nearly enough of it. All the same I hope that I may get the chance to do it again for it takes one off the main roads and one runs up against all sorts of interesting places which the guide books know not.

I have wished a hundred times that I had sent your F1 seeds out when you suggested it. We had not reckoned on Russia petering out quite so suddenly

---

[500] Biffen's improved varieties of wheat, resulting in the release of *Little Joss* in 1912, and *Yeoman* in 1916 set the standard for yield and quality until 1957.

though, and there seemed a good chance of your being back in time to sow here. Now they will have to wait till we get through with the job. I am off prophesying when that will be. We all go on the assumption that it may last forever and plot and plan accordingly. The people are wonderfully good and make light of their difficulties. The Missus says it's due to the fact that they never were so well off before and there seems to be a good deal in it.

The farming goes well now-a-days. I had no idea that How Hill was so good: we actually averaged 48 bushels with the wheat last season. The whole secret seems to be slag. Fields that had the reputation of being useless do really well with a fair dressing. But we are getting weedy and we cannot afford to fallow much at a time. We put up a silo this summer and now we are running fattening trials; silage versus roots. The bullocks are making a close fight for it but I fancy that roots will win.

As for pigs, we are the experts on the job now and put on half a crown a week on each of them. I want to salt one down but cannot spare the bath for a long enough period.

That seems to be about all of the news, such as it is!

Yours sincerely

R. H. Biffen

……………………

Correspondence from others

Adolf Engler to MSP:

Berlin-Dahlem,

12nd Nov. 1917

Very dear Sir,

Many thanks for being so kind as to send me the recent biography and the collection of letters of Charles Darwin who, like you, I hold in great respect. I am happy to hear that you have been able to make use of the plants I sent you from the botanical garden for your teaching at Ruhleben. I am prepared to send more plants in March and in the following months, but I would be even happier if we were into peace time by then.

Sincerely

A Engler

……………………

Professor Erwin Baur to MSP:

Institute for Agriculture,

Potsdam

11 January 1918

Dear Mr. Pease,

Thank you for your letter of 26th Nov. I apologise for the late reply, caused by the pressure of office work. It will be a pleasure for me to help you with the literature you asked for and the research material. I have put in a request at central command to allow you to visit me in the next few days in Potsdam or Berlin where I am giving lectures at the Institute of Agriculture on Thursdays from 4 to 6 pm.

I also enclose the recent numbers of the *Zeitschrift für induktive Abstammungs- und Vererbungslehre* [Journal for Inductive Science of Descent and Inheritance]. You can keep them until the beginning of February. For any requests concerning literature please do not hesitate to contact me.

With best regards, yours faithfully,

Erwin Baur

....

Professor Erwin Baur to MSP:

Institute of Genetics Research, Potsdam.

15th Oct. 1918

Dear Mr. Pease!

Many thanks for your letter of 29 September. I have only just moved into a new flat, so I haven't been able to reply sooner. Regarding the zoological material, I have contacted Prof. Hymons at the Zoological Institute of the Royal Agricultural College. The material you requested will be sent in a parcel and it will be ready for collection at the gate of the College by a representative of your camp.

The latest issues of *Zeitschrift für induktive Abstammungs- und Vererbungslehre*, nos. 17, 18, 19 and vol. 1 of no. 20 are bundled together in a parcel and on their way to you. Will you be so kind as to send them back after use to the address of the Institute. I would also be grateful to you if I could see the most recent editions of the *Journal of Genetics*. The last issue I had was vol. 4, no. 1.

At present it looks like a peace treaty could be on the way. I'm sure you will be glad if that period of boredom you had to go through at Ruhleben will be coming to an end.

With best wishes, yours sincerely,

E. Baur

....

William Bateson to MSP:

The John Innes Horticultural Institution, Mostyn Road, Merton, Surrey

28th Dec. 1918

Dear Pease,

We heard of course that you had been in Ruhleben – you must be thankful to get out after all. I am glad Baur made some effort, unsuccessful though it was.

Come and see me by all means. As at present planned, I mean to go to Cambridge on Wed Jan 1st probably returning on Mon morning; I may come back on Sat. Any day in the week beginning 5th Jan suits me except the 8th. Perhaps you would come for a night (no luggage). Probably we could do better so, but as you please.

Sunday 11th is perhaps too far off, or I would suggest that week-end.

Yours truly,

W. Bateson

....

Professor Erwin Baur to MSP (at the Cambridge School of Agriculture):

Potsdam, Sedanstrasse 7

16th Dec. 1919

Dear Mr. Pease,

Yesterday the food parcel which some time ago you said you would send me has arrived here. I thank you so much for your kindness. Since I personally do not suffer any hardship, I have shared out the contents among the gardeners of the institute, some of whom are in dire need. I find it a bit strange of the English nation that on the one hand they block the ports and the docks and thus cause a famine and a severe crisis in the big cities, and on the other they found charitable societies to organise food relief. My feeling is that England and France are spreading the seeds of evil. You have no idea how hatred and bitterness is growing among our people in regard of the extortion and the chicanery forced on us through this “peace treaty”.

In return for your parcel I am going to send you a copy of the latest edition of my “*Introduction*”.

With best wishes, yours sincerely,

Erwin Baur

....

Microscopy at Ruhleben, by Paulson, Lechmere and Pease

Article in the Journal of the Royal Microscopical Society, Volume 38, Issue 1, 1918

II.—*Microscopy at Ruhleben.*

By R. Paulson, F.R.M.S.

(*Read* November 21, 1917.)

Those who are acquainted with the internal government of the civilian camp at Ruhleben through letters and printed matter, received from interned relatives and friends, know already something of the educational work that has been going on there for the past two and a half years.

Prisoners have been permitted to send a copy of the prospectus of the work of the organized classes for each successive term, and the various numbers of the camp magazine.

As an introduction to the prospectus of work for the autumn term, 1916, we find among other notices the following:—

"In most subjects the tuition provided at the school ranges from that required by absolute beginners to that required by Advanced University Students."

"The Term consists of fourteen weeks; the total subscription of 3.50 marks should be paid in advance, if possible."

Roughly the camp is made up of students from the Public Schools and Universities, numbers of our best pioneers in commerce, trade and industry—men who had gone to health resorts.

Some five months ago Mr. E. J. Sheppard received a letter from Dr. Lechmere in reference to a paragraph in "Nature," respecting a slide exhibited at the Meeting in December 1916 of the Royal Microscopical Society.

It was the preparation of the anther of *Lilium candidum*, showing the extrusion of nuclear chromatin during mitosis in the pollen mother-cells.

As the letter was reported to the Council it was suggested that Dr. Lechmere should be communicated with, and that he should be asked to give some account of the microscopical work done in the camp.

A letter was written to this effect, and after a period of eighty-seven days an answer was received, together with a report by Mr. Michael Pease on "Biological Activities at Ruhleben."

Before reading the report it might be well to mention that the camp is situated on a bleak plateau on the site of the well-known race-course to the west of Berlin. This fact will account for the mention of betting-booth, hay-loft and grand-stand. The rigours of winter here are extreme. With inadequate heating it is impossible to carry on the necessary work of embedding and cutting with the microtome. Without knowing these facts the account of the equipment of the laboratory might conjure up a view of semi-luxuriance.

These men are living under most depressing conditions, and it is only due to a dogged determination to weather the storm that any scientific work is systematically carried on.

Letter from Dr. A. Eckley Lechmere to R. Paulson, F.R.M.S., dated August 14, 1917.

I am very pleased to supply further information as regards the microscopical equipment. When the laboratory started in the spring of 1915, we were fortunate enough to have several microscopes at our disposal. These were supplied by people in the Camp who had their instruments in Germany. I had been working at plant diseases in Munich with Prof. von Tubeuf, and at the cytology of sex in insects with Dr. Büchner, so I was fortunate in having both instruments and a certain amount of material at hand which Prof. von Tubeuf kindly sent me here. Since then several more instruments have been obtained by other students. We have now an excellent microscopical outfit for general laboratory work. The instruments include the following items:—

One Leitz binocular, two Leitz C, two Leitz GH, two Winkel, one Seibert, and one Nietsch, one Baker Diagnostic, and a set of eight dissecting lenses, two polariscopes, micrometer eye-pieces, camera lucida and microspectroscope, one Leitz Minot microtome.

For sitting accommodation we use a large deep bench, fitted under the windows in the wall of the loft. The windows themselves have been much enlarged, and this year we have had skylights let into the roof. For work in the evenings I have arranged a small transformer to work from the main electric supply, which gives sufficient current to run twenty 4-volt lamps; at the same time it can supply current for heating a small drying-box for the microtome slides, and is further used for an electric needle for orientation of sections in wax.

The general instruction in laboratory work and the preparation of lectures do not leave much time for original work. The only things I have attempted here have been a series of stages in the development of the Orange Scale Insect (*Aspidotus*), and a few preparations of a curious mite infesting the earwig. The body of each mite has a long stalk which forms a branching meshwork gradually covering the body of the host. I have never seen it before, and do not know the genus. During the months of May and June this year I kept a series of eggs of *Limnæa stagnalis*,

Planorbis corneus and *Valvata piscinalis* under observation for the early stages of development. I have a large number of eggs embedded for future cutting, after using pereny and acetic sublimate as fixing reagents. Towards the end of an egg-laying period in *L. stagnalis* I frequently found some of the egg-capsules with numerous eggs, up to fifteen in number, instead of the normal single egg. I also managed to hatch out several cases of two embryos from one capsule. A curious incident occurred with the aquarium in which there were specimens of *P. corneus*, and the only specimen of *Paludina vivipara* I have been able to find. One night five of these snails, including the *Paludina*, were dragged out of the aquarium and devoured by a rat. The aquarium is now removed to a safer place for protection from further invasion.

Report on Biological Activities in Ruhleben. From Michael S. Pease, B.A. Cantab., dated August 14, 1917.

The first outward sign of biological activity in Ruhleben appeared in the spring of 1915, when Dr. A. E. Lechmere started a series of lectures on Elementary Biology. These were held in a disused betting-booth, and attended by half-a-dozen enthusiasts. In the summer, one of the grand-stands was set aside for lectures, and Dr. Lechmere continued his course on the Protozoa, while I contributed a course of twenty lectures on Heredity. At Christmas, 1915, the loft of Barracks 6 became available for educational purposes, and the first weeks of the new year saw the conversion of a corner of a somewhat dilapidated hay-loft into a biological laboratory. By the end of January the accommodation for eight microscopes was provided. The necessary glass-ware and reagents were got in from Messrs. Leitz, and practical botany, of a necessarily elementary character, was started with twenty-one students.

In the following terms regular lecture courses in botany were given by myself, and the corresponding practical work was of a more thorough and extensive nature. The ground covered has been as follows:—

Bryophytes and Pteridophytes (Summer, 1916).
Gymnosperms (Autumn, 1916).
Algæ (Lent, 1917).
Angiosperms (Summer, 1917).

Spirit material was kindly presented to us by Prof. A. C. Seward, Dr. Darbishire, and Prof. Tubeuf.

We are indebted to Prof. Engler for a weekly supply of flowers from the Kgl. Botanischer Garten, Dahlem, for the systematic course. A pond within the race-course has been our source of fresh material for Algæ and Protozoa.

The equipment of the laboratory has been continuously improved. A cable was laid on to give us electric current day and night. A transformer was constructed on the premises, and each microscope provided with a 4-volt lamp for work after dark.

Several electrically heated incubators were also fitted up, and last Easter permission was obtained to put in sky-lights and to fit up a water-supply.

With the possibility of a continuous source of heat, we were able to consider paraffin embedding.

Serious difficulty has been encountered in the construction of a satisfactory automatic electric thermostat for the embedding bath. We have recently secured a Hearson's capsule, and an improved model of embedding bath is now being made. Nevertheless, a considerable quantity of material has been satisfactorily embedded, and a beginning is being made with the technique of Cytology. Last Christmas a first-class microtome (Minot model by Leitz, cutting to 1μ) was purchased, but the rigours of the winter, followed almost instantly by those of a phenomenally hot May and June, has made it impossible to start microtomy until recently.

It has been impossible to do practical work in Zoology, but Dr. Lechmere's lectures have continued to draw an enthusiastic band of students. His course so far has covered :—

Protozoa (one term).
Cœlenterata (one term).
Vermes (three terms).
Echinodermata (one term).

And he has just finished the second term of his course on Mollusca.

At the same time, he has also started a course on Invertebrate Embryology. Animal physiology has been very exhaustively treated (again only theoretically) by Mr. S. R. Edge, B.A. Cantab. Practical instruction has been given in the testing of agricultural seeds by Mr. A. Hill, B.Sc. Aberdeen, and for this course a large electrically-heated incubator was constructed.

This summer new space was alloted to Science, and this was made use of to accommodate a library, shared jointly by the biologists, chemists, and physicists. The library provides seating accommodation for working, and contains over 500 volumes, mostly the property of the science staff, but many also supplied by the Board of Education.

At present "Nature" is at once our only periodical and only link with scientific activity outside.

Appendix 3. Correspondence about parcels

....

(13162/P/1250)

The Secretary of the Prisoners of War Department presents his compliments to Mrs. Pease, and is directed by Lord Newton[501] to acknowledge the receipt of her letter of the 15th instant respecting the regulations in connection with the despatch of parcels to civilian prisoners of war in Germany.

The Secretary is to state that the matter in question is under consideration, and that a further communication will be addressed to Mrs. Pease in due course.

PRISONERS OF WAR DEPARTMENT,

DOWNING STREET, S.W.1

25th January, 1917.

....

(22481/1250/P)

The Secretary of the Prisoners of War Department presents his compliments to Mrs. Pease and is directed by the Controller to refer to the letter from this Department of the 25th ultimo, regarding the regulations for the despatch of parcels to civilian prisoners of war in Germany.

The Secretary is to state that there is no objection to the articles, mentioned in Mrs. Pease's letter of the 15th ultimo being sent to her son in Ruhleben through the Central Prisoners of War Committee, except that blankets are prohibited for reasons connected with the blockade.

The Secretary is to add that the Central Prisoners of War Committee regret that the parcel mentioned above was returned to Mrs. Pease, owing to a mistake.

PRISONERS OF WAR DEPARTMENT,

DOWNING STREET, S.W.1

February 2nd 1917

---

[501] Lord Newton (Thomas Legh, 2nd Baron Newton) who was appointed Controller of the newly established Prisoner of War Department in October 1916.

....

29 Eaton Place, London S.W.

February 16th, 1917

Dear Mrs. Pease,

I will worry the war office with pleasure about sending things to Ruhleben. The War Office is perfectly hopeless in every way. Their stupidity and narrow-mindedness is beyond belief.

Yours sincerely

Henry Bentinck[502] [Lord Henry Cavendish-Bentinck]

....

(99226/1218/P)

The Secretary of the Prisoners of War Department presents his compliments to Mr. E. R. Pease, and is directed by the Controller to acknowledge the receipt of his letter of the 14th respecting the despatch to his son, a prisoner of war at Ruhleben of materials for research work in Biology.

Lord Newton is disposed to give favourable consideration to Mr. Pease's application for a permit to export the materials in question, and the Secretary is therefore to request Mr. Pease to forward to this Department a list giving the quantities of the various materials which he desires to send monthly to Mr. Michael Pease.

PRISONERS OF WAR DEPARTMENT,

DOWNING STREET, S.W.1

23rd May, 1917.

....

ERP to The Secretary, Prisoners of War Department, Downing Street, S.W.1

The Pendicle, Limpsfield, Surrey

29th May, 1917

Ref. (99226/1218/P)

---

[502] An article in the *Evening Despatch* on 9th February 1917 states that Lord Bentinck will raise the question in the House of Commons about the growing pressure from relatives and friends of Ruhleben prisoners to exchange them for all the German civilians in the UK.

Sir,

I am obliged for you letter of 23rd May stating that Lord Newton is disposed to give favourable consideration to my application for permission to send chemicals to my son in Ruhleben. I have been enquiring how the chemicals in question are supplied, and of Professor Biffen what quantities should be sent. According to his advice, my son should have:–

1 lb. (about a pint) of Absolute alcohol

1 lb. (about a pint) of Xylol

1 pint of Glycerine

1 pint of Turpentine

These, Professor Biffen states, should last about 6 weeks.

1 lb. Paraffin wax, hard.

½ lb. Paraffin wax, soft.

These should last a year.

In view of the uncertainty of the posts perhaps I might have an order to send the first four monthly, but I shall be satisfied, if it seems better to you, for once in 6 weeks.

I am, Sir,

Yours Faithfully

E.R.Pease

....

The Secretary, Prisoners of War Department, Downing Street, S.W.1 to ERP:

5th June, 1917

Ref 107863/1218/P

Sir,

I am directed by Lord Newton to transmit to you herewith a copy of correspondence, as marked in the margin [vis: From Mr. Pease 14th May ref 99226, to Mr. Pease 23rd May ref 99226, From Mr. Pease 29th May ref 107863], respecting the despatch to Ruhleben of materials for research work on Biology.

I am to state that the Committee are authorised to despatch at once the quantities desired by Mr. Pease and if the first consignments are duly delivered, to despatch the same quantities of absolute Alcohol, Xylol, Glycerine and Turpentine every six weeks until further notice.

It is requested that this Department may be informed of the date and method of consignment in order that steps may be taken to check the delivery of the first consignment.

A copy of this letter is also being sent to the Chief Postal Censor.

I am, Sir,

The Secretary,

Central Prisoners of War Committee.

....

(107863/1218/P)

The Secretary of the Prisoners of War Department presents his compliments to Mr. E. R. Pease, and, with reference to his letter of the 29th ultimo, is directed by the Controller to transmit herewith a copy of a letter which has been addressed to the Central Prisoners of War Committee respecting the despatch to his son at Ruhleben of materials for research work in Biology.

Mr. Pease will observe that the Committee have been authorised to despatch the articles in question, and it is suggested that Mr. Pease should communicate with the Committee with regard to the purchase of the items.

PRISONERS OF WAR DEPARTMENT,

DOWNING STREET, S.W.1

5th June, 1917.

....

ERP to The Secretary, Prisoners of War Department, Downing Street, S.W.1:

6th June, 1917

Ref. 107863/1218/P

Dear Sir,

I beg to acknowledge, with many thanks, receipt of letter intimating that permission has been granted for the dispatch of the chemicals required by my son who is a prisoner in Ruhleben.

I am,

Yours faithfully

E.R. Pease

....

Appendix 3

ERP to The Secretary, Central Prisoners of War Committee, Thurloe Place, S.W.7

6th June, 1917

Dear Sir,

The Secretary of the Prisoners of War Department, Downing Street, has sent me a copy of his letter addressed to you dated the 5th inst., and numbered 107863/1218/P, authorising you to send to my son, Michael S. Pease, Baracke XI, Box 17, Ruhleben, the chemicals he requires for microscopic research, as indicated in my letters, copies of which you have received.

May I ask you to inform me at once whether you will purchase the articles in question yourself, or whether I shall procure them and hand them over to you for transmission.

A week or so ago I saw one of the principals of British Drug Houses Ltd., 22-30 Graham Street, City Road, E.C., who informed me that absolute alcohol and xylol must be put in bottles and packed in closed tins for transmission abroad, and they kindly undertook to do this for me if they received the order, on my behalf, through a retail agent. No doubt they could supply the whole of the goods required but Professor Biffen gave me the name of another firm where I could procure the sort of wax required. This name I have not with me now.

As the matter has taken a long time to reach the present stage, your prompt attention will oblige,

Yours faithfully,

E.R. Pease

....

BRITISH RED CROSS SOCIETY. | THE ORDER OF ST. JOHN OF JERUSALEM IN ENGLAND.

CENTRAL PRISONERS OF WAR COMMITTEE.

The Rt. Hon. Sir STARR JAMESON, Bart., C.B., Chairman
A. C. DUFF, Esq., Secretary

Cheques should be made payable to Sir Starr Jameson, and crossed Barclay & Co., not negotiable.

Telegrams: Prisoners, South Kensington, London
Telephone: Kensington 7040.

Nearest Stations: BROMPTON ROAD TUBE. SOUTH KENSINGTON.

Please reply to:
THE SECRETARY,
Central Prisoners of War Committee,
and quote V.W/V.A.

4, THURLOE PLACE,
[Nearly opposite the Brompton Oratory]
LONDON, S.W.

Special Department.

June 8th 1917

Edward Pease, Esq.,
25, Tothill Street,
Westminster,
S.W.1

Dear Sir,

In reply to your letter of the 6th instant we heard a couple of days previously from the Secretary of the Prisoners of War Department, and when your letter came we had already written to the Army & Navy Stores, Victoria Street, asking them if they could supply the chemicals required by your son. We have not yet had a reply from them and will let you know directly we hear. Our reason for selecting the Army & Navy Stores was that this firm is one of our authorised shops and therefore they would be able to pack and despatch the chemicals under Red Cross Label direct to your son. A special arrangement will have to be made if the goods cannot be sent from one of our authorised shops.

Yours faithfully,

L. IMPEY
Lt. Colonel

Secretary
p.p. V.W.

Central Prisoners of War Committee to ERP:

4 Thurloe Place, London S.W.7

29th June 1917.

Ref. EMC/LB.

Dear Sir,

In answer to your letter of the 28th instant, we have been informed by the Army and Navy Co-operative Society that they are able to despatch the Chemicals authorised by the Prisoners of War Department, and we have instructed them to despatch same as soon as possible.

Yours faithfully,

L. IMPEY,

Lieut. Colonel.

Secretary, p.p.

....

ERP to The Secretary, Prisoners of War Department, Downing Street, S.W.1.

9th July, 1917

Dear Sir,

Ref. 107863/1218/P.

In reference to the above correspondence, Mrs. Pease has just received the following postcard:–

(From) Michael Pease, Baracke XI, Box 17, Ruhleben.
June 16th, 1917.
Delighted to hear about the reagents. The minimum quantities are as follows:-

Absolute Alcohol	½ litre
96% "	½ litre
70% "	1 litre
Xylol	½ litre
Clove oil	¼ litre

Should be sent in sealed tins. Please send twice the above quantities in the first parcel.

The Central Prisoners of War Committee, in response to enquiries, wrote to me on June 29th that they had not yet despatched the first lot of chemicals (!) but had instructed them to be sent as soon as possible.

The above list differs substantially from the list supplied me by Professor Biffen, in accordance with which your instructions were given to the Central Prisoners of War Committee. The card does not state the period of the parcels contemplated, but I understand them to be once a month, as that was the proposal you originally accepted, and the six weeks period was suggested later by Professor Biffen.

I write now to ask if it would be possible for you to have the order to the Central Prisoners of War Committee varied to meet my son's desires? I should add that a half litre is about equivalent to 1 lb., and alcohol and Xylol are sold by weight here. For clove oil, 1 quarter litre is about half a pint.

I am, sir,

Yours faithfully,

Edward R Pease

....

Central Prisoners of War Committee to ERP:

4 Thurloe Place, London S.W.7

July 18th 1917

Ref V.W/V.A.

Special Department

To Edward R Pease, Esq., 25 Tothill Street, S.W.1 [Fabian Society headquarters]

Dear Sir,

We have had a further communication from the Prisoners of War Department, Downing Street, with regard to the chemicals to be sent to Mr. Michael Pease at Ruhleben. As the matter is rather complicated we should be very much obliged if you could call at this office any day between 11a.m. and 5p.m. so that we can settle this matter satisfactorily. We are very sorry that the first lot of chemicals have not yet been despatched to Mr. Pease, this was owing to a misunderstanding in this office.

Yours faithfully,

L. IMPEY.

Lt. Colonel.

Secretary. p.p.

....

Appendix 3

Central Prisoners of War Committee to ERP:

4 Thurloe Place, London S.W.7

July 23rd 1917

Ref V.W/V.A.

Special Department

To Edward R Pease, Esq., Cote Bank, Westbury-on-Trym, Bristol.

Dear Sir,

In reply to your letter of the 21st instant, the position about the chemicals is as follows:-

On June 29th the order was given to the Army & Navy Stores and we only learnt last week from the American Express Company that the goods had not yet gone through. We have now been in communication with the Army & Navy Stores and find that their difficulty is they have not yet been able to obtain the Xylol. They have sent a special messenger to the City today to try once again if they can procure it and they are to inform us directly, and if they cannot get it, we will endeavour ourselves to do so. Of course if they had informed us sooner that there would be this special difficulty about Xylol we would have taken steps in the matter. We regret the delay exceedingly, but you will understand that once a definite order to the Army & Navy Stores had been given the matter was thought to be completed.

The following is a list of the quantities we shall in future send monthly to Mr. Michael Pease, and we shall be glad to hear from you if they are correct.

Absolute Alcohol	½ litre
96% "	½ "
70% "	1 "
Xylol	½ "
Clove Oil	¼ "
Glycerine	1 pint
Turpentine	1 pint

If this is not what you wish please let us know.

We think you may be interested to see the enclosed statement which was handed to us by Dr. K. E. Markel, 20 Queen's Gate Terrace, S.W. Dr. Markel [who ran the Prisoners of War Relief Agency] takes a great interest in prisoners both here and in Germany, and we think it possible that you may like to get into communication with him.

Yours faithfully,

L. IMPEY.

Lt. Colonel.

Secretary. p.p.

....

(159878/1218/P)

The Secretary of the Prisoners of War Department presents his compliments to Mrs. Pease and is directed by the controller to refer to her letter of the 30th ultimo relative to a consignment of chemicals for her husband [*sic*] at Ruhleben.

The Controller is informed that it was stated in error in a letter from the Central Prisoners of War Committee that the delay in despatching the chemicals was due to a misunderstanding in their office, and that in reality it was occasioned solely by the inability of the Army and Navy Stores to procure the Xylol required.

The Secretary is to add that the materials were despatched upon July 25th as soon as they were received from the Stores.

It is understood that the matter has already been explained to Mr. Pease when he called at No. 4, Thurloe Place.

PRISONERS OF WAR DEPARTMENT,

DOWNING STREET, S.W.1

20th August, 1917.

....

Appendix 4. Release petitions

....

Martin Lutherstr 59

Berlin Schöneberg,

9 February 1915

Dear Frau Paky

Hearty thanks for your friendly communication. I beg that you will send the following information to Mrs. Pease as soon as possible.

We have continued our efforts on behalf of Michael and believe we have made a step forward. Mrs. Pease should get into touch with Herr Marc Muller, 47 Brondesbury Park, N.W. He is the representation of Herr Wulfing whose son is in London. If this young man has the same work as Michael, Mrs. Pease could speak to Mr. Acland[503] and then let us know what the latter is prepared to do. We, that is my husband, will then approach the German Government. We assume that both Governments will make the conditions which are usual in such cases. At the same time please convey to Mr. and Mrs. Pease our hearty greetings.

[no name or signature]

....

ubiaja via. Sapele., S. Nigeria

22-5-16

Dear Mrs. Pease,

It would interest me very much to know how your son is getting on. I suppose that he is still at Ruhleben, as he is far too robust to be included in any category of persons unfit for military service.

I have received letters from various people asking me to use an influence which I entirely lack to further a scheme under which prisoners from both countries should be allowed to reside in Switzerland under the guarantees of their own and the Swiss authorities that they should not attempt to return to their own countries until the end of the war. There seems to be no doubt in my

---

[503] Francis Dykes Acland; Liberal MP for Camborne, Under Secretary for Foreign Affairs 1911-15 and in June 1915 appointed Parliamentary Secretary to the Board of Agriculture and Fisheries.

mind that such an arrangement would be quite practicable at least for certain classes of civil prisoners. In fact I understand that French and German sick military prisoners have already been handed over to the Swiss Government during convalescence under an arrangement of mutual guarantees.

As you are in touch with public affairs at home perhaps it would be possible for those who are interested in the fate of the Ruhleben prisoners to get into touch with one another, form a strong committee to prepare the ground in the press and then interview the Foreign and Home Office as well as the War Office authorities and subsequently also the Diplomatic representatives of the U.S.A. and the Swiss Federation. The branch of the Geneva Society which has done so much for prisoners of war of all nations might also be able to assist in formulating a scheme.

There should be no difficulty in framing one which would not clash with the interests of any party concerned. It seems needless to dwell on the amount of unnecessary suffering which such a mutual agreement might relieve.

Believe me, with kind regards to your son,

yours sincerely,

Edward M Falk[504]

....

The Pendicle, Limpsfield, Surrey

11th Aug. 1916

Dear Commander Wedgwood,

I am so grateful to you for your kind letter and for the very prompt and practical steps you have taken to urge the Government to clear out all Germans now.

I know you carry great weight in the House and your question will help matters greatly. I have a letter from Michael written on July 16th. He never under any circumstances would whine, and he always could make the best of things for my sake, but I know how he suffers mentally and he once said "the hideousness of the place was enough to drive one mad".

Please do ask you daughter to write to him again. Her letter gave him real pleasure. He told me that she seemed to realise exactly how he felt.

---

[504] Edward Morris Falk (1878–1946), a District Commissioner in Nigeria who, with Geoffrey Pyke, escaped from Ruhleben in July 1915.

With heartfelt thanks

yours sincerely

Marjory Pease

....

Foreign Office,

August 11th, 1916.

(P.1218/16).

Dear Acland,

In reply to your note to Rumbold[505] of the 7th enclosing a letter from Mrs. Pease, I do not think that for the moment we can say more than that the Government are doing their utmost to obtain the release of all the Ruhleben prisoners, and that proposals have been put before the German Government which will bring this about – if we can get them accepted by the other side. I am sure you will let Mrs. Pease understand that, so far as we are concerned, no stone is being left unturned to attain this happy result.

Unless I hear from you to the contrary, I am keeping Mrs. Pease's letter in our files.

Yours sincerely

[illegible]

....

R S Langford (Board of Agriculture and Fisheries) to MGP:

Board of Agriculture and Fisheries

4, Whitehall Place, S.W.

15th August, 1916.

Dear Madam,

Mr. Acland asks me to send on the enclosed note [above] which he has received from the Foreign Office, which he is sure you will like to see.

Yours faithfully,

R S Langford[506]

---

505 Possibly Sir Horace Rumbold, the F.O. attaché to Berlin in 1913-14, then Berne.

506 Robert Squire Langford, Secretary to the Agriculture and Fisheries Board.

....

Robert Cecil to Gershom Stewart:

August 15th, 1916.

My dear Gershom Stewart,[507]

I greatly sympathise with Mrs. Pease in her desire to obtain the release of her son from Ruhleben. As you know, we have now proposed to the German Government that all civilian prisoners over 45 shall be exchanged, and that the British prisoners under 45 should be exchanged for an equal number of Germans interned in this country. I trust that this will lead to the release of all our prisoners.

I am afraid that the Government cannot contemplate exchanging the British civilians in Germany for all the Germans here, as to do so would make the Germans a present of at least a division of men of military age to be used to fight our troops in the field.

Yours sincerely,

Robert Cecil[508]

Gershom Stewart to MGP:

17 Aug. 1916

My dear Cousin,

The enclosed letter [above] will show you that I done something - however little it may be - for your boy Michael, and I earnestly hope that he won't have to spend another winter in Ruhleben. I told Lord Robert that Michael belonged to very important folk! I am quite certain that he will do what he can to get him back.

Yours very sincerely,

Gershom Stewart

You can keep the letter

....

Robert Cecil to Gershom Stewart MP:

---

[507] Gershom Stewart, M.P. for Wirral 1910 to 1923. A distant cousin of Marjory Pease.

[508] Lord Robert Cecil, Under-Secretary of State for Foreign Affairs, 1915-1919.

November 3rd, 1916

My dear Stewart,

Very many thanks for your letter of November 2nd respecting Mrs. Pease's son.

As you doubtless know by now the Foreign Office have severed all connection with prisoners questions, which are now under the control of Lord Newton [Prisoners of War Department], to whom I am passing your letter asking him to consider it carefully.

Yours sincerely,

Robert Cecil

[The following handwritten note was added when this letter was forwarded to Marjory]:

Cousin – for your information!

I will see that Lord Newton does not lose sight of your boy. G

....

(220689/1218/P).

The Secretary of the Prisoners of War Department presents his compliments to Mr. Gershom Stewart and is directed by Lord Newton to reply to Mr. Stewart's letter to Lord R. Cecil of the 2nd instant, respecting the question of the transfer to Switzerland of British civilians of military age interned in Germany.

The Secretary is to explain that the German Government would no doubt refuse to transfer to Switzerland all the British subjects of military age interned in Germany on a strictly reciprocal basis and that they would stipulate that all German civilians of military age in the United Kingdom should be sent to Switzerland.

The transfer to Switzerland of the British subjects concerned would be comparatively easy for the German Government to effect but the transfer of the Germans to Switzerland from this country would present great difficulties at a time when all available ships and rolling stock are required by the Allies for the transport of troops and ammunition and for other essential purposes. There are also strong military objections to the internment of civilians in any country contiguous to Germany.

The negotiations for the exchange of the British and German civilians over forty five are not yet finally concluded and when concluded the transport of the men from this country to Holland and vice versa will require some time to effect.

Even on the assumption that the difficulties in the way of the transport of the Germans under forty five to Switzerland could be overcome, it would be undesirable to make any fresh proposals to the German Government until the repatriation of the older men has been accomplished.

Lord Newton is however most anxious to secure the release from Germany of all British civilians interned there and will do all he can as far as the interests of the country permit to bring this about.

The Secretary is to add that proposals have been made to the German Government which, if accepted, should result in some improvement in the machinery for repatriating British and German civilians who are invalids.

FOREIGN OFFICE.

November 20th, 1916.

....

Appendix 5. Family trees

In the following family trees, generations are indicated by numbers and indents. The + sign indicates marriage. Names in bold italic font are relatives mentioned in the diaries, letters or footnotes. Where a person was known by their second name this is underlined, and when known by another name this is in brackets.

Michael Stewart Pease's family (maternal side)

1-Rev George Smyttan Davidson (1816-1901) of Kinfauns Manse, Perthshire
+***Mary Gammell Stewart*** (1830-1923)
2-George Harcourt Davidson (1856-1880)
2-James Stewart Davidson (1858-1950)
+Agnes Finlayson McLaren (1862-1934)
3-George Stewart Davidson (1892-1960)
3-Peter McLaren Davidson (1902-1993)
2-Harcourt Morton Davidson (1860-1926)
+Jane Primrose Wylie Hutchinson (1864-1952)
2-***Mary (Marjory) Gammell Davidson*** (1861-1950)
+***Edward Reynolds Pease*** (1857-1955)
3-**Michael Stewart Pease** (1890-1966)
3-***Nicolas Arthington Pease*** (1894-1984)
2-John (Jack) Stewart Davidson (1863-1952)
+***Marie Louise Heuston*** (1883-1953)
3-Mary E A Davidson (1919-1922)
2-female Davidson (1865 - stillborn)
2-William Smyttan Davidson (1867-1906)
+***Catherine (Kate) Alice Riach*** (1869-1952)
3-***George William Smyttan Davidson*** (1897-1916)
3-***Mary Gammell Stewart Davidson*** (1900-1970)
3-***Betty Kathleen Riach Davidson*** (1904-1962)
2-***Roger Stewart Davidson*** (1869-1955)
+***Janet Drummond McLaren*** (1872-1955)
3-***Roger Alastair McLaren Davidson*** (1900-1983)
3-***John (Jack) Harcourt Stewart Davidson*** (1903-1964)
2-Andrew Gammell Davidson (1872-1907)
+Annie Reade (1874-1917)
3-***Reginald Harcourt Davidson*** (1900-1982)
3-***Ralph Stewart Davidson*** (1902-1977)
3-***Beatrice Davidson*** (1903-1978)
3-Gordon Davidson (1906-1993)

Appendix 5

Michael Stewart Pease's family (paternal side)

1-Thomas Pease (1816-1884) of Cote Bank, Westbury-on-Trym, Bristol
+Lucy Fryer (1820-1844)
2-***Katharine Aldam Pease*** (1843-1920)
+Thomas Hanbury (1832-1907)
3-Cecil Hanbury (1871-1937)
3-Hilda Beatrice Hanbury (1872-1939)
3-Daniel Hanbury (1876-1948)
3-Horace Hanbury (1880-1939)
2-Lucy Ann Pease (1844-1910)
+Robert Robinson (1838-1915)
3-***Enid Lucy Pease Robinson*** (1881-1975)
+Martha Lucy Aggs (1824-1853)
2-Mary Gertrude Pease (1851-1909)
+George Dymond (1828-1873)
3-Sylvia Dorothea Dymond (1873-1931)
2-Margaret Pease (1852-1913)
+***Jonathan Hogg*** (1847-1930)
2-***Thomas Henry Ormston Pease*** (1853-1937)
+Mary Ellis Cave (1866-1945)
3-***Eleanor Mary Pease*** (1889-1976)
3-Thomas Ormston Cave Pease (1890-1974)
3-***Margaret Barbara Pease*** (1892-1966)
+***Susanna Ann Fry*** (1829-1917)
2-***Edward Reynolds Pease*** (1857-1955)
+***Mary (Marjory) Gammell Davidson*** (1861-1950)
3-**Michael Stewart Pease** (1890-1966)
3-***Nicolas Arthington Pease*** (1894-1984)
2-***Marian (May) Fry Pease*** (1859-1954)
2-***Rosa Elizabeth Pease*** (1860-1951)
2-***William Benson Pease*** (1861-1953)
+Bessie Mary Nicholas (1861-1894)
+***Mary Ann (Nancy) Hutchinson Swanton*** (1870-1950)
3-Dora (Dolly) Ann Swanton Pease (1898-1997)
3-Mary Elizabeth Pease (1901-1993)
2-***Joseph Gerald Pease*** (1863-1928)
+***Winifred Amy Hudleston*** (1872-1943)
3-Anne Purefoy Rosa Pease (1906-1977)
3-Monica Dionis Hudleston Pease (1909-1987)
2-Robert Aldam Pease (1864-1946)
+Grace Constance Begbie (1880-1949)
3-Jocelyn Susan Pease (1909-1996)
3-Robert Charles Pease (1919-1997)
2-***Anna Dorothea (Dora) Pease*** (1865-1955)
+***Charles Percy Sanger*** (1871-1930)
3-Daphne Theodora Sanger (1905-1991)
2-Caroline (Cara) Susan Pease (1866-1908)
+John Bright Clark (1867-1933)
3-John Anthony Clark (1908-1985)
2-***Cyril Arthington Pease*** (1868-1923)
+***Margaret (Peggie) Russell Heath*** (1867-1917)
+Lily Page (1890-1980)
2-***Oswald Allen Pease*** (1871-1917)
+Evangeline Agnes Begbie (1881-1966)
3-Mary Evangeline (Lallie) Margaret Pease (1908-2006)
3-Thomas Exham Vincent Pease (1910-1964)
3-Charles Ormston Hugh Pease (1910-1989)
3-Roger Begbie Pease (1913-2005)

1-Hannah Pease (1814-1866) of Adel Grange, Leeds
+Robert Lawson Ford (1809-1878)
2-***Elizabeth (Bessie) Helen Ford*** (1848-1919)
2-***Emily Susan Ford*** (1850-1930)
2-***Isabella Ormston Ford*** (1855-1924)
2-five other children

Helen Bowen Wedgwood's family

1-Clement Francis Wedgwood (1840-1889) of Barlaston Lea, Stoke-on-Trent
+Emily Catherine Rendel (1840-1921)
2-Francis (Frank) Hamilton Wedgwood (1867-1930)
+Katharine Gwendoline Pigott (1868-1958)
3-Frances Dorothy Joy Wedgwood (1903-1996)
3-Cicely Stella (Star) Wedgwood (1904-1995)
3-Clement Tom Wedgwood (1907-1960)
2-Clement Henry Wedgwood (1870-1871)
2-***Josiah Clement Wedgwood*** (1872-1943)
+***Ethel Kate Bowen*** (1869-1952)
3-**Helen Bowen Wedgwood** (1895-1981)
3-***Rosamund Wedgwood*** (1896-1960)
3-***Francis Charles Bowen Wedgwood*** (1898-1959)
3-***Josiah Wedgwood*** (1899-1968)
3-***Camilla Hildegarde Wedgwood*** (1901-1955)
3-Elizabeth Julia Wedgwood (1907-1993)
3-Gloria Wedgwood (1909-1974)
+Florence Ethel Willett (1878-1969)
2-Ralph Lewis Wedgwood (1874-1956)
+Iris Veronica Pawson (1887-1982)
3-John Hamilton Wedgwood (1907-1989)
3-Ralph Pawson Wedgwood (1909-1909)
3-Cicely Veronica Wedgwood (1910-1997)
2-Cicely Frances Wedgwood (1876-1904)
+Arthur Wigram Money (1866-1951)
2-***Arthur Felix Wedgwood*** (1877-1917)
+***Katharine Longstaff Longstaff*** (1880-1976)
3-Katharine Frances Wedgwood (1912-2004)
3-Felicity Emily Wedgwood (1913-2003)
3-Cecil Felix Neville Wedgwood (1916-1996)
1-Godfrey Wedgwood (1833-1903) of Idle Rocks, Moddershall, Staffordshire
+Mary Jane Jackson Hawksaw (1836-1863)
2-Cecil Wedgwood (1863-1916)
+Lucie Gibson (1864-1939)
3-***Phoebe Sylvia Wedgwood*** (1893-1972)
3-***Doris Audrey Wedgwood*** (1894-1969)
1-five other children

Appendix 6. Sources

Selected web resources

The Ruhleben Story – http://ruhleben.tripod.com

Hoover Institute – https://digitalcollections.hoover.org/search/ruhleben/null/list

Leeds Library Special Collections – https://explore.library.leeds.ac.uk/special-collections-explore?query=ruhleben&selection=

RHS Linday library archive – https://archiveshub.jisc.ac.uk/search/archives/59079105-fa9a-3b97-a7d1-78195115b711

Camp magazines and other pulications– https://archive.org/search.php?query=ruhleben

Harvard Archive – http://library.law.harvard.edu/digitalexhibits/ruhleben/exhibits/show/ruhleben

Imperial War Museum – https://www.iwm.org.uk/search/global?query=ruhleben&pageSize=

Repatriation of Prisoners – http://www.thedanishscheme.co.uk/Articles/Dissertation.pdf

Records of Civilian POWs in the National Archives – https://spw-surrey.com/MT9/?s=ruhleben

Genealogy sites – www.ancestry.co.uk *and* www.findmypast.co.uk

Wikipedia – https://en.wikipedia.org/wiki/Main_Page

Selected bibliography

Bilton, David. 2016. *Allied POWs in German Hands 1914-1918.* (Chapter 5 on Ruhleben). (Barnsley: Pen & Sword Military.)

Cohen, Israel. 1917. *The Ruhleben Prison Camp.* (London: Methuen & Co. Ltd.)

Elliot, Brent. 2014. A tale of two societies: the Royal Horticultural Society and the Ruhleben Horticultural Society. *Occasional Papers from the RHS Lindley Library,* Vol. 12, 31–76.

Ketchum, J. Davidson. 1965. *Ruhleben – A Prison Camp Society.* (Toronto: University of Toronto Press.)

Liddle, Peter (editor). 2015. *Britain Goes to War: How the First World War Began to Reshape the Nation.* (Chapter 10 on Ruhleben). (Barnsley: Pen & Sword Military.)

Paulson, R. (with contributions from A. E. Lechmere and M. S. Pease). 1918. Microscopy at Ruhleben. *Journal of the Royal Microscopy Society,* Vol. 38, Issue 1, 26-29.

Powell, Joseph, and Gribble, Francis Henry. 1919. *The History of Ruhleben.* (London: W Collins.)

Richards, Derek (editor). 2014. *Wyndham's War: being the Diaries of Thomas Wyndham Richards, a Cardiff Schoolmaster interned in Ruhleben and Havelberg 1914-1918.* (Newport: Vine Press.)

Stibbe, Matthew. 2008. *British Civilian Internees in Germany.* (Manchester: Manchester University Press.)

Swale, W. Eric. 1977. *Memories of Ruhleben Camp, Berlin, 1914-1918.* Unpublished manuscript (copy held in the Liddle Collection, University of Leeds).

Index of Names

The following index is confined to the names of internees, military staff, German academics and other people linked to the camp, together with Michael's acquaintances from school days. Pages numbered in bold have a footnote, and those in italic have a photo.